DEVELOPMENTS IN
RUSSIAN POLITICS 9

DEVELOPMENTS IN RUSSIAN POLITICS 9

EDITED BY

RICHARD SAKWA

HENRY E. HALE

AND

STEPHEN WHITE

DUKE UNIVERSITY PRESS
DURHAM AND LONDON
2019

This edition was published in the United States in 2019
by Duke University Press.

Library of Congress Cataloging-in-Publication Data
Names: Sakwa, Richard, editor. | Hale, Henry E., [date] editor. |
White, Stephen, [date] editor.
Title: Developments in Russian politics 9 / edited by Richard Sakwa,
Henry E. Hale and Stephen White.
Other titles: Developments in Russian politics nine
Description: Durham : Duke University Press, 2019. | Includes
bibliographical references and index.
Identifiers: LCCN 2018057888 |
ISBN 9781478004196 (hardcover : alk. paper) |
ISBN 9781478004806 (pbk. : alk. paper)
Subjects: LCSH: Russia (Federation)—Politics and government—1991–
Classification: LCC DK510.763 .D48 2019 | DDC 947.086—dc23
LC record available at https://lccn.loc.gov/2018057888

First published in English by Palgrave Macmillan, a division of Macmillan
Publishers Limited under the title *Developments in Russian Politics 9*,
edited by Richard Sakwa, Henry E. Hale, and Stephen White. This edition
has been published under licence from Palgrave Macmillan. The authors
have asserted their right to be identified as the authors of this Work. For
copyright reasons this edition is not for sale outside of United States,
Canada, and Dependencie.

Printed in the United States of America on acid-free paper ∞

CONTENTS

List of Figures and Tables   ix

Preface   x

Notes on Contributors   xii

List of Abbreviations   xvi

1   Politics in Russia   1
      Richard Sakwa

      The Soviet system   2
      Perestroika: from rationalisation to disintegration   5
      Post-communist Russia: the Yeltsin years   8
      Putin: the politics of stability   11
      Challenges of democratisation   15
      Conclusion   17

2   Presidency and Executive   18
      John P. Willerton

      Putin and the legacy of a strong executive   19
      Institutions of the federal executive   25
      The Putin team   31
      The continued Putin presidency   35

3   Political Parties   38
      Ora John Reuter

      Political parties and Russia's stalled democratization:
      1991–2003   38
      The emergence of a dominant party system   42
      United Russia as the dominant party   43
      United Russia and the electorate   45
      Opposition in Russia   47
      Conclusion   52

4   Parliamentary Politics in Russia   **54**
Ben Noble

History   54
Federal Assembly   56
The law-making process and outputs   60
Recent parliamentary developments   64
Conclusion   65

5   National Identity and the Contested Nation   **67**
Marlene Laruelle

The contested identity of the Russian Federation   67
Stabilising Russia's national narrative knots   70
Nationalist movements   74
The interplay of state nationhood and non-state nationalism   77
Conclusion   79

6   Protest, Civil Society and Informal Politics   **80**
Graeme B. Robertson

Political protest and contentious politics in Russian history   81
Putin and protest   85
The protest cycle of 2011–12   88
Protest, civil society and politics since 2012   89
Protest, civil society and the presidential election of 2018   92
Conclusion   93

7   Russia, Media and Audiences   **94**
Ellen Mickiewicz

Television   94
Radio   98
Newspapers   99
The internet   100
RT: Russia projected abroad   102
The critical importance of scale   104
Cognitive processing and state messages   106

8   Assessing the Rule of Law in Russia   **108**
Kathryn Hendley

The heritage of Soviet law   108
The institutional structure of the Russian legal system   110
The Russian legal system in action   112

Russians' expectations of the legal system 114
Prospects for the rule of law in Russia 117

9 A Federal State? 119
Darrell Slider

Putin's vertical of power 120
Interactions between governors and the president 127
Federal agencies in the regions and the problem
of decentralisation 130

10 Managing the Economy 133
Philip Hanson

Russia's recent economic performance 133
The domestic sources of stagnation 139
Recent economic policy in Russia 142
The future: reform for the sake of faster growth? 146

11 Inequality and Social Policy in Russia 150
Thomas F. Remington

The challenge of social policy 150
Rising inequality 153
Evolution of the social welfare system 157
Income inequality and access to social services 161
The challenge of policy reform 162

12 Russian Foreign Policy 165
Valentina Feklyunina

The making of Russian foreign policy 165
Russia's foreign policy priorities 167
Russian foreign policy: from integration to confrontation
with the West 171
Russia's foreign policy dilemmas 176
Conclusion: explaining Russian foreign policy 178

13 Security, the Military and Politics 180
Bettina Renz

Yeltsin, security and the military 181
Putin, security and politics 184
Putin, the military and politics 186
A Russian military resurgence? 188
Conclusion 191

CONTENTS

14 Russia and its Neighbours   **192**
Samuel Charap

A diverse region   192
Pushing and pulling   193
Conflicts heat up and freeze   195
Integration gets serious   197
Conclusion   203

15 The Continuing Evolution of Russia's Political System   **205**
Henry E. Hale

A social context of patronalism   206
Power networks in Russian politics   207
The emergence of Russia's single-pyramid system   207
The problem of presidential succession   208
Tightening the political machine   209
Dilemmas of governance facing Putin   211
Putin's appeal   211
Putin's strong-hand rule: more subtle than brutal   213
So, what kind of regime is Russia and what lies ahead?   215

Guide to Further Reading   217
Glossary   223
References   224
Index   242

LIST OF FIGURES AND TABLES

Figures

2.1	Major institutions of the Putin executive	27
2.2	Major informal groups of the Putin team	32
3.1	Popular support for major Russian political parties: 2002–17	46
4.1	The partisan distribution of the State Duma, 1994–2017	58
4.2	Key venue-stages of the law-making process	60
4.3	Bill passage statistics, second to sixth State Duma convocations	62
8.1	The Russian court system	110
10.1	Ceasing to catch up, Year-on-year growth in the GDP of Russia and of the Group of 7 countries, 2000–16 actual and 2017–20 projected (% p.a.)	135
10.2	The price of Urals oil ($ per barrel) and the rouble–dollar exchange rate (cents per rouble), quarterly data 2010–17 (indices, 2010 Q1 = 100)	136
10.3	Money wages and the consumer price index, annual data, 2010–16 (end-year inflation) (% annual change)	136
10.4	Federal budget revenue and expenditure, 2010–17 (% of GDP)	137
10.5	Russia's international assets and international liabilities, 2010–17, at the start of each year ($ billion)	139
10.6	Employment and investment in Russia, 2010–16 (% per annum change)	140
11.1	Distribution of pretax income by percentile group	154
11.2	Distribution of national wealth by percentile group	154
11.3	Incomes, poverty and inequality, 1995–2016	155
15.1	Percentage of the Russian population believing Russia is a democratic country, by year	214

Tables

1.1	Tsarist, Soviet and Russian leaders	3
2.1	Russian Public Opinion Survey Results (Levada Center, August 2000–August 2017)	22
3.1	Post-Soviet Russia's main parties	41
11.1a	Shares of wealth owned by top strata of households, 2016	156
11.1b	Top decile's share of national wealth	156

PREFACE

Russia is – by a considerable margin – the world's largest country. It spans two continents and 11 time zones. It has one of the world's largest economies, and one of its most formidable concentrations of military might. It is a founding member of the United Nations, with a permanent seat on its Security Council, and a member of the various groupings of the world's leading industrial nations. It is also now at the centre of policy attention in Western countries, where Russia has been excoriated for everything from annexing the Crimean peninsula to engaging in a social media effort to influence Western election outcomes. So it hardly needs to be said today that Russia matters and that we need to understand it now more than ever, including how its leaders are chosen, what influences them, and how the country they lead interacts with the rest of the global community.

We have assembled a new team to explore such issues in this ninth edition of *Developments in Russian Politics*. As always, it is largely a new book: partly because it reflects the start of Vladimir Putin's fourth term in the Russian presidency and far-reaching changes in the wider society, but also because it draws on a new set of contributors. Eight of them appear in this *Developments* volume for the first time; others have taken on new subjects; and the remaining chapters have been entirely rewritten and updated. So this is, in substance, a new book. But it has the same objective as its predecessors, which is to provide an accurate and up-to-date analysis of the contemporary Russian system with a special emphasis on the issues that are currently most topical and that are likely to be of the greatest interest to other scholars as well as to the university and college students for whom it is primarily intended.

We start, as we must, by placing contemporary Russian politics within a longer-term perspective, and then move to the core institutions of the Russian state: the political executive (including the presidency and government), the political parties and their electoral and political performance, and the legislature. Further chapters consider the wider relationship between Russians and their political system: questions of national identity and state building, the protest politics and patterns of opposition that remain as important as in the last edition of this book, and political communication in electronic as well as more conventional forms. We also consider the extent to which a rule of law has been able to develop that might place some limits on the exercise of central authority and how far the federal system prescribed in the constitution is a political reality.

We then move on to policy formation: in the economy, as slowing growth rates in the era of sanctions pose new challenges; in dealing with the consequences of inequality and social policy in a changing and increasingly divided society; in foreign affairs; and in defence and security. A new chapter examines Russia's relations with its neighbours, an especially important issue following the continuing crisis in relations with Ukraine. A final chapter places the entire system within wider debates about 'democratization' and considers the trajectory of change. We conclude, as in earlier editions, with a guide to further reading and a comprehensive list of references.

We complete this book as Vladimir Putin settles into his fourth term as president, and what may be the start of an extended period of succession, since according to the constitution he will have to give up office in 2024. We hope the pages that follow will help to set out more clearly the nature of the office he once again controls, and the kind of challenges he will confront in the years to come.

Richard Sakwa
Henry E. Hale
Stephen White

NOTES ON CONTRIBUTORS

Samuel Charap is a senior political scientist at the RAND Corporation, in Washington, D.C. His research interests include the political economy and foreign policies of Russia and the former Soviet states; European and Eurasian regional security; and US-Russia deterrence, strategic stability and arms control. Charap's book on the Ukraine crisis, *Everyone Loses: The Ukraine Crisis and the Ruinous Contest for Post-Soviet Eurasia* (co-authored with Timothy J. Colton), was published in January 2017. His articles have appeared in *The Washington Quarterly, Foreign Affairs, Survival, Current History* and several other journals.

Valentina Feklyunina is Senior Lecturer in Politics in the School of Geography, Politics and Sociology at Newcastle University. She is the author of *Identities and Foreign Policies in Russia, Ukraine and Belarus: The Other Europes* (2014, co-authored with Stephen White) and numerous articles on Russian foreign policy, identity and soft power in the *European Journal of International Relations, British Journal of Politics and International Relations, International Politics* and *Europe-Asia Studies*. Her current research focuses on Russia's international status and narratives of Russian history.

Henry E. Hale is Professor of Political Science and International Affairs at George Washington University, co-director of the Program on New Approaches to Research and Security in Eurasia (PONARS Eurasia), and author of the books *Patronal Politics: Eurasian Regime Dynamics in Comparative Perspective* (Cambridge, 2015), *The Foundations of Ethnic Politics* (Cambridge, 2008), and *Why Not Parties in Russia?* (Cambridge, 2006). Specializing on political regimes, ethnic politics, and post-Soviet politics, he is also editorial board chair of *Demokratizatsiya: The Journal of Post-Soviet Democratization* and vice president of the American Political Science Association's section on qualitative and multi-method research.

Philip Hanson is an Emeritus Professor of the University of Birmingham and an Associate Fellow of the Chatham House Russia and Eurasia Programme. His most recent publications include 'Import Substitution and Economic Sovereignty in Russia', a Chatham House research paper co-authored with Richard Connolly, 2016, and 'The State of the Russian Economy: Hopeless but not Politically Serious?', *The Russian Review* (October 2017).

Kathryn Hendley is William Voss-Bascom Professor of Law and Political Science at the University of Wisconsin-Madison. She is the author of *Everyday Law in Russia* and has written extensively on Russian legal reform in journals such as the *American Journal of Comparative Law, Europe-Asia*

Studies, *Law & Social Inquiry*, *Law & Society Review*, *Post-Soviet Affairs*, and *Slavic Review*. She has been a visiting scholar at the Kennan Institute and the Woodrow Wilson International Center for Scholars in Washington, D.C., the Program in Law and Public Affairs at Princeton University, and the Kellogg Institute for International Studies at Notre Dame University. She was a Fulbright Scholar at the New Economic School in Moscow in 2011–12. Her current research focuses on the Russian legal profession.

Marlene Laruelle is Associate Director and Research Professor at the Institute for European, Russian and Eurasian Studies (IERES), Elliott School of International Affairs, The George Washington University. Dr. Laruelle is also co-director of PONARS Eurasia (Program on New Approaches to Research and Security in Eurasia). She has authored *Russian Eurasianism: An Ideology of Empire* (Johns Hopkins University Press, 2008), *In the Name of the Nation: Nationalism and Politics in Contemporary Russia* (Palgrave, 2009), and *Russia's Strategies in the Arctic and the Future of the Far North* (M.E. Sharpe, 2013). Her next book, *Russia and the Symbolic Landscape of Fascism*, will be published by the University of Pittsburgh Press in 2018.

Ellen Mickiewicz is James R. Shepley Emeritus Professor of Public Policy and Political Science at Duke University. She is the author, most recently, of *No Illusions: The Voices of Russia's Future Leaders* (Oxford University Press, 2014) and *Television, Power, and the Public in Russia* (Cambridge University Press, 2008). She is currently researching Kazakhstan's elite university students' attitudes and their use of the internet, as well as the standards of evidence applied to Russia's international communications medium, RT.

Ben Noble is Lecturer in Russian Politics at University College London in the School of Slavonic and East European Studies (SSEES). He is also Senior Research Fellow in the Laboratory for Regional Political Studies at the National Research University – Higher School of Economics, Moscow. His published works include articles in the *Journal of European Public Policy* and *Post-Communist Economies,* as well as chapters in *The New Autocracy: Information, Politics, and Policy in Putin's Russia* (Brookings Institution Press) and *Building Justice in Post-Transition Europe? Processes of Criminalisation within Central and Eastern European Societies* (Routledge). He is currently working on a monograph exploring the resolution of intra-executive policy disputes in the Russian State Duma. This draws on his doctoral dissertation research, which was awarded the Political Studies Association's Sir Walter Bagehot Prize.

Thomas F. Remington is Visiting Scholar at Harvard University. He is Goodrich C. White Professor (Emeritus) of Political Science at Emory University and a Senior Research Associate of the Higher School of Economics in Moscow, Russia. He is author of a number of books and articles on Russian and post-communist politics. Among his publications are *Presidential Decrees in Russia: A Comparative Perspective* (Cambridge University Press, 2014) and *The Politics of Inequality in Russia* (Cambridge University Press,

2011). He is currently conducting research on inequality and social policy in the United States, Russia and China.

Bettina Renz is Associate Professor in International Security at the University of Nottingham's School of Politics and International Relations. She is co-author of *Securitising Russia: The Domestic Politics of Putin* (Manchester University Press, 2006, with Edwin Bacon and Julian Cooper) and the author of *Russia's Military Revival* (Polity Press, 2018). She has also written numerous articles and chapters on the Russian force structures, military reforms, military doctrine and strategic thought, and civil-military relations.

Ora John Reuter is Associate Professor of Political Science at the University of Wisconsin-Milwaukee and Senior Researcher at the Centre for the Study of Institutions and Development at the Higher School of Economics, Moscow. He is the author of *The Origins of Dominant Parties: Building Authoritarian Institutions in Post-Soviet Russia* (Cambridge University Press, 2017). His articles on elections, parties, political economy, and authoritarianism have appeared in journals such as *Journal of Politics*, the *British Journal of Political Science*, *World Politics*, *Comparative Political Studies*, *Comparative Politics*, *Europe-Asia Studies* and *Post-Soviet Affairs*.

Graeme Robertson is Professor of Political Science at the University of North Carolina at Chapel Hill. He has published a number of recent articles on what shapes popular support for the Putin regime. He is currently working on a book that traces how Putin's political system has been jointly constructed by the Russian state and Russian society.

Richard Sakwa is Professor of Russian and European Politics at the University of Kent and an Associate Fellow of Chatham House. He is a graduate of the London School of Economics (BA Hons) and the University of Birmingham (PhD). He held lectureships at the University of Essex and the University of California, Santa Cruz, before joining the University of Kent in 1987. He has published widely on Soviet, Russian and European affairs. Books include *Communism in Russia: An Interpretative Essay* (Macmillan, 2010), *The Crisis of Russian Democracy* (Cambridge University Press, 2011), *Putin and the Oligarch: The Khodorkovsky-Yukos Affair* (IB Tauris, 2014), *Putin Redux: Power and Contradiction in Contemporary Russia* (Routledge, 2014), and *Frontline Ukraine: Crisis in the Borderlands* (IB Tauris, 2016). His latest book is *Russia against the Rest: The Post-Cold War Crisis of World Order* (Cambridge University Press, 2017).

Darrell Slider is Emeritus Professor of Government and International Affairs at the University of South Florida (Tampa). He is the author of a number of works on Russian regions, elections, federalism and decentralization. Dr. Slider was a Fulbright research scholar at the Higher School of Economics in Moscow for the 2017–18 academic year.

John P. Willerton is Professor of Political Science at the University of Arizona, Tucson. He is the author of *Patronage and Politics in the USSR* and 60 articles and chapters dealing with various facets of Soviet and post-Soviet Russian domestic politics and foreign policy. His current research focuses on post-Soviet political elites, the Russian federal executive, and Russia's relations with the Commonwealth of Independent States (CIS) and former Soviet Union (FSU) countries. He is currently engaged in a project on Vladimir Putin and Russia's search for a national idea.

LIST OF ABBREVIATIONS

AA	association agreement
ABM	anti-ballistic missile
BRI	Belt and Road Initiative
BRIC(S)	Brazil, Russia, India, China (South Africa)
CBR	Central Bank of Russia
CIS	Commonwealth of Independent States
CPD	Congress of People's Deputies
CPRF	Communist Party of the Russian Federation
CPSU	Communist Party of the Soviet Union
CSR	Centre for Strategic Research
CSTO	Collective Security Treaty Organisation
DCFTA	Deep and Comprehensive Free Trade Area
DNR	Donetsk People's Republic
EAEC	Eurasian Economic Commission
EaP	Eastern Partnership
EEU	Eurasian Economic Union
EU	European Union
FAPSI	Federal Agency for Government Communication and Information
FAR	Fatherland-All Russia party
FOM	Public Opinion Foundation
FSB	Federal Security Service
FSKN	Federal Service for Control of the Drug Trade
FSNG	Federal National Guards Service
FSO	Federal Guard Service
GATT	General Agreement on Tariffs and Trade
GDP	gross domestic production
G8	Group of Eight leading industrialised nations (now G7)
KGB	Committee of State Security (Soviet security agency)
KMT	Kuomintang (China)
LDPR	Liberal Democratic Party of Russia
LGBT(Q)	lesbian, gay, bisexual and transgender (queer)
LNR	Lugansk People's Republic
MAP	membership action plan
MChS	Ministry for Emergency Situations
MVD	Ministry of Internal Affairs
NATO	North Atlantic Treaty Organisation
NGO	non-governmental organisation
NPT	new political thinking
NTV	Independent TV
OSCE	Organisation for Security and Cooperation in Europe

PA	Presidential Administration
PACE	Parliamentary Assembly of the Council of Europe
PAYG	pay as you go
PR	proportional representation
PRI	Party of the Institutional Revolution (Mexico)
RNU	Russian National Unity party
RSFSR	Russian Soviet Federative Socialist Republic
RT	formerly Russia Today TV station
SBP	Presidential Security Service
SCO	Shanghai Cooperation Organisation
SPS	Union of Right Forces liberal party
START	Strategic Arms Reduction Treaty
SVR	Foreign Intelligence Service
UAV	unmanned aerial vehicle
UK	United Kingdom
UN	United Nations
UNSC	United Nations Security Council
UR	United Russia
US	United States
USSR	Union of Soviet Socialist Republics
VKP(b)	All-Union Communist Party (Bolsheviks)
VPN	virtual private network
VTsIOM	Russian Public Opinion Research Foundation
WTO	World Trade Organisation
YeGE	unified state examination

1 POLITICS IN RUSSIA
Richard Sakwa

Russia re-emerged as an independent state in 1991, and in the course of nearly three decades it has been engaged in a monumental act of nation and state building. It was never going to be easy to create a capitalist democracy from scratch, but in the event the process has been dramatic and contradictory. Everything had to be created anew, including the party and parliamentary systems, legally defensible property rights, a new class of entrepreneurs, and above all the constitutional framework and the rule of law. The adoption of the constitution proved protracted and divisive, accompanied by a violent conflict between the last Soviet parliament (the Congress of People's Deputies) and president Boris Yeltsin in October 1993. The constitution adopted in December 1993 still bears the scars of this conflict. Having defeated the parliamentary forces, Yeltsin introduced strengthened powers for the executive presidency that remain to this day. In addition, Russia needed to find a new place in the international system, one that corresponded to its own vision of itself as a great power but also took into account the concerns of its new neighbours, the 14 former Soviet republics that were now independent states.

In the years since the collapse of communism there have been great achievements, yet the process remains incomplete and contradictory. The Soviet legacy of an enormous security apparatus, a vast dependent bureaucracy and an over-extended welfare system remains a potent force in politics, as do the rather more intangible factors of attitudes and political culture. The new Russian political elite remains steeped in the mores and prejudices of the Soviet era. This encounters an increasingly impatient younger generation, a growing proportion of whom have grown up in the post-Soviet years and for whom communism is something to be read about in the history books.

The transformation of the economy and polity, moreover, has spawned new interests and concerns, demanding a more open political system, free and fair elections, and genuine accountability of the authorities to the institutions of representative democracy and the law. While Vladimir Putin, who has been in power since 2000, remains legalistically committed to the black letter of the constitution, his commitment to the spirit of genuine constitutionalism is more questionable. These demands spilled out into the streets in December 2011, in protest against the widespread fraud in the parliamentary elections in that month. The rebirth of an active opposition prompted a number of significant reforms, including the return of elections for regional governors, but the power of the regime was soon re-asserted. Russia remains what is called a 'managed democracy', with political processes closely monitored and controlled from the Kremlin.

In March 2018 Putin was elected for a fourth term, and if he remains in office until his six-year term runs out in 2024, he will have been one of the longest-serving Russian leaders. Although Putin's return to office signals continuity, profound changes are taking place in the country and even within the Putin system, and these will be analysed in this book.

The Soviet system

Contemporary Russia cannot be understood without some understanding of what went before. As in any study of a political system, historical contextualisation is crucial, and Russia has had rather a lot of history over the last century. In the space of not much more than 100 years Russia has endured two world wars, four major revolutions, a civil war, and the collapse of two major political systems. The Russian Empire, ruled by the Romanov dynasty from 1613, proved remarkably resilient in the Great War, which Russia entered in July 1914 in alliance with France and Great Britain, even though it suffered a series of defeats. In the end, though, the strain proved too much, and the abdication of Nicholas II in February 1917 ended the rule of the Romanovs after 300 years in power. In the next eight months Russia tried to fight a war while making a revolution. While it was notably unsuccessful in the first endeavour, it shocked the world with the scale of the second. The Provisional Government at last began to fulfil the potential of the long-gathering Russian revolution. Since at least 1825 and the Decembrist movement there had been growing pressure for the introduction of an accountable government, and now genuine constitutionalism appeared finally to have arrived. However, at the same time socialism had also arrived, in the form of the soviets (councils) of workers, peasants and soldiers. Dual power represented not only two contending sets of institutions but also two ideologies of revolution – what Marxists call the 'bourgeois democratic' and the socialist.

Only six months after the fall of the autocracy, on 7 November 1917 (25 October in the Old Style Julian calendar), the radical Bolshevik party under the uncompromising leadership of Vladimir Il'ich Lenin came to power. It was too late for the new authorities to stop the planned elections to the Constituent Assembly, and the Bolsheviks found themselves in a minority in the new body. This was the first genuinely democratically elected legislature in Russian history, with 370 seats going to the Socialist Revolutionary party, and 175 to the Bolsheviks. The Assembly met for 13 hours, from 4pm to 5am, on 18–19 January 1918 (5–6 January, Old Style). Early in the morning, when the guard was 'tired', the Assembly was dissolved – never to meet again. Thus Russia's first major experiment in democracy ended in a dismal failure. Three years of brutal Civil War ended in a Bolshevik victory, and the stage was set for one of the greatest experiments in political and social engineering in history. The dominant rule of the Communist Party was now established by Lenin, and once victory in the Civil War of 1918–20 was assured, the regime was able to consolidate its power. This required making concessions to the peasantry, in whose name the revolution had been made, and the country revived remarkably quickly in the period of the

New Economic Policy (NEP) from 1921 to 1928. For Joseph Stalin, who after a struggle following Lenin's death in 1924 achieved dictatorial power, accelerated industrialisation soon became the overriding aim, and forced collectivisation of the peasants into collective and state farms was accompanied by unimaginable misery and famine, including the *Holodomor* in Ukraine in 1932–34. The intensification of coercion peaked in the terror of the 1930s. However, victory over Nazi Germany and its allies in the Great Patriotic War of 1941–45 appeared to vindicate all the sacrifices of the early Soviet period. Hopes for the end of mass coercion were disappointed, and terror remained prevalent until the death of Stalin in March 1953.

Table 1.1 Tsarist, Soviet and Russian leaders

Date ruled	Name of leader
1894–17	Nicholas II
1917–24	Vladimir Il'ich Lenin
1924–53	Joseph Vissarionovich Stalin
1953–64	Nikita Sergeevich Khrushchev
1964–82	Leonid Il'ich Brezhnev
1982–84	Yuri Vladimirovich Andropov
1984–85	Konstantin Ustinovich Chernenko
1985–91	Mikhail Sergeevich Gorbachev
1991–99	Boris Nikolaevich Yeltsin
2000–08	Vladimir Vladimirovich Putin
2008–12	Dmitry Anatolevich Medvedev
2012–	Vladimir Vladimirovich Putin

Stalin's successor, Nikita Khrushchev, allowed what was called 'the thaw', including the release of millions of people from the labour camps, what the great Russian writer Alexander Solzhenitsyn called the *gulag archipelago* in his massive historical study of the origins and conduct of the system. In his 'Secret Speech' of 25 February 1956 at the Twentieth Party Congress Khrushchev provided a devastating critique of the man – Stalin – but failed to give a systemic critique of how this man had been able to commit so many crimes for so long. This was also a period of optimism that the Soviet socialist system would be able to out-compete the capitalist West. The new Party Programme of 1961 promised that socialism 'in the main' would be built in the Soviet Union by 1980. Khrushchev's erratic course in domestic and foreign policy (including the Cuban missile crisis of October 1962) provoked his ouster in October 1964.

He was replaced by the dour Leonid Brezhnev, under whose long rule (1964–82) the question of political renewal was suppressed. Even the modest economic reform plan envisaged by the Prime Minister, Alexei Kosygin, in the 1960s ran into the sands of the Soviet bureaucracy, a force which jealously guarded its powers over property and policy. The Prague Spring in Czechoslovakia in 1968 tried to introduce 'socialism with a human face', but the attempt to renew the communist system by establishing a more humane and democratic form of socialism was crushed by Soviet and allied tanks in August of that year. Nevertheless, 'reform socialism' was placed firmly on the agenda and raised issues that would later be taken up by Mikhail Gorbachev, but by then it was too late. Instead, the last years of Brezhnev's rule gave way to the period of stagnation (*zastoi*) as the high hopes of *détente* with the West gave way to an intensified and extremely dangerous renewed phase of the Cold War.

By the time of Brezhnev's death in November 1982 it was clear that the accumulating problems of corruption, declining growth rates, increasing technological backwardness and general societal malaise needed to be addressed. Yuri Andropov headed the Committee of State Security (KGB) from 1967, and he was in a unique position to observe society's ills. He briefly took over as leader between Brezhnev's death and his own death after a brief period in office in February 1984. He posed the fundamental question: 'We do not know the country we live in'. Andropov's response was a programme of 'authoritarian modernisation', including the intensification of labour discipline, the struggle against corruption and the restoration of a more ascetic form of communist morality. On Andropov's death the ailing Konstantin Chernenko clawed his way to power for a brief period. Chernenko's death in March 1985 finally allowed a new generation to assume the reins of leadership.

For seventy-four years, between 1917 and 1991, the Soviet Union sought to create an alternative social order based on its own interpretation of Marxist thinking combined with a Leninist understanding of the need for a dominant party. The Soviet system endured far longer than most of its early critics thought possible, but ultimately between 1989 and 1991 it came crashing down. The legacy of the failed experiment lives on in Russia today. The Union of Soviet Socialist Republics (USSR) was established in December 1922 as a union of allegedly sovereign republics to give political form to the diversity of the new republic's peoples and nations, and this was then given juridical form in the adoption of the Soviet Union's first constitution in January 1924. The system worked as long as there was a force standing outside the ethno-federal framework, the All-Union Communist Party (Bolsheviks) (VKP(b)), renamed the Communist Party of the Soviet Union (CPSU) at the Nineteenth Party Congress in 1952. With the launching of perestroika (restructuring) by the new General Secretary of the CPSU, Mikhail Gorbachev, in 1985, the Party gradually lost its unifying potential as its own internal coherence dissolved. Gorbachev launched an ambitious programme of reform, known as perestroika, which by 1989 had not only transformed the Soviet Union but also allowed the liberation of the allied Soviet bloc countries and put an end to the Cold War. However, his reforms also allowed dormant national aspirations to come back to life, led (surprisingly) by Russia, which allowed the country to fall apart by the end of December 1991. Gorbachev's reforms precipitated a twofold process, each with its own distinct logic but devastating when they came together, namely the *dissolution* of the communist system and the *disintegration* of the country.

Perestroika: from rationalisation to disintegration

The appointment of a reforming CPSU General Secretary in March 1985 set in motion a period of 'transition' that continues to this day, even though Putin repudiates the term. Gorbachev came to power as Andropov's protégé, but his programme of reform quickly transcended even a residual notion of 'authoritarian modernisation'. In domestic politics full-scale reforms were adopted, while at the same time he sought to put an end to the Cold War with the West, a struggle that he increasingly considered both futile and damaging for all concerned. Gorbachev came to power with a clear sense that the old way of governing the Soviet Union could no longer continue, but his plans for change swiftly came up against some hard realities. He achieved some significant success in democratising the system and by around 1989 the communist order had effectively been dismantled and the country was moving towards constitutional democracy, but the accumulation of economic and national problems provoked the country's disintegration in December 1991. Reform communism had given way to the communism of reform, and by the end to no communism at all.

On a visit to Canada in May 1983, Gorbachev and the Soviet ambassador, Alexander Yakovlev (who was later to play a large part in shaping the reforms), argued that 'We cannot continue to live in this way' (Remnick 1993: 294–5). Gorbachev came to power committed to modernising the Soviet system. In the space of six years perestroika moved through five main stages: initial attempts to *rationalize* the system included some ambitious economic goals, a programme known as 'acceleration' (*uskorenie*); the focus then moved to a phase of *liberalisation*, including the rapid development of *glasnost'* (openness), in which the country's tragic past was exposed in all its savagery and glory; fundamental political questions began to be addressed in the next phase known as *democratisation* (*demokratizatsiya*), which began to transform the society and polity through relatively free and fair elections and the creation of a genuine legislature freed from CPSU control; but all this began to provoke the *dissolution* of the foundations of the communist order, as its past was discredited and the basis of its rule delegitimised; culminating in 1991 in a final stage of *disintegration* of the country itself. Once changes began they could not be limited by regime-led reform, and pressure for radical renewal became overwhelming. The attempt in August 1991 by a group of conservatives to hold back the tide of change precipitated the result that they had sought to avert: the total dissolution of the communist system of government and, by the end of the year, the disintegration of the USSR.

Gorbachev did not come to power with a clear set of policies; but he did have an attitude towards change to which he remained committed to the bitter end. He intended to achieve a modernisation of the communist system through perestroika, and within that framework launched what he called a 'revolution within the revolution' to save the system and not to destroy it. Gorbachev understood that the system was suffering from major problems, including declining economic growth, social decay, excessive secrecy in scientific and political life, and the degeneration of the ruling elite into a venal and incompetent class. Gorbachev never repudiated the basic idea that the communist system remained a viable, and in some ways a superior, system to capitalist democracy. His aim was to provide Soviet communism with the dynamism enjoyed by capitalism, but without its defects. He certainly never set out to undermine what was called the 'leading role' of the Communist Party or to destroy the planned economy. Perestroika, he insisted, was 'prompted by awareness that the potential of socialism has been underutilized' (Gorbachev 1987: 10).

In the economic sphere he got off on the wrong foot right away: the policy of acceleration sought to achieve economic transformation and increased output at the same time, and in the event was unable to gain the long-term achievement of either. This was accompanied by an anti-alcohol campaign that deprived the country of nearly one-third of tax revenues (Miller 2016). Equally, *glasnost'* was intended at first not to be freedom of speech but to expose the failings of a corrupt bureaucracy, and thus to strengthen the Soviet system. However, openness soon became a devastating search for the truth about Leninist and Stalinist repression and took on a life of its own, escaping from the constraints that Gorbachev had initially intended.

Gorbachev's own views about the past were filtered through a romantic Leninism, believing in an allegedly more democratic and evolutionary late Leninist model of the New Economic Policy of the 1920s. By the end of 1987 *demokratizatsiya* came to the fore, with the gradual introduction of multi-candidate elections accompanied by a relaxation of the Leninist 'ban on factions', the formation of groups in the Communist Party. Gorbachev's own views at this time were eloquently developed in his book *Perestroika: New Thinking for Our Country and the World* (1987), in which he talked of perestroika as a revolution both from above and below. The 'from below' element was by now taking hold in the form of thousands of 'informal' associations, representing the rebirth of an independent civil society (Lewin 1988).

The changes begun by Gorbachev began to out-run his ability to control them. The proliferation of *neformaly* (unofficial social associations) and an independent press reflected a distinctive type of negative popular mobilisation against the old regime that proved very difficult to channel into positive civic endeavour. The establishment of the Democratic Union on 9 May 1988 marked the beginning of the renewed era of multiparty politics, but its radical anti-communism signalled that Gorbachev's attempts to constrain and control political pluralism within the framework of 'reform communism' would fail and the communist order would dissolve. In some non-Russian republics the informal movement took the form of popular fronts, with Sajudis in Lithuania one of the largest representing aspirations for national autonomy and, later, independence.

The high point of Gorbachev's hopes that a humane and democratic socialism could replace the old moribund system was the Nineteenth Party Conference in June–July 1988, where he outlined a programme of democratic political change and a new role for the USSR in the world. Soon after, in September, institutional changes weakened the role of the Party *apparatus*, and constitutional changes in November created a new two-tier parliament, with a large Congress of People's Deputies meeting twice a year selecting a working Supreme Soviet. The first elections to this body took place in March 1989, and revealed the depths of the unpopularity of Party rule. The early debates of the parliament riveted the nation, as problems were openly discussed for the first time in decades. The Congress stripped the Communist Party of its constitutionally entrenched 'leading role' in March 1990, and at the same time Gorbachev was elected to the new post of president of the USSR. His failure to stand in a national ballot, and thus demonstrably gain the support of the people, was a fundamental mistake. Lacking a popular mandate, he was sidelined by those who did – above all Boris Yeltsin, who became head of the Russian Congress of People's Deputies in May 1990 and then went on to face a popular ballot in June 1991 to become Russia's first president.

What was called the 'nationalities question' now threatened the unity of the country. Although Gorbachev was responsive to calls for greater autonomy for the 15 union republics making up the USSR, he had no time for any talk of independence. Through an increasingly desperate attempt to negotiate a new Union Treaty Gorbachev hoped to transform what was in effect a unitary state into a genuinely confederal community of nations. These hopes were dashed by Lithuania's declaration of independence on 11 March 1990, followed by that of Georgia on 9 April 1991 and all the other republics by the end of the year. In foreign affairs Gorbachev advanced the idea of 'new political thinking' (NPT), based on the notion of interdependence and a new co-operative relationship with the West. On a visit to the European Parliament in Strasbourg in September 1988 he talked of the establishment of a 'common European home', but it was not clear what form this would take. By 1989 the Eastern European countries in the Soviet bloc took Gorbachev at his word when he called for change, and from the autumn of that year one after another the communist regimes collapsed. The fall of the Berlin Wall on 9 November 1989 marks the symbolic end of Soviet power in Eastern Europe. This deeply affected a KGB operative in the German Democratic Republic at the time, Vladimir Putin. Gorbachev facilitated the unification of Germany, although he is much criticised for failing to guarantee in treaty form the demilitarised status of the Eastern part of the new country and of Eastern Europe in general. The enlargement of NATO to fill the perceived security vacuum would be one of the most controversial issues of the post-communist era.

At home, resistance to Gorbachev's policies grew to the point that a group prepared to seize power in a coup. The specific issue was the planned signing of the new Union Treaty on 20 August 1991, but the plotters were also concerned about economic disintegration and the loss of political control. For three days in August (19–21) Gorbachev was isolated in his dacha in Foros in the Crimea, while his nemesis, Boris Yeltsin, emerged much strengthened. Yeltsin had been elected president of Russia with 57% of the vote on 12 June 1991, and thus he had the popular legitimacy to speak for the country. The image of Yeltsin standing on a tank outside the Russian White House (the seat of its government) has come to symbolise the high point of unity between the people and the Russian leadership. In the days following the coup Yeltsin put an end to Communist rule by banning the Party in Russia. Attempts to save the Soviet Union in the last months of 1991 failed. The pressure for increased sovereignty for republics grew into demands for independence. A meeting of the leaders of Belarus, Russia and Ukraine in the Belovezhskaya Pushcha nature reserve in Belarus on 7–8 December agreed to put an end to the USSR, and in its place created the Commonwealth of Independent States (CIS). The CIS was broadened on 21 December to include most (with the exception of the Baltic republics and Georgia) former Soviet states. Gorbachev formally resigned as president on 25 December 1991, and on 31 December the USSR formally ceased to exist.

Gorbachev's reform of the Soviet system provoked its demise. The debate over whether the Soviet Union could have been reformed while remaining recognisably communist continues to this day (Cohen, 2004). Gorbachev's perestroika clearly showed the system's evolutionary potential, but this was an evolution that effectively meant the peaceful transcendence of the system it was meant to save. From one angle, Gorbachev's reforms were a great success. By 1991 the country had become relatively democratic, staging the freest and fairest elections that the country has yet seen, it was moving towards becoming a market economy, the union was changing into a confederation of sovereign states, and the Cold War had been overcome largely by Soviet efforts. However, the terminal crisis of the system in 1991 revealed deep structural flaws in Gorbachev's conception of reform and in the system's capacity for change while remaining recognisably socialist in orientation. Gorbachev remained remarkably consistent in his commitment to a humane democratic socialism with a limited market in a renewed federation of Soviet states (Brown 1996; Taubman 2017). However, his attempts to limit change to his preconceived notions soon crashed against some harsh realities: the aspirations for independence in a number of repub-lics, notably of Estonia, Latvia and Lithuania, forcibly incorporated into the USSR by Stalin in 1940 and again in 1944; the inherent instability of a semi-marketised system – it either had to be one thing or another, a planned or a market economy; and ultimately the lack of popular support for any socialism, irrespective of how humane or democratic it may have become. The attempt to reform the Soviet system exposed its many contradictions, and these ultimately destroyed the system. The country reformed itself out of existence.

Post-communist Russia: the Yeltsin years

Russia entered the twenty-first century a very different country from the one that had entered the twentieth. The Tsarist empire had disintegrated, the autocracy had been overthrown, the Soviet communist system had been and gone, and the USSR had also disintegrated leaving fifteen separate successor republics. Independent Russia for the first time developed something akin to a nation state rather than an as empire or part of a confederation. It was form-ally the 'continuer' state to the Soviet Union, and thus assumed responsibility for the earlier state's treaty and debt obligations, but it also inherited a permanent seat in the United Nations Security Council (UNSC) and the nuclear weapons of the whole union. The economy was severely distorted by the Soviet planned economy and absence of private ownership of the means of production and the legal framework for a market order. Above all, the country now engaged in an extraordinary act of political reconstitution intended to establish liberal democracy. Democratic politics, defined as the procedural contest for political power and governmental accountability to a freely elected legislature and subordinate to the rule of law, accompanied by a public sphere of debate, criticism and information, had finally arrived in Russia. Whether the so-called transition actually achieved democracy is another question, and one to which we shall return.

The Yeltsin administration was committed to Russia becoming a democratic market state allied with the advanced Western nations and integrated into the world economy. There was far less agreement, however, on how these three goals – democratisation, marketisation and international integration – were to be achieved. Bitter debates raged throughout the 1990s, and will be discussed in later chapters of this book. On one thing, however, there was broad agreement: the borders of the Russia that emerged as an independent state in 1991 should not be changed, however unfair and arbitrary many considered them to be. Some 25 million ethnic Russians found themselves scattered across the 14 other newly independent states, yet Yeltsin's refusal to exploit the real and imagined grievances of the Russian diaspora to gain political capital stands as one of his major achievements (for a general review of Yeltsin's leadership, see Aron 2000; Colton 2008). Politics in the post-communist era would be in *Russia*, and not in some mythical re-established Soviet Union in whatever guise.

The nature of these *politics* is less clear. For the first two years following independence Russian politics was wracked by the struggle to adopt a new constitution (Andrews 2002; Sakwa 2008a). The two-tier parliament that Russia inherited from the Soviet Union proved unworkable, and ultimately replicated the situation of dual power of 1917, with both the president and the parliament endowed with executive powers. On 21 September 1993 Yeltsin unilaterally dissolved the Congress of People's Deputies, sparking an armed confrontation that only ended when Yeltsin sent in the tanks on 3–4 October. Yeltsin took advantage of his victory to strengthen the powers of the presidency. The constitution was finally adopted in a referendum on 12 December 1993 in what set the pattern for flawed ballots. A new legislature was also elected, which in subsequent elections came to be dominated by new-grown populists, nationalists and the reconstituted Communist Party of the Russian Federation (CPRF). Russia now entered a period of relative political stability, although the legitimacy of the new polity was questioned because of the violence accompanying its birth and the flawed elections through which it was constituted. The constitution nevertheless is a fundamentally liberal document, proclaiming a range of freedoms that would be expected of a liberal democratic state, although the division of powers between parliament and president remains unbalanced. The presidency effectively stands outside the formal description of the separation of powers, and many of the ills of Russian democracy are ascribed to the excessively strong executive, often dubbed 'super-presidential' (Fish 2001, 2005).

The presidency emerged as the guarantor not only of the constitutional order (as stated in the constitution), but also of a reform process that under Yeltsin was driven forwards with a single-mindedness that at times threatened to undermine democracy itself (Reddaway and Glinski 2001). This was an inverted type of 'Bolshevik' radicalism, seeking to establish the foundations of capitalist democracy in the shortest possible time. Fearing the revenge of the Communists, state property was disbursed in a chaotic process that did indeed create a new class of owners, but many deserved the title of 'oligarch' rather than entrepreneur. The pattern was set of entwined economic and political power that remains to this day, fostering corruption and a neo-Soviet economic statism. This is most in evidence when it came to elections. Fearing that neo-communists and other opponents of moves towards the market and international integration would come to power in the 1996 presidential elections, Yeltsin toyed with the idea of cancelling them altogether. Instead, he drew on the resources of his new oligarch friends and launched an expensive propaganda barrage (with the help of American advisers) that propelled him to office for a second term. Later, President Dmitry Medvedev conceded that Yeltsin had not really won the election against his Communist opponent, Gennady Zyuganov, but at the time no one was in a position to do anything about it. Although in ill-health for much of the time, Yeltsin dominated politics to the end of the decade (McFaul 2001).

Although Yeltsin formally remained committed to Russia's democratic development, several features undermined this ambition. The first was the unhealthy penetration of economic interests into the decision-making process. Rapid and chaotic privatisation from the early 1990s gave birth to a new class of powerful economic magnates, the oligarchs. Their support for Yeltsin's re-election in 1996 brought them into the centre of the political process, and gave rise to the creation of what was known as the 'family', a mix of Yeltsin family members, politicians and oligarchs. Most notorious of them was Boris Berezovsky, who used political influence as a major economic resource. Many others at this time exploited insider knowledge to gain economic assets for a fraction of their real worth. It was in these years that the empires were built of Mikhail Khodorkovsky (the Yukos oil company), Roman Abramovich (with Berezovsky at the head of Sibneft), Vladimir Potanin (Norilsk Nickel), Vladimir Gusinsky (the Media-Most banking and media empire), and many others (Fortescue 2006). Their heyday were the years between the presidential election of 1996 and the partial default of August 1998, and thereafter oligarchical power as such waned, although as individuals they remained important players.

The second feature was the exaggerated power of the presidency. Granted extensive authority by the 1993 Constitution as part of a deliberate institutional design intended to ensure adequate powers for the executive to drive through reform, the presidency lacked adequate constraints. Too many decisions were taken by small groups of unaccountable individuals, notably in the case of the decision to launch the first Chechen war in December 1994.

We will return to this question below, but associated with that is the third problem, the weakness of mechanisms of popular accountability. Although far from powerless, the State Duma (see Chapter 4) is not able effectively to hold the executive to account. This is related to the weakness of the development of the party system (Chapter 3). The fourth issue is the question of the succession. Earlier drafts of the constitution limited a president to two terms, but following his victory in October 1993 Yeltsin inserted the word *consecutive* (Article 81.3), thus making it possible for a president to return after a gap. While all incumbent leaders try to perpetuate their power by ensuring a transfer to favourable successors, in Yeltsin's case the stakes were particularly high. He feared that a new president could mean a change of system in its entirety, with the possibility of personal reprisals being taken against him and his family. For this reason the Kremlin engaged in a long search for an individual who would ensure continuity and the personal inviolability of Russia's 'first president' (as he liked to style himself) and his associates.

Putin: the politics of stability

They found this guarantee in the person of Vladimir Putin. He was nominated prime minister on 9 August 1999, acting president on Yeltsin's resignation on 31 December 1999, formally elected for his first term on 14 March 2000, for a second term on 14 March 2004, becoming prime minister on 8 May 2008 under the presidency of Dmitry Medvedev, and was re-elected to the presidency (with the term now increased from four to six years) in March 2012 and March 2018. Putin respected the letter of the constitution, which stipulates a maximum of two consecutive terms, but with a gap he was allowed two more terms. Putin is now set to remain in power until 2024, at which point he will be 72 years old. He could theoretically run again in 2030, or he could change the constitution to allow an earlier fifth term, to create some sort of supervisory role, or shift power from the presidency to a strengthened prime minister. As things stood, as soon as Putin was elected for his fourth term, speculation over the succession intensified.

Putin's accession to the presidency in 2000 did not at first represent a rupture in the system inherited from Yeltsin, but changes in leadership style, policy orientations and ideological innovations effectively marked the beginning of a distinct era. Putin's programme of 'normal' politics, accompanied by attempts to build a state based on 'order' and 'stability', represented a new stage in Russia's endlessly unforgiving attempts to come to terms with modernity (Sakwa 2008b). Putin pursued a politics of stability. The polarisation that attended Yeltsin's rule gave way to an explicitly consensual and 'centrist' approach. This represented not simply an avoidance of the extremes of left and right but sought to generate a transformative centrism on which a new developmental model for the country could be based. The new approach allowed the regime to reassert its predominance while establishing a framework for socio-economic transformation to continue. The regime adopted a pragmatic and technocratic approach that allowed society to get on with its business as long as it did not challenge the leadership's tutelary claim that it knew what was best for the country. A relatively coherent and durable new political order emerged.

While Putin was undoubtedly a reformer, his approach to change was no longer one of systemic transformation but of system management. In other words, he was a transactional rather than transformative leader. His speeches and interventions are peppered with the concept of 'normality'. The concept of normality suggests a certain naturalness of political debate and choice of policy options, relatively unconstrained by the formal imposition of ideological norms. This represented a strategic depoliticisation that reduced structured political choice and allowed the regime to rule on behalf of society. Putin's strategic goal of modernisation of the economy was accompanied by the attempt to consolidate society. Although these goals were not always compatible, a common principle underlay both: the attempt to avoid extremes in policy and to neutralise extremist or alternative political actors. Putin's rule was technocratic and based on the exercise of administrative power. Putin's politics of stability was characterised by the refusal to accept changes to the constitution (apart from lengthening the presidential and parliamentary terms), the acceptance of the privatisations of the Yeltsin years, and the explicit repudiation of revolution as a form of achieving positive political change.

This echoed Putin's sentiments voiced in his *Russia at the Turn of the Millennium* in December 1999, where he noted that the communist revolutionary model of development not only had not delivered the goods but could not have done so (Putin 2000: 212). Although regretting the break-up of the Soviet Union (but not the dissolution of the Communist system), Putin never considered the restoration of anything resembling the USSR as remotely possible, let alone desirable. In his 25 April 2005 address (*poslanie*) to the Federal Assembly (the two houses of parliament, the State Duma and the upper chamber, the Federation Council) he called the break-up of the Soviet Union 'the greatest geopolitical disaster' of the twentieth century and a 'tragedy for the Russian people', but this did not mean that he sought to restore the old state. At the heart of Putin's politics of stability was the attempt to reconcile the various phases of Russian history, especially over the last century: the Tsarist, the Soviet and the democratic eras. In foreign policy, Putin insisted that Russia should be treated as a 'normal' great power. He argued that Russia's foreign policy should serve the country's economic interests, a policy that was evident in debates over the union of Russia and Belarus.

At the heart of Putin's leadership was the reassertion of the constitutional prerogatives of the state (what he called the 'dictatorship of law'), accompanied by the struggle to ensure that the regime did not fall under the influence of societal actors. In particular, the 'oligarchs' under Yeltsin had exercised what was perceived to be undue influence; this was now repudiated. Equally, the independent regional governors were reined in, and between 2005 and 2012 they were appointed by the Kremlin. The gap between the regime and the state became increasingly apparent as the 'dual state' became consolidated. The distinction between the constitutional state and the administrative regime is central to understand the contradictions of the Putin system (Sakwa 2010, 2011). Putin claimed to be strengthening the state, but in practice this meant intensifying the tutelary prerogatives of the administrative regime. The regime increasingly became insulated from all political actors, including independent political parties and parliament. Accountability mechanisms were weakened, and what was gained in the ability of the government to act as an independent force was lost in its lack of interaction with society. Instead, the regime's pedestal party, United Russia (see Chapter 3), and other state-sponsored movements, such as the Russian Popular Front (ONF), acted as neo-Leninist 'transmission belts' between the regime and society.

Putin's supporters advance the argument that stability and security should come before democracy. Russia, they suggested, should not be expected quickly to achieve a high-quality democracy, given its authoritarian past, its political culture and the weakness of civil society. They echo the argument advanced by Samuel Huntington in his classic work of 1968, *Political Order in Changing Societies*, which argued that modernising societies were in danger of being overwhelmed by societal demands and social pressures if authoritarian restraints were released too fast. Hence there was a need for constraints to allow adequate structures and institutions to take shape and for the polity to form in a manner capable of aggregating and controlling these pressures (Huntington 1968). Following the Beslan school massacre of 1–3 September 2004, Putin on 13 September announced a range of reforms to the state system, including the appointment of governors and wholly proportional parliamentary elections. The return to the themes of 'authoritarian modernisation' reflected the intensification of 'managed democracy', the term used to describe the tutelary politics that had emerged under Yeltsin.

Although Russia had formally gained all the institutions of a capitalist democracy, the spirit of pluralism and accountability was lacking. Democratisation theory often assumes that once the authoritarian burden is lifted, society will automatically spring back into some sort of democratic shape. However, in the Russian case the 'totalitarian' experience had devastated civil society and the foundations of liberalism, hence society itself has to become an object of the transition process. This tends to justify the displacement of sovereignty from the people to some agency that can carry out the necessary transitional measures, theoretically on behalf of the people who are considered not yet fit to govern themselves. In the Russian case this was the elite group around Yeltsin, and under Putin the administrative regime. The fear in the Kremlin was that left to themselves, the people would elect a radical nationalist, a populist, or some other demagogue; but control over popular choice also extended to more liberal candidates.

The term 'sovereign democracy' was used to describe the system following the Beslan hostage crisis, but this was only part of a larger debate about democracy and Russia's place in the international system. The key point was to achieve state sovereignty in the international system, accompanied by what Vladislav Surkov (at the time responsible for the management of political affairs) called the democratisation of international relations

(Surkov 2006a: 31–32). By now the economic situation had improved, with the country registering an average of seven percent annual growth throughout Putin's first two terms as president, the standard of living was rising, poverty was decreasing and Russia was becoming a consumer society on the Western model. The growing confidence based on domestic economic and political stabilisation and windfall energy revenues was, paradoxically, accompanied by a deep-rooted insecurity about Russia's international position and domestic integrity. The 'orange' revolution in Ukraine in late 2004 saw a massive popular mobilisation that forced a third-round run-off presidential contest between Viktor Yushchenko, favoured by the West, and Viktor Yanukovich, the candidate promoted by Russia. The Kremlin was deeply alarmed by what it considered to be the West's use of civil society to force regime change, and fear of 'orange techniques' provoked a clampdown on Russian NGOs and popular mobilisation.

The tension between stability and order now came to the fore. This was a feature of Brezhnev's rule that in the end gave way to stagnation. Stability is the short-term attempt to achieve political and social stabilisation without having resolved underlying problems and contradictions. Thus Brezhnev refused to take the hard choices that could have threatened the regime's precarious political stability. Order in this context is something that arises when society, economy and political system are in some sort of balance. To a large extent an ordered society operates according to spontaneous processes, whereas in a system based on the politics of stability administrative measures tend to predominate. Political order in changing societies may sometimes require the firm hand of the military or some other force that is not itself subordinate to democratic politics, as Huntington argued, but in the end most authoritarian modernising regimes give way to more inclusive democratic systems. Too much authoritarianism tends to result in rather too little modernisation.

Putin on a number of occasions explicitly sought to distance himself from this sort of tutelary politics as he tried to maintain a balance between the two wings of the dual state – the administrative regime and the constitutional state – but overall the *leitmotif* of his leadership was the technocratic assertion that the regime knows best. To achieve this, a system of 'managed democracy' applied administrative resources to manage the political process, undermining the spontaneous interaction of pluralistic political and social forces. This was in evidence as Putin managed the succession in 2007–08 to allow Medvedev to assume the presidency. The aim was continuity, and this was confirmed by Putin taking up the office of prime minister, creating what became known as the 'tandem'.

In his four years in the Kremlin Medvedev was constrained by the tandem form of rule, but he nevertheless articulated a liberal and less tutelary approach to politics. Medvedev condemned 'legal nihilism', and stressed a rather more liberal path towards modernisation. Medvedev rejected the term sovereign democracy, insisting that democracy did not need any adjectives. His article 'Russia, Forward!' of September 2009 provided a devastating critique. He described Russia as a semi-Soviet social order, 'one that unfortunately combines all the shortcomings of the Soviet system and all the difficulties of contemporary life' (Medvedev 2009). The fundamental question was whether Russia, with its 'primitive economy' and 'chronic corruption', has a future? Medvedev attacked not Putin but the system that Putin represented, a balancing act that blunted his message. This pusillanimity characterised his entire presidency, but although it is now common to disparage his achievements, the principles enunciated by Medvedev – for greater political pluralism, economic competitiveness and international engagement – are challenges that Russia objectively faces, whoever the leader.

The negative popular reaction to the 'castling' move of 24 September 2011 made this all the more visible. On that day it was announced that Putin planned to return to the presidency, and Medvedev would become prime minister. Russian politics appeared to have become an elite affair, with citizens little more than bystanders. The frustration burst out into mass demonstrations following the blatant fraud in the parliamentary elections in December, forcing the regime to move towards political deconcentration, although not genuine liberalisation. The registration of political parties became much easier, gubernatorial elections were restored, the electoral system was once again reformed and a degree of competitiveness returned to Russian politics. In other words, the programme espoused by Medvedev was implemented, although in very different circumstances to that originally envisaged. Following Putin's return to the Kremlin in May 2012 there was a period of 'tightening of the screws', but in the end mild political reform continued. Society had changed as a result of the relative prosperity of the Putin years, and an increasingly powerful popular constituency emerged demanding inclusion in the management of public affairs, above all through free and fair elections.

Challenges of democratisation

The scope of transformation in post-communist Russia has been unprecedented. A monolithic society was converted into a pluralistic one, a planned economy was reoriented towards the market, a new nation was born, and the state rejoined the international community. None of these processes is complete, and by definition never can be. The reform process itself generated new phenomena that raise questions about the received wisdom of the political sciences and economics. There has been rapid divergence in the fate of post-communist countries, with the majority of Central and East European countries joining the European Union in May 2004 with a second wave in January 2007 and Croatia entering in June 2013. Most of these countries have also joined NATO, creating what in the Kremlin's view is a security challenge of the first order. The failure to create an inclusive and what in Russian parlance is called an 'indivisible' post-Cold War security order in Europe and globally is perhaps the greatest failure of the period, reinforcing domestic insecurities and justifying the perpetuation of administrative forms of rule.

The 'third wave' transitions, to use Huntington's (1991) term to describe the mass extinction of authoritarian regimes following the fall of the dictatorship in Portugal in April 1974, prompted a renewed interest in problems of democratisation. The dissolution of communism encouraged political scientists to look again at the theoretical literature on democratisation and to compare the transitions in the post-communist bloc with earlier transitions in Latin America and Southern Europe (O'Donnell et al. 1986). The insights garnered in the study of the democratisation process elsewhere provide a theoretical framework to study the problem of the reconstitution of central political authority on principles of democratic accountability. The degree to which this literature has anything to offer when political regime change is accompanied by economic transformation, state and nation building and societal reconstruction in conditions of what some call a new Cold War remains a moot point.

The view that democracy is the inevitable outcome of post-communist transition is clearly mistaken. There is far too much that is contingent in processes of systemic change to allow any firm teleological view to be convincing. While about 100 countries have set out on the path of democracy during the 'third wave', at most three dozen have achieved functioning democracies (Carothers 2002). The contrary view – that the legacies of communist and even pre-communist authoritarian political cultures, economies and social structures doom the attempt to build democracies where there had at best been weak traditions of pluralism, toleration and political competition – is equally misleading. Deterministic views of democratisation leave out of account national political cultures, level of economic development, strategic concerns, leadership choices and elite configurations, economic dependencies and proximity to zones of advanced capitalist democratic development (above all the European Union). Rather than a *teleological* view about the inevitability of democracy, the *genealogical* approach takes into account concrete questions of political order, constitutionalism, state building, social structure and social justice, interacting with the practice of democratic norms and good governance (Sakwa 2012). Despite the efforts of political scientists, there is no agreement on one single factor that determines the success or failure of a democratisation process.

The relationship between liberalism, democracy and constitutional order remains contested in the post-communist context. Instead of government being accountable to the representative institutions of the people and constrained by the constitutional state and its legal instruments, the government assumed an independent political existence. It is at this point that a politically responsible and accountable government becomes a regime; formal institutions are unable to constrain political actors and informal practices predominate (North 1990). The outward forms of the constitutional state are preserved, but legality and accountability are subverted. A set of para-constitutional behavioural norms predominate that while not formally violating the letter of the constitution undermine the spirit of constitutionalism. Para-constitutional behaviour gets things done, but ultimately become counter-productive because of the reliance on the personal intervention of the leadership rather than the self-sustaining practices of a genuinely constitutional system. The regime is constrained by the constitutional state, but the system lacks effective mechanisms of accountability.

The contrast between the informal power relations established within the framework of regime politics, and the institutionalised competitive and accountable politics typical of a genuinely constitutional democratic state characterises Russian politics. Particularistic informal practices have been in tension with the proclaimed principles of the universal and impartial prerogatives of the constitutional state. Under Yeltsin personalised leadership came to the fore, with the power system and its oligarchical allies operating largely independently from the formal rules of the political system outlined in the constitution. Behind the formal façade of democratic politics conducted at the level of the state, the regime considered itself largely free from genuine democratic accountability and popular oversight. These features, as Hahn (2002) stresses, were accentuated by the high degree of institutional and personal continuity between the Soviet and 'democratic' political systems. A party-state ruled up to 1991, but the emergence of a regime-state in the 1990s created a system that perpetuated in new forms the arbitrariness of the old order. Under Putin the regime-state consolidated its power, but as a result of changes in society, and the elite came under increasing challenge. Putin in his fourth term was challenged to find more inclusive forms of political management, or he could find himself the target of a popular movement of the sort that emerged in the 'Arab spring' in 2011. A 'Russian spring' is not immediately in prospect, but the longer a 'thaw' is delayed the more likely that the contradictions between stability and order will intensify.

Conclusion

A democratic transition is usually considered to be over when democracy becomes the only game in town and where there is 'definiteness of rules and indefiniteness of outcomes'. Russia's transition is indeed over, but instead of democratic consolidation Russia's 'managed democracy' reversed the formula to ensure 'definiteness of outcomes and indefiniteness of rules'. Nevertheless, the scope for democratic development in Russia remains open. The government does seek to deliver a set of public goods, and although it practices an extra-democratic logic to achieve them, its fundamental legitimacy is derived from its formal commitment to the logic of the constitutional state. The regime is legitimate precisely because it claims to be democratic, and thus elections are not mere charades. Putin's government is undoubtedly considered legitimate by the great majority of the Russian people, as evidenced by his convincing electoral victories and consistently high personal ratings. However, too much is settled not in the framework of competitive politics but within the confines of the power system, leaving government only weakly accountable to society and its representatives. Nevertheless, the sinews of constitutionality are developing, and politics is not yet entirely subsumed into the administrative order. It will take an active citizenry and political pressure from below and courage from the leadership to ensure that the promise of Russia's democratic development is fulfilled.

2 PRESIDENCY AND EXECUTIVE

John P. Willerton

When Vladimir Putin passed Leonid Brezhnev on 12 September 2017 to become the longest-serving Russian leader since Joseph Stalin, he was fully positioned within the polity and society as Russia's paramount leader. As a paramount leader, Putin enjoyed the strong – unchallengeable – support of both the governing elite and the mainstream population that ensured he could govern Russia regardless of the official position held. In September 2017, the Russian population and elite were already anticipating the next presidential election, held in March 2018. The electoral outcome was clear, even if the particulars of the candidates running, voter turnout, and margin of Putin's assumed victory were to be determined. In all public opinion surveys of the period 2014–early 2018, strong majorities of Russians indicated they would vote for Vladimir Putin's return to a second term of his second presidency (and hence, his fourth term overall). In fact, Russians did vote in overwhelming numbers to re-elect him, with Vladimir Putin winning nearly 77% of the vote. Observers, especially foreign, understanding Russia as an authoritarian polity, found this outcome unexceptionable. Even granting institutional and electoral pressures that strongly favoured Putin's continued tenure as president, it was nevertheless important that this favoured incumbent enjoyed daunting public support. A lacklustre campaign did not preclude a 67% voter turnout, as candidate Putin articulated a 'guns and butter' policy agenda that built upon his earlier presidential terms. Especially encouraging for Putin and his team was the fact that, as opinion surveys had indicated, Russian late teens and young adults were the age cohort that proportionately most supported the incumbent president (*The Wall Street Journal*, 17 March 2018). The institutional powers of the presidency, joined with the leadership prowess and formidable popularity of Putin, combine to make the federal executive the focus of decision-making in contemporary Russia. Vladimir Putin will dominate Russian politics for the duration of his life, or for as long as he chooses: a fact that inspires his supporters, while frustrating his opponents.

One is loath to understand the politics of a country through the prism of elite politics, let alone the leadership of one individual. Yet one has little choice but to do so in understanding contemporary Russian politics. As the post-Soviet Russian polity and society move towards the third decade of Putin's and his team's governance, the Russian President's command of that polity and society is stronger than ever. It is incumbent upon the observer to understand the interests and perspectives of Russia's paramount leader, while also being attentive to his multifaceted and complex team, and the institutions of the hegemonic (i.e., overwhelmingly powerful) federal presidency and executive that he and his team control. Western observers and domestic Russian critics of Putin's regime are understandably critical of the Russian elite's claims of having established a post-Soviet Russian variant of a twenty-first-century democratic political system. But simplistic discussions of a new authoritarian Russian political system miss nuanced elements of top-down political consultation, representation within the governing team of diverse and competing interests, and bottom-up pressures to which the well-ensconced Putin elite are responsive. If the concentration of power and authority with the hegemonic presidency appears surprisingly simple, the complexities and nuances by which that presidency and related federal executive operate are more difficult to gauge.

Putin's May 2018 return to a fourth term (2018–24), sequentially broken by his one-term stint as prime minister (2008–12), when a loyal protégé, Dmitry Medvedev, held the presidency, only reaffirmed the unassailable dominance of both this paramount leader and his team across all decision-making settings. Beyond the formal institutions of the presidency, the Putin team fully directs the federal government, and the Putin platform party, United Russia, enjoys electoral pre-eminence, while the mass organisation, the All-Russian People's Front (ONF), further ties the governing team to various societal elements. These federal-level state and non-state institutions structure Russian political realities, to which sub-federal, down-to-local officials respond. When an election is held in an out-of-the way locale, such as the remote northern region Chukotka, only Putin's United Russia party flies in a candidate laden with 'pork' (i.e., resource giveaways) for the locals. Predictably, the local political establishment and population enthusiastically line up to vote for Putin and his allies: this is the political reality that so favours the long-governing leader and his regime. After the transformative changes and chaos of the late 1980s and 1990s, the Putin 2000s have entailed the complete reestablishment of top-down political order, with the hegemonic presidency and federal executive in the commanding position (Gel'man 2015). The Russian presidency and federal executive, with Putin and team firmly in charge, merit our careful attention.

Putin and the legacy of a strong executive

A broad overview of the past 1000 years of Russian politics reveals Russia has had a decided proclivity towards strong leaders, heading an authoritarian state, even granting fluctuations in the power of the central government (Moscow or St Petersburg) vis-à-vis the vast diversity of regions (which now span 11 time zones). Vladimir Putin came to power in the complicated and troubling environment of the post-Soviet 1990s, when the federal government was relatively weak vis-à-vis the regions, and competing elements both inside and outside Moscow pressed their interests. In a 1990s characterised by most Russians as a 'time of troubles', with 'wild west capitalism' and a socio-cultural scene described as a 'societal carnival' (i.e., 'anything goes'), political authorities were weakened and policy outcomes unreliable. For most Russians, perhaps the most important contribution Putin made to the evolution of the Russian polity was to restore the stability of the federal state, resting on the power of the presidency and the executive branch. Supporters and critics differ in their assessment of the longer-term consequences of Putin's state consolidation and policy efforts. Where supporters emphasise the rebuilding of a solid polity that delivers coherent policy, critics see the return of authoritarian institutional arrangements and policy-making norms that favour the elite. All agree, however, that the political chaos and policy uncertainty of the late 1980s and 1990s were replaced by a domestic political context of stability, regularity, and routinisation.

In personality, leadership style, and policy preferences, Putin proved able not only meeting, but exceeding, public expectations; his 50% approval rating at the time of his January 2000 elevation to the presidency rapidly moving into the 60–70 and even 80% range throughout his first two-term presidency (2000–08). Russian public opinion survey research results reported in Table 2.1 are illustrative, with the public's assessment of Putin's performance as president (panel 2 of Table 2.1) compared here with the public's assessment of the Russian government's performance (panel 3), and juxtaposed with the public's assessment of the Russian domestic situation (panel 1). The mainstream Russian public's considerable confidence in Putin as leader is revealed throughout the 18 years that Putin has dominated Russian politics, including when he served, 2008–12, as prime minister. With the exception of a moderate drop in public support of Putin into the mid-60% range in the late Medvedev and early second Putin presidency years (2011–14), Putin's approval figures have slowly risen or held constant, ultimately reaching into the 80% level after 2013.

A closer examination of Table 2.1 is useful as we consider the Russian public's strong support for Putin, contrasted with that public's more varied – and occasionally negative – assessment of the performance of the [Putin] government over the same time period. Drawing upon these Levada Centre survey results, it was only eight years into the Putin period that a majority of those surveyed came to approve the government's performance (59%, in August 2008), and this was when Putin had left the presidency and assumed the position of prime minister. The contrast between the public's assessment of Putin's performance, and that of his government (when someone else was prime minister), is striking: over the periods 2000–08 and 2012–17, there is an average 31-point difference in the positive assessment of Putin's and his government's performance. And Putin consistently holds this advantage even when the public's assessment of the situation in Russia is negative, when more citizens indicate Russia is on the 'wrong path' rather than moving in the 'right direction.' Supporters and critics emphasise different phenomena in understanding Putin's popularity. If supporters point to Russia's long-term economic turnaround and the country's heightened global leadership position under Putin, critics note Putin's good fortune in the timing of record energy prices (in the first two presidencies) or domestic payoffs of the annexation of Crimea (in the third presidency). Yet at the heart of Putin's strong domestic standing was a broad public assessment that he is a strong leader and that he has been able to deliver a coherent policy programme while mastering the institutionalised hegemonic presidency. Once again, Russia was led by the publicly desired resolute leader, what in pre-Soviet times was termed the 'tsar-father' ('tsar-*batiushka*'), standing atop a less trusted (and oft-perceived ineffectual) government, but firmly in charge of the strong state.

If leadership style matters, then Putin's modest background and assertive manner have fitted with Russian preferences in the post-Soviet era. Putin was born into a working-class family and was a product of the post-Stalinist period. He made a career in the Soviet intelligence services that entailed an elite education, travel and work abroad, and a broader awareness of both the Russian society and the outside world. His life experiences of the late Soviet and early post-Soviet periods left him subject to divergent and conflicting influences that were evident both in his rise to power and in his presidency. As an intelligence officer, Putin was well conditioned to a chain-of-command culture that emphasised loyalty and strict subordination, public order, and commitment to a strong state. Working as a key associate of the reformist St Petersburg mayor Anatoly Sobchak, however, he personally experienced the need for root and branch system change, and he became sensitive to bottom-up societal pressures, notions of elite and governmental accountability, electoral procedures, and the messiness of democracy building (Hutchins 2012). Where many observers understandably emphasise Putin's KGB past, his experience in the early days of reformism in his native St Petersburg should not be discounted. Is it suggestive that the only occasion during which Putin publicly expressed emotion was the funeral (in February 2000) of his mentor, the reformist Sobchak, who died of cancer at age 62?

Meanwhile, Putin has always exhibited an uncanny ability to express appreciation for past Soviet experience while simultaneously engaging post-Soviet thinking. Putin's life and career experience provided him a strong awareness of the complexities of system change and of governmental administration, and not only of commercial life but of civil society. Putin's institutional and policy preferences would be partly drawn from the Soviet past, but they would also rely on an evolving set of post-Soviet ideas and a willingness to make adjustments as dynamic conditions dictated. Putin's 'trial and error' approach to policy making bolstered his ability to adjust to evolving domestic political and socioeconomic realities. These preferences and skills proved true during the first Putin presidency, and his subsequent prime ministership, and they have been no less true for his second two-term presidency. The economic modernisation programme of the second presidency has built on the substantial and holistic reforms of the first presidential term (2000–04), while expanding on the more tempered and piecemeal efforts of the second presidential term (2004–08), and even of the Medvedev presidency (2008–12). Similarly, the expansion of state power in high-priority military-industrial sectors in the 2000s would contrast with the targeted privatisation efforts of the third presidency. As we will note later, Putin's fourth presidency's emphasis on raising salaries, wages, and pensions builds on initiatives set out at the beginning of his third term; initiatives stymied

Table 2.1 Russian Public Opinion Survey Results (Levada Center, August 2000–August 2017)

1. Russian Public Assessment of Situation in Russia
"Russia moving in the right direction or going down the wrong path?"

	8/2000	8/2001	8/2002	8/2003	8/2004	8/2005	8/2006	8/2007	8/2008	8/2009	8/2010	8/2011	8/2012	8/2013	8/2014	8/2015	8/2016	8/2017
Right direction	29	37	37	36	38	34	43	47	55	44	48	42	41	40	64	55	51	57
Wrong path	54	42	47	49	50	52	42	34	29	36	32	40	41	43	22	29	33	29
Don't know	17	21	16	15	12	12	15	19	16	20	20	18	18	17	14	17	17	13

2. Russian Public Assessment of Vladimir Putin as President
"Do you approve the activities of V. Putin as the president (prime minister) of Russia?"

	8/2000	8/2001	8/2002	8/2003	8/2004	8/2005	8/2006	8/2007	8/2008	8/2009	8/2010	8/2011	8/2012	8/2013	8/2014	8/2015	8/2016	8/2017
Approve	65	74	76	74	68	70	78	82	83	82	78	68	63	63	84	83	82	83
Disapprove	26	19	20	23	30	27	21	16	15	16	20	30	35	36	15	17	18	15
No Answer	10	7	5	3	3	3	1	1	2	2	2	2	2	1	1	1	1	1

3. Russian Public Assessment of the Government

"Do you approve the activities of the Russian Government?"

	8/2000	8/2001	8/2002	8/2003	8/2004	8/2005	8/2006	8/2007	8/2008	8/2009	8/2010	8/2011	8/2012	8/2013	8/2014	8/2015	8/2016	8/2017
Approve	38	39	35	38	32	29	37	43	59	53	52	44	47	41	62	54	46	50
Disapprove	49	45	54	54	60	66	59	53	38	44	45	54	52	58	36	44	53	49
No Answer	13	16	11	8	8	5	4	4	4	3	3	2	1	1	2	2	1	1

Source: Created using data from Levada Centre (http://www.levada.ru/en/ratings/) [Accessed 27th September 2019]

in the period 2014–17 by the drop in Russian governmental revenues (tied with the economy's contraction, oil price drops, and the Western sanctions and Russian counter-sanctions).

Perspectives on Vladimir Putin, his leadership style, and his legacy as Russia's paramount leader have varied, with especially divergent judgements separating mainstream Russian elite and public perspectives from those of many Western observers (Petersson 2014 and 2017). At the heart of Russian assessments have been widespread elite and public perceptions of significant domestic and foreign policy successes. Russians highlight the country's considerable national economic growth, the resultant, evident rise in citizens' standard of living, and Russia's return as a major global player. Putin team initiatives reversed the conditions and developments associated with Russia's 'failing state'; the 'failing state' signifying a state that is losing its vibrancy and legitimacy as it fails to carry out the tasks or provide the services to which it is committed (Willerton, Beznosov and Carrier 2007). A combination of factors was responsible for this turnaround, but forceful political leadership must be included among them. This turnaround, albeit with ups and downs, especially during the Medvedev and Putin second presidency first term, is a hallmark of the entire period since 2000. During the first presidency, Putin's modest style and 'samurai warrior' personal ethic won him considerable public sympathy (Solovyov 2008). Meanwhile, his decisiveness from the onset to tackle complex problems (such as taking on the influential oligarchs, beginning the process of reining in regional power barons, and crafting an intelligible tax programme), his ability to manage the bureaucracy while simultaneously strengthening the state and providing tangible returns to the population, predictably secured him consistently high marks. Indeed, the extent of Putin's authority – that is the legitimacy of his governance – was revealed in the second term (2004–08), when his government advanced unpopular reforms that trimmed the welfare state while Putin's popularity went unaffected.

Russians' confidence in Putin's leadership abilities continued during his four-year tenure as prime minister (2008–12) and subsequently during his third presidency (2012–18). As prime minister, and once again as president, Putin maintained a high profile in tackling numerous domestic economic problems while presenting himself as a strong manager overseeing a diverse array of officials. Well-publicised encounters with industrial managers, high-visibility trips throughout the country, and lengthy sessions with interested publics enabled Putin to simultaneously exhibit his forceful manner and his detailed command of the wide range of issues on the country's agenda. Equally important were Putin's regular, lengthy presentations before the State Duma, not to mention his very active agenda of interactions with foreign leaders and luminaries. Indeed, in the wake of the 2014 Russian annexation of Crimea, Western sanctions, and Russian counter-sanctions, Putin became active in engaging a range of potential foreign economic partners. High-visibility meetings, trips, or agreements involving a wide array of countries (e.g., Brazil, China, India, and Turkey, among others), reinforced Putin's positioning as a major global leader.

In contrast, Western observers' views of Putin and his leadership impact were and continue to be negative (e.g., Hill and Gaddy 2013). Enhanced power concentration and related decision-making 'streamlining', hallmarks of the Putin period, were seen as undercutting democratic impulses, with the four-year interlude of a Medvedev presidency having no discernible impact on this predominant Western judgement (Dawisha 2014). A new corporatism enabling the state to dominate key industries was joined with the state's control over the media and its enhanced ability to shape public opinion. Meanwhile, corruption continued to be widespread and appeared to include elements of the ruling Kremlin team itself. Putin himself had acknowledged that his regime's failure to address the country's epidemic of corruption had been the biggest failing of his first presidency, though Westerners questioned the seriousness of his regime's efforts. Finally, fledgling impulses for creating a Russian civil society had been undercut by the sum impact of the above-noted developments. Indeed, a vociferous minority of Russians would publicly express negative assessments of the Putin style and legacy similar to those of most Westerners, their opposition keenly evident in public demonstrations in Moscow and other urban centres in 2011–12.

Putin's return to the presidency in May 2012, and his actions during his third presidency, only reinforced the judgment of critics, foreign and domestic, that renewed authoritarian-system norms and centralised decision-making within the federal executive were core hallmarks of the Putin leadership approach. An assertive foreign policy, symbolised by the dramatic Russian move into Crimea in March 2014, was joined with domestic policy discussions dominated by Putin team elements. Indeed, it was the President himself, whether in formal presentations to the Duma, appearances before the influential Valdai Discussion Club (Moscow-based think tank), or the annual across-Russia live (often four-hour long) question-and-answer sessions, 'Direct Line with Vladimir Putin', who set out initiatives, stimulated discussions, and framed policy questions. For most Western observers, the bottom line was a renewed authoritarianism, one that came with a more forceful foreign policy and that was grounded in Russia's quest to be a Eurasian and even global leader (Myers 2015). For critics, the onset of Putin's fourth presidency in May 2018 looked to offer more of the same.

Institutions of the federal executive

There has been considerable continuity in the organisation and institutional configuration of the federal executive and the presidency across the Putin, Medvedev and restored Putin presidencies. There were some modest alterations for the Medvedev presidency (2008–12), with those changes reinforcing the position of the office of prime minister, then held by Putin. Any bolstering of the power of the prime minister was short term. Since Putin's return to the presidency in May 2012, the strong position of the office of president has only been reinforced, with the position of prime minister clearly subordinate.

The Russian Federation has a semi-presidential political system, with executive political powers divided between a president (and related institutions), who is head of state and who sets out the broad contours and directions of policy, and a prime minister and government, which are responsible for developing, implementing, and managing policies. This system is formally grounded in the 1993 Constitution, but its *de facto* logic stems in part from the Soviet experience, where the executive was divided between policy-making bodies housed in the Communist Party apparatus and policy-implementing bodies housed in the Soviet government. In today's Russia, the prime minister and other ministers who form the government are responsible to both the president and the national legislature. In Russia and in other contemporary semi-presidential systems, it is the head of state, the president, who nominates the prime minister, who must enjoy majority support within the legislature. That support is ensured by the president nominating the leader of the majority party or coalition, with the prime minister then forming a government comprised of ministers who must be approved by the legislature. The experience of the Putin period, 2000–present, fits with this institutional logic, with the pre-eminence of the presidency assured. Putin, his team, and his platform political party, United Russia, have dominated the political system, limiting institutional cleavages and ensuring decision-making continuity.

The president

An array of institutions and officials comprise the federal executive, with the hegemonic presidency at the helm. Informal arrangements, involving various sectoral interests, bureaucratic elements, and groupings of person-nel, also structure the president's decision-making primacy. The federal presidency has been hegemonic not only because its position is constitu-tionally superior to that of other institutions, but because it has possessed independence and freedom of manoeuvre. Since 1992, the president, through presidential decrees, legislative proposals, and vetoes, has been able to direct the decision-making process. While these formal abilities have not been essential in the Putin period, when the president had strong elite and public support, and when his platform party dominated the parliament, they are available if needed. Meanwhile, the president is able to appoint and guide the work of the prime minister and government, with key cabinet members (such as the foreign, defence, internal affairs, and justice ministers) appointed by and directly accountable to the head of state. The president is supported by a large set of agencies and officials that link him to all federal and major sub-federal institutions (Figure 2.1).

The 1993 Yeltsin Constitution specifies that the president 'defines the basic directions of the domestic and foreign policy of the state', while the president also represents the country domestically and internationally (see Articles 80–93). As the head of state and commander-in-chief of the armed forces, the president has the right to declare a state of emergency and mar-tial law, call for referendums, and even suspend the decisions of other state

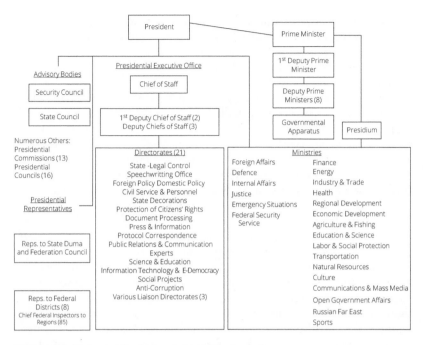

Figure 2.1 Major institutions of the Putin executive

bodies if their actions violate the constitution or federal laws. Changes during the Putin leadership strengthen the president's ability to direct Russia's centre-periphery relations, this in a country that is as vast as it is varied in its regional and ethnic composition.

Much decision-making initiative comes out of the Presidential Administration, but the president directs the federal government through the appointment and supervision of the prime minister and other ministers. The president, acting through the vast structure of supporting agencies, initiates legislation and reports annually to a joint parliamentary session on his government's domestic and foreign policy. Meanwhile, there are conditions under which the president can dissolve the lower house of the parliament, the State Duma, but these entail unusual circumstances that to date have not arisen. Likewise, the rival legislative branch has the formal ability to remove the president for malfeasance, but the procedures for impeachment are cumbersome and involve numerous federal bodies including the Constitutional Court and upper house of the parliament, the Federation Council. Since a two-thirds majority of the full membership of both houses is required to remove a president, the probability of ouster is low by any standard; the dominant position of the Putin's United Russia Party only further ensures the near-invulnerability of the head of state. The more compelling constraint on a president's tenure in office comes with the constitutionally mandated consecutive-two-term limit, with Putin's 2008 decision to step down after two terms, following upon President Boris Yeltsin's 1999 decision to retire after nearly two terms, setting a precedent.

The late 2008 Medvedev-initiated legislation to extend the presidential term to six years (previously four years) signifies that the second two-term Putin presidency will last until 2024. It is unclear whether Putin will consider, at that point, changing the constitutional constraint to permit his fourth presidency to continue with a third consecutive term.

An important, constitutionally permitted, means by which the chief executive can manoeuvre unilaterally is through the issuing of presidential decrees (*ukazy*), which have the force of law. The constitution (Art. 90) provides the president extensive leeway in issuing decrees to make institutional and policy changes, and while such decrees are inferior to laws, they are binding so long as they do not contradict the constitution or federal laws. In the face of a massive state bureaucracy, with its numerous and often-conflicting ministries, there is a need for powerful top-down mechanisms such as presidential decrees to direct its activities. While policy-making decrees may be overridden by parliament, a two-thirds vote of both chambers is needed, and this is highly unlikely to occur, given not only the parliament's highly fragmented structure and the weakness of the party system, but the contemporary strength of President Putin's United Russia Party. In the past, most notably during the Yeltsin period, decrees had a significant impact on Russian politics, and Putin relied on them during his first term to advance important initiatives (such as the establishment of the country's seven [now eight] federal districts and restoration of the system of presidential envoys, efforts to 'normalise' Chechnya, and energy and economic reforms). Yet as the Putin team strengthened its federal position, decrees became less necessary and Kremlin initiatives were advanced through legislation. This pattern continues in the Putin second presidency, as the President's agenda is advanced via legislation and not decree.

Presidential Administration

A critical institutional reality that highly favours the unilateral power of the federation president is the vast Presidential Administration (Figure 2.1). This administration both supports the activities of the country's chief executive and supervises the implementation of presidential decisions. Originally built on the organisational resources of the defunct Soviet Communist Party central apparatus, this extensive set of institutions is comprised of dozens of agencies and includes more than 3,000 full-time staff members: a number suggesting it is larger than the comparable support structure of the US president. The 21 directorates that are at the heart of the Presidential Administration reflect the decision-making and supervisory interests of the federal executive. The complex and often hidden manoeuvrings of the varied organisations and informal groups of officials constitute a sort of 'checks and balances' system within the federal executive. Since the Russian Constitution is silent on the organisation and functioning of this administration, it is up to each president to structure and manage it according to his own power and policy needs. Elite and public expectations of a chief executive being able to direct this administration – along with the federal government and the political process overall – are critical to positive evaluations of strong leadership. Occasional ruptures during the Medvedev presidency (e.g., Medvedev's public squabble with Finance Minister Alexei Kudrin that led to that powerful minister's September 2011 ouster) reflected the challenges of managing the large presidential team, with Medvedev's own public standing suffering as a result. In contrast, Putin has proven decisive and nimble in managing the Presidential Administration, and all evidence reveals both the elite and the population have confidence in his administrative prowess.

Management of the Presidential Administration requires a team of reliable subordinates, and Putin has had such a team throughout his presidency. Critical is the head of the Presidential Administration, the president's chief of staff, who oversees both administrative and personnel matters and operates as a sort of *éminence grise* of the federal executive. A number of skilled protégés have held this top post, and considered together these trusted loyalists reflect the diversity of the Putin team (see Figure 2.2). From the more reformist (and current Prime Minister) Dmitry Medvedev, to the long-time *silovik* (intelligence-security sector) ally, Sergei Ivanov, to the current youngish administrator, Anton Vaino, Putin has relied on lieutenants who bring different career backgrounds and associations with the President, and whose careers tap contrasting elements in the broader Putin-team constellation. Today, little-known Anton Vaino's reputation as a loyal and effective administrator makes him a key figure, not only in linking the President to the extensive set of institutions below, but in connecting the President to the government, Prime Minister Medvedev, and senior government officials. Born in 1972, Vaino is of a different generation than Putin (born 1952), and he reflects an increasingly important cohort of younger, up-and-coming officials in the Putin team. Indeed, as the Putin team continues to age, having been in power for nearly 20 years, other senior members (e.g., first deputy chiefs of staff, Sergei Kirienko and Aleksei Gromov) bring careers less tied to Putin's career past. These officials may be loyal, but they appear to hold top positions based on their abilities to address organisational or policy needs.

Figure 2.1 also indicates that the federal executive includes numerous presidential representatives to all important federal and sub-federal organisations, with these representatives serving as liaisons to coordinate those bodies' actions with presidential preferences. Especially notable are the presidential representatives to the eight federal districts, and the chief federal inspectors to the 85 regions, officials directly linking the federal executive to the most important administrative units of Russia's vast periphery. The federal executive also includes numerous advisory bodies that deal with selected policy areas while formally linking the president and his executive team to other institutional actors. These bodies also do not have a constitutional status, they operate at the president's pleasure, and similar to the Presidential Administration can be reorganised or abolished as the chief executive sees fit. Several of these bodies have now accrued some institutional history, encompass senior officials, and facilitate the president's handling of high-level policy matters. This is true of the Security Council (created 1994), which deals with foreign and security issues and includes the prime minister, relevant ministers, and the heads of the eight federal districts. Meanwhile, the State Council (created 2000) includes the heads of Russia's 85 regions and is the main institutional setting where regional leaders can deal directly with the president. The State Council addresses centre-periphery and sub-federal policy issues through meetings held every three months; a smaller presidium – or governing council – of eight rotating regional leaders, one from each of the federal districts, meets monthly.

Prime minister and government

The president's power and authority has also been traditionally grounded in his direct influence over the prime minister and cabinet, which form the government and define the 'basic guidelines of the government's activity'. The constitution does not specify which ministries shall be formed, leaving it to the president and prime minister to make the desired choices, but it does identify the policy areas with which the government will deal. The government crafts the federal budget and implements fiscal and monetary policies. It is responsible for the conduct of the economy and has oversight of social issues. The government implements the country's foreign and defence policies, administers state property, protects private property and public order, and ensures the rule of law and civil rights.

At the government's helm stands the prime minister, who is nominated by the president and must be approved by the Duma. While the Duma can remove the prime minister through the passage of two 'no confidence' votes within three months, there are political constraints on the parliament doing so; while the Duma for its part must be dissolved by the president if it does not approve his prime minister designate three times in a row. Traditionally, the prime minister's power is grounded in presidential approval rather than parliamentary support. The position and power of Prime Minister Medvedev, while formally nominated by President Putin and approved by an overwhelming vote of the State Duma, is certainly grounded in the strong support given to him by President Putin, even granting the assessment by many that Medvedev is an experienced manager and thoughtful politician. Prime Minister Medvedev's ability to advance the Putin agenda is certainly bolstered by the presence of a vast array of Putin protégés and allies in top governmental and presidential posts.

Having served as President, Dmitry Medvedev's past experience in the Presidential Administration and federal government has yielded nuanced knowledge of both policies and high-level elite politics that is valuable to a prime minister. A lawyer-academic who first met Putin while working in the St Petersburg government of reformist mayor Anatoly Sobchak, he moved to Moscow shortly after Putin became prime minister (1999), and during the first Putin presidency Medvedev held a number of highly influential positions; especially notable was his service as head of the Presidential Administration (2003–05), first deputy prime minister (2005–08), and his chairmanship of Gazprom (through most of 2000–08), the world's most powerful energy conglomerate. Medvedev's presidency proved unexceptional in its lasting impact, the high point being his oversight (with Putin's support) of the decisive Russian response to the summer 2008 Georgian conflict. While there were a few policy achievements (e.g., the 2010 nuclear arms agreement with the US), Medvedev proved unable to manage the complex constellation of political-bureaucratic forces that comprise the Russian executive and state. Meanwhile, throughout most of his presidential tenure, Medvedev's own public support always lagged behind that of then Prime Minister Putin, and this pattern continued as Prime Minister Medvedev's approval ratings consistently fell well below those of President Putin.

The prime minister chairs the Cabinet of Ministers, which oversees the state bureaucracy and has both political and law-making functions. Individual ministers set objectives for their ministries, craft their own subordinate bodies' budgets, and oversee policy implementation, but they do not have independent power bases. While most ministers report to the prime minister, five 'power' ministries (Foreign Affairs, Defence, Internal Affairs, Justice, and Emergency Situations) are directly accountable to the president. The prime minister's power over the ministries is further consolidated through the Cabinet Presidium, led by the prime minister and including the first and deputy prime ministers and other senior ministers. The Presidium coordinates and manages the government's work and, with it including three of the power ministers (foreign, defence, and internal affairs) who also report directly to the president, it reinforces the interconnected executive supervisory roles of the president and the prime minister. The institutional arrangements and responsibilities of the federal executive are becoming increasingly routinised, as both Presidents Putin and Medvedev have exhibited similar preferences in the setting out of ministerial portfolios during the past administrations. Putin now has in place a vertical, top-down administrative arrangement which his supporters contend streamlines the policy process.

The Putin team

The ability of Putin and his allies to manage the presidency, federal executive, and the Russian polity overall is grounded in the stable functioning of a large and multi-faceted team of officials. Informal politics – the politics of personalities, career networks, regional and sectoral interests, and competing institutions – are central to the conduct of Russian politics, as they were in Soviet times. Core to the informal politics of the twentieth-first-century federal government is the constellation of contrasting yet interconnected forces comprising the governing Putin team (Zygar 2016). Analysis of informal politics is difficult: definitive evidence is generally lacking, with the necessary interpretation always subject to sceptical judgement. We proceed cautiously in assessing contemporary Russia's informal politics, our focus on the core elements and logic of a Putin team that has dominated Russian politics for two decades. In broadly characterising these elements we may note their business-like manner, but an essential feature is loyalty to Vladimir Putin. As the Putin team has aged over the course of roughly 20 years, there has been rotation and retirement of officials. New, younger career administrators have moved into important executive positions, operating in tandem with long-term Putin protégés. Figure 2.2 sets out the important informal groups of officials who comprise the Putin team. The groups identified have been critical components of the governing team since its beginning, with the senior officials identified in the Figure ranging from long-time Putin protégés to younger professionals who have only interacted with Putin since he has been at Russia's helm.

Considerations of space preclude a full-blown analysis of all the officials noted in Figure 2.2, but the major informal groups listed reflect the diversity of elements comprising the governing team. These groups reflect Vladimir Putin's own career past, as he ascended through the KGB, worked in St Petersburg in the tumultuous 1990s, and then came to Moscow to assume a senior position in Russia's intelligence-security service. As the governing Putin team has evolved over nearly two decades, its composition has necessarily changed as the country's policy needs and Putin's power interests have evolved. If a broad characterisation of the governing team includes the informal groups detailed here, officials with more profound past career associations with Putin have given way to younger officials whose positions seem to reflect administrative expertise or achievement rather than strong personalistic ties to the President. Illustrative, at the highest political level, is the replacement as head of the Presidential Administration of the long-term protégé Sergei Ivanov with the little-known and younger Anton Vaino.

Turning to the major informal groupings comprising the governing team, the so-called St Petersburg lawyers and economists include a highly educated group of academics and specialists, trained and starting their

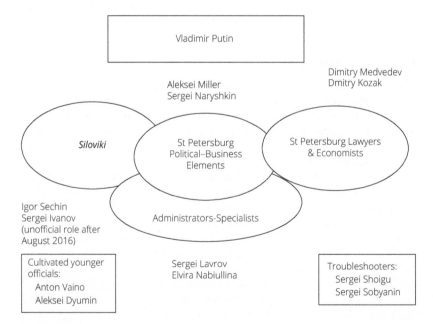

Figure 2.2 Major informal groups of the Putin team

careers in the northern capital, who have been central to the crafting and implementation of Russia's economic and political transformation. Generally educated in the late or immediate post-Soviet period, they ascended to federal importance under Putin, though older figures tied with them were important in the Yeltsin years (such as Anatoly Chubais). Here are officials often focused on the technical complexities of the country's economic and political overhaul, they are generally committed to a market economy, privatisation, careful structuring of the state's role in the country's socio-economic life and full engagement of Russia with the global system, but nested in a putatively democratic political system. We should distinguish another grouping, 'St Petersburg political-business elements', as these officials, also from Putin's hometown, have backgrounds more grounded in practical business experience and politics, but their policy preferences generally have been aligned with those of the St Petersburg lawyers and economists. These individuals have constructed complicated careers that span the political-administrative and business worlds that have dominated a fast-changing post-Soviet Russia.

Overall, while organising officials into these groups, there are differences in background and articulated priorities: we must differentiate Gazprom chair Aleksei Miller from the Foreign Intelligence Services Director (and one-time head of the State Duma and one-time head of the Presidential Administration) Sergei Naryshkin. Likewise, the policy trouble-shooter, Dmitry Kozak, who has tackled high-profile policy responsibilities (e.g., one-time oversight both of the troubled North Caucasus Region and the 2014 Sochi Winter Olympics), brings tremendous hands-on experience as a deputy prime minister, now serving under the one-time president and prime minister, Dmitry Medvedev. There may be personal-career rivalries among such elements and individuals, but it is difficult to assess the dynamics. Meanwhile, all of these officials appear committed to the governing team's power and policy agenda.

The other major group in the governing Kremlin team that draws upon Putin's career past is the *siloviki* (derived from the Russian word for power), officials from the intelligence-security services who have constituted a dominant force throughout the Putin period. It is challenging to accurately identify a common interest or shared set of perspectives for all *siloviki*, but many observers would conclude they have a natural preference for a strong state and less sensitivity to the nuances of the democratic system. *Siloviki* have presented themselves as disciplined professionals, they are generally highly educated, and some have brought past commercial experience to their governmental positions. A view of many in Russia, if not in the West, is that the *siloviki* are generally non-ideological, have a pragmatic law and order focus, and emphasise Russian national state interests. Today, there are a few holdover *siloviki*, such as Igor Sechin (the head of Russia's leading oil company, Rosneft), who have long-term connections with President Putin. There are influential members of the Putin team, such as defence minister Sergei Shoigu, who have career connections with the intelligence-security forces, but their formative careers were not in this area and were not tied with Putin.

The restored Putin presidency commencing in May 2012 and continuing into its fourth term has entailed a more pronounced shift in the composition of the governing elite, as a widening array of younger officials, without personal ties to the president, have risen to senior positions. Many of these officials fall into the Figure 2.2 category, administrators-specialists, though this category also includes some older and highly experienced officials such as Foreign Minister Sergei Lavrov (serving since 2004). Many of these officials who ascended into the senior ranks of the governing team during its second decade are highly educated, with careers involving considerable experience in a specialised area. Elvira Nabiullina (born 1963) constructed a promising career in economic development and trade, she has ties with senior St Petersburg economists such as the influential Aleksei Kudrin, she has held several top-level ministerial posts, and she now chairs the Central Bank of Russia (CBR). Anton Siluanov (born 1963), Minister of Finances, is a similarly well-educated and experienced economist who has become a key member of the leadership dealing with the intricacies of a complex and evolving economy. A relatively young Medvedev protégé and holdover from Medvedev's presidency is Justice Minister Aleksandr Konovalov (born 1968), who similarly brings educational credentials and a career as a tough prosecutor to the capstone post in his area of expertise. A final notable example of such administrator-specialists is Vladimir Kolokoltsev (born 1961) who, having made a career in the police sector, ascended from being Moscow police commissioner to a top post as Minister of Internal Affairs (i.e., domestic security-crime issues).

Finally, there is an important group of Putin team officials whose careers have revealed considerable organisational-decision-making prowess and a 'jack-of-all-trades' set of abilities and who have assumed a trouble-shooting role in tackling institutional or policy matters of the highest order. Sergei Shoigu merits attention, as he not only had a successful past tenure as the Minister for Emergency Situations, but was tapped to be Moscow Oblast governor, and then was called upon to assume the defence minister's portfolio when Putin protégé Anatoly Serdyukov was dismissed early in the third Putin presidency (2012). Over the course of his tenure as defence minister, Shoigu has assumed an ever-higher public profile, and he is one politician to whom some observers point in thinking about a Putin heir. Another such talked-about potential Putin heir, Sergei Sobyanin, has made a trouble-shooting career that has included service as governor of the important Tyumen province, deputy prime minister, head of the Presidential Administration, and mayor of Moscow (since 2010), with all of these posts held in the span of less than two decades. Neither Shoigu nor Sobyanin has strong personal ties with Putin from the formative years of Putin's career. But they have been cultivated by Putin during his presidential tenure, and they must be considered as among the most important figures in the Putin team.

Considered overall, the governing Putin coalition is large, multi-faceted, has exhibited a good level of continuity, and shows no sign of weakening or fracturing. The dilemmas that Dmitry Medvedev faced in supervising this team during his presidential tenure reinforce the conclusion that a priority concern for a Russian chief executive must be the management of both personnel and institutions. The team that will continue to govern Russia for the foreseeable future is clearly aligned to the career past, power interests, and policy preferences of Putin. From the long-term loyalist, one-time St Petersburg governor, and current Federation Council chairperson, Valentina Matvienko (born 1949), to the up-and-coming military-security officer, one-time Putin bodyguard, and governor of Tula province, Aleksei Dyumin (born 1972), this is a coalition that is highly effective for President Putin's purposes. By all appearances, Vladimir Putin continues to successfully manage his second two-term presidency team.

The continued Putin presidency

Most observers, whether inside or outside Russia, expect the fourth term of the Putin presidency to entail continuity in regime political efforts and policy outcomes. As indicated in the preceding discussion of the hegemonic presidency, federal executive, and governing elite cohort, the Putin team is powerfully positioned to direct the Russian polity. Yet Putin and his team confront at least two important challenges that could result in more interesting policy-making developments as the presidency continues.

First, while Putin as paramount leader commands a domineering political position, there is no doubt he must deal with the reality of what could be termed a 'Putin fatigue' that would naturally come with leading the Russian state for two decades. There is no strong evidence of meaningful opposition to Putin within the Russian polity, either from the elite or the general public. Even the presumed strongest opponent to Putin in the 2018 presidential election, Pavel Grudinin, of the Communist Party of the Russian Federation (CPRF), failed to record an expected solid vote (coming in second, but earning less than 12% of the vote). But there is suggestive evidence of public restiveness, if especially suggested by the public's more reserved and even critical assessment of the Putin government and its policy performance (Willerton 2016 and 2017). If high-profile Putin critic Aleksei Navalny's popularity has receded from its high in the early 2010s, his criticisms of both Putin (e.g., 2011 characterisation of Putin's platform party as the 'party of swindlers and thieves') and Putin's top ally, Medvedev (e.g., a widely viewed 2017 YouTube video), have made their mark on public opinion. Putin's seemingly unassailable leadership position is helped by the absence of viable alternatives. But complacency and even smugness with two decades of continuing governance could give way to more meaningful disillusionment were the domestic political or economic environment to be rocked with new challenges.

Second, as Putin finds himself in his fourth presidential term, not including his two terms as prime minister (1999, 2008–12), he and his team confront the real challenge of what could be termed 'making something old, *new* again'. One could argue that making something old *new* again was the challenge of the incumbent Putin seeking re-election in 2004. But now, with two more presidential re-elections under his belt, the challenge of defining a policy agenda or set of initiatives as *new again* is all the more difficult. What do Putin and his team offer as new, in what is effectively the eighth presidential term of the combined Putin-Medvedev tenure, having directed Russia since 2000?

Speeches from the December 2017 16th Congress of Putin's platform party, United Russia, which nominated Putin as its presidential election candidate, along with Putin's own campaign addresses, offer insight into efforts to present initiatives that could distinguish the Putin's fourth presidency from the preceding third term. Indeed, a high-profile Putin presentation to the Federal Assembly, delivered on 1 March 2018 only days before the presidential election, provided Putin with the opportunity to offer a *tour d'horizon* of the Russian political, economic, societal, and foreign policy scene, while setting out his own record and his second presidency second term agenda. With even his election rivals shown to be in attendance on Russian television, Putin identified a number of new initiatives, albeit much of the two-hour address surveyed what Putin saw as past policy successes. Other chapters in this volume review some relevant policy fields. Here I touch upon one broad area: initiatives to increase the salaries of public sector employees, doctors, and educators, with related spending increases in health care (e.g., a special national cancer programme) and education. These initiatives have widespread appeal to the Russian public, and they have their roots in the so-called 2012 May Directives, when Putin had returned to the presidency. While the 2012 directives had instructed the government to develop the conditions for the creation of 25 million jobs, they had gone essentially unfulfilled. The lack of government allocations had not only reflected government inefficiencies and even corruption. The lack of allocations had resulted from the domestic economic recession that occurred 2014–16, as related both to the drop in world energy prices and to the sanctions and counter-sanctions that arose in the wake of the 2014 Ukraine crisis. Indeed, if millions of jobs were not created, and most salaries not significantly raised, even the value of pensions dropped. By the onset of the 2018–24 Putin presidential term, the domestic economy was growing again, state revenues were increasing, inflation was low, and a Putin effort to make good on a set of promises left unfulfilled from May 2012 was serious. Meanwhile, talk of continuing to raise the average life expectancy of Russians (combined female and male) to 80 years by 2030, built on advances realised 2000–18, provided an identifiable goal for an over-arching second presidency second term programmatic thrust: what Putin termed the 'preservation of the people'. Perhaps the four-time Russian President would indeed make something old, *new* again.

The hegemonic presidency and strong executive branch will remain hallmarks of the Russian political system. Likewise, the long-governing Putin team will continue to dominate all institutions of the policy process. Mainstream Russian and foreign observers continue to disagree as to the putative democratic, authoritarian, or hybrid (i.e., mix of democratic and authoritarian features) character of the twenty-first-century Russian polity. However, the continued dominance of a paramount leader, standing atop a hegemonic presidency fully legitimated by the country's constitution, is furthered by the strong support offered by the Russian public and elite.

Public opinion surveys have revealed the following conclusions that, when summed, underscore the formidable political and institutional position of Putin and his team:

- 55% of Russians judge the president 'is the source of power and the holder of Sovereignty' (VTsIOM survey, November 2014);

- 81% believe 'strong leaders do many more good things for the country than any laws or discussions' (VTsIOM survey, November 2015);

- 74% indicate that 'everything is changing so quickly that you cannot figure out which laws you need to abide by' (VTsIOM survey, November 2015);

- 67% determine Russia is a democratic country (ROMIR survey, October 2014);

- 71% prefer to 'break democratic principles for the country to achieve order' (VTsIOM survey, March 2014); and

- 79% conclude Vladimir Putin believes in democracy (ROMIR survey, October 2014).

Many factors underlie the continuing power both of the presidency and federal executive and of Putin and his governing team. These factors include a historical tradition of the strong leader, the 1993 Constitution, the consolidated power position of Putin and his team, the overwhelming support of the country's elite, and the consistently demonstrated support in elections and surveys of the Russian citizenry. Observers will continue to offer varying judgements of how Putin's leadership and policy-making legacy factor into an overall assessment of that power. Uncertainties, however, remain, as the ageing Putin regime moves into his fourth term. Supporters and critics alike will need time to assess whether the experienced paramount leader and supporting team will, indeed, make something old *new* again, avoid Putin fatigue, and set out a programmatic course responsive to Russia's continuing twenty-first-century policy challenges.

3 POLITICAL PARTIES
Ora John Reuter

The story of Russian democracy can be told through its political parties. Observers had high hopes for democracy when the Soviet Union broke apart. After all, Russia's new leaders seemed committed to building a democratic state and a stable multi-party system. But these hopes were soon dashed. Many parties did emerge, but they were disorganized and effervescent. Outside the State Duma, political parties played little role in politics. As a result, Russia's weak parties were unable to serve as reliable mechanisms of accountability and representation.

In the 2000s, Russia's party system careened in the opposite direction: it became highly stable, but also more authoritarian. Under Vladimir Putin, the Kremlin has actively curated the party system. It created a single pro-Kremlin party, United Russia, that dominates elections and legislatures at all levels. Under Putin, opposition parties are still allowed, but many of the regime's most vocal critics are effectively excluded from electoral politics. Those opposition parties that remain 'in the system' are caught between a need to remain on good terms with the Kremlin and a need to maintain their oppositional credibility.

This chapter explores these metamorphoses in Russia's party system. It begins by exploring how Russia's underdeveloped party system undermined democracy in the 1990s and how the vestiges of that system laid the groundwork for the creation of United Russia. The second part of the chapter explores the role of political parties in an electoral authoritarian regime. What is the role of the ruling party in such a system? What is the role of the opposition? And can such a party system link citizens to the government?

Political parties and Russia's stalled democratization: 1991–2003

The collapse of the Soviet Union led to drastic changes in Russia's party system. Until perestroika, the only legal party had been the Communist Party of the Soviet Union (CPSU), and Yeltsin banned it in 1991. Thus, when the Soviet Union broke apart Russia did not have anything resembling a functioning party system. Nonetheless, Russia's new rulers intended for the state to have a multi-party system, and many parties soon sprang up to take part in elections.

The new parties were arrayed across the political spectrum. On the left there were communist parties, including the Communist Party of the Russian Federation (CPRF), which billed itself as successor to the CPSU. On the other end of the spectrum, there were several liberal parties that supported market reforms. There were also far-right, nationalist parties, as well as niche parties, which appealed to groups ranging from environmentalists to farmers to pensioners to car-owners. And in between, there were a succession of centrist parties. Some of these centrist parties were known as 'parties of power' because they were created by the government. At each State Duma election – in 1993, 1995, and 1999 – the Kremlin extended its support to a different party of power.

These new parties formed the rudiments of a democratic party system. Surveys found that many voters could distinguish the major parties from each other and understood where the major players stood on the issues. Party allegiances formed among a significant share of the electorate, although only a handful of parties were able to attract a stable following. In the State Duma, meanwhile, parties acted as surprisingly well-disciplined organizations.

And, yet, even though many parties emerged, the party *system* was inchoate and failed to effectively link citizens with government. Democratic theorists have long tied successful democracy to strong political parties. By aggregating diverse preferences, parties stabilize policy making and make it more predictable. Strong party labels also allow voters to discern what individual candidates stand for and help voters assign responsibility for policy outcomes. Unlike individuals, party organizations have long time horizons. Thus, strong parties should always have electoral incentives to be responsive; individuals often lack those incentives.

In Russia's first post-communist decade, parties mostly failed in these tasks. For one thing, many important areas of government were non-partisan. The president and most of the government were non-partisan. The same was true of the Federation Council. In the regions, most governors and even most regional legislators were non-partisan. The State Duma was the only institution where parties played a significant role.

The party system was also highly fractionalized. In 1995, 43 parties were on the ballot and 49% of the vote went to small parties that failed to overcome the electoral threshold to receive seats. There was also high volatility. In both the 1995 and 1999 Duma elections, more than 40% of the vote went to parties that were brand new. From election to election, the major party players changed drastically. Indeed, only the CPRF managed to win more than 6% of the vote in 1993, 1995, and 1999. And only the CPRF, Yabloko (liberal, pro-market party) and the Liberal Democratic Party of Russia (a far-right nationalist party) competed in all three elections. In the midst of all this party volatility, politicians switched from party to party.

Most of Russia's parties had vague programmes and weak organizations as well. They received few donations and had difficulty collecting dues, so most were chronically underfinanced. The activist base of most parties was narrow and few party leaders were under the collective control of the rank and file.

The constant emergence of new parties, combined with the lack of distinct programmatic platforms, made it hard for voters to determine what a particular candidate or party stood for. Thus, parties often failed to perform their core function of helping voters make informed choices at the ballot box. And because parties came and went with such speed, voters had a hard time using their vote to sanction (or reward) candidates. In turn, candidates had little use for poorly organized parties. This reduced campaigns to personalized contests between individuals or bitter clashes between powerful financial industrial groups.

Thus, many scholars view party underdevelopment as one of the reasons for Russia's incomplete transition to democracy. Why were parties so underdeveloped in the 1990s? Much of the system's underdevelopment simply had to do with its newness. With no history of democracy prior to 1991, Russia's parties had to start from scratch in building their organizations and making linkages with voters. Others have pointed to institutional factors (Ishiyama 1999), social antipathy towards parties (Hough 1998), and the global decline of mass parties as culprits (e.g. Dalton and Wattenberg 2002).

Henry Hale (2006) has advanced the argument that parties remained weak in Russia because politicians could rely on other organizations to achieve their electoral goals. In democracies, candidates usually affiliate with parties for two main reasons. First, parties provide candidates with resources that they need to get elected – money, organization, connections. Second, parties provide candidates with a political reputation, so that voters know what candidates stand for. If candidates can secure these benefits without having to pay the costs of joining a party – for example having to adhere to a partisan ideology or being under the thumb of party leadership – they will not join parties. In post-Soviet Russia, Hale argues, candidates often relied not on parties, but on so-called party substitutes to provide them with the resources they needed to win elections (Table 3.1).

One set of party substitutes were the regional political machines that were headed by powerful governors. During the 1990s, regional leaders took advantage of the power vacuum created by the Soviet collapse to create semi-sovereign fiefdoms. Governors proved adept at using their expansive patron-client networks to get their favoured candidates elected. Another class of substitutes were the expansive corporate conglomerates headed by prominent oligarchs. In the 1990s and early 2000s many candidates relied on these organizations, rather than parties, to provide them with the name recognition and campaign resources that were necessary to win elections.

Finally, some have argued that parties remained underdeveloped in the 1990s because the Kremlin chose to eschew party politics. President Yeltsin never joined a political party and barely even endorsed one. Some argue that if Yeltsin had chosen to make the office of the presidency a partisan one, it would have given impetus to party building (e.g. McFaul 2001). Moreover, if the Kremlin had created a strong political party it would have legitimized party competition as a means of exercising and achieving political power. As we will see in the next section, however, state investment in a strong political party can also be bad for democracy if the state wields the party as a tool to limit political competition. Either way, one of the most distinctive facts about party development in Russia is that the authorities maintained an arm's-length relationship with parties throughout the 1990s. Rather than rely on a stable pro-presidential

Table 3.1 Post-Soviet Russia's main parties

Party	Leader(s)	Years in Duma	Main policy stands	Status vis-à-vis Kremlin	Share of party list vote in 2016 State Duma election
United Russia	Vladimir Putin, Dmitry Medvedev	2001–	Anti-communism, guarded pro-Westernism, conservatism	Pro-Kremlin, Ruling Party	54
CPRF	Gennady Zyuganov	1993–	Socialism, nationalism	Anti-Kremlin Systemic Opposition	13
LDPR	Vladimir Zhirinovsky	1993–	Far-right nationalism	Loyal Systemic Opposition	13
Just Russia	Sergei Mironov	2006–	Moderate leftism	Loyal Systemic Opposition	6
Yabloko	Grigory Yavlinsky	1993–2003	Pro-democracy, social market, pro-Western	Anti-Kremlin, sometimes systemic, sometimes non-systemic	2
Progress Party	Alexei Navalny	Never	Pro-democracy, anti-corruption, pro-Western	Anti-Kremlin, non-systemic	Not-registered

majority party in the Duma, the Kremlin chose to (or was compelled to) legislate via shifting coalitions of deputies.

We can now summarize the main features of Russia's party system as it existed when Vladimir Putin came to power. The Kremlin played a relatively limited role in party politics. The party system was shaped less by the state than it was by 'market' forces and socio-economic factors. Much of electoral politics was dominated not by parties, but by individuals, regional power brokers, and oligarchic financial-industrial groups. The party system was unstable, with only a few consistent players.

The emergence of a dominant party system

Russia's party system experienced a sea change at the beginning of the twenty-first century. The highly volatile system of the 1990s was replaced by a rigid system dominated by one party, United Russia. United Russia was created in the aftermath of the 1999 State Duma elections. In those elections, Yeltsin's inner circle faced an existential threat from a new party called Fatherland-All Russia, which was formed by a coalition of powerful regional governors – most notably, Moscow Mayor Yuri Luzhkov and Tatar-stan President Mintimer Shaimiev. It survived the election, largely thanks to then Prime Minister Putin's emergent star power (see Chapter 4). But the "Kremlin's" latest party of power, Unity, controlled only 18% of seats in the Duma. Thus, as with previous Dumas, it looked as if the Kremlin would not be able to count on a pro-presidential majority in the Duma.

However, rather than muddling through, as previous administrations had done, the Kremlin chose to build a pro-presidential majority. At the urging of Deputy Presidential Administration Chief Vladislav Surkov, FAR and Unity began negotiations to merge their parliamentary factions. Two groups of non-partisan deputies – Regions of Russia and People's Deputies – also joined the negotiations. Although initially hesitant about the idea, the merger soon gained the blessing of Putin. In December 2001, a merger of the blocs was sealed and a founding congress was held for the All-Russian Party 'Unity and Fatherland – United Russia.'

The new pro-presidential party controlled 234 Duma seats, a majority. The new party then set about extending its reach into the regions, establishing factions in regional legislatures and recruiting powerful governors to join its ranks. These efforts paid off; in the 2003 State Duma elections, UR won an absolute majority. After a number of independent deputies joined its parliamentary, it came to control a two-thirds majority.

The Kremlin invested much more heavily in United Russia than it did in any previous party of power. Although he has never officially joined the party, Putin associated himself with his party of power much more closely than Yeltsin had ever done. Putin spoke at party congresses, headed its party list in 2007, and served as party chairman from 2008 to 2012. His advisors, meanwhile, sent signals to the elite that the Kremlin was serious about placing all its eggs in the United Russia basket. At a 2006 gathering of activists from another pro-Kremlin party, Just Russia, Vladislav Surkov proclaimed that the political system would be 'built around United Russia' for the foreseeable future (Reuter 2017: 144).

These words were turned into action. Rather than bargain with multiple deputy groups, the Kremlin began working almost exclusively with United Russia in the Duma. In the regions, the Kremlin privileged United Russia over other parties. Between 2005 and 2012, over 75% of newly appointed governors were United Russia members.

Why did the Kremlin choose to build a dominant party? The main reason was that it wanted to co-opt Russia's powerful elites and bring order to its relationship with them. This was especially true in the regions and in the Duma. No authoritarian leaders are able to rule alone. All must enlist the cooperation of other political elites in order to secure their rule. Leaders seek elite cooperation because elites provide essential political services that help the regime govern cost effectively. They are opinion leaders, power brokers, and influencers. Dictators often bring such elites into the regime in order to draw on their political resources.

As noted in the previous section, Russia's regional elites had accrued immense power and influence over the course of the 1990s. In order to govern the country, the Kremlin would have to engage with these elites somehow. After all, they were too powerful to repress. Thus, it launched United Russia as a way to harness together the political machines of regional elites and put them to work for the regime. In particular, these machines would be used to help the regime win elections.

The Kremlin might have liked to do the same in the 1990s, but Yeltsin was highly unpopular and, with oil prices at record lows, the state had few resources at its disposal. Thus, regional elites had little reason to link their fates to any centralized dominant party that would have been created. In the early 2000s this situation changed: Putin was widely popular, the economy was growing, and the coffers of the federal treasury were swelling with oil revenues. In this setting, elites had ample incentive to link their fates to the Kremlin and the Kremlin had ample incentive to co-opt them. The result was United Russia.

United Russia as the dominant party

What is United Russia's role in Russia's political system? The answer to this question is complicated by the hybrid nature of Russia's political regime. On the one hand, United Russia serves certain functions as an *authoritarian* dominant party. In particular, it helps the Kremlin manage and structure relations with elites, especially in legislatures and the regions. On the other hand, it also performs some of the same functions that parties in democracies do. It has an extensive grassroots organization that helps the Kremlin mobilize supporters, and its brand helps pro-Kremlin voters identify their preferred candidate. This section begins by discussing United Russia's position among the political elite.

One way to conceive of an authoritarian dominant party is as a coalition of pro-regime elites. The function of the party is to organize relations with and among these elites. Indeed, it is clear that United Russia is the most important party among the Russian political elite. In 2017, it controlled 75% of the seats in the Duma and 80% of seats in the Federation Council. Fifty-seven of Russia's 85 governors are UR members. The party has a majority in all 85 regional legislatures and supermajorities in 78 of those regions. Current data on party penetration in local politics is not easily available, but in 2012, 86% of the mayors of cities with populations over 75,000 had United Russia mayors. Ninety-two percent of those city councils had UR majorities.

However, party penetration in the federal executive branch is limited. Although Prime Minister Medvedev is party chairman and a few government ministers are members, most of the government is non-partisan. The same is true for most high-ranking members of the Presidential Administration, Putin's inner circle. Most importantly, Putin himself has never become a member of the party. He endorses the party, speaks at party congresses, and was Chairman of the party for four years (2008–12), but he does not owe his career to the party and is not subject to its collective control.

Why does Putin not become a member? Putin seeks to retain maximum freedom of manoeuvre. Being under the control of a party would limit his flexibility to make decisions and respond to challenges. Moreover, by associating too closely with the party, Putin could be tainted by scandals or crises that attach to the party. Thus, while Putin clearly favours UR over other parties, he has not put himself under the party's control.

The fact that the most important office in Russia is non-partisan places severe limitations on the influence of United Russia. In the Soviet Union, policy was made by collective party organs and transmitted for implementation to government institutions. This does not happen in Russia today. On the one hand, United Russia does have its own leadership organs – the Presidium of the General Council and the Bureau of the Higher Council – which are populated by prominent Duma deputies, governors, businessmen, and ministers. These organs make important decisions that affect party cadres, but they do not make political decisions that are carried out by the Kremlin. It is the Kremlin that sets policy direction in Russia. United Russia's role is limited then to managing pro-Kremlin deputies in legislatures and elites in the regions. In this way, United Russia is less like the CPSU or the Chinese Communist Party and more like dominant parties in other electoral regimes such as the PRI in Mexico or the KMT in Taiwan.

United Russia has provided a number of important benefits to the Kremlin. Perhaps most importantly, it has helped the Kremlin dominate elections. Aside from providing a party brand and organizational resources (discussed below), the strategy of co-opting regional political machines proved wildly successful. Throughout the 2000s and early 2010s, United Russia consistently performed best in those regions where it had inherited a strong political machine from a co-opted governor (Reuter 2013; Golosov 2011).

The party also helps coordinate the campaigns of pro-regime candidates. In 1995, as many as nine parties split the pro-Yeltsin vote among themselves. This provided openings for opposition parties to win in races where a majority of voters were actually pro-Kremlin. This no longer happens since the vast majority of pro-regime candidates run with UR affiliations.

The other main benefit that United Russia has provided is elite loyalty. This is most evident in legislatures. In the 1990s, the Kremlin had constant difficulty passing its legislative initiatives because it had to coordinate independent deputies and shifting factions. This is no longer a problem. Pro-regime deputies are consolidated in United Russia factions and party discipline is strict. Almost all Kremlin legislation is passed easily, usually with the unanimous support of the United Russia faction.

The party helps ensure loyalty outside legislatures as well. The party rewards loyalty with career advancement. Thus, even those elites who end up on the losing end of a particular political bargain can expect that they will be rewarded in the future if they just stick with the party. Unstable autocracies are often characterized by high rates of elite defection, but Putin-era Russia has seen few such defections.

United Russia and the electorate

In addition to being an elite party, United Russia is the primary electoral vehicle of the Kremlin. The party has a massive grassroots organization consisting of 85 regional branches, 2,595 local branches and 82,631 primary party organizations. Regional and local branches have permanent staffs, but primary party organizations do not. Rather, these organizations are staffed by hundreds of thousands of party activists, usually local government officials, teachers, and mid-level factory managers. These activists are deployed at election time to agitate on behalf of UR candidates. Between elections, they hold meetings, rallies, and trainings. On paper, activists are able to exert control over higher party organs through the selection of delegates to higher-level party conferences, but in practice, the selection of delegates is often dictated from above.

The party also has a youth wing – Young Guard (*Molodaya Gvardia*). With 170,000 members, Young Guard claims to be the largest youth organization in the country. It agitates during elections and holds seminars and political lectures. Modelled on the CPSU's youth wing, Komsomol, the Young Guard has been an important conduit of elite recruitment for United Russia. Indeed, the current chairman of the party's General Council, Andrei Turchak, was head of the Young Guard in 2007–08.

Surveys consistently show that United Russia is the most popular party in the country (see Figure 3.1). United Russia owes much of its popularity to state manipulation. Biased state media provide ample and positive coverage for United Russia, while ignoring or discrediting the opposition. Moreover, the state puts pressure on opposition parties – limiting their ability to hold protests, denying ballot access, repressing their leaders – so that the playing field is skewed in United Russia's favour.

Still there are some important elements of United Russia's popularity that are not directly attributable to authoritarian manipulation. One is its relationship with Putin. The party has always been keen to highlight its close relationship with Putin, who consistently has approval ratings in the 60–80% range. United Russia officials never miss an opportunity to mention that Putin founded the party and often refer to him as their 'moral' leader. In 2007, the party called its election platform 'Putin's Plan.' According to one survey from the 2016 State Duma elections, 26% of United Russia voters listed the party's support for Putin as the primary reason that they chose UR.

But the party has other sources of support as well. Surveys find that voters credit both Putin and United Russia for improvements in living conditions over the past 18 years. And perhaps surprisingly, the party has developed a core of strong supporters that feel psychologically attached to

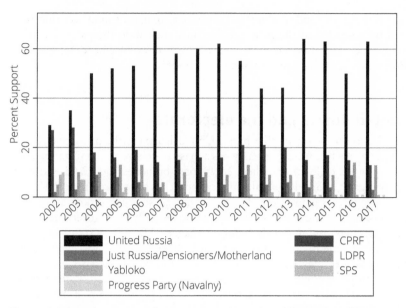

Figure 3.1 Popular support for major Russian political parties: 2002–17

Source: Created using data from Levada Center (http://www.levada.ru/en/) [Accessed 18 July 2018].
The question wording is: If elections to the State Duma were held this Sunday, would you vote? If
so, which of these parties would you vote for? The bars indicate the share of respondents stating
their intention to vote for a particular party, as a share of those who would vote. All polls are from
November of the given year, except 2009, 2016, and 2017. Data are from September, August, and
June for those years. November polls were not available in those years

the party. In Western democracies, party identification is one of the most powerful predictors of voting behaviour. Citizens form bonds with particular parties and those partisan attachments often colour their view of politics. Although multi-party politics is relatively new in Russia, surveys indicate that many voters have begun forming such attachments. In 2016, 27% of Russian citizens could be considered loyalists of UR. Other parties have much smaller sets of loyalists (surveys indicate that the CPRF is able to claim 8% of Russian adults as its loyalists).

Surveys indicate that voters can discern United Russia's position on the ideological spectrum. On the whole it occupies a centrist position in Russia's party system. Voters perceive it as slightly right of centre on economic issues (more pro-market) and more pro-Western on foreign policy issues. Indeed, Putin's party is actually more liberal than the average Russian voter. This is true on social issues as well, although it has grown considerably more conservative over time.

Ideologically, United Russia is a broad tent. As a party that unites much of the political elite it has many different types of politicians in its ranks. To accommodate this diversity UR has encouraged the creation of ideological wings within the party. There is a liberal wing, which is more pro-democratic and more market oriented. There is a social-conservative wing, which focuses on social issues. And there is a state-patriotic wing for those who are most focused on issues of national identity and defence. At various points, these informal clubs have been given institutional form, but as of this writing, there has been a trend away from allowing these wings to create their own organizations.

Of course, at election time the various wings must create a single platform. This leads to the creation of non-ideological platforms with little specific policy content. Many criticize United Russia for lacking ideological cohesion, but it is rational from an electoral standpoint. United Russia is what political scientists call a catch-all party. Rather than taking a strong ideological stance, it tries to appeal to voters from across the ideological spectrum. Some of the world's most long-lived dominant parties were catch-all parties. Their centrist position prevented the opposition – which is positioned on opposite ends of the ideological spectrum – from coordinating against them. This is what United Russia does.

Another aspect of United Russia's electoral strategy is clientelism – the exchange of selective inducements for political support. United Russia is much less clientelist than some other dominant parties, but it still uses such techniques to gain votes. At election time, it is not uncommon to find party logos emblazoned on new public works projects, such as roads, schools, churches, swimming pools and the like. The party also administers its own 'Party Projects,' a series of social and infrastructure projects that are funded by the federal budget. In 2014, there were 43 such projects at the federal level and over 400 at the regional level. In some campaigns, United Russia has given itself the moniker 'Party of Real Deeds' (*Partiya Realnykh Del*). The implication is that UR is the party of the government, and as such, it can provide tangible benefits to voters in a way that opposition parties cannot.

Finally, United Russia secures votes by capitalizing on the precarious position of the opposition. In 2016, a cache of United Russia's agitator training materials was leaked to the press. One of the arguments that activists were encouraged to use was: 'Who, if not United Russia? Can you imagine Russia being ruled by any of the existing opposition parties?' Because it is marginalized by the state, the opposition is an unknown quantity for many Russian voters. United Russia seeks to benefit from this. The party also paints its majority status as an inherently positive trait. Another slogan that agitators used was: 'United Russia is the party of the majority; the majority can't be mistaken'. Thus, United Russia uses the pressures of social conformity to its advantage.

Opposition in Russia

The opposition is weak in Russia. As Figure 3.1 shows, only the CPRF and LDPR ever poll above 10%. Recent surveys indicate that most opposition parties have support levels that hover around 1%. Some of this weakness is due to Putin's popularity, but much of the opposition's weakness is due to obstacles created by the Kremlin. Fraud, biased state media, onerous registration requirements, institutional manipulation, clientelism, and repression combine to keep the opposition at bay in Russia.

Scholars of Russian politics often distinguish between systemic opposition parties and non-systemic parties. Systemic opposition parties – such as Just Russia and the LDPR – may oppose certain policies, but do not usually call for the overthrow of the system. Often called the 'loyal opposition', these parties moderate their criticism of the regime and sometimes even lend their support to Putin. In return for their loyalty, they may be granted certain institutional perks (such as prominent leadership position in a legislature, a governorship, air time on state television).

By contrast, non-system opposition parties, such as Alexei Navalny's Progress Party (now called Russia of the Future), position themselves as uncompromising rivals of the regime. They call for regime change and do not cooperate with the authorities on matters of policy making. Indeed, because of their radical stance, non-system opposition parties often find themselves entirely excluded from the formal political process.

In practice, the distinction between systemic and non-systemic parties is not always stark. The systemic–non-systemic distinction is more of a continuum than a dichotomy. One on end are parastatal 'opposition' parties, which are created and directed by the Kremlin. On the other end, are hardcore revolutionary movements that are illegal. In between, Russian opposition parties adopt various stances towards the regime and participate in elections to varying degrees. The paragraphs below discuss several of the major opposition players in Russia.

Just Russia

Russia's most 'systemic' opposition party is Just Russia. Just Russia was created in 2006 at the initiative of the Kremlin. It came together as a merger between three smaller systemic opposition parties – the Russian Party of Life, Rodina, and the Russian Pensioners Party. Each of these parties had been founded in its time as state-sanctioned left-leaning opposition parties that could draw votes away from the CPRF without threatening the regime. Just Russia occupies a centre-left position in the ideological space. It is slightly less pro-market than United Russia and is more anti-Western. Its campaigns emphasize issues of social justice. However, like United Russia, its stated ideology is somewhat diffuse, and ambitious politicians of many stripes join its ranks.

Just Russia's leader, Sergei Mironov, is a long-time Putin ally, going back to their days working together in St Petersburg. From 2001 to 2011, he was speaker of the Federation Council. Thus, Just Russia can barely be considered an opposition party. At various times since its founding, rumours have surfaced that the Kremlin intended to transform Just Russia into a second party of power. But this has yet to happen. The party usually polls in the single digits.

Vladimir Zhirinovsky's Liberal Democratic Party of Russia (LDPR)

The LDPR is one of only two parties (the other being the CPRF) that have secured seats in all seven Dumas since 1993. The party is primarily a vehicle for its controversial, extreme nationalist leader Vladimir Zhirinovsky.

Zhirinovsky's political career began in 1991 when he finished third in presidential elections for the Russian republic. In the State Duma elections two years later, his newly formed party finished in first place with 23% of the vote. That a party could win 23% of the national vote with a leader whose political style consisted of rambling nationalist rants and drunken tirades shocked observers in Russia and abroad. Among Zhirinovsky's many outlandish policy proposals: Russia should annex Alaska; all Chinese immigrants should be expelled from the Russian far east; Russia should ban all political parties and introduce an 'elected' monarchy; Russia should legalize polygamy to solve its demographic crisis. His personal style is controversial as well. He has been known to throws handfuls of money to crowds, and he has been involved in no less than five physical altercations with deputies and reporters.

The LDPR has never been able to duplicate its success of 1993. Its electoral support oscillates in the 5–15% range. Most Russians view Zhirinovsky as some complicated blend of offensive, entertaining, and ridiculous. Few take his antics seriously. Indeed, some suggest that Zhirinovsky himself does not believe what he says and that his absurd antics are just designed to grab attention.

On paper, the LDPR's ideology is ethnic nationalist It takes a hard anti-Western line on foreign policy issues but does not take a clear stand on economic issues, disavowing both economic liberalism and communism. Despite its brazen rhetoric, the party actually votes with the government quite frequently. Its relationship with the Kremlin is almost as cosy as that of Just Russia. It often receives leadership positions in regional legislatures, and, in 2012, Putin even appointed one of its members to be governor of Smolensk Oblast.

Communist Party of the Russian Federation (CPRF)

After Yeltsin banned the CPSU in Russia in 1991, several communist groups sprang up to carry the communist banner. The CPRF emerged in 1993 as the largest of these, and most importantly, the only one that managed to register for Duma elections that December. The party took third place in those elections. Its support grew as the economic crisis deepened and some voters soured on the idea of reform. It reached the peak of its power in 1996 when its presidential candidate and long-time leader, Gennady Zyuganov, won the first round of the presidential elections against Yeltsin. Yeltsin won narrowly in the second round, but some argue that this was only due to fraud.

The CPRF was the largest party in both the second and third Dumas and it remains Russia largest opposition party. Although it is a communist party in name, it has softened its stance on state ownership and now accepts a significant role for private enterprise. It has also deviated from the ideology of the CPSU by embracing Russian nationalism and defending the rights of the Russian Orthodox Church.

Until United Russia came on the scene, the CPRF had the strongest grassroots organization of any Russian political party. It had, and to some extent still has, a devoted core of activists, mostly drawn from those who 'lost' in the transition from communism (e.g. older voters and the working class).

The CPRF's relationship to the state is complicated. On the one hand, it is often a vociferous critic of United Russia, especially on issues related to economic reform. At the same time, it sometimes votes with the government and has been hesitant to call for regime change. During the 2011–12 protest wave, Zyuganov conspicuously rejected street protests as a strategy for contesting the election results, claiming that the protest movement aimed to return power to the 'ultra-liberal forces … who destroyed the USSR and created the current system of electoral falsification.' The CPRF participates actively in elections and holds seats in legislatures at all levels. Indeed, in the regions, United Russia often shares important legislative leadership positions with it. In 2015, a CPRF member won a competitive election to become governor of Irkutsk Oblast, one of the most important regions in Siberia. In 2017, Putin nominated a CPRF member to be governor of Oryol Oblast. Thus, the CPRF benefits from moderating its opposition to the regime. The difficulty for the party is that if it moderates its opposition too much, it risks losing its core voters. This is a perennial conundrum for systemic oppositions under authoritarianism.

Liberal parties

Russia has had a number of liberal parties over the years. In the Russian political vernacular, liberal parties are those with pro-market, pro-Western, pro-democracy platforms. Liberals had their best showing in 1993 when 34% of the vote was captured by such parties. The liberals capitalized in the early 1990s on anti-communist sentiment and an appetite for change.

Since the early 1990s, however, their vote share has gradually declined and, since 1999, no liberal party has won enough votes to form a faction in the Duma. Their decline is due to several factors. For one thing, many liberals went into government in the early 1990s. Thus, liberal parties have lost voters and leaders to the various parties of power. Indeed, in the early 1990s a young Vladimir Putin worked on the staff of one of Russia's most prominent liberal politicians, St Petersburg mayor Anatoly Sobchak. And yet, by 1995, Putin was running the St Petersburg branch of Our Home is Russia, a party of power. In Putin-era Russia, the liberal opposition continues to be hamstrung by the fact that United Russia is situated to the right of centre. Thus, some moderate liberal voters and politicians are UR supporters.

The liberals have also underperformed because they have been divided. Some of these divisions have been ideological, but more often it has been personal conflicts that have prevented the emergence of a unified democratic coalition in Russia. Finally, as with other parties, the liberals have suffered from administrative pressures. This has been especially true in the past ten years.

Russia's longest-standing liberal party is Yabloko (an acronym for the party's founders that literally means 'apple'). Yabloko's founder and long-time leader is Grigory Yavlinsky, who first gained fame as a market reformer in the late Soviet period. Personal feuds and policy disagreements soon led Yavlinsky and his allies to part ways with Yeltsin and other liberals. The party has remained committed, however, to market reform and West-ern integration. However, its programme tends to focus more on issues of human rights, social justice, and economic equality than do other liberal parties. In the 1990s, Yabloko had the reputation of being the party of the old Soviet intelligentsia.

Yabloko has been a vocal critic of creeping authoritarianism under Putin. In the early 2000s, it rejected a coalition with another democratic party – Union of Right Forces (*Soyuz Pravykh Sil*, SPS) – on the grounds that the latter was too supportive of Putin. Unlike some other democratic parties, Yabloko is usually allowed to participate in elections, but it has not had a deputy in the Duma since 2003.

Historically, market-liberal, pro-business parties have formed the other major flank of the liberal opposition. One of the most prominent was the SPS, a conglomeration of liberal parties formed to contest the 1999 elections. One of its leaders was Boris Nemtsov, a well-known market reformer and former deputy prime minister under Yeltsin. Among other things, SPS was distinguished from Yabloko by its willingness to work with the Kremlin – several of its former leaders are now high-ranking officials in Putin's government – and by its special focus on appealing to the business community. With the implicit backing of the Kremlin and an effective, youth-focused campaign, SPS won a respectable 9% of the vote in 1999 and was the fourth largest party in the Duma. As the regime became more authoritarian, however, SPS became more oppositional. In the process, it lost both its Kremlin support and many of its voters. It failed to clear the threshold for representation in 2003 and subsequently splintered. Since then, the market-liberal opposition has been persistently fractured and marginalized.

SPS's former leader, Boris Nemtsov, went into extreme opposition in the mid-2000s and became one of the leaders of Solidarnost, a loose coalition of liberal politicians and organizations that is one of the central players in the non-system opposition. The groups that make up Solidarnost are among the Kremlin's harshest critics. They focus primarily on issues related to democracy, the rule of law, civil rights, and corruption. Several of their constitutive organizations and leaders have been banned from participating in elections. On 27 February 2015, Nemtsov was murdered on a bridge near the Kremlin while returning home from dinner. The killing inflamed passions among the opposition, many of whom believe that someone in the Kremlin either ordered the killing or is engaged in a cover-up to conceal the identity of those behind it.

One of the most important figures to emerge from the liberal, non-system opposition is Alexei Navalny. The 35-year-old Navalny came to prominence in 2010 as an anti-corruption campaigner. His anti-corruption blog was one of the most popular pages on the Russian blogging service,

Live Journal. Navalny quickly transformed his online star power into one of Russia's most potent political brands. In 2011, he coined an epithet for United Russia, 'The Party of Crooks and Thieves,' which gained wide currency online. In 2013, he ran for mayor of Moscow and finished second with 28% of the vote. In the same year, he founded his own party, the Party of Progress, (Russia of the Future) which he continues to lead.

Navalny distinguished himself from other opposition leaders by capitalizing on new media. His YouTube channel – which has 1.5 million subscribers – produces slick videos exposing the corruption dealings of high-ranking Russian officials that get tens of millions of views. He maintains an active presence on Twitter, Instagram, Facebook, VKontakte, and Live Journal, and his organization has become adept at using these tools to attract large, enthusiastic crowds for his rallies. In 2017, *Time* magazine named him one of the 25 most influential people on the internet.

Navalny attracts support from young, well-educated Russians in large cities. Although his support base remains limited, the Kremlin is clearly concerned with the threat posed by Navalny. Although narrow, his base of support comes from the country's intellectual and cultural elite, groups with influence beyond their numbers. Navalny's support base also seems to be growing, and his main issue, corruption, is one that concerns even many pro-regime voters.

Thus, the Kremlin makes every effort to keep Navalny from becoming too threatening. He is banned from appearing on state television, and newscasters are reportedly forbidden from even using his name. When his supporters try to organize rallies in the regions, they are often denied permission on suspicious pretexts. In 2017, a scheduled rally in Samara was cancelled because regional authorities said it would interfere with a belly-dancing competition. In 2013, he was convicted on corruption charges in a case that appeared political. Although his prison sentence was later suspended, the conviction prevented him from running for office for a period of five years. He repeatedly expressed his desire to run for president in 2018, but the authorities would not register his candidacy.

Conclusion

Like Russian democracy, Russia's party system in the 1990s was disorganized and chaotic, but it was, at least, functioning. Russia's authoritarian turn in the 2000s was accompanied by a fundamental transformation of its party system. With United Russia at its centre, the system became rigid and uncompetitive. But how stable is this system? Some see the system as inherently unstable because Putin has never fully committed himself to United Russia. Indeed, Putin appears to want to keep his options open. In 2018, he declined to run as United Russia's nominee, and instead ran as an independent. At the same time, others point out that the current system offers a win-win arrangement for the current political elite. Some see the current party system as an equilibrium that, absent some external crisis or unforeseen event (e.g. Putin's sudden death or a massive economic crisis), will remain stable in the near future. Others see signs that the system is undermining itself. For instance, United Russia was initially constituted as an organization that could harness together the electoral machines of regional governors. But in recent years the Kremlin has been replacing these regional patrons with colourless bureaucrats from Moscow. This could have the dual effect of obviating United Russia and making it harder to win elections in the regions. These questions will be answered in Putin's fourth term.

4 PARLIAMENTARY POLITICS IN RUSSIA
Ben Noble

In the early 1990s, parliamentary politics was at the heart of Russian politics. It was the deadlocked battle for supremacy between the Russian president, Boris Yeltsin, and the chairman of the Supreme Soviet, Ruslan Khasbulatov, that ended with the shelling of the White House – the then-seat of Russia's permanent parliament. This violent confrontation ultimately claimed the lives of many in Moscow, with upper estimates reaching 1,000 people (see Chapter 6). Now, the Federal Assembly is dismissed as a mere 'rubber stamp' – a body that unthinkingly nods through decisions made by the Presidential Administration and the government. What changed? How did we get from violence to passivity, from parliament being at the centre of political life, to it (apparently) playing a largely peripheral, symbolic role?

This chapter will tell the story of federal-level parliamentary politics in post-Soviet Russia. Although it might be tempting to narrate a simple account, moving from violence and confrontation to conformity and control, the chapter will also underscore events that complicate this narrative. The chapter will also touch on a more fundamental question: Does it even make sense to approach studying the Russian Federal Assembly as a 'real' parliament – as a branch of government that plays a meaningful, independent role in the political life of the country? Just because we call a body a legislature, does it follow that we should assume it performs the 'roles' and 'functions' traditionally associated with such institutions in democracies? In engaging with this issue, the chapter will discuss the recent literature on political institutions in non-democratic regimes, which is part of wider scholarship on neo-institutionalism. Before getting there, however, the chapter will begin with some necessary historical context: the place of parliaments in the Soviet Union.

History

Parliamentary politics in the Soviet Union

A deep chasm separated the rhetoric and reality of Soviet parliamentary politics. Article 2 of the 1977 Soviet Constitution stated that, 'All power in the USSR belongs to the people. The people exercise state power through Councils of People's Deputies, which constitute the political foundation of the USSR. All other bodies are under the control of, and are accountable to, the Councils of People's Deputies.' In other words, Soviet ideology located power in parliaments (or councils – *sovety,* in Russian). This was, however, a legal fiction. In reality, power was exercised by the Communist Party. Votes in the 'soviets' were unanimous – symbolic affirmations of the Party line; there was no real opportunity for substantive debate of, and resistance to, decisions already made.

Things began to change with General Secretary Gorbachev's reforms in the second half of the 1980s: *perestroika, glasnost'*, and *demokratizatsiya*. In March 1989, elections for the Congress of People's Deputies were held, giving people in the Soviet Union a relatively meaningful choice of candidates for the first time. Many candidates endorsed by the Communist Party of the Soviet Union failed to gain seats in the Congress, losing to vocal, reform-minded individuals, including Yeltsin. The first sessions of the Congress in May 1989 proved sensational, with Soviet citizens able to watch on television real, passionate, and heated debate, with open criticism of the Soviet system.

Although the USSR Congress of People's Deputies dissolved itself following the attempted August 1991 coup, the Congress of the Russian Soviet Federative Socialist Republic (RSFSR) continued to operate *after* the collapse of the Soviet Union (albeit changing its name slightly). (For a helpful chronology of legislative institutions in the transition across the fall of the USSR, see Remington 2001: 2.) However, the blurred lines of authority associated with the operation of the hangover 1978 Russian Constitution in the early, chaotic post-Soviet period led to ratcheting tension between the legislature and the executive. Who had the final say? Who *truly* represented the interests of the people?

The 1993 constitutional crisis

Things came to a head in 1993. Following decision-making gridlock, Yeltsin took the nuclear option on 21 September, issuing decree number 1400 to dissolve the Congress and Supreme Soviet. On 22 September 1993, members of the Committee for Protecting the People's Power and the Constitution issued an appeal to 'the people', denouncing Yeltsin's decree. This plea to the people, issued from within the White House, echoed another document in Russian parliamentary history. On 9 July 1906, members of the first Imperial State Duma issued an appeal to 'the people', protesting against the dissolution of the Duma by decree on 8 July. History appeared to be repeating itself.

Continuing a flurry of astonishing events – including the declared impeachment of Yeltsin, a ruling by the Constitutional Court finding decree 1400 null and void, the barricading of the White House, and a battle over the Ostankino television tower – Russian army tanks shelled the White House on 4 October. This proved to be the decisive blow against the resistant pro-parliamentary actors. Yeltsin was now able to forge ahead with plans for a new post-Soviet constitutional order.

The 1993 Constitution was, therefore, formed in the shadow of the fire-ravaged White House. Yeltsin had beaten the legislature into submission, allowing him to shape constitutional details from a position of strength. A referendum on whether to adopt the new constitutional text took place on the same day as elections to the Federal Assembly on 12 December 1993. (Note how odd this was: people were asked to vote for parliamentarians, who would fill a body which did not yet exist – and might never exist in case the people did not support adoption of the con- stitutional text.) The 1993 Constitution was adopted, and quickly dubbed 'super-presidential' (Holmes 1993/1994; see Chapter 2 on executive pol- itics). This was hardly surprising given the conditions of the document's genesis. And yet, Yeltsin did not dominate the Federal Assembly after it began operating in January 1994. To understand how this was possible, we need to cover the basics of institutional rules and the shifting compo- sition of the new parliament.

Federal Assembly

The new post-Soviet constitution created a bicameral (two-chamber) national-level legislature – the Federal Assembly – consisting of the State Duma and the Federation Council. Article 100.1 of the 1993 Constitution states that these two chambers 'shall hold separate sittings', although the two bodies sit together for the president's address to the collected Assembly – a Russian equivalent to the 'state of the nation' address by the president of the US. The geography of these two chambers' buildings is indicative of their relative current importance. Whereas the State Duma is in the very centre of Moscow, within eyesight of the Kremlin, the Federation Council is slightly further out – still within the capital's central boulevard, but in a far less prominent position.

State Duma

Unlike the English words 'parliament' and 'legislature' – which are derived from the French for 'to speak' and the Latin for 'law', respectively – the Russian verb '*dumat*', from which the word 'Duma' is derived, means 'to think'. Although we should be careful not to read too much into the significance of this etymological difference, it is interesting, at least, to bear in mind as we look at the lower chamber's structure and activities.

The State Duma contains 450 seats. Each seat is filled by a 'deputy' (syn- onymous with 'legislator' or 'parliamentarian'). The rules governing the elec- tion of State Duma deputies have varied over the post-Soviet period. Between the 1993 and 2003 federal parliamentary elections, half (225) deputies were elected on the basis of achieving a plurality of votes in single-mandate districts (constituencies). The other 225 deputies were elected according to a party-list proportional representation (PR) system. The 2007 and 2011 elections, by contrast, moved to a pure PR system. But – in a prominent example of insti- tutional instability in modern-day Russia – the 2016 elections saw a return to the mixed electoral formula. The rules of the game have, clearly, changed. On one reading, such instability should be expected in a society still getting used to the operation of elections; tweaks are needed in order to ensure that rules match social conditions. On another reading, however, these changes to electoral legislation stem from the Kremlin's desire to manipulate institutions to suit its own ends, rather than to foster conditions favourable to healthy democratic competition.

There have been seven legislative terms – known as 'convocations' (*sozyvy*) in Russia – since the creation of the Federal Assembly by the 1993 Constitution. The length of these convocations has varied. The first convocation lasted two years, from the beginning of 1994 to the end of 1995; the second to the fifth convocations lasted four years each; the sixth convocation was slated to last five years (in line with a 2008 constitutional amendment), but finished slightly earlier than planned for reasons discussed below; and the seventh convocation started at the end of 2016, with a view to sitting for five years. Each parliamentary year is further broken down into two sessions, spring and autumn.

The State Duma has a leadership hierarchy, including a chairperson (colloquially known as a 'speaker'), first deputy chairs, and deputy chairs. There have been five chairmen of the State Duma so far: Ivan Petrovich Rybkin (first convocation – Agrarian Party deputy); Genadii Nikolaevich Seleznev (second and third convocations – Communist Party of the Russian Federation (CPRF), then Party of Russia's Rebirth deputy); Boris Vyacheslavovich Gryzlov (fourth and fifth convocations – United Russia deputy); Sergei Evgen'evich Naryshkin (sixth convocation – United Russia deputy); and Vyacheslav Viktorovich Volodin (seventh convocation – United Russia deputy).

Each deputy serves as a member of one parliamentary committee – bodies which focus on a particular policy area, and which deal, *inter alia*, with bills falling in that particular area. As of 2017, there were 26 committees, ranging from the committees on defence, culture, and education, to the committees on energy, budget and taxes, and health protection. Each committee has its own leadership structure, with a chairperson, as well as deputy chairs. There are also a number of Duma commissions, including the commission on questions of deputy ethics.

Deputies are assisted in their jobs by a body of technical civil servants. This body – or *'apparat'*, in Russian – of professionals consists, for example, of the Legal Department (*Pravovoe upravlenie*), which provides legal expertise on draft legislation. Reports from the Legal Department sometimes contain scathing criticism of submitted bills, although the visibility of this criticism depends largely on the willingness of committee chairmen to draw attention to the Department's reports. It is unlikely, therefore, that a United Russia chairman will draw attention to criticism relating to a bill submitted by the president or the government. On money matters, the Federal Assembly is also assisted by the Audit Chamber (*Schetnaya palata*), which provides expertise on, for example, federal budget bills, as well as presenting reports on the implementation of budget laws.

The partisan composition of the State Duma has varied considerably over time. Figure 4.1 presents information on all seven Duma convocations, 1994–2017. Each segment within each bar relates to a different formal legislative grouping. Rather than focus on the details of party and deputy groups names, the pattern is of particular importance.

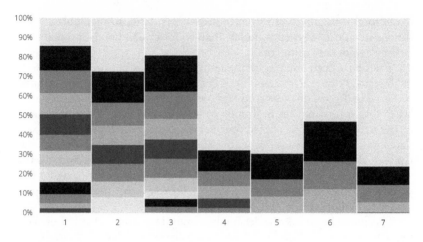

Figure 4.1 The partisan distribution of the State Duma, 1994–2017

Notes: Each segment within each bar relates to a different formal legislative grouping. Segment shades do not indicate the same formal legislative groups across bars. The data presented in this figure are taken from a selection of various records on the State Duma's online voting record archive: http://vote.duma.gov.ru [Accessed 18 July 2018]. Given that the party affiliations of certain Duma deputies can, and have, changed during convocations, data on the first to the sixth convocations are taken from the final vote during that convocation's final plenary session. For the seventh convocation, data is taken from 24 November 2017.

In the first three convocations of the State Duma, the 450 seats were divided between a relatively large number of parties and deputy groups, with no one political bloc forming a majority. This clearly changed, how-ever, with the fourth convocation, when United Russia achieved more than the two-thirds majority required to amend the constitution. Figure 4.1 also makes clear United Russia's loss of this 'constitutional majority' in the sixth convocation. (Although United Russia won a majority of seats (238) in this convocation, it secured this majority on the basis of less than a majority of votes cast – 49%.)

It is difficult to overstate the importance to the Kremlin of securing a pro-executive majority in the State Duma in order to achieve its policy goals. (See Chapter 3.) When the Kremlin lacked a stable, disciplined majority of deputies in the Duma who could be relied upon to support the executive's policy initiatives, the government and the president had to rely on shifting, *ad hoc* coalitions of deputies. Engineering these majorities was costly, since votes had to be 'bought' through, for example, promises of career advance-ment or access to rents.

The emergence of a pro-executive majority had clear effects on the vibrancy of debate. On 29 December 2003, the then-chairman of the State Duma, Boris Gryzlov, stated that the State Duma 'is not a venue in which it is necessary to hold political battles, to assert political slogans and ideologies' – something that became popularised in the catchier form, the Duma is 'not the place for political discussions' (Chaisty 2012: 97). This claim angered and puzzled observers in equal measure. If the Duma was not the place for political debate, then what was it meant to do? Wasn't the lower chamber of the national legislatures *precisely* the place for such discussions – in a vibrant, pluralistic political system, at least?

Russians do not hold the State Duma in high regard. Opinion polls have repeatedly shown that large majorities disapprove of the activities of Russia's parliament.

Over the last decade a majority of respondents report a *negative* view of the lower chamber. And, according to data collected in a 2012 survey by the Public Opinion Foundation (*Fond Obshchestvennoe Mnenie*, FOM) – a Russian polling organisation that is widely regarded to be Kremlin friendly – 73% of respondents were simply not interested in the State Duma's work (FOM 2012).

Federation Council

As originally conceived, the Federal Assembly's upper chamber was meant as a venue for the expression of *regional* voices in the national-level decision-making process. Each region is constitutionally guaranteed two representatives in the Council, with the basic law further stipulating that one of these representatives should be from the executive branch and the other from the legislative branch of a region's political system. However, the *overall* number of Federation Council members – known colloquially as 'senators' – has varied along with changes to the number of federal subjects in Russia. (See Chapter 9.) There were, therefore, initially 178 senators, but the number of regional representatives now stands at 170 (166 if we exclude the representatives from Crimea and Sevastopol). And, according to a July 2014 amendment to the 1993 Constitution, the president is able to appoint a certain number of senators directly.

The method for filling Federation Council seats has also changed over time. In 1993, there were concurrent elections for senators and Duma deputies. But this was the only time Russian citizens have been able to vote directly for Federation Council members. Following legal changes in 1995, the regional heads of the executive and legislative branches were granted *ex officio* membership of the Council. This authority gave regional elites a place at the centre of federal decision-making – a power that they used frequently in the second half of the 1990s (see Chapter 3). However, in an effort to reduce the influence of regional interests, the rules were changed again in 2000, which meant that regional executive and legislative branch leaders lost this automatic seat, instead choosing representatives. And, in 2012, the formula was amended yet again, allowing the Kremlin a tighter grip on the choice of senators.

Although party factions are not allowed to form in the Council, the majority of senators are United Russia members. Exceptions in 2017 include Vyacheslav Mikhailovich Markhaev – a CPRF senator representing the executive branch of Irkutsk *oblast'* – and Arsen Suleimanovich Fadzaev – a 'Patriots of Russia' member and representative of the legislative branch of North Ossetia–Alania.

Such has been the shift in the balance of power between the federal cen-tre and the regions that experts have concluded the following: the Coun-cil 'effectively represents the federal government in the regions rather than providing the regions representation in federal policy-making' (Ross and Turovsky 2013: 59). And, when it comes to the law-making process (on which more below), these same scholars have dubbed the Federation Council a 'rubber stamp' (*ibid.*).

The law-making process and outputs

How a bill becomes a law – theory

In order to become a federal law, all bills must be introduced into the State Duma. According to article 104.1 of the 1993 Constitution, 'The power to initiate legislation shall belong to the President of the Russian Federation, the Federation Council, members of the Federation Council, State Duma deputies, the Government of the Russian Federation, and the legislative (rep-resentative) bodies of the subjects of the Russian Federation'. The higher courts – now, the Supreme Court and the Constitutional Court – also have the right to introduce bills in their areas of competence. Particular, fine-grained rules governing the consideration and passage of legislative initia-tives are contained in the standing orders (*reglamenty*) of both chambers of the Federal Assembly.

All bills pass through three key venue-stages: the State Duma, the Federation Council, and the president's office (see Figure 4.2). Of these three stages, the review requirements are most elaborate in the Duma, with most bills required to go through three readings in plenary sessions of the lower chamber. Beyond these hurdles, initiatives must also pass a number of 'gatekeepers'. Following registration in the lower chamber, all initiatives are sent to the Duma speaker, following which they are sent to a com-mittee related to the initiative's subject matter. This committee is known as a 'profile' committee. If an initiative satisfies the committee's prelimi-nary review, the committee can propose to the whole Duma – or Duma 'in plenary' – that the initiative be taken up for consideration. Otherwise, the bill is returned to its author. Initiatives taken up for consideration are then sent to the Duma Council, which appoints a 'lead' committee that is responsible for coordinating work on the initiative as it passes through the State Duma. Additional co-committees can also be appointed if a bill covers a range of policy areas. The Council also calls for initial reactions from a variety of actors on the initiative. The lead committee then makes a decision as to whether to recommend the bill be adopted by the Duma

Figure 4.2 Key venue-stages of the law-making process

in first reading, and the Duma Council schedules the first reading on the Duma floor. The bill can be rejected at this stage, but, if it is adopted in first reading, amendment proposals are called for, to be presented within a specified timeframe. Before the second reading of a bill, the lead committee collects these amendment proposals, sorting them into those it thinks should be adopted and rejected. The Duma Council once again schedules the bill for consideration on the Duma floor, and deputies discuss, and vote on, whether to allow the bill to progress. If the bill is not rejected, it moves on to the third reading stage, which is largely used to tidy up linguistic and legal details.

Once a bill is approved by the State Duma in third reading, it is officially referred to as a federal law (*federal'nyi zakon*) and moves on to the Federation Council. The Council is not required to review all laws. Indeed, if the upper chamber does not act on a piece of legislation within 14 days, the law moves on to the president. The Council can, however, reject an initiative, returning it to the Duma, following which a special commission comprised of both deputies and senators works on resolving points of contention. Alternatively, the Duma can overturn the Council's rejection with a two-thirds vote. Once laws reach the president, the head of state can either sign or not sign the text. In the case of the latter, the law returns to the lower chamber. If the Duma wants to override the president's veto, this requires two-thirds of all deputies to vote in favour of an override, following which two-thirds of the Federation Council must also vote for an override in order for the initiative to be promulgated into law.

How a bill becomes a law – practice

Figure 4.3 presents data on the number of bills introduced and adopted by the State Duma between the second and sixth convocations, as well as the number of laws rejected by the Federation Council or president and the number of laws signed by the president.

As shown by the lower-left graph in Figure 4.3, the frequency with which bills are vetoed (or returned) to the State Duma by the president or the Federation Council has decreased markedly. (For a discussion of the reasons for bill vetoing, see Noble and Schulmann 2018: 62.) This means that, once a bill is adopted by the State Duma, the overwhelming likelihood is that it will be signed into law by the president. This contrasts with earlier post-Soviet experience, especially during the second Duma convocation, in which initiatives sometimes 'ping ponged' between the three venue-stages, as policy disagreements dragged on.

According to Tkachenko (2017: 523), 6,717 federal laws were adopted in Russia between 1 January 1994 and 31 July 2016. Although this figure includes laws amending existing pieces of legislation, this is still an exceedingly large number of laws, with clear (negative) implications for realising the rule of law. Put yourself, for example, in the shoes of a criminal defence lawyer, who will have to keep on top of the constantly shifting content of the Criminal Code and Criminal Procedure Code, never mind focusing on the specifics of a case and defending their clients.

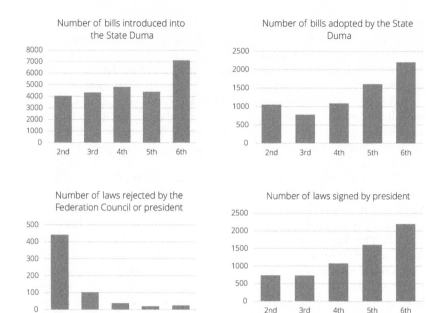

Figure 4.3 Bill passage statistics, second to sixth State Duma convocations

Source: The data presented in these graphs are taken from the State Duma's website, http://www. duma.gov.ru/legislative/statistics/ [Accessed November 2017]

We should be cautious, however, in blaming parliamentarians for this legal instability. Malaev and Shkurenko (2017) report that, in the fifth and sixth convocations of the Duma, the government and the president were responsible for 55% and 61% (respectively) of all bills that became laws. Moreover, the vast majority of executive-sponsored bills are signed into law, with infrequent cases of bill failure more often explained by differences between executive actors, rather than resulting from successful opposition from deputies (see Noble and Schulmann 2018). As such, although the Russian constitution can be seen as providing for a 'separation of powers' system, a United Russia (super-)majority in the State Duma, as well as a loyal corpus of senators, allows the Kremlin to reap the rewards of a 'unity of purpose' system (see Haggard and McCubbins 2001).

The data presented in Figure 4.3 do not include information on the level of debate over bills or voting results. Existing analysis of a sub-set of legis-lative initiatives – budget bills – gives some impression of trends over time, however. When it comes to the discussion of federal budget bills, a proxy for the level of debate on the Duma floor suggests a notable decline over time (see Noble 2017b: 507). This apparent reduction in scrutiny is, moreover, associated with lower levels of amendment to the text section of budget bills. To be sure, we cannot discount the possibility that the proxy measure of scrutiny fails to capture meaningful legislator activity. In addition, it is tricky to present conclusive proof causally linking apparent reduced scrutiny with fewer amendments. However, the existing analysis suggests that the contemporary State Duma does not act as a significant player in the budget process. To the degree that review of the yearly budget is a key task of parliament – a moment during which any autonomy from, and criticism of, executive plans should be on display, even if it is absent in other policy areas – then we have reasons to suspect that the vigour of debate in the Russian parliament on key policy questions has waned over time. (For further information on the parliamentary passage dynamics of Russian budget bills, see Noble 2017b.)

Tkachenko (2017: 522) provides a critical summary of the current law-making situation in Russia: 'inadequately prepared bills are introduced to the Duma and become law very quickly: often they are adopted in the first reading in one day, and from one to seven days are allocated for amendment. The stage for discussion, where the shortcomings of the bills could be identified and addressed, is in fact skipped.' According to a Communist Party (CPRF) State Duma deputy, Victor Ilyukhin, '[l]egislation is not made in the Duma, but by the Kremlin and the government [...] All decisions about whether or not to pass bills are made there' (quoted in Feifer 2010). In line with this account, a video was circulated in May 2010, purportedly showing people racing around the Duma's main hall, frantically voting for absent deputies (*ibid.*).

At the same time, although deputies themselves might be excluded from many consequential law-making discussions, policy disputes can rage between executive actors and powerful economic interests during the legislative stage of law-making. Although these debates take place in non-legislative venues, their outcomes are inserted as second-reading amendments, sometimes drastically altering the content and scope of bills (see Noble and Schulmann 2018).

Although there are now fewer opportunities for deputies and senators to influence decision-making on key pieces of legislation as they pass through the Federal Assembly, there is still evidence of lobbying in the federal parliament (Chaisty 2013). Beyond opportunities to help shape the content of federal policy, however, there are other powerful incentives for achieving a seat in the Assembly. These include immunity from prosecution and access to high-ranking officials.

In light of the above, the Federal Assembly has been referred to with a number of disparaging terms, including 'rubber stamp' and 'mad printer'. The suspicion that the federal legislature is not a 'real' parliament is either stated bluntly or hinted at (see, for example, Feifer 2010). In fact, the question of whether 'nominally democratic institutions' (including parties, elections, and parliaments) in hybrid or non-democratic regimes play the same 'roles' and 'functions' as their namesake institutions in democracies has received a good deal of attention recently from political scientists (see, for example, Gandhi 2008, and Svolik 2012). A common starting point is that these institutions are not simply 'window dressing' – efforts to create a Potemkin democracy for international observers and domestic opposition – but, rather, serve meaningful roles, including co-opting members of the political opposition, transmitting information about citizen grievances to the regime elite, and co-ordinating intra-elite relations.

What is the solution to this apparently poor state of affairs from the point of view of democracy? According to Tkachenko, it is nothing less than the introduction of meaningful competition between parliamentary actors: 'Without competition there is no incentive for thorough discussion of bills' (2017: 523). And Ekaterina Schulmann – a Russian political scientist and leading political commentator – has argued that '[t]here is only one way to fix this: hold free, fair elections' (quoted in Antonova 2014).

Recent parliamentary developments

Following his installation as speaker of the State Duma in October 2016, Vyasheslav Volodin – former first deputy chief of staff of the Presidential Administration – set about instituting a range of reforms. These measures focused on four areas: improving discipline in the corpus of deputies, raising the prestige of Duma deputies, carving out an independent place for the legislature in national-level decision-making, and increasing the law-making efficiency of the lower chamber. Examples of these include a clampdown on deputy absenteeism from Duma plenary sessions; returning to deputies the right to use VIP lounges in airports; taking a critical stance against certain government-sponsored bills (or, at least, holding up their consideration in the lower chamber); and removing the backlog of bills under consideration for decades.

The evidence so far suggests the limited effectiveness of these changes. There are reports, for example, that deputies continue to vote by proxy during plenary sessions (albeit possibly not on the scale previously seen). Moreover, there is evidence that Russian citizens' perceptions of the State Duma have *worsened* since Volodin introduced his reforms. As for taking old bills off the books, although this might help portray an image of efficiency and order, it is not clear that it will significantly free up time for Duma actors to focus on more pressing concerns. (For an early assessment of Volodin's reforms, see Noble 2017a.)

Deputies have grumbled about Volodin's new regime. In November 2017, for example, LDPR State Duma deputy Sergei Ivanov protested against the 'complete unanimity' observed when deputies voted during plenary sessions, saying that such unanimity was only possible in a 'cemetery' (Samokhina 2017). Ivanov protested about the difficulty experienced by deputies in voting according to their own consciences and preferences, stating that legislators were required to write explanatory letters every time they voted against the party line. (It is worth mentioning that this same Duma deputy proposed a bill on 1 April 2013 that called for protections for civilians from the effects of garlic consumption, including people's bad breath in public places. Ivanov argued that the introduction of the bill (on April Fool's Day) was meant as a bit of light relief, following the adoption of too many serious, 'draconian' laws (RIA Novosti 2013).)

Displays of open criticism of the national parliament during a plenary session are exceedingly rare nowadays, however. And it is not surprising why. In response to Ivanov's comments on voting unanimity in the State Duma, Vyacheslav Volodin made a thinly veiled reference to the possibility that Ivanov might lose his mandate. Indeed, *Kommersant'* journalist Sofya Samokhina called Ivanov's speech 'brave' (Samokhina 2017). Should we expect legislators to have to be brave when commenting on parliamentary practices?

Conclusion

Parliament's place in post-Soviet Russian politics has varied significantly. From the deadlock and dissolution of the Congress of People's Deputies and the Supreme Soviet, to the unnerving uniformity of deputy behaviour in the State Duma's seventh convocation, it is not possible to come up with a cover-all description of legislative politics in post-Soviet Russia. The story of post-Soviet Russian parliamentary politics clearly reflects, and constitutes, broader dynamics, including the institutional uncertainty, decentralisation, and fractiousness of the 1990s and the efforts at recentralisation in the 2000s. Much, however, like claims of the recentralisation of the state under Vladimir Putin have been overstated (see, for example, Monaghan 2012 on the power *'vertikal'*), so too would it be too simplistic to claim that the conflict apparent in legislative affairs in the Yeltsin years have been replaced by perfect order. Conflict is still very much present in the legislative stage of law-making, although legislators are not the primary actors; and members of the Federal Assembly are not all unthinking, loyal voting automatons.

Scholars of legislative politics sometimes disaggregate various 'roles' or 'functions' of parliaments. Kreppel (2014: 85), for example, notes the 'traditional' classification of legislative activities into 'four primary functions: linkage; representation; control/oversight; and policy-making'. This chapter has focused on the policy-making process, but it is worth mentioning the other roles as they apply to the Russian Federal Assembly. Regarding linkage and representation, deputies' schedules certainly block off time for 'work with voters' – a time that should provide an opportunity for parliamentarians to hear, and respond to, citizens' issues. However, legal changes in 2017 mean that deputies need to seek approval to hold meetings with voters under certain conditions. Regarding oversight, executive actors are periodically called to answer questions in both the State Duma and the Federation Council during 'Government hour'. These events, however, rarely result in stinging, meaningful critique. Following the posting of Aleksei Navalny's YouTube video, accusing Dmitry Medvedev of large-scale corruption, there was some discussion among Duma deputies about whether to raise the issue during the prime minister's query session in the lower chamber. This potentially awkward situation did not arise, however.

What are the prospects of meaningful change in parliamentary politics? At a 2017 meeting of the Inter-Parliamentary Union Assembly in St Petersburg, President Vladimir Putin stated, 'We will strive consistently to raise the authority and importance of parliament' (quoted in Churakova 2017). The reality does not, however, match the rhetoric. As long as a majority of deputies and senators regard pleasing Kremlin principals as the optimal strategy for career advancement (and survival), then things will likely not change much. In spite of speaker Volodin's claims that the Duma is once again a 'place for discussion', this fact is disputed by the State Duma's very own deputies, as well as being reflected in the low regard Russians have for the federal parliament.

The next federal parliamentary elections are scheduled for September 2021. As with so much else in Russian politics, the fate of parliamentary politics before (and after) then will, no doubt, depend to a large degree on the choices of President Putin, who secured a fourth presidential term (2018–24) on 18 March 2018. However, as questions of leadership succession become even more central, the attractions of diffusing power – either by making government more manifestly accountable to the Federal Assembly or by transferring powers from the executive to the legislature – could help move parliament closer to the centre of political life. That being said, the safest option for the current elite might be to keep parliament as a safely subservient body – although this option, in turn, runs the risk that maintaining an ersatz body will only kindle hopes for the return of a legislative branch of power with its own will.

5 NATIONAL IDENTITY AND THE CONTESTED NATION

Marlene Laruelle

In this chapter, I define nationalism as the ideology of promoting the interests of a particular nation. Among these 'interests' are that the territory of the nation should correspond to a state, and that the nation should govern itself and protect its identity. This definition of nationalism can therefore include both movements that contest the status quo by stating that these two conditions are not met, on the one hand, and state initiatives to consolidate statehood by merging it with nationhood, on the other. In the case of Russia, these two trends exist in parallel, with several interplays at work.

The chapter first discusses the difficulties of establishing the country's 'identity' and the regime's actions to elaborate and stabilise the national grand narrative. It then looks at the various movements in pursuit of more nationalistic policies, before exploring their interaction, competition, overlap and mutual borrowings with state strategies. Ultimately, it concludes that Russia's national identity is a joint construction with bottom-up and top-down dynamics.

The contested identity of the Russian Federation

The Russian Federation as it emerged in December 1991 had never existed as a state within those borders. The first question that needed to be answered was the very designation of the new nation. There were two options from which to choose: a Russian nation-state (*russkoe gosudarstvo*), as proposed by the Russian nationalists very active since the 1980s; or a Russian Federation (*Rossiiskaia Federatsiia*) with a more inclusive nationhood (Tolz 2001). It was this more open option that reformers around Yeltsin selected, with the aim of following the path of Western liberal democracies, but also – and more pragmatically – mitigating the risk that the country would divide along ethnic fault-lines. The Kremlin quickly developed the project of a civic identity modelled on the Russian term *rossiiskii*, or 'Rossian', which designates that which is related to the Russian state, as distinct from *russkii*, the term that applies specifically to the Russian language, culture, or ethnicity. This Rossian identity was meant to unite all citizens of the Federation around a European-style civic patriotism, symbolised by the removal of ethnicity (*natsional'nost'*) from the Russian passport in 1997. Until the adoption of the

1993 Constitution, the Soviet identity card (*vnutrennyi pasport*, or internal passport) registered the ethnic origin (*natsional'nost'*) of each individual.

The Rossian civic identity does not eliminate the multiplicity of local ethnic identities, which are recognised by a variety of disparate rights inherited from the Soviet system. Russia thus remains a federal state: it now consists of 85 subjects, of which 27 originate directly from the ethnic specificities of their populations. This count of 85 federal subjects includes the Republic of Crimea and the Federal City of Sevastopol, whose annexation in March 2014 is not recognised by the international community. As of 2018, there were a total of 46 *oblasts* (regions); 1 autonomous *oblast*; 9 *krais* (territories); 22 republics; 4 autonomous *okrugs* (districts), of which 3 are simultaneously components of *oblasts*; and 3 federal cities (Moscow, St Petersburg, and Sevastopol). The 2010 census distinguished 194 'nationalities', among which about 50 ethnic groups have public policies that preserve their vernacular language and ethnic culture in the local education system, as well as giving 'titular' individuals (representatives of eponymous peoples) priority access to high-level positions in local government (Tishkov 2013). Non-ethnic Russian citizens of the Federation represent about 20% of the population, and have quite varied symbolic statuses, from the brotherly nations of Ukrainians and Belarusians to the assimilated Siberian people, to those perceived as 'culturally foreign', such as North Caucasians.

The Rossian civic identity promoted during the Yeltsin era was both a success and a failure. It was a success inasmuch as the citizens of the Russian Federation very widely recognise themselves as part of the Russian state, whatever their ethnicity. Rarely is public opinion divided along ethnic lines, with the exception being specific issues related to an ethnicity's own symbolic status and Russia's multinational identity (Gerber and Zavisca 2017). Yet it was a failure because the term *rossiiskii* did not take root. Indeed, it was increasingly challenged, first in the 1990s, by Chechen leaders seeking independence, and then by nationalist elites in the republics, for whom Russia remained too 'Russian' and the state identity insufficiently federal and multiethnic. On the other side, the Rossian identity sparked harsh criticism from Russian nationalists, who denounced it as a 'de-Russification' of Russia and the submission of ethnic Russians to minorities' *diktat*, a theme that dated back to some 1960s dissident circles (Brudny 2000; Mitrokhin 2003).

In the 2000s, the debate between Russian and Rossian underwent a series of changes. First came the formalisation of a new political discourse that expanded the space for patriotism, based primarily on the rehabilitation of the Soviet past, as the objective and the engine of consensus under Putin (Laruelle 2009). This state-sponsored patriotism has resulted in the revaluation not only of the Soviet past, but also of imperial Russian history. The state committed significant funds to commemorating the great symbolic battles of Russian history (Alexander Nevsky against the Swedes, Dmitry Donskoi against the Mongols, Mikhail Kutuzov against Napoleon, Alexei Yermolov commanding the imperial army in the Caucasus, etc.). Second, there has been a gradual formalisation of the Russian Orthodox Church as the right arm of the state. The Church is increasingly visible at official ceremonies, in the military, and in educational institutions, thus weakening the

Russian civic consensus, the explicit corollary of which is the secular nature of the state and equal rights for the so-called traditional religions (Orthodoxy, Islam, Buddhism, and Judaism). Third, some influential intellectuals and politicians, tapping into Russian nationalist sensitivity, have continued to raise the spectre of the de-Russification of Russia. Many legislative projects, sometimes adopted but never implemented, have identified ethnic Russians as the carriers of state and formal Russian culture, and thus as *primus inter pares*. Meanwhile, use of the term *rossiiskii* has gradually declined; it is increasingly common to use *russkii* even in reference to civic identity.

The elites of the national republics – and most minority groups – have reacted strongly to what they interpret as the breakdown of the Russian civic contract. Many advocate a proactive policy of preserving ethnic languages. Some want ethnicity to be reinstated in passports, in order to protect minorities from assimilation or – in the case of Russian nationalists – to avoid the possible 'dissolution' of 'Russianness'. Others argue for strengthening federalism in order to give more autonomy to the national republics. For their part, Islamic institutions claim rights equal to those of the Russian Orthodox Church in terms of their access to military and educational institutions (Dannreuther and March 2011; Verkhovsky 2008). Despite Moscow's centralising will, local situations are very diverse. Official secularism no longer applies in Chechnya, where Sharia, the Islamic law, has been partially introduced, forcing women to veil themselves and allowing polygamy. In Tatarstan and Bashkortostan, Islam is increasingly being taught in public schools. In several other republics, textbooks offer a schizophrenic reading of history, presenting the federal perspective – 'peaceful integration' into the Russian Empire – in the class on Russian history but celebrating local resistance to 'Russian colonialism' in the class on local history.

Not only is Russia an ethnic mosaic that reproduces the national diversity of the former Soviet Union on a smaller scale, but it is also increasingly a territorial and cultural archipelago, characterised by large regional variations in living standards, socio-economic dynamics and societal values. The country is deeply divided. Moscow is the undisputed capital in all regards, a showcase for both the country and the regime. It is followed by several dynamic regions with oil and gas production and the rich agricultural south, essentially the 15 'millionaire cities' – those with more than one million inhabitants – plus some less populated administrative capitals. The rest of the country, especially rural areas and small towns, is comprised of depressed regions, which endure mass depopulation, dying industries and weak connections to the rest of the country (Zubarevich 2014).

The country's internal balance accentuates the impression of an archipelago. The Far East, Siberia, and Arctic regions are experiencing massive desertion. The Far East, which covers 36% of the territory of the country, has lost 22% of its population since 1990. Rural northern Russia, the so-called non-black soil areas, is also dying, creating a veritable 'shrinking skin' that sees whole villages disappear. The 2010 census found that 36,000 of 133,700 Russian villages had fewer than 10 permanent inhabitants (Nefedova 2012). Arable land is abandoned: the total sown area fell by 36% between 1990 and 2012, from 118 million hectares to 76 million, before beginning a slow recovery that saw 79 million hectares cultivated in 2015 (Rosstat 2015, p. 399, 2016, p. 282). More central regions, such as the Urals and some oblasts along the Moscow–St Petersburg axis, are also facing depopulation, often due to the decline of one-industry towns. At the opposite end of the spectrum, 20 regions are enjoying population increases. Of these, 19 are national republics or autonomous districts with relatively high percentages of non-ethnic Russian citizens, mostly Muslim and Buddhist regions (namely the North Caucasian republics and Tuva). The demographic balance between ethnic Russians and other ethnicities is thus shifting in favour of the latter. At the same time, many national republics are among the most economically disadvantaged regions of the country, creating nodes of political and interethnic tensions, such as in the North Caucasus.

In addition, the identity of the Russian Federation has been dramatically affected by massive waves of emigration and immigration. Between 4 and 6 million people left the country since the fall of the Soviet Union, mostly for Europe, North America and Israel, while several million left other post-Soviet republics for Russia – an in and out population movement of unprecedented scale. In the 2000s, ethnic returnees have progressively been replaced by labour migrants searching for better job opportunities in the flourishing Russian economy: several million migrants from Central Asia, Azerbaijan, Moldova and, since 2014, Ukraine have sought to settle in Russia. Given the unregistered nature of much of this migration, precise numbers are difficult to determine. Migrants fill specific niches neglected by Russian citizens: construction, road services, minor commercial activities, hotel and restaurant work, taxi-driving and, increasingly, human services (working as home health aides and providing child and elder care) (Schenk 2018).

These migrations have fundamentally changed the urban landscape, with the emergence of ethnic neighbourhoods (not on a par with the segregation of American cities, but new for Russia), often in the suburbs of large cities, and the establishment of 'ethnic' restaurants and mosques, including in Russian regions that have not traditionally had Muslim populations (Zaionchkovskaya 2009). This has given rise to a high level of xenophobia: two-thirds of the population believes that Russia welcomes too many migrants. Migrants are blamed for rising crime and health risks; they are also accused of being unwilling or unable to integrate and of not respecting Russian values and lifestyles (Schenk 2010). The feeling of being 'invaded' by 'coloured people' has been on the rise, at least until the Ukrainian crisis. This has partially reshaped the country's identity by weakening the traditional narrative of Russia's multinationality being an asset.

Stabilising Russia's national narrative knots

Faced with societal changes on such a broad scale, the Russian authorities have been concerned about the lack of a unified grand narrative that would prevent ideological conflicts. In the wake of the turbulence of perestroika and the early 1990s, when Soviet narratives were dismantled, the Kremlin has worked to create a new identity language and rebuild a national discourse that makes sense of Russia's history and current situation.

Yet the regime has been reluctant to commit to an official ideology, since it is fully cognisant that such a project would face two major difficulties. First, since the fall of the USSR, Russian society has diversified and fragmented in terms of lifestyles and ideological references. Second, imposing ideological constraints entails the corresponding development of a large-scale repressive apparatus tasked with verifying the application of dogma and punishing those who are recalcitrant. The Putin team itself is a product of the fragmentation and globalisation of Russian society. It remembers the failure of the Soviet tools of repression in the last decades of the regime, as well as the exorbitant cost associated with attempting to maintain a coercive system. The question thus became how to promulgate a new ideology without overly assailing a fragmented society that mistrusts any new attempt at indoctrination – without the need for costly mass coercion. The solution was found, firstly, in saturating the media space with official discourses in a bid to marginalise dissenting opinions, and, secondly, in the interplay of the implicit and the explicit about 'Russianess' (Laruelle 2017).

This phenomenon of 'constructing' the nation's symbols can be observed in every country. For Russia, it is now comprised of five foundations or cornerstones, of which only the last is highly evolutionary and context dependent.

1. Russia is defined by its historical continuity and its geographical scope. The country's continuity (*preemstvennost'*) over time, since the Christianisation by Vladimir in the ninth century, is stressed through the slogan of a country of '1,000-year history': whatever changes there may be to the country's political regime and territorial borders, there is one – and only one – Russia. This notion is particularly important for managing the memory of the twentieth century and the difficult historical junctures of 1917 and 1991 (Omelicheva 2017). The Sochi Olympics' opening ceremony offered a visually powerful representation of claiming Russia's historical continuity.

   The celebration of Russia's territories has also become routine for political elites. Putin is honorary chair of the Russian Geographical Society; several senior officials, mostly those linked to the *siloviki* world, are also directly involved in celebrating Russia, its extreme conditions and its diversity, from the Arctic to the Far East and the Black Sea region (Radvanyi 2017). Putin's personal involvement in extreme outdoor sports and his cross-country journey behind the wheel of a Lada confirm the heavy symbolism of Russia as a territory.

2. The nation's historical pantheon is organised to offer the maximum possible inclusiveness. As long as the continuity of the state in its different political and territorial embodiments is respected, almost all hierarchies within the pantheon are accepted. At the top of it is the memory of the Second World War, the nation's foundational myth since the 1970s, whose cult has been re-instated as post-Soviet Russia's central historical commemoration (Wood 2011). Then come several dozen events and figures who are accorded more or less similar importance; Saint Vladimir,

Peter the Great, Nicholas II, Stolypin, Lenin, Stalin, Gagarin or Putin himself can be seen as the main hero of national history.

The pantheon is state-centric: everything that consolidated Russia as a state is positively valued, while everything that weakened Russia as a state is denigrated. As such, Stalin is judged positively for having modernised the country, whatever the price of repressions, while revolutions, in particular those of 1917 – grouped with the 1991 Soviet collapse – are seen as negative because they caused drama for the country (Malinova 2018). The pantheon is given life through massive state-funded historical commemorations and re-enactments; rehabilitation of the architectural heritage; subsidies for historical films and miniseries; and, more recently, through historical parks such as 'Russia—my history', which is backed by the Russian Orthodox Church and makes impressive use of multimedia technologies (Laruelle forthcoming).

3. Russia's mainstream political culture is based on a Soviet-lite nostalgia made to fit post-Soviet conditions, especially the acceptance of the market economy and a now deeply embedded consumerism. Although outright nostalgia for the Soviet regime is rare (the Communist Party collects fewer votes each year), nostalgia for the Brezhnev era, the golden age of Soviet culture, is massive and exists across class and age divisions (White 2010; Sullivan 2014). This Soviet nostalgia is reflected in diverse modalities: films, songs, and literature from that time have been largely rehabilitated, as have some fashions and consumer products. Soviet vintage, too, has been a commercial success (Kalinina 2014).

Although the Brezhnev years give rise to a large consensus, the Stalin years continue to be interpreted in contrasting ways: state violence is condemned at the rhetorical level but justified by the need to modernise the country and win the war; perpetrators are non-existent; and only mourning the victims – increasingly under the Church's patronage, and therefore with a clear Orthodox tone – is permitted. This Soviet nostalgia has left little room for the imperial past: though it has been rehabilitated in the historical pantheon as part of Russia's greatness and continuity, support for tsarism per se remains limited, even if the Church and some groups around it are pushing for a more straightforward restoration.

4. Russia's nationhood is projected abroad through several notions: compatriots, Russian World, and Eurasia. These are used in different contexts and directed towards different audiences, yet they are not contradictory and show some level of articulation. Russia presents itself as the pivot of Eurasia, a Eurasia synonymous with post-Soviet space, which it claims to lead naturally by virtue of its geographic, demographic and economic power. This Eurasian space is asked to demonstrate geopolitical loyalty to Russia in the name of a common historical destiny; states which take pro-Western stances are deemed to be under anti-Russian influence (Laruelle 2015a). This Eurasian identity is also used to stimulate Russia's relationship to Asia, especially to the Asia-Pacific region, as well as

to boost the image of Russia as a Muslim country: Russia is a member of the Organisation of Islamic Cooperation (OIC) and now an influential power in the Middle East. The notion of Eurasia therefore plays a dual role, indicating Russia's dominance over the post-Soviet space and its inclusion in the non-Western world of Asia and the Middle East.

The concept of Russian World targets more specific constituencies: the Russian-speaking communities of the post-Soviet region, the historical diasporas of émigrés in the 'far abroad', and non-ethnically Russian but Russia-oriented secessionist regions such as South Ossetia and Abkhazia (O'Loughlin, Toal and Kolosov 2016). It also reaches out to conservative groups in Europe and the US that exhibit pro-Russian positions, seeking to include them as 'fellow travellers' of the Russian World (Shekhovtsov 2017). The notion of compatriots, which emerged very early in the 1990s and which gave birth to the idea of the Russian World, now largely determines access to Russian citizenship (Shevel 2011). Despite evolutions in legislation and legislative practices, Russia continues to offer citizens of post-Soviet countries comparatively simple access to its citizenship. The compatriot repatriation programme, launched in 2006, has allowed many such individuals, regardless of ethnicity, to emigrate to Russia through official channels. The theme of protecting Russian minorities abroad was one of many used to justify the annexation of Crimea; other justifications included Kosovo's independence, the US invasion of Iraq, and NATO's eastward expansion (Teper 2016; Suslov 2014).

5. Once these four foundations are secured, the state's promotion of national ideological products appears quite eclectic and evolutionary. It offers a broad ideological palette, aiming at a 'pick and choose' policy that will allow it to achieve a broad consensus. The core of this ideological palette is 'patriotism', revived through state programmes since 2001 and present at every level of public discourse (Goode 2018): no one, even opposition figures, can have public and political legitimacy without insisting on his or her patriotic feelings. This is the only tool necessary to disqualify liberals: economic liberalism can be defended, but political liberalism, especially when it supposes 'submission' to Western geopolitical interests, is rejected on the grounds of being unpatriotic.

Once liberalism has been excluded, the kaleidoscope is broad and plural: anti-Americanism is revived during periods of international crisis with the US and the West more globally; the idea of Russia as a globalised country creating a multipolar world with its BRICS (Brazil, Russia, India, China and South Africa) allies alternates with the notion of Russia as a besieged fortress in need of protection and isolation (Engström 2014; Lipman forthcoming). The narratives of Russia as the protector of Russian ethnic minorities abroad and of its Orthodox brothers, including Eastern Christians in the Middle East, and of Russia as leading a Eurasian world connected to Central Asia and open to the

Asia-Pacific coexist in parallel. Post-modern narratives combining public relations- and marketing-inspired vocabulary go hand in hand with references to conservative Christian values. In this mosaic, references to Russia as the 'other' Europe, the 'authentic' one – rooted in Byzantium and the Slavophile tradition – seem to dominate (Neuman 2017; Engström 2017), yet pluralism remains the guiding principle.

Nationalist movements

While state authorities work to elaborate the nation's grand narrative and give it its current architecture, several non-state actors are also engaged in activating narratives around the topic of the nation and in capitalising on them. Several such narratives can be identified, divided into three main chronological periods.

The 1990s

In the 1990s, four ideological forces opposed Yeltsin's government by advancing arguments that can be described as nationalist: they denounced the Kremlin for not protecting the Russian nation, for letting it being 'infected' by non-Russian – read: Western – values, and/or for not defending Russian diasporas in the 'near abroad'. All of them called for the establishment of a 'genuinely Russian' government. These groups constituted what has been called the national-patriotic opposition.

The first to promote the notion of a Russian nation in danger and needing to protect its values from Western influence was the Russian Orthodox Church, which set itself up in opposition to the Yeltsinite liberal trajectory in the early 1990s. This was a dramatic change from the perestroika years, when the Church worked hand in hand with dissidents and liberal opponents to Mikhail Gorbachev in order to bring down the regime and its atheist ideology.

Two political parties also engaged in defending the Russian nation: the Communist Party of the Russian Federation (CPRF), led by Gennady Zyuganov, and Vladimir Zhirinovsky's Liberal-Democratic Party of Russia (LDPR). Both constituted serious opposition to Yeltsin's presidency; thanks to their electoral successes, they controlled the Duma for years. Zyuganov was the first to elaborate a narrative that combined nostalgia for the Soviet regime, references to Orthodox spirituality, and the claim that Russia was the pivotal force in Eurasia (March 2002). This narrative would later be adapted and transformed by the Putin regime. Zhirinovsky, known for his provocative stances, was ideologically more eclectic, presenting himself first as a Russian Hitler ready to seize power – a reference he rapidly abandoned, as it was very negatively received by a Russian society shaped by the memory of the 'war against fascism' – and then calling for Russia to reconquer Central Asia and create a large Eurasian empire. He also inaugurated xenophobia towards North Caucasians with his virulently anti-Chechen narratives (Umland 2008).

The fourth group was comprised of parties or institutions that did not participate in 'high politics', lacked Duma representation – even if some of their leaders were elected for a short period – and were active at the civil society level. Chief among these was Russian National Unity (RNU), a paramilitary movement led by Alexander Barkashov that sent volunteers to post-Soviet conflicts (Transnistria, South Ossetia, Abkhazia and Chechnya). Its brigades received paramilitary training through the RNU's connections to the Ministry of Defence (Shenfield 2001; Likhachev and Pribylovskii 1997).

The 2000s

This landscape of the 1990s was dramatically transformed in the 2000s with Putin's arrival in power. The new president immediately proposed a more consensual reading of the Soviet past and rehabilitated several of its symbols, thus shrinking the space available to the national-patriotic opposition. The Communist Party and the LDPR were progressively captured by the new 'power vertical', making them part of the 'systemic' or co-opted opposition; a segment of their electorate shifted to the new presidential party, United Russia.

The RNU and other nationalist groups, which were already very divided and in competition with one another, likewise lost much of their appeal after Putin came to power, as the president's masculine glamour captured a good share of their supporters. Yet it was the emergence of a new generation that most profoundly transformed the nationalist opposition. This generation adopted new counter-cultural methods of action and ways of life, best embodied by the skinhead movement. The 50,000-strong skinhead movement began to gain power in Russia in the mid-2000s, where they organised street violence against North Caucasians and migrants (Tipaldou and Uba 2014; Arnold 2016). Contrary to the previous nationalist generations, their goal was not so much to take political power as to develop a counter-culture that would acquire authority in the streets. This new nationalist opposition, with even less capacity for institutionalisation than its predecessors, was regularly divided and reshaped by internal competitions between its leaders (Verkhovskii 2014).

The only nationalist institution of the 1990s to gain from Putin's arrival in power was the Church. Step by step, the Moscow Patriarchate built new connections with Putin's inner circles and the Presidential Administration, presenting itself as an indefatigable ally of the Kremlin in its quest to stabilise Russian society ideologically and anchor it in so-called patriotic values. At the same time, the Church was also fighting for its own cause, lobbying for the return of property, exemption from certain taxes, and the right to penetrate state institutions such as the army and the school system. Some of these efforts were successful, but the Church was defeated on other points, and state institutions have remained largely secular (Richters 2012; Papkova 2011).

2011–14: A turning point

The years 2011–14 constitute a turning point in the evolution of the nationalist landscape, marked by the emergence of a third generation of leaders, such as Aleksandr Belov. These leaders stressed the need to move away from radicalism and called for a new nationalism, 'not with a beard and enormous boots, but in a suit and tie' (Kozenko and Krasovskaia 2008). This was part of nationalist groups' general trend towards looking at European far-right parties as models to follow and attempting to integrate into pan-European networks. Many nationalist groups also moved from attacking migrants to criticising the Putin regime for not doing enough to combat illegal migration and corrupt North Caucasian elites, particularly the Ramzan Kadyrov regime in Chechnya. These two elements – looking at Europe as a model and denouncing the Kremlin – opened the path for nationalist groups to collaborate with liberals and participate in the anti-Putin protests of winter 2011–12. The protests saw the formation of surprising ideological coalitions of nationalists and liberals, who were united in their denunciation of Putin's third term (Kolstø 2016). Blogger and lawyer Aleksei Navalny, the leader of the liberal opposition, combined his sharp criticism of the regime's corruption with an admixture of xenophobia that was well received by the nationalist opposition (Laruelle 2014; Kolstø 2014).

But this dual opposition was destroyed by the Ukrainian crisis and Putin's *coup de maître* of annexing Crimea. Nationalists found themselves divided. Some recognised Putin as having contributed to reunifying the Russian nation and therefore softened their opposition to him, as in the case of Eduard Limonov, the leader of the now-forbidden National-Bolshevik Party. Some criticised the Kremlin for not 'finishing' the job of annexing Donbas and possibly the rest of eastern Ukraine and organised the deployment of volunteer fighters to Donetsk and Lugansk, putting themselves in the ambiguous position of serving unspoken state interests while continuing to complain about the Kremlin's lack of genuine pro-Russian policies. The fight for Novorossiya – the name given to the territories of eastern Ukraine that were supposed to 'rejoin' Russia – became the new battlefield for radical nationalists looking for war theatres (Suslov 2017; Laruelle 2015b). A third, minority group decided to support Ukraine against Russia, seeing in Ukrainian far-right and paramilitary movements such as the Azov battalion the embodiment of their ideological convictions. Since then, and due also to tighter legislation, the nationalist landscape has remained heavily divided, with no new organisation able to take leadership and narratives that have difficulties finding their niche (SOVA annual reports).

Once again, the Moscow Patriarchate has benefitted from this change of atmosphere. Having been at the forefront of preserving so-called traditional values and Russian spirituality since the early 1990s, the Church easily found its niche in the 'conservative turn' taken by the regime during Putin's third term (Østbø 2017; Sharafutdinova 2014). It became increasingly involved in the domain of morality, pushing legislation to make it harder to divorce or have an abortion, supporting anti-homosexuality laws, reintroducing the notion of 'causing offense to religious feelings' into the penal code, and influencing debates on juvenile justice. Some leading figures, such as Bishop Tikhon (Shevkunov), head of the powerful Sretensky Monastery and a best-selling writer often presented as Putin's personal confessor, embodies this political Orthodoxy. He made the Church the ideological avant-garde of the regime and took the lead in historical policy by fostering a new anti-Soviet narrative that rehabilitates the Tsarist regime. Even if this ideological positioning goes against the state's inclusive national narrative, it still enjoys official support from the Presidential Administration and gained visibility in 2017 during the centenary of the 1917 revolutions.

The interplay of state nationhood and non-state nationalism

These nationalist movements are grassroots trends not initiated by the Kremlin, and their agenda is mostly one of 'national revolution' against the current regime. They have been working hard to develop a bottom-up influence strategy to transform the state from within. There is clearly an ambivalent relationship between some of them and the Kremlin: groups of people, ideas and notions have been co-opted by certain groups in power while being ignored and even repressed by others. Some do work as 'ideologically binding agents': a good example is the Night Wolves, Putin's biker leather club, which blends heavy patriotism, anti-Americanism, Putin's personality cult, Orthodoxy and biker culture, and which received state funding until 2017 (Yatsyk 2018). Yet in this mutual instrumentalisation, the Kremlin has always maintained control over its use of these grassroots movements, succeeding in implementing a 'carrot-and-stick' policy, whereas the movements have been unable to win over the ruling institutions.

The articulations between grassroots nationalist tendencies and the Russian state are multi-layered and exist in several realms. First, in time: there are moments when the Kremlin is more active in co-opting these groups against its main competitor, the liberals, and others when it is disinterested or more repressive. The best example of such an evolution is probably the first months of the war in Ukraine, when the Kremlin let all groups, including the most radical, defend the notion of Novorossiya, then closed this window of opportunity as early as July 2014, when it retook control of the Donbas war. Second, in space: Russia is a huge country and location matters. Local contexts play a critical role in the everyday relationship between the state at regional and municipal level, on the one hand, and grassroots movements, on the other. Three regions seem to dominate in terms of deep interactions: Moscow and the Moscow region under mayor Yuri Luzhkov, at least until 2007–08; St Petersburg; and southern cities such as Krasnodar, Stavropol, and Rostov-on-Don, known for their conservative atmosphere and Cossack traditions. In many other regions, local authorities display greater opposition to radical groups, including by regularly cancelling the nationalist Russian Marches of 4 November.

Third, and the key layer: ruling groups. The Russian state is plural, and the Kremlin is itself comprised of several groups. Nationalist leaders often have a patron in the establishment, mostly in the security services or law enforcement agencies, but they can be targeted and repressed by other state structures. Some para-state actors – who have their own ideological niche not always in tune with the Presidential Administration's narrative, but who operate under its umbrella in the grey zone of the Kremlin's 'ecosystem' of interest groups, lobbies, and personal connections – perform a go-between function, co-opting not so much people as narratives and trying to get them integrated into the state ideological portfolio. Among the main 'go-betweens' is the Moscow Patriarchate, which maintains contact with several Orthodox civil society organisations, some with very fundamentalist agendas or of monarchist persuasion, as well as with several paramilitary groups (even funding its own vigilante militia, the *Sorok sorokov*). The Ministry of Defence and the military-industrial complex, too, fund some ideological groups that deploy pro-Soviet and pro-army narratives, for instance Aleksandr Prokhanov's Izborsky Club (Laruelle 2016).

Through their charitable foundations, businessmen Vladimir Yakunin, longtime head of Russian Railways until his dismissal in 2015, and Konstantin Malofeev, founder of Marshall Capital Partners investment fund and supposedly one of the main financial backers of the Donbas insurgency, support groups with a more Orthodox and monarchist orientation. They also act as the vanguard of the policy to reach out to the European far right. These figures can be defined as nationalist entrepreneurs, in the sense that they have genuine room for manoeuvre; they can determine their ideological preferences and cultivate their own networks. But their entrepreneurship remains a fragile one, in permanent negotiation and tension with competing groups and the Presidential Administration. Just as oligarchs' empires are not secure but remain dependent on individual loyalty, the ideological empires of these entrepreneurs are unstable and can be challenged and dismembered.

All these articulations confirm how skilled the Kremlin is at co-opting movements and ideas that might compete with its own legitimacy. It considers everything related to Russian nationalism to be a potential rival for legitimacy and therefore as something it should bring 'under control'. Yet 'control' does not mean repression and coercion – far from it. On the contrary, it means giving a space for expression, allowing the movement to answer the mobilisation needs of some segments of the population and thereby defuse the threat of a coalition of the unsatisfied. The Kremlin excels at capturing a *Zeitgeist* and taking inspiration from grassroots initiatives, the latest example being its co-option of the Immortal Regiment, a memory initiative in which citizens display photos of family members who died in the Second World War.

In consolidating the Russian national narrative, the state corners the market on some topics that were previously the province of nationalist movements. Once integrated into a state-run narrative, themes that formerly belonged to nationalist groups lose their divisive nature and become part of a more inclusive and plastic architecture, which diminishes their mobilisation potential. The same happens in foreign policy. Nationalists are not part of any decision-making structures. Russia may use a nationalist post hoc *explanation* for its strategic decisions, but it does not advance a nationalist *agenda*. With the important exception of Crimea, the state does not call for changes to Russia's borders and therefore does not advance the nationalist agenda of equating the nation with its territory. Yet it exhibits discursive ambiguities about the symbolic borders of Russianness, uses some nationalist mediators for 'hybrid' war purposes in the 'near abroad' and in the West, and pushes domestically for a narrative focused on marginalising the 'inner enemies' of the nation.

Conclusion

As this chapter argued, the interplay between Russia's nationhood process – in many ways similar to those happening worldwide – and nationalist potential for mobilisation has been shaping the country's ideological scene since the collapse of the Soviet Union. The authorities focus on building a resilient grand narrative that is consensual enough to be broadly supported by the population, elude difficult moments that may polarise public opinion, and advance interpretative grids that favour the regime's own legitimacy and stability. Nationalist movements' ideological room for manoeuvre has reduced dramatically since the 1990s, as topics previously part of their agenda have infiltrated the state discursive portfolio and thereby been 'neutered'. In this joint construction with bottom-up and top-down dynamics, the state has so far largely kept control over the mobilisation potential of nationalists; the annexation of Crimea has forestalled the nationalist-liberal axis of protest that was emerging in 2011–12.

While state-sponsored nationhood offers impressive examples of creativity, plasticity and inclusiveness, its ability to keep the balance in the coming years remains to be seen. Some influential actors, such as the Church, are pushing for more rigid narratives; xenophobia, weakened since the Ukrainian crisis, may reappear as a dividing line between ethnic Russians, Russia's Muslims, and migrants; and the younger generation, for the moment very pro-Putin, will probably develop a set of values that will challenge the status quo. Ideological polarisation therefore has the potential to abruptly re-emerge and dramatically reshuffle the cards of Russia's contested identity.

6 PROTEST, CIVIL SOCIETY AND INFORMAL POLITICS

Graeme B. Robertson

June 12 is a holiday in Russia to mark the anniversary of the declaration of independence of Russia from the Soviet Union. In 2017, the holiday offered tourists and visitors to the Russian capital the opportunity to view two different narratives about Russian politics. One narrative told the story of the great victory in World War II. The central streets of the capital were filled with hundreds of people dressed in World War II uniforms, with period weapons, tanks and military installations. Many of the people came from Russia's vibrant community of war re-enactors – people whose hobby it is to re-enact famous military battles from Russia's history – and they were there for (yet another) state-sponsored celebration of Russia (and the Soviet Union's) victory in World War II, a period that is increasingly being used as a legitimizing story for Russia's current rulers.

Right alongside the re-enactors, however, quite a different story was on offer. Here the focus was on corruption in government and what the thousands of protesters in attendance saw as the morally bankrupt system of rule in the country today. Taking advantage of the holiday to add legitimacy to their claims, the protesters, many of them teenagers, waved the Russian tricolor flag even as they criticized those in power at the highest levels of the Russian government. These protests were the second major set of anti-corruption protests in Russia in a short period of time. On 26 March of the same year, some 60,000 people had participated in protests in 80 towns and cities across the country. The 12 June protests were even bigger with somewhere between 50,000 and 100,000 people protesting in 154 cities. Worried that what they were seeing was the beginning of a new wave of anti-government protests, the authorities cracked down hard. At least 1,720 protesters were arrested around the country, including more than 900 in Moscow alone. With presidential elections less than one year away, the protest wave was the first major sign of potential political problems for the Russian leadership since 2014.

However, the 2017 anti-corruption protests are far from the first time that protest and politics outside of formal political institutions represented a real challenge to the status quo in Russian politics. In fact, as we will see in this chapter, politics in Russia is often more about what happens outside formal channels than it is about participation in elections and voting. In thinking about unconventional politics, or to use the term social scientists prefer, 'contentious' politics, scholars have in mind a very wide variety of actions in which people come together, often unexpectedly, to make public demands on the state or the political system. These actions range from a vast array of different kinds of protests, to strikes, to using violence to change the expected order of politics in new and often dramatic ways. As we will see, such acts of contention have played a crucial role in shaping how the contemporary Russian state came into being, how its constitution was written and how its current political institutions operate. We will see too how those institutions have, in turn, shaped the nature and frequency of protest and how contentious politics and more conventional politics are likely to continue to shape each other in the years to come.

Beyond the issue of political protest and contention, in this chapter we will also consider the development of civil society in Russia. Often seen as an indicator of democratic development, civil society and non-governmental organizations (NGOs) typically play an important role in organizing and defending the rights of a broad range of people and groups in society. We will see how the economic collapse that followed the end of communism stifled the nascent civil society in Russia. However, as the economy started to grow again in the 2000s, civil society groups began to flourish across the country. For the most part this process took place without either help or hindrance from the Russian state. However, as we will see, in recent years the government has intensified efforts to try to make sure that civil society is contained within spaces that do not represent a challenge to the political system.

Political protest and contentious politics in Russian history

Like Eskimos and snow, Russians have a lot of words for protest, rebellion and civil unrest and over the centuries of its existence, the political fate of Russia has more often been decided in the streets and fields than in parliaments or elections. A number of such periods in Russian history continue to inform how politicians, journalists and citizens think about politics today. In the 1990s, the favoured historical reference in newspapers and television was to the so-called Time of Troubles, which lasted from the death of Tsar Fyodor Ivanovich in 1598 to the establishment of the Romanov dynasty in 1613. The Time of Troubles saw devastating famine, civil war, mass uprisings and foreign occupation. The Russian state that had emerged over the preceding 500 years almost disappeared entirely. Another key period of contention often referenced by Russian politicians and commentators is the Pugachev Rebellion (1773–75), a revolt that took place at a time of foreign war and tremendous peasant unrest, which has become a symbol of the cruelty and violence that ensues when order breaks down and the Russian masses become involved in politics. Finally, of course, the tempestuous events of the Russian Revolution of 1917 and the ensuing Civil War continue to influence how Russians think about popular participation in politics and its consequences. For conservatives, the Revolution is the clearest illustration of the costs of chaos and disorder. For radicals, the Revolution remains a symbol of the political possibilities of popular participation and of resistance against a corrupt elite.

Far from being of purely historical interest, contention also played a crucial role in creating Russia as the independent federation it is today. Formerly the most populous part of a much larger state, the Soviet Union (USSR), Russia broke off in a huge wave of contention that swept across the USSR. Between 1987 and 1991, nationalist and other protests severely undermined the political viability of the Soviet state and brought the Soviet Union to the brink of collapse. However, it was an act of contention of a different kind – a failed coup launched by senior Communist officials – that pushed the Soviet state over the edge and led to the emergence of a new independent Russia on 1 January 1992.

Politics and writing the Russian Constitution

Although Russia was suddenly independent, the shape of the new country and its political institutions was still to be defined, and action on the streets once again proved decisive. The constitution inherited from the Soviet era was unclear on the powers of the president and the parliament. The result was a stand-off in which president and the parliament both claimed to be the legitimate democratic power in the country and where each sought to pursue very different policies.

With no obvious institutional solution in sight, Boris Yeltsin resorted to extraordinary measures. Though he had no constitutional mandate to do so, on 21 September 1993, Yeltsin decreed the parliament to be dissolved and called for new elections. The head of Russia's Constitutional Court duly announced that Yeltsin's decree was unconstitutional. The parliament in turn voted for Yeltsin's impeachment and appointed the vice-president in Yeltsin's place. In response, Yeltsin dispatched police units to surround the parliament building. After an 11-day siege, parliament members and their supporters who had been trapped in the building broke through the police cordon. Along with other supporters, the parliamentarians attempted to seize key government buildings in Moscow, including the main television station, where a gun battle ensued. For some hours the outcome looked in doubt, but finally Yeltsin succeeded in persuading the Russian military leadership to support him and ordered tanks to attack the Russian parliament building. When the siege was over on 4 October, somewhere between 187 (according to the government) and 1,000 (according to parliamentary supporters) had been killed. Now Yeltsin had a free hand to draw up a constitution that centralized power in his own hands.

Economic crisis, protest and society

Although Yeltsin had effectively established a dominant place for the president in the constitution, many writing at the beginning of the 1990s still expected him to be seriously tested by protest in the streets. After all, they argued, severe economic challenges would impoverish millions of people who now enjoyed new democratic rights and the freedom to protest. This, scholars thought, ought to lead to massive waves of unrest that would destabilize the new political settlement.

Russians did indeed suffer enormous social and economic upheaval, but the expected waves of protest never materialized. It was not that Russians did not take action to address the economic catastrophe that was engulfing much of the country – thousands did, participating in strikes, hunger-strikes, road and railway blockades and even, in a few extreme cases, public acts of suicide. However, though there were many thousands of protests, these events had little in the way of political consequences. There were many reasons for this. First, the depth of the economic crisis affecting the country meant that Russian workers had little leverage or bargaining power. Stopping working in a situation in which factories were largely at a standstill anyway had little effect. Second, in the 1990s it was extremely difficult to create organizations that could represent workers or put political pressure on the state. The independent civil society organizations that had flourished in the late Soviet period disappeared in the economic crisis and political disappointment of the first years of Russian independence. Moreover, in their place, state-affiliated organizations dominated the field of associations, and state-sponsored labour unions in particular continued to try to pacify rather than organize workers. Third, and most paradoxically of all, democracy made it more difficult, not less, for workers, pensioners and others to hold the state responsible for their economic situation. Under communism, the state took upon itself direct responsibility for the economic condition of its citizens. When coal miners in 1989 struck over a lack of soap, the head of the Soviet government himself came to negotiate with them. However, in Yeltsin's Russia, the state explicitly downplayed its responsibility for the economy, turning things over, rhetorically at least, to the market. Moreover, electoral democracy meant that legitimate political power derived from the process of winning elections (by fair means or foul), rather than from economic performance, as it had in the Soviet era.

Ethnic and regional politics and contention

In addition to the economic crisis, Russia also faced a major challenge from many of its own ethnic minorities and regions that claimed autonomy from Moscow. Challenges from restive regions and minorities were common and, in many ways, dominated politics in the first half of the 1990s. Most prominent amongst these were the Volga republics of Tatarstan, Bashkortostan, the Siberian region of Sakha (Yakutia) and the Caucasus region of Chechnya. However, for the most part, the politics of regional and ethnic autonomy were contained within negotiations between political leaders without large-scale mobilizations on the streets. Yeltsin and his team were able to buy off the leadership of most regions with a combination of special bilateral treaties and financial transfers.

The major exception to this pattern was the Republic of Chechnya, located in the Caucasus mountains in the south of Russia. In November 1991, the Chechen parliament declared Chechnya's independence from Russia. Initially, the Russian government was too concerned with the myriad other problems it faced at the moment of the Soviet collapse to do much more than complain. However, in late 1994 Yeltsin and his team could no longer ignore the existence of a *de facto* autonomous state within Russia that had become a centre of lawlessness and instability. In December 1994, Yeltsin opted to launch a full-scale military intervention in order to reestablish Russian control. Despite the overwhelming advantage the Russian military had in terms of numbers and equipment, they were unable to defeat the Chechen forces. After a bloody and fruitless conflict, the Russians were forced to accept a peace deal in August 1996 that allowed *de facto* Chechen independence.

However, the uneasy coexistence between Russia and Chechnya was shattered in 1999, when a large group of militants, closely associated with international Islamic fighters, invaded Dagestan, a region of Russia bordering on Chechnya. This provocation came on top of years of cross-border raiding from Chechnya and the kidnapping of dozens of citizens of neighbouring regions. Faced with this escalation, the Russian government launched another full-scale invasion. In contrast to the street fighting of the first war, this time Russian forces rapidly seized control of the main population centres, including the Chechen capital, Grozny. While successful, the Russian assault was also brutal, inflicting thousands of civilian casualties and committing innumerable human rights violations. Facing defeat on the conventional battlefield, Chechen fighters resorted increasingly to attacks on civilian targets outside the borders of Chechnya, the most horrifying of which involved the taking hostage of an entire elementary school in Beslan, North Ossetia, on the first day of classes in September 2004. In the fighting that followed, some 350 hostages, many of them young children, were killed. Other atrocities have included hostage-taking in a central Moscow theatre and bombings of apartment buildings, airliners, subway trains, rock concerts, hospitals, trains, and markets. More than a thousand people have been killed in terrorist incidents in Russia since 1991, with some 600 killed in Moscow alone by 2007 (Taylor 2011). Although by 2010 the federal authorities had largely defeated pro-independence Chechen militants and established a Chechen-led regime in power, acts of terrorism and violence have continued, especially in the North Caucasus region, and isolated incidents have also occurred elsewhere in Russia.

Aside from the obviously disastrous impact within Chechnya itself, the conflict has made the task of building a law-bound and democratic state in Russia much harder. Both the fighting in Chechnya and terrorism in the rest of Russia have been used to justify limitations on media freedom and human rights. Civilians and conscripts alike have suffered in the brutality of a civil war. Famous journalists and human rights activists and ordinary men, women and children have been killed, with the finger of blame often being pointed at Russian forces. Media freedom has suffered as limits on reporting about the conflict have been justified on grounds of state security. In Chechnya, peace has been restored at the cost of installing a repressive and often violent Chechen regime. In the rest of Russia, fear of terrorism has sometimes led to reprisals against ethnic Chechens and other Caucasians. More generally, Russian citizens have for the most part been willing to support their government in actions that have frequently breached both democratic and human rights norms. In short, the bloody Chechen conflict has made the environment much more difficult for democracy in Russia.

Putin and protest

As awful as the Yeltsin years were for all but a small minority of Russians, by the turn of the millennium the economy had started to bounce back. With the economy recovering, the opportunities for local organization and participation increased and civil society organizations started to play a small but nonetheless noticeable role in many places in Russia. The government responded to this development by creating new institutions designed to integrate civil society into political and administrative decision-making. The new economic and political context of the Putin years also saw the re-emergence of political protest and the beginnings of a more coherent opposition to the existing political system.

With the wrenching economic crisis of the 1990s over, voluntary organizations and NGOs began to emerge in different parts of the Russian Federation. Thousands of new organizations were registered and began to participate in local politics and society (Evans et al. 2006). The Russian government was aware of this development and took a number of measures to channel this emerging civil society sector in directions that would help the government rather than challenge it. At the federal level, a new assembly, known as the Public Chamber, was created to give representatives of NGOs a voice on public policy. The Public Chamber sat for the first time in 2005 and consists of representatives of civil society chosen by the government, who in turn elect further members. The Chamber is supposed to increase citizen involvement in both legislative and executive action and comment on draft legislation and the implementation of existing law. The Public Chamber also manages a system of competitions for federal funding of NGO projects throughout Russia. In addition to the federal level Public Chamber, similar bodies were set up at the regional level all across the country.

Opinions have been divided on the role of the Public Chambers in practice. Supporters argue that the Chambers provide a unique voice for the third sector in Russia and give civil society organizations unparalleled influence over policies that affect NGOs directly. These supporters also cite the intervention of the Public Chamber in a number of important cases over the years. Critics, on the other hand, argue that the system is intended to promote only pro-government organizations and to provide incentives for groups to avoid criticism of the government in return for access to funding and positions in the Chamber. What is clear is that the creation of the Public Chambers constitutes recognition on the part of the Russian government that a thriving state in the contemporary world needs a thriving society. However, by creating formal state institutions to which some have access and others do not, the system creates in society an insiders/outsiders divide that may make the development of that thriving society harder rather than easier to achieve.

Alongside the growth in civil society, the Putin years also saw the re-emergence of contention as an important part of Russian politics. The first sign that politics was returning to the streets of Russia came in January 2005. As part of a package of liberal economic reforms, the government introduced a new system whereby benefits in kind – particularly free transportation – that were provided to pensioners, war veterans and others were to be replaced by cash payments. The reforms were highly controversial, and protests quickly spread in Moscow, St Petersburg and across much of Russia.

The government responded with a mixture of concessions and repression of activists, and the protests gradually petered out. However, the protests represented a turning point. For the first time since Putin had come to power, the government had looked vulnerable to a challenge from the streets. Policies created by the executive and pushed through Russia's sleepy parliament had mobilized tens of thousands of angry citizens and had been partially reversed due to action on the streets. Moreover, the protests had included a broad range of groups from pensioners and liberal human rights activists to nationalist and neo-Bolshevik youth and had impressed upon these diverse groups the possibilities offered by creating a united front. Consequently, in the aftermath of the protests, especially in the biggest cities, Moscow and St Petersburg, meetings to coordinate non-parliamentary opposition activity began for the first time.

The non-system opposition that emerged from these meetings formed from two primary sources – alienated former parliamentary parties and politicians, and supporters of parties and movements at the right and left fringes of Russian politics. The initiative to coordinate was primarily local and so the character of the emergent opposition varied from place to place. In St Petersburg, for example, activists got together to form a united opposition bloc that stretched from liberals supported by businessman and philanthropist George Soros to members of the National Bolshevik Party, whose activists celebrate Stalin. Achieving cooperation across an opposition that spans such an enormously broad spectrum was a difficult and slow task, so activists focused on opportunities where a united front against the incumbent regime could be presented. The G8 summit of major world leaders in St Petersburg in 2006 was one such event, and though the protesters were kept far from the official meetings, the non-system opposition used the occasion to launch itself politically. Similarly, in Moscow, a parallel organization, 'Other Russia', was created around the time of the G8 summit. Other Russia included an extraordinary array of people and groups. Prominent amongst the leadership were liberal and former world chess champion Garri Kasparov, Yeltsin's former Prime Minister Mikhail Kasyanov, Viktor Anpilov, a Stalinist who had fought on the side of the parliament against Yeltsin in 1993, National Bolshevik Party leader Eduard Limonov and a former head of the neo-liberal Union of Right Forces, Irina Khakamada. Other Russia began a regular series of protests by holding a 'Dissenters' March' in Moscow on 16 December. The march was followed by others the following year in Nizhny Novgorod, St Petersburg and Moscow. In 2009, Limonov and others also began 'Strategy 31', a series of protests held on the 31st day of each month to mark the alleged violation by the authorities of article 31 of the Russian Constitution, which guarantees freedom of assembly.

Over the next few years, the non-system opposition continued to focus on non-parliamentary tactics. Deprived of access to television, activists sought creative ways of attracting attention. Traditional street protests were supplemented with flash mobs and other creative 'happenings' intended to destabilize the authority of the ruling administration. A key feature of the protests is the broad range of issues that have brought people together. Instead of the almost uniformly economic demands of the 1990s, protests now feature a much broader range of demands reflective of a rapidly trans-forming and changing society. Much of the energy behind street protests in Russia since the late 2000s has been driven by economic development and the environmental and distributional challenges that growth tends to gener-ate. Urban building projects are one of the most common causes of protest in recent years as developers seek to make more profitable use of crowded urban space, often violating the rights of former tenants. Similarly, civil rights complaints and especially problems with the criminal justice system and with corruption have come to play a bigger role.

Environmentalists have also played a big role in the development of civil society and informal politics. Russia has a tradition of environmental protests, dating back to the Soviet period and efforts to preserve the pristine environment of Lake Baikal in Siberia. In recent years, the environmental movement has continued to focus on Lake Baikal but has also been involved in a wide range of issues, including protesting against pollution from gas production facilities, environmental destruction resulting from construction projects associated with the 2014 Winter Olympics in Sochi, and exploita-tion of natural resources in the Arctic. From a political perspective, the most significant environmental protests of recent years took place in 2010, when thousands of activists fought a summer-long campaign involving civil disobedience in an attempt to stop the construction of the Moscow-St Petersburg motorway through the Khimki Forest, part of the greenbelt on the outskirts of Moscow and home to elk, wild boar and several endangered plant and insect species. By the end of the summer, then President Dmitry Medvedev ordered a suspension of construction, marking a rare climb-down on the part of the authorities. Many of the activists involved in the Khimki protests have continued to participate in civil society and local politics.

By contrast, labour unions have played a somewhat marginal role in civil society and politics. Although workers' strikes and independent labour unions played a major role in bringing down the Soviet Union, in the post-communist era the largest unions have generally been co-opted by employers and the state, depriving workers of genuine representatives. Nevertheless, as the economy grew in the 2000s, efforts at independent labour organizing began again to spread across the country, focusing in particular on flourishing industrial and natural resource enterprises, transportation and foreign-owned industrial plants. So far, the government and employers have worked hard to repress the new unions, and labour organizing remains a difficult and sometimes dangerous task.

The protest cycle of 2011–12

In December 2011, the nascent protest movement in Russia took centre stage in the international news for the first time. On 4 December 2011, elections took place to the lower house of Russia's parliament, the State Duma. Russian and international observers condemned the elections, as they had done in the past, citing barriers to candidate registration, ballot-box stuffing and violations in counting the votes. As the results came in that evening, the perception that the elections had been marred by fraud was widespread in opposition circles. The reaction to fraud, however, differed between those who had a place in Russia's divided political system and those who were excluded. Communist Party leader Gennady Zyuganov, whose party had won the second largest number of seats in the Duma, at first condemned the elections on television. Later, after his party was awarded a number of key committee assignments in the new parliament, Zyuganov changed positions and the Communists duly took up their seats.

By contrast, the non-parliamentary opposition quickly took to the streets. On the day after the elections, Monday, 5 December, a few thousand activists protested in Moscow, denouncing the elections as unfair. Since no permit had been granted for the protest, the gathering was technically illegal and police arrested some 300 participants. More than 100 activists were also arrested at a similar event in St Petersburg. The gathering attracted a number of politicians who had been active in Other Russia, as well as other activists and cultural figures. Finding themselves together, an informal committee was quickly formed to coordinate protests against the elections.

The following day unsanctioned protests continued in the centre of Moscow, and a number of protest leaders were arrested. At the same time, pro-government supporters rallied in front of the Kremlin and the authorities moved large numbers of police and security officials into the capital. Nevertheless, the number of people willing to participate in protests seemed to be growing rapidly. One opposition group, Solidarity, had a permit for a legal demonstration of 300 people on Saturday, 10 December. However, as the date approached it became clear from social media that many thousands more were intending to participate. As a result, the authorities agreed to a much larger demonstration on an island in the Moscow River, in a place called Bolotnaya (Swamp) Square. On the day, somewhere between 25,000 and 80,000 people participated in a peaceful gathering. Leading cultural figures, authors and rock stars joined the politicians in addressing the crowd. Similar, if much smaller, protests were held in St Petersburg and other cities across Russia. Two weeks later, on 24 December, between 28,000 (the police estimate) and 120,000 (the opposition estimate) people gathered on Prospekt Sakharova in central Moscow. A third mass event took place in Moscow on 4 February 2012, with a march culminating in Bolotnaya Square. Between 40,000 and 160,000 people braved the –20 Celsius temperatures to participate.

Though the authorities in the Kremlin had initially seemed rattled by the protests, by March the situation seemed back under control. Vladimir Putin ran for and was duly elected president on 4 March with little challenge either on the streets or at the ballot box. With Putin firmly back in office, the authorities also began to take a tougher stance towards the protesters. A demonstration at Bolotnaya Square on 6 May, the day before Putin's inauguration, took place in the context of a massive police presence. At the rally, scuffling broke out between police and protesters and about 400 protesters were arrested and 80 injured. This was the first significant violence of any of the protest events and was indicative of a more aggressive line being taken by police.

Protest, civil society and politics since 2012

Many international and Russian commentators celebrated the protests as a new stage in Russian politics and argued that the event marked the beginning of the end of the Putin regime. While they were right on the first count, they were wrong on the second. Russian politics definitely took a decisive turn in a different direction after the protests, but rather than mark the beginning of the end of the Putin regime, the protests prompted a transformation in the Russian leadership's political strategy aimed at aggressively reasserting control.

Over the course of the next few months, the Putin administration launched the most intensive set of repressive measures seen since the end of the Communist era. Dozens of low-profile, ordinary citizens were rounded up in dawn raids, tried in politicized tribunals and imprisoned for alleged offenses related to previous protests. Protests were broken up and protesters arrested. Protest leaders were arrested and held under trumped-up charges. Members of parliament who had been sympathetic to the protesters were stripped of their mandates and removed from parliament. On 27 February 2015 a leading opposition figure, Boris Nemtsov, was gunned down on a bridge in the shadow of the Kremlin.

However, the campaign to reestablish control was not limited to arrests and direct repression. Instead, the arrests were part of a broader political campaign to discredit the opposition and to establish the Putin regime's legitimacy in the eyes of the broader Russian population. Central to this strategy was a clear effort on the part of the Kremlin to cast the opposition as anti-Russian, foreign supported, effete and deviant. These classic populist tropes were evident in a range of different ways.

Perhaps most obvious was the campaign to discredit election protesters as foreign stooges. Statements by President Putin accusing the United States of paying for the protests, and television 'documentaries' condemning independent election observers for taking foreign money, were part of a broad campaign to convince Russians that allegations of fraud at the elections were generated by foreign governments. While surveys suggest that these charges were not generally accepted by the population at large, they did have some resonance within sub-groups.

The regime also sought to portray the opposition as deviating from traditional Russian values. Early in the protest cycle, President Putin compared the white ribbons worn by protesters to condoms and called the protesters indecent. Over time, this trope has been developed into a full-scale effort to change the subject from electoral fraud to a broad defence of 'traditional' values. At the core of this strategy has been a sustained campaign against the rights of LGBT people in Russia. Local bans on LGBT Pride marches and vigourous enforcement of laws seeking to criminalize 'propaganda' that 'promotes' homosexuality has become increasingly common in Russia over recent years. In the aftermath of the protests, the Putin administration chose to make such initiatives a centrepiece of policy. This use of political campaigns aimed at stigmatizing opposition, and especially to villainize a distinct sub-group, is clearly not a new phenomenon in Russia or elsewhere. Nevertheless, in the Russian context these efforts represented a significant invigoration in legislative, political, and law enforcement efforts to create a zone of 'healthy' social groups and forces working for Russia and one of 'unhealthy' or 'unpatriotic' forces who can be banned, harassed or legally pursued (like Russia's LGBT community).

A key part of the government's political strategy has consisted of establishing a legal framework within which the state would have the ability to target whatever individuals or groups were politically expedient at the time. Creating a legal framework for repression is not the same as building the rule of law. In fact, the essence of the legalistic approach to repression is the adoption of vaguely worded legislation that can be used to attack political targets backed up by a compliant judiciary that can be relied upon to provide the kind of judgments the state desires. In this sense, the understanding that underpins the state's approach to the law is purely political – laws are there not to inhibit and limit agents of the state, but to facilitate the achievement of their goals.

A particularly flagrant example of this is the so-called Foreign Agents law signed by President Putin on 21 July 2012. The Foreign Agents Law requires NGOs that engage in 'political activity' and that receive funding from foreign entities (either public or private) to register with the Russian state as 'foreign agents'. The law provides exemptions for a range of different kinds of organizations, including those involved in health, environmental protection or science, culture and art, but was interpreted by most commentators and, more importantly, by the Russian courts, as having a wide application. In practice, the law has been used to target high-profile groups, in particular, the election monitoring organization Golos, the public opinion polling company the Levada Center, and the human rights organization Memorial. However, the pressure has not been limited to groups with an international presence. Smaller local groups including numerous research organizations focusing on women's rights, LGBTQ issues and anti-discrimination in general have also been targeted. By cutting off the flow of funds to NGOs from abroad, Russian organizations are likely either to have to close down or become increasingly dependent on the state for support.

Part of the new strategy of the Putin administration has also been to try to isolate any emerging leaders among the street opposition. Most of the protest leaders before 2011 were people with a long history of association with the opposition and so were old news and little feared in the Kremlin. However, the election-related protest cycle brought forward some new faces who represented more of a challenge to politics as usual in Russia.

Amongst the most prominent was Sergei Udaltsov, leader of a group called Left Front. With his allegiance to leftist and even revolutionary positions, Udaltsov is far from the political mainstream in Russia, but he nevertheless represents a challenge to the current system and, in particular, to the comfortable place of the Communist Party within it. Consequently, Udaltsov has faced serious intimidation from the Russian authorities, including frequent periods of detention. This pressure culminated in February 2013, when Udaltsov was placed under house arrest on the quite fantastical charge of having conspired with Georgian agents in a plot to overthrow the Russian president. Udlatsov was convicted and jailed until his eventual release in August 2017.

Most prominent of all the new oppositionists is the anti-corruption blogger and sometime nationalist rabble-rouser, Alexei Navalny. Navalny has an aggressive, irreverent political style that matches well in competition with the macho image of President Putin. Navalny's most famous contribution to Russian political debate so far has been his relabelling of Russia's ruling United Russia Party as the 'Party of Crooks and Thieves', a label that has stuck and become common currency amongst the opposition. Over recent years, Navalny has steadily emerged as the figurehead of the non-parliamentary opposition. In October 2010, Navalny won 'virtual elections' held online to elect a 'Mayor of Moscow' in protest against the appointment of a long-time Putin associate (Sergei Sobyanin) to that job. Then, in October 2012, he had the biggest support in the election to the opposition Coordinating Council, with 53% of those who participated selecting him for the council.

In response to Navalny's rising profile, the authorities launched a series of investigations into Navalny's activities in an attempt to bring down the anti-corruption campaigner with corruption charges of their own. By the summer of 2013, Navalny was the defendant in three different trials – accused of embezzling money from a forestry company (Kirovles), from the Post Office (the Yves Rocher case) and from a right-wing political party. In July 2013, Navalny was convicted in the Kirovles trial and sentenced to five years' imprisonment. Bizarrely enough, the authorities promptly released Navalny pending appeal – something that almost never happens in Russia – and he returned to Moscow to run in the real elections for mayor of Moscow in September 2013. After a lively campaign of meeting voters and engaging directly with citizens – he was largely excluded from television during the campaign – Alexei Navalny polled a very creditable 27% of the vote, coming close to forcing the winner and incumbent mayor, Sobyanin, into a run-off vote.

Finally, the political campaign to re-impose order and to marginalize opposition was enormously helped by events in Ukraine and the Putin administration's response. In February 2014, after months of protest and disorder on the streets of the capital and across the country, the sitting President of Ukraine, Viktor Yanukovych, abandoned his post and fled to Russia. Yanukovych had run a violent and corrupt regime in Ukraine and was widely seen as having the support of Moscow. In response to the revolution in Ukraine, Russia moved quickly to annex the Crimean

Peninsula that was part of Ukraine. The Russian state also provided support to separatist rebels in two other eastern provinces of Ukraine. These actions were buttressed by a massive propaganda campaign on Russian television, mongering fear amongst the population for the safety of ethnic Russians in Ukraine.

Despite significant protests from anti-war groups in Moscow and elsewhere, the Putin administration's rapid actions in Ukraine received an overwhelmingly positive response amongst Russians in general. Putin's approval ratings that had been stagnant in the low 60s percent, shot up to the high 80s, where they have remained since. The rise in support was largely the result of nationalist and patriotic Russians who had previously been sceptical of Putin, rallying to his side. This served to further marginalize opponents, whom the administration had already sought to portray as treasonous.

Protest, civil society and the presidential election of 2018

Navalny has since continued his campaigning, and although he was banned from running for the presidency in March 2018, he acted as though he was a candidate. His campaign was based on promises of more open and honest government and the adoption of western practices to end corruption. He travelled the country, despite frequent physical and legal harassment, holding quite well-attended public meetings and engaging in discussion with citizens. There is clearly a constituency, albeit a limited one for now, that craves change of the kind that Navalny is promising.

However, it is equally clear that the Kremlin feared that if Navalny appeared on the ballot he would garner real support. While Putin's popularity remains extremely high, the Kremlin seems anxious about the future. Navalny's anti-corruption campaigns, including extremely well-documented videos exposing alleged massive corruption on the part of top leaders such as Prime Minister Dmitry Medvedev, have obviously struck a chord in the country. Millions and millions of people have watched the videos and hundreds of thousands have turned out for anti-corruption protests, such as those with which this chapter began.

Moreover, other signs of discontent are evident. Thousands of young and middle-aged Muscovites protested in 2017 against an extravagant and grandiose plan to demolish and rebuild aging apartment buildings in the city. Although the government claims widespread support for one of the most ambitious programmes of urban renewal ever undertaken, many citizens who are affected are suspicious that the real beneficiaries of the massive project will be contractors close to the Putin administration rather than residents. It is thought that distrust of the reconstruction plans contributed to opposition groups winning about a quarter of the seats in Moscow city council elections in 2017.

Nor is discontent limited to the capital or to the middle classes. A long-running series of protests by Russian truckers – part of Putin's core working-class base – over a new taxation system for trucking has brought them directly into conflict with the Kremlin. There is also some evidence that strike activity amongst other Russian workers may have increased in recent years.

All these factors make the Kremlin extremely nervous of allowing any unpredictable factors to be at play during election periods. The script for elections is taken from the parliamentary elections of 18 September 2016, which were dominated by the ruling party, United Russia. Here a key feature was to control the media and to limit discussion of the issues to the minimum. The goal, successfully achieved, was to make the elections as dull as possible to put the population to sleep, while mobilizing key supporters and engaging in widespread fraud.

Conclusion

Within the corridors of power in Russia, President Putin's position looks more consolidated than ever. His popularity in the country remains high and there is no overt sign of discontent within the ruling elite. The view from inside the Kremlin suggested, correctly as it turned out, relatively plain sailing for Putin as he embarked upon the campaign for his fourth term as Russia's President. Yet, looked at more broadly, from the streets and workplaces of Russia, the future seems less certain. Challenges for the regime and discontent with economic outcomes are not hard to find.

Politics in Russia continues to change. The extraordinary turmoil and devastation of the 1990s scarred Russian society and contributed to the construction of a closed, hierarchical political system. This system was designed to minimize contestation and to seal politics off from contention and pressure from below. However, as the economy recovered, Russian society has grown wealthier, better organized and more like societies in countries to Russia's west. At the same time, activists and others excluded from the political system sought to use protests and other forms of politics to gain a voice. The protest cycle of 2011–12 was a watershed moment in this process and was a loud wake-up call to the authorities that politics as usual has to change. The authorities responded to that call with a combination of repression and efforts to mobilize conservative and nationalist forces in society. So far, this repressive turn has been largely successful. However, the question is whether this is a sustainable strategy in the longer term. Pressure from below for a greater liberalization of the political environment continues to build, even as the regime works to isolate and exclude its opponents. What balance is struck between liberalization and repression will be a crucial feature to watch in Russian politics in the coming years.

7 RUSSIA, MEDIA AND AUDIENCES

Ellen Mickiewicz

In contemporary Russia, the media scene is one of demoralization of many and struggle to preserve professional standards for fewer. The decade of the Yeltsin administration in the 1990s, though rife with corruption, is viewed by journalists as a 'golden time'. Compared to what came after, it is accurate. Paradoxically, it was the *lack* of institutions and the incapacity of the state that allowed more room to manoeuvre, space to adopt new ways, openness to expressions of new sets of values. It is that phenomenon that made the period one of freedom of the press that the journalists snatched from the dying Soviet empire and the chaotic administration of the first years of the Russian Federation.

Television

The vast majority of Russians say they get most of their news and information from television. With the landmass spread out over 11 time zones, a system of communications satellites makes it possible for signals to reach the population. Most Russians can access the three big national channels, as well as channels for sports, movies, 'nostalgia' (Soviet-era old movies and personalities), and other entertainment programmes. Still, in some places, the Far Eastern and Maritime provinces, for example, viewers can often receive only two channels: Channel One and Channel Two, the principal channels during the Soviet era.

Because of the huge audience numbers, television is the most closely watched and monitored of media. Television is particularly important, because of the very large numbers it attracts and partly for two other reasons. In seeking to put forward a single Kremlin-devised and -approved line, the state is, in effect, subscribing to the hypodermic needle model. Viewers will, in the model, absorb the message as intended by the central government and uphold its values and policies. Most people will, it is assumed, be exposed only to this message and therefore will not be exposed to counter-messaging. The third important reason the state is so concerned about television relates to the capacity conferred on television in modern times to declare the 'legitimacy' of a regime. Legitimacy is not meant here literally. Rather it refers to the phenomenon that because of television's enormous reach, and its importance for the government, any takeover of the medium and claim to successful replacement of the government by an aspiring new regime is apt to be believed. It is the takeover of television that opponents of the regime seek, because it has become the proof – sent widely and instantly to the whole nation – of the success of insurgency.

In Russia, as in many other countries, television headquarters are protected by armed guards. In 1993, when a rebellion against Boris Yeltsin was hatched in parliament, rebels rushed to Ostankino, where state television transmitters are located, and attempted to take it. A deadly gun battle was fought at the entrance. The head of Channel One became alarmed and after unanswered telephone calls to city officials, shut down the channel in the middle of a soccer game. A technical manoeuvre permitted Channel Two to switch frequencies and continue on air all through the night and next day, reassuring the population that the president was in control. The message of continuity of government also dampened and ultimately is credited with preventing a possible mass movement from the provinces to support the rebels. Boris Yeltsin in his memoirs declared that television 'saved Russia'.

Channel One operates as a joint stock company, comprised of a majority state-owned bloc of shares and the rest of the shares held by government-friendly big businessmen. 'Rossiya', the second channel, is state owned and operated. These two channels had the biggest audiences in Soviet times and continue that domination. NTV, a third channel, is owned by Gazprom, the energy conglomerate close to the Kremlin. It was the first private news-gathering station in post-Soviet Russia and made its reputation with courageous reporters, such as Elena Masyuk, who at great risk discredited the state's narrative that the war in Chechnya, as reported by the other two channels, was a Kremlin project to provide aid to the region. Instead, Masyuk showed what was not reported by the state: corpses from Moscow's bombs and ruins of buildings where terrified civilians tried to take cover. A fatal weakness underlay the station's existence: continuously delayed payments on substantial loans. NTV's audience quickly grew; the news agenda became determinedly adversarial. The country's best journalists were there, and President Vladimir Putin put an end to it, portraying the station's demise as an economic failure. On Easter Sunday 2001, Gazprom called in its loans; tax police raided NTV's headquarters and the channel was shuttered. Under Gazprom, the new owner, programming was altered to resemble that of the other two channels.

In a country where many are living close to the bone and do not expect much change, the free news and entertainment on television is the only alternative to more expensive choices: going out to movies, plays, concerts and buying newspapers. In the Soviet era the main television news programme on Channel One from its inception captured the Soviet audience; it is still traditional in many families to sit in front of the screen to watch 'Vremya' (Time), the first and still the most important TV news programme. College students coming home for a holiday or living at home join in the ritual. Afterward, they return to their computers as soon as possible. Only the first two channels penetrate the whole country; both are partially or wholly state owned. The period of viewpoint diversity ended when the government of Yeltsin was replaced by the leadership of Vladimir Putin. The channels remain: content, owners, and many staff do not. Instead, news content on the national channels tends to be similar and the news replays a version of past uniformity upholding government policy. As in most countries, audiences for television are by far the most heterogeneous, bringing together the less educated and the well-educated, reaching rural and urban viewers instantaneously, and with pictures, which, in terms of cognition, are far more persuasive than text only.

None of the news sources strays from the agenda of the Kremlin, which regularly gathers television heads and most noted journalists to synchronize stories. Big business figures aligned with the Kremlin serve on the governing boards of most media. Self-censorship is widely practiced; editors and heads of departments are chosen for their experience, both in television and in understanding the limits imposed by the central government. Even more damaging to diversity was the drastic drop in oil prices. The Russian economy as a whole contracted; the standard of living fell. Rubles for television advertising plummeted. It no longer made sense to advertise foreign products that had become too expensive or were no longer available because of sanctions the West applied to punish Russia's actions in Ukraine. Some independent regional stations had become first rate, but when their loans were called in and advertising dropped, they were constrained to close down. Tomsk-2, an independent regional television station in Siberia, did superlative work and served a vital need to inform the region; it was forced to close by its creditors. While it lasted, the station had received rare national recognition (four TEFI – equivalent to the US Emmy and the British BAFTA awards), not shunted off to the special category reserved for regional television but in direct competition with the big networks.

The viewing day has much more than news, even though news programmes remain extremely popular, in spite of their retreat into a more Soviet style of presentation and content. Ratings for cities with populations over 100,000 in January 2017 showed that a talk show came in first. 'Let Them Speak' takes place in a TV studio, where two young hosts keep the tide of passionate talk from overflowing. Real-life personal dramas unfold. On one show, the plight of children dying from overdoses of alcohol and inadequate societal responsiveness was argued at a high emotional pitch. This show, lasting nearly an hour on Channel One, had the highest ratings in urban Russia, followed by 'Vremya'. There are stunningly resilient Soviet-era entertainment game shows and comedies, such as 'Field of Miracles', 'KVN' (acronym for Club of Spirited People), and 'The Person and the Law'. Viewers like detective and crime shows, popular music concerts, and Western clones, such as 'Who Wants to Be a Millionaire?'.

By following the old Soviet model of exaggerating positive news and minimizing or skipping protests and marches, as well as negative factors in the economy, the government, as before, creates a dilemma: Russians can look through their windows, go to markets, see what their neighbours have and draw conclusions for themselves about the health of the economy and the needs of their families. No amount of whitewashing and exaggerated successes can erase daily life. Russians have lived through decades of two realities that don't match: what the television screen shows them and what they experience for themselves. As a result, they are well schooled in scepticism. Even decades after the end of the Soviet Union, viewers approach what television shows them with caution. Even young people, who never knew Soviet reality, match what they see on television with other coverage, comparing what they experience and what the internet's broader palette provides. Almost half of the Russians responding to a national survey said the economic situation was worse than what television portrayed.

Coverage of international stories is a different issue. Most viewers have no personal knowledge of the situation in Syria or Iraq; some get impressions about Ukraine from relatives and friends, but it is much less feasible to evaluate news taking place far away. When the pollsters come around to ask about support for foreign ventures, they often get positive responses. But the professed agreement with government policy and television news about these far-off places can mask a basic fact: On average, people care most about their own and their families' livelihood. Military ventures abroad are distant and back in Russia, citizens lose interest quickly. In 2016, a national poll probing Russians' interest in contentious events in Ukraine, so often dramatically portrayed on television news, found that only 9% said they followed events in Ukraine 'very attentively'; 60% said that they either did not follow Ukraine stories at all or they paid little attention. In 2014, when Russia forcibly took the Crimean peninsula from Ukraine, Moscow celebrated the return of historically Russian territory, where the Russian navy is berthed and from whose shores some of the greatest battles in history were fought. Soviet leader Nikita Khrushchev had transferred it from the Russian Soviet Republic to the Ukrainian Soviet Republic in 1954. When the territory of Crimea was annexed, Russia rejoiced with fireworks; streets filled with joyful demonstrations celebrating the annexation and many fewer protesting the violation of law. Television kept up the patriotic programming. Soon, the polls would show that when the national budget was announced, ordinary people were dissatisfied with continued cuts in social welfare and blamed the decline of oil prices, Western-imposed sanctions, and the costs of supporting Crimea. The constant drumbeat of patriotism from television did nothing to offset problems of health and welfare at home.

A remarkable station called TV Rain started up in 2010 as a cable channel. It was like nothing else. Its young hosts and reporters covered what was deliberately ignored by the big three channels: protests, demonstrations, interviews with activists opposed to the Kremlin, news of the economy; and it covered high culture, which had virtually disappeared from state-controlled television. Its audience is upscale and well educated. The young reporters are thoroughly professional and do not shrink from pressing hard-hitting questions. One such interviewer is Ksenia Sobchak, whose sharp questions and stubborn tenacity get answers. She even went on to run against Vladimir Putin in the 2018 presidential election. Knowing she could not win, she could voice liberal positions on a national stage. Every certified candidate was granted free time on national television. TV Rain was most notable, independent, and important during the enormous demonstrations of 2011 and 2012. It was on all day and night, talking to all stripes of political parties and speakers. The small staff of the station was knowledgeable about the politics and history the speakers invoked, and its explanations helped viewers understand what was happening in real time. After the demonstrations, some of its leading figures attempted to form an internet-based method to gather preferences from people around the country, and from these concerns to design an agenda that a web-based counter-parliament might develop ways to implement. TV Rain showed live all the meetings formulating the new experimental strategy.

On the solemn 70th anniversary of the siege of Leningrad, a deeply emotional commemoration of the 900-day horror when one million people died and the surrounding Nazi military kept the city's population penned in, cold and starving, TV Rain made an ill-considered decision to show a call-in poll asking whether Leningraders should have given in to the Germans and avoided the massive suffering and death or hold out, as, in fact, they did, at great cost. The Kremlin found it intolerably offensive and successfully put pressure on the cable operators to drop the station. TV Rain had been a thorn in the side of the leadership, in any case, and this error of tact provided the chance to wound it badly. Revenues fell abruptly; a downsized TV Rain team had to leave their studio and set up in a small space. The station continues on a subscription basis. In 2017, long-haul truckers from all over Russia – thousands of them – launched a wildcat strike protesting new fees and taxes and drove their enormous rigs to Moscow, where they enacted the 'snail'; moving at a snail's pace to block traffic. This was a working-class, leaderless movement and TV Rain covered it fully. Several reporters were on site; others analyzed the issues from the studio. It was barely visible on state-controlled television.

Radio

Radio is an inexpensive medium, convenient for the growing number of car owners. There are hundreds of stations: some state owned and some private. The most popular is a private radio station broadcasting music. There is one programme, though, that is unique. *Ekho Moskvy* (Moscow Echo) is a discussion show hosted mainly by its founder, Alexei Venediktov. Venediktov has a keen sense of balancing political controversy with Kremlin demands. Typically, a programme features a group made up of officials from government ministries, film critics, writers, and the host. Many have wondered how Venediktov does the programme time after time without the Kremlin's taking action to shut him down. He has managed to convince the government that ministers and directors of agencies will have a chance to explain and advocate for government policies. The other guests offer some rather pointed and critical positions. Venediktov succeeds by keeping the tone of the discussion moderate and cool. As a matter of fact, the largest number of guests over time have come from the government. Their bureaucratic droning does not compete very well with the acerbic wit of the writers and critics. Venediktov is always under scrutiny. He meets weekly with political officials to apprise them of plans for the week's show. But this clever, careful strategy is unstable. The Kremlin put Gazprom officials on the board of directors. Venediktov is willing to make compromises. At times, he goes first to the authorities before undertaking something controversial. None of these strategies, however, interferes with the diversity of viewpoints and the presence of some of the most articulate, liberal voices. It is a rare balancing act, the success of which is due to Venediktov himself. Even so, the regime has changed his board of directors, and it is always possible that the future will be increasingly precarious. Especially whenever elections approach, Venediktov must be careful.

Both TV Rain and *Ekho Moskvy* have comparatively small audiences. They are very far from even a fraction of the audiences for the big stations. But their audiences are elites, and many live in Moscow. That demographic alone gives pause to the Kremlin overseers, because Soviet and post-Soviet leaders have always been focused on Moscow and on protecting their own status in the capital.

Newspapers

The newspaper market is struggling in many countries: significant amounts of advertising revenues have migrated to the internet. Additionally, where household disposable incomes have declined, newspapers may be an unnecessary expenditure. Newspapers are more attractive to the well educated and, in turn, newspapers attract their audiences with long-form investigative journalism and analyses. Newspapers have a particular attraction for readers who seek long and thorough coverage instead of predictable, short, news capsules of domestic television channels and many websites. Newspapers also have a tradition of importance in making history. In Tsarist Russia, Lenin made the newspaper a powerful force in centralizing his movement to make revolution. In present-day Russia there are hundreds of newspapers appealing to different tastes and pastimes, but there are only a few that are large, respected, and enjoy editorial independence. Others have come under the control of tycoons and banks close to the government. Still, substantial investigative journalism continues at *Nezavisimaya Gazeta* (*Independent Newspaper*), *Novaya Gazeta* (*New Newspaper*) and *Vedomosti* (*News*). *RBC*, a well-regarded business daily, came under pressure for investigative reporting on corruption among top officials. *Novaya Gazeta* has lost advertisers, as the Kremlin warned off investors and advertisers, but it still provides a platform for good journalists who have been unable to continue working at other newspapers in Moscow. *Kommersant*, a business newspaper, downsized and has online daily editions in several Russian regions and in the UK.

The dynamic of change in press outlets of all kinds is a continual tightening of control from the Kremlin and strong negative reactions to investigative pieces that appear to implicate the top leadership in corruption. *RBC* came under pressure and threat of a fraud investigation, which resulted in the resignation of the three top editors. Wealthy businessman Mikhail Prokhorov, reacting to the threat, sold *RBC*. The new owner's journalism values effectively mean the end of *RBC*'s excellence and purpose. *Lenta.ru*, the most popular news aggregator on the Russian internet, was warned in

2014 that a hyperlink in a story on Ukraine led to extremist sources, and the managing editor was dismissed by the largest shareholder. 'Extremism' is both prohibited by a plethora of exceptionally broad laws and virtually undefined in legal terms. That strategy enables prohibitions to be elastic in their implementation and leaves ordinary citizens or organizations in a weak position to challenge them. In the case of *Lenta.ru,* nearly the whole staff of editors and reporters – 80 of them – resigned in protest. Many moved to Latvia and from Riga founded the online Meduza project, continuing their investigative work. The media landscape is more barren, but by no means without strong areas of news gathering and investigative journalism: *Vedomosti, Nezavisimaya Gazeta* and *Novaya Gazeta* still uphold journalistic values and ethics and employ some of the best professionals, as do TV Rain, *Ekho Moskvy,* and the Meduza project.

Individual journalists are also at considerable risk when they investigate corruption, especially among those in high offices. A number of journalists have been murdered: some shot point-blank, some killed by a bomb planted in the office. Others have been beaten, and many have gone to prison. The cases and appeals are rarely given timely and fair resolution.

The internet

In 2000, internet penetration in Russia was 2%; in 2016, it had reached 70.1%. Eighty-five percent of Russian internet users access it with their mobile (cell) phones. The most important social media site is VKontakte (In Contact). Facebook, though growing, has not yet caught up to sites introduced and developed in Russia. VK, a domestic product, is a giant amalgam of social networks, bloggers, and communities. In 2017, it ranked first in Russia and 15th globally.

In universities, assignments are usually put on their intranets. Mobile (cell) phones leapfrogged the slow expansion of broadband. Younger Russians led the way to the internet, and many use Instagram, Twitter, and more specialized and often less expensive ways of communicating, such as WhatsApp. The older generation of political leaders appears increasingly divorced from the emerging generation and is suspicious of this unknown population invisible behind computer screens. When politicians attempt to imitate youth by starting their own blogs, the attempt is dismissed as amateurish and simply an exercise in public relations.

Putin's approach is increasingly to try to control this massive interconnected, distributed universe. In December 2011, news of outright vote fraud enraged Muscovites. They assembled in an organized fashion in massive numbers in the capital and gathered also in St Petersburg and smaller cities. Moscow's demonstrations were peaceful, organized, and orderly. But the last of them turned violent. The route agreed to by both city and marchers was altered without informing the demonstrators trapped inside a space surrounded by heavy security. Sergei Udaltsov, a far-left leader, began fighting; riots broke out. A number of prohibitions followed. During a five-year period, one after the other, rules regarding online freedom and, more generally, distribution and publication of certain kinds of speech were expanded and penalties made harsher:

- Slander is recriminalized. The law chills the democratically inclined media by creating harsh punishment for ill-defined, elastic categories of speech.

- 'Extremist' speech, vaguely defined, is banned.

- Children are to be prevented from harm by pornography. Anything resembling pornographic speech in any form is prohibited. Further, under the 'Law on the Protection of Children', internet websites may be black-listed for 'information containing explicit language; justifying unlawful conduct; encouraging children to commit acts that endanger their lives and/or health, such as suicide; promoting among children a desire for drug, tobacco or alcohol use, gambling, prostitution and vagrancy; justifying violence to humans and animals; promoting non-traditional sexual relationships and disrespect to parents; pornographic information and information containing personal data on minors who became victims of illegal actions.' (Richter, Andrei and Anya Richter 2015)

- Non-governmental organizations receiving funding from the US or other foreign sources must cease operating or change the source. For the press, this had grave consequences: *Kommersant* could no longer share costs with the *Financial Times*; some regional media outlets and public opinion survey organizations lost funding.

- Foreign entities may not establish a media outlet or broadcast in Russia and may not own stock exceeding 20% of the charter capital nor may foreigners control or direct media outlets or determine policies and decisions.

- Roskomnadzor (acronym for Russian Committee for Oversight), the internet oversight agency, requires that internet companies processing Russian citizens' personal information must store that user data on servers inside Russia. LinkedIn did not comply. The court banned access. Others created servers in Russia and put some data in them, but how much and what kind is unclear.

- News aggregators with more than one million daily users are to be held accountable for the content, except when the content is a verbatim reproduction of materials published by media outlets registered in Russia. If the website targets Russian entities in its advertising, it is subject to the law against 'extremism, propaganda or pornography, cult of violence, use of curse words, defamation, etc.' All news information must be stored for six months, so that it can be accessed by Roskomnadzor (Richter, Andrei and Anya Richter 2015).

By broadening the scope of the prohibitions and leaving definitions imprecise, the new tightening of rules governing the internet becomes a supple method of control that warns of stiff punishment for largely undefined behaviour. Whether or to what degree the laws will or can be fully implemented is a real question. It might be sufficient to make examples of notable offenders.

RT: Russia projected abroad

Mikhail Gorbachev, the last Soviet leader, recognized that many of the country's young people had turned away from their history: revolutionary zeal had dissipated; possessing material things trumped ideology; and the lure of youth cultures elsewhere appeared more attractive than the drab future at home. Channel One could help. It created a new kind of news and talk show, anchored by young people speaking the fast-paced jargon of actual street-talk. As a safety measure it was scheduled for very late at night. The hosts, wearing T-shirts, sat around a kitchen table and talked with each other and guests. Western rock music (officially banned) was performed. Yegor Ligachev, second-in-command of the Soviet ruling Politburo once asked me rhetorically, 'Where did they get these people? From jails? They are nothing like our upstanding Komsomol [Communist Youth League]'. Soviet officials were not yet ready to seek such a shocking solution. The show was closed down more than once and finally pulled off the air.

Extending a country's message to the world is not a new phenomenon. Before digital technology made transmitting sophisticated visual data economically manageable, radio served the purpose. Radio Moscow, Voice of America, Radio Liberty, the BBC, Deutsche Welle, Vatican Radio and many other short-wave radio enterprises made it possible to send news, music, and a narrative to other countries in their own languages. In effect, it was a competitive world market: not for money, but for influence, soft power.

The post-Soviet Russian Federation uses Sputnik, a news agency redesigned with modern graphics, to replace an older, stodgy, organization. Rossiya (Channnel Two) transmits its programmes abroad. In December 2005, Russia Today debuted as a television channel. Its policy would be to present what it called a more balanced picture of Russia, as opposed to the version presented in the Western media. An Arabic-language channel was started in 2007 and in 2009, a Spanish one. In 2017, a French bureau was added. In 2009 the station had been re-branded as 'RT' and given a modern look and rapid-fire bold graphics. In 2010 RT America, in English, based in the US, began to transmit programmes more contentious, polemical, and harshly critical of the West, and recruited some well-known television personalities from the US and elsewhere, along with its Russian personnel. Some interviews and talk shows also brought on American guests with opposing views.

Attention to RT changed markedly in the US and Western Europe during the 2015–16 presidential campaign and general election. The Democratic National Committee discovered it had been hacked. The hackers delivered the material to WikiLeaks, and the public read about petty infighting and plans to favour the candidacy of Hillary Clinton over her opponent Bernie Sanders. Interference of this kind, in such an important election, shocked policy makers and the press. US intelligence agencies had a 'high degree of confidence' that the source was in Russia. Hacking into American systems is extremely serious. RT's way of seeking to influence audiences outside Russia is different. In hearings before Congress, in the State Department, and in NATO, RT has been dubbed the leading instrument of 'weaponized' information. It was said to describe a process entirely new in international affairs and exponentially more dangerous than anything experienced before. Testifying before a committee of the House of Representatives, a witness from a Washington think tank said, 'it's not like old fashioned propaganda, aimed solely at making Putin and Russia look good. It's a new kind of propaganda, intended to sow doubt about anything having to do with the US and the West; and in a number of countries, unsophisticated audiences are eating it up' (Dale, Helle 2015). NATO created a new department to counter the weaponized information of RT. Lieutenant Colonel Patrick Vermer, head of NATO's Information Operations Groups, believes that there is a new conflict in which information is turned into a weapon; RT, is, as he put it, 'the primary vector.' Power attributed to RT's programs can be very great, so much so, that when the 17 agencies making up the US intelligence community issued their report on Russian hacking in January 2017, the report devoted most of its text to warnings about RT: its close association with the Russian government, the budget, the type of content it favoured, the journalists, its audience reach, YouTube presence, and the profound danger it posed to the free West.

These claims describe an immensely powerful propaganda tool that exerts an enormous effect on anyone who is exposed to its message. These are questions about persuasive communication that social scientists have studied for decades. Between the World Wars and after, the 'hypodermic needle' model appeared, asserting that media messages were so powerful that they could be seen as a hypodermic needle, injecting into the audience a message from the sender, and that message would have immediate, direct, and uniform effects on everyone who was exposed to it. The message would be injected and absorbed exactly as intended by the sender and to everyone, in exactly the same way. This model was disproved and discarded long ago. It lives on in another world altogether, where social media blogs, comments, and advertisements as well as press reportage are thought to produce a deep, immediate, and lasting effect on the whole population exposed to it. Another basic and obvious premise is the *cum hoc* or *post hoc, ergo propter hoc* fallacy. The fallacies warn that because two things happen together (*cum hoc*), or because one thing happens after another, they are not thereby causally related. When Swedish citizens critically questioned the Minister of Defense about joining NATO, his press secretary attributed the scepticism to RT's programmes without acknowledging Swedish determination to remain neutral ever since the Napoleonic Wars (while having achieved interoperability and cooperation with NATO after the Second World War).

Substantial research has been conducted on the *content* of RT's transmissions. Analysis of content is helpful in expanding understanding of Russia's official agenda and estimating the importance Russia's political leaders might be placing on different issues and different places in the world. The missing term, obviously, is about the receiver of the message: does anyone receive the message is the first question. RT's own statistics often refer to the number of people in a region who *are able* to receive the programmes. This would be the *potential* audience, but not the people in the area who have actually turned it on and are watching. When we look at the numbers of those people who are viewers of the station we find in the UK, RT's share was 0.5% of the population, with per-person weekly viewing at zero hours and one minute. The Welsh-language public service channel S4C attracted 0.6% of the market. In the US, the Nielsen rating organization ranked the top 94 cable news channels (this would exclude the biggest news operations, which are not cable only). RT did not make it into the list. In Europe, RT's audience is less than 0.1% of the potential audience. Of all *foreign* broadcasters, in every country, the BBC far outpaces all competitors.

On YouTube, at first glance, it is a different story. RT was the first news channel to reach one billion views. In 2016, it had achieved three billion views overall. The figures are true but need to be interpreted. RT's strategy is to put up on YouTube mainly videos of catastrophes and violence. They draw an audience. When a catastrophe occurs, such as the March 2011 tsunami and subsequent explosion at the Fukushima nuclear energy plant in Japan, RT quickly bought the rights to show it under its logo. The audience was huge, but the video was not about Russia and it was not political. Eighty-one percent of the 100 most popular RT videos over five years were purchased from foreign countries. One percent of RT's total exposure on YouTube is political.

The critical importance of scale

As the US Congressional committees and the intelligence community studied the Russian threat to elections, attention shifted to social media: blogs, posts, accounts (from unknown sources and bots), and inventions termed 'fake news'. Content was not directly partisan, favouring one candidate over another, but homed in on subjects such as social ills, racial tensions, unemployment, and inequality; their purpose and threat lay in what policy makers called sowing discord, even though these issues had been deeply troubling to the US for decades, even centuries. Introduce scale into the analysis, and the issue assumes a different form: Between 2015 and 2017, 80,000 Russia-linked posts appeared on Facebook, but, during those same years, people in the US saw more than 10 *trillion* posts of all sorts on Facebook. During the same years, likely Russian video uploads reached 1,100 videos with 43 hours of content. Keeping scale in mind, these were not popular videos: only 3% had more than 5,000 views. Twitter found that the 1.4 million election-related posts linked to Russia, were less than *¾ of 1%* of all the election-related tweets between September 2016 and November 2016 (*The New York Times* 2017, emphasis added).

In 2017, *The New York Times* put on its front page this headline: 'To sway vote [in the US] Russia used an army of fake Americans Flooding Twitter and Facebook…' As of 2017, there were 3.74 billion internet users in the world and 1.24 billion websites. Fifty-one percent of all internet traffic comes from computer-generated messages [bots] and only 51.8% from actual human beings. Eighty-five percent of email globally is spam. If we narrow the cosmos of the internet to focus on social media, we find that there are 2.79 billion active social media users in the world. As of 2017, during a single month, 2 billion monthly active users logged in to Facebook. The figure for Twitter is 328 million. Neither Russians' nor any other party's attempt to 'flood' the internet or 'flood' Facebook and Twitter is remotely possible. The vastness of the internet and the rapidly-changing world of interacting messages would overwhelm strategies designed to ensure saturation. Blog posts may appear numerous. 'Might have seen' is how RT has often inflated its audience numbers, but it is also how Facebook portrayed a category of users to the US Congress, saying that more than 126 million users 'potentially' saw posts linked to Russia on Facebook, but as the company's general counsel made clear, many reached this way may not have seen the posts.

It might be argued that 'selling' a message on the internet is of special importance; advertising, it is argued, can be shaped to propel the message to particularly vulnerable or ideologically attuned users. US intelligence agencies concluded that Russia was linked to the purchase of advertisements on a number of networks, including Facebook and Twitter. They, too, were about contentious social issues in the US, but not directed specifically to support either candidate and focused on divisive issues central to the US throughout its history, issues that have yet to be resolved. Putting the ad buys in the context of scale: for the third quarter of 2016 alone, Facebook's revenue from advertisements was more than $6.8 billion. The likely Russian ads totalled 3,000, but only 2,250 actually ran, because the features the buyer specified for the targeted audience were so many that no existing population could be identified. As with Twitter, too, there are levels of advertising. At the level of least expensive, the ad is small and runs usually once before it drops down to be overrun by the fast-paced flow of incoming tweets and messages. Spending more money could have bought a 'promoted trend' on Facebook and a 'promoted' ad on Twitter. With this type of ad, the buyer gets much better placement and length of time to be seen. In addition, the advertising department assists in the creation of a more effective ad. At Twitter, this option can run from $200,000 up to $750,000.

The internet has opened an enormous alternative. In fact, it is so enormous and so competitive and kaleidoscopic, it is difficult for a post or message or advertisement to rise above the clutter. So far, the advertisements bought by apparently Russia-related entities have been modest and fleeting: modest, in the sense of level of complexity and favorable placement. Every message is fleeting without sufficient repetition that features changes in format and video content. Inevitably, unless the ad buyer spends considerable amounts of money, new ads push down the ones that appeared a nanosecond before. Each competitor in this vast market is vying for the user's attention, followed up, it is hoped, by behaviour in actually purchasing the product or choosing the favoured choice. Online advertisements must make their way through the jumble of competitors. RT has its audiences on cable and online. The rebranding increased the tempo of shows and certainly of the graphics, which are sometimes dizzying. What we cannot know at this point is, with what effect on the individual, not only of RT, but also of posts, blogs, ads, and "news" that may be wholly or partially made up? Without that link – what, if any persuasion takes place – we do not yet have the concrete evidence to draw a conclusion. Content tells us much, including what values and strategies the Russian government may be promoting. But content does not equal effect. And the large field of messages pushing contrasting ideologies and products for purchase created by specialists with more experience and expertise in targeting and emotionally arousing audiences makes for an internet space crammed with competition.

Cognitive processing and state messages

An internet message or television news programme that is tasked with persuading is much more likely to be at least partially persuasive if it reaches the audience first, before any other communication on the same topic. Being first makes it far more difficult for competitors to engage in counter-persuasion and counter-messaging. Even when it appears that there is no competition, as is the case for that number of Russians in Russia who depend solely on their own television news, there is always experience, phone calls to relatives in other areas, analogies with similar situations – these are heuristics or cognitive shortcuts – that enable a viewer to come to a judgement about a salient piece of news. How do Russian television audiences make sense of state-controlled television news? They are consumers in large numbers, but many of them have lived through decades of a low-information government strategy of news programmes lacking diversity of viewpoints. Under these conditions, viewers often unconsciously draw on the store of heuristics built up over time. Where political parties compete, their labels usually serve as one type of heuristic, if the label stands for a particular combination of values (e.g. Labour or Tory, Democrat or Republican). Other heuristic principles are availability (how readily it is brought to bear on the situation), and liking (the communicator is liked, rather than disliked).

When they watch the news, average Russians use heuristics as a check on the veracity of the story. They also quickly see trade-offs when a news story presents wholly positive news about new construction, food production, and modernization, to name a few. The viewer comes to the news with the attitude that there will always be trade-offs and if, as is likely, the news story shows none, the viewer will usually contribute several from previous experience. When the completion of a pipeline was a news story, viewers in focus groups in several cities immediately added that it will spring leaks and pollute the land or that some corrupt big businessmen are always involved in the energy sector, or, when profit from the pipeline was described, viewers reacted negatively: they would never see a ruble from it. One Russian viewer noted that the pipeline lay in an earthquake-prone zone. None of these 'counter-messages' was in the story. In addition to what is stored in individuals' long-term memory, audience members have friends and relatives, who can shed light on the thin information coming from the news story. They cannot do that for stories about Iraq and Syria, because they lack the knowledge, but those stories are least salient for typical television viewers and also have the least staying power. It is the world around them, the family, the basics of life that are important.

Russians have to work if they want to amplify the news. If they are older and well educated, they might prefer to read print or online newspapers. If they are younger, they increasingly use the internet and often access information they care about from social networks and news aggregators, very often on their cell phones. English speakers look for British and American sources. They will see contradictions among those sources and between them and Russian sources. They continuously search and compare. The term 'state-controlled' media is accurate up to a point. Freedom of the press is narrowing but is far from extinguished; new elastic legal prohibitions produce uncertainty for accuser and accused. Information from television is skeletal. But viewers, readers, and followers – if the issue is personally important – can rely on habits, relatives, friends, and experience to enlarge what is publicly available.

In messages meant to persuade international audiences, the task of persuasion is even more difficult: many fewer people are exposed. Those who consume them are usually already persuaded by many other sources and seek a diet of similar messages. The US intelligence community revealed in February 2018 that the same kind of internet activity was again aimed at the next American elections, because the previous actions were judged successful. In February 2018, the special counsel investigating the charges opened a grand jury indictment of 13 Russian officials, who had stolen identities of American citizens, broken laws regarding impermissible expenditures favouring political candidates and parties, identity fraud, bank fraud, visa application fraud, and others. Details showed a concerted effort to favour the candidacy of Donald Trump and then to favour *and* disparage both candidates. There is clear evidence of conspiracy and lawbreaking in the activities of the indicted group. An *impact* on US individuals, and proof of attitude change resulting from the hostile activities, is not present in the indictment. That would be the most important link in the Russians' strategy and necessary proof of effectiveness. There is no evidence of attitude change expressed in changing votes, much less a power to sway elections. Even so, unlawful actions to interfere in the functioning of democratic institutions should be judged seriously.

Quite different is the end-point – the purpose of the activity is to cause individuals exposed to the messages to change their votes, attitudes, and related behaviour entirely because of particular messages. Information in social media, pseudo-information, fakes, half-truths can be accessed and passed on with ease. But the effect on today's multi-tasking individuals is not so clear, wrapped, as they are, in a swirl of chaotic information competition on the web. Each added task, such as new claims and narratives, lowers the overall efficiency and quality of an individual's understanding and retention of messages. How to distinguish the real, durable effect of any information, however packaged, on individuals – after taking account of all other influences, past and present – is the critical question for now and the future.

8 ASSESSING THE RULE OF LAW IN RUSSIA

Kathryn Hendley

Recent years in Russia have witnessed a series of politicized arrests and trials in Russia that have left the reputation of law and the courts in tatters. The widespread arrests of participants in anti-Putin protests in 2017, including the detention of organizer Alexei Navalny as he left his house, are only the latest examples. Navalny was also tried and convicted on embezzlement charges in 2014 as part of a series of high-profile cases, the outcomes of which were generally thought to be preordained by the Kremlin. It followed the convictions of the members of Pussy Riot for their anti-Putin stunt in a Moscow cathedral in 2012, and the fraud conviction of Mikhail Khodorkovsky for tax evasion and fraud in 2005 and subsequent dismantling of his oil company, Yukos. These cases and others like them have created an image of Russian law as an instrument used by the state to impose its will on dissenters. That is, of course, part of the story, but the focus on the sensational has obscured the role of law in the everyday lives of ordinary Russians. Despite their misgivings about the inability of judges to stand up to the Kremlin, Russians are taking their mundane disputes to the courts in ever-increasing numbers, suggesting that the story of law is more complicated than it might appear at first glance.

This chapter begins with an historical overview of the somewhat peripheral role of law in the Soviet Union and the effort to revitalize it that was begun in the late 1980s under Gorbachev. That institutional transformation continued through the decades that followed. A comparison between the Soviet legal system and that of the present day serves to highlight the many changes. The bulk of the chapter is devoted to an evaluation of the extent to which these reforms have moved from good intentions to being implemented in practice. The chapter concludes with some reflections on the prospects for the rule of law in Russia.

The heritage of Soviet law

The Soviet Union is sometimes thought of as a lawless state, but at least at the formal level it was not. The USSR had a series of constitutions that, much like constitutions elsewhere, laid out the structure of the government and established a wide range of rights for citizens. It also had a full complement of statutory laws and administrative regulations. Yet this formal structure mostly failed to take account of the role of the Communist Party.

In reality, whenever the law proved inconvenient, the party elite were able to bend it to suit their interests. This made law an instrument to be used by the state (in the guise of the Party) and stripped law of its predictability. The idea that citizens could use law as a shield to protect themselves from arbitrariness was laughable. The long list of rights included in Soviet-era constitutions (which were more extensive than those available through the US Bill of Rights) turned out to be illusory because their exercise had to be consistent with citizens' duties to the Soviet state. Efforts by political dissidents to defend themselves by citing the constitution were uniformly unsuccessful.

One reason efforts to realise constitutional rights fell on deaf ears was the composition of the Soviet judicial corps. Judges were elected, but in single-candidate elections that were controlled by the Communist Party. Not surprisingly, virtually all judges were party members. Judicial terms lasted only five years; gadflies were quickly tossed aside. Likewise other legal professionals knew better than to challenge the system. Yet law was not entirely irrelevant in the Soviet Union. Though the looming presence of the Communist Party undoubtedly had a chilling effect on the behaviour of all participants in judicial processes, reality dictated that party officials took an active interest in relatively few. The vast majority of cases proceeded according to the written law, especially when the issues involved were mundane. The flaw with this sort of dualistic system in which law matters sometimes but not all the time is that predicting when outside influence will swoop in is perilous. As a result, Russians were reluctant to take their disputes to courts, preferring to resolve them informally.

The virtual non-existence of acquittals in Soviet criminal trials is sometimes cited as evidence of the politicization of justice. The explanation is more complicated. After World War II, Communist Party officials mounted a campaign to improve the work of the criminal justice system. Acquittals became seen as a failure of effort of all involved. They were a stain on the work records of judges, prosecutors, and police, and tended to stymie their rise in the ranks. As a result, once a criminal case was initiated, the institutional incentives pushed in favour of keeping it going until a conviction was obtained (Solomon 1987). Politics certainly played a role, but they operated at an abstract level that mooted the merits of individual cases.

When Gorbachev, the first law-trained leader of the Soviet Union since Lenin, came to power in 1985, a thorough rethinking of the role of law followed. At the 19th Party Conference in 1988, he advocated the introduction of a 'socialist rule-of-law-based state' (*sotsialisticheskoe pravovoe gosudarstvo*) in which law and not political connections would dictate the outcome of cases. Under his leadership, the Communist Party was stripped of its influence in the judicial selection process, a key prerequisite to building greater independence among judges. This period also witnessed the first, albeit tentative, steps towards judicial review with the creation of the Committee on Constitutional Supervision, which was charged with reviewing the acts of the legislative and executive branches.

The institutional structure of the Russian legal system

Many of the ideas put forward during the Gorbachev years were actualized in the decades that followed. Figure 8.1 presents an organizational chart of the current legal system. The introduction of the Constitutional Court in 1991 (as a successor to the Committee on Constitutional Supervision) institutionalized judicial review. In doing so, Russia followed the example of many of its European neighbours who shared the civil law legal tradition (under which judicial decisions are binding only on the participants, and do not have precedential value for others) by creating a stand-alone court that is empowered to hear challenges to the constitutionality of statutes and administrative regulations from legislators and ordinary citizens. In a decisive break with the Soviet past, its decisions have the force of law and, if they go against the government, can invalidate laws or regulations. On paper, the Constitutional Court gives substance to the proclamation of the 1993 Constitution that the judicial branch is equal to the legislative and executive branches (Trochev 2008). A number of regions have created their own constitutional courts, which are charged with maintaining the constitutionality of regional legislation and are not part of a formal hierarchical system.

The early 1990s also witnessed the creation of a hierarchy of courts, known as *arbitrazh* courts, designed to resolve the sorts of commercial

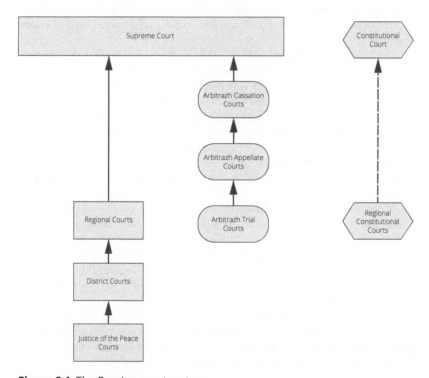

Figure 8.1 The Russian court system

disputes that would inevitably arise with the transition from a command economy to a market economy. These courts also handled bankruptcy claims. Over the two decades of their existence, the *arbitrazh* courts have repeatedly revised their procedural rules in an effort to respond to the needs of their constituency. In 2015, their jurisdiction was expanded to include personal bankruptcy.

The vast majority of claims, including criminal prosecutions, divorces and child custody, and labour disputes, continue to be handled by the courts of general jurisdiction. The basic structure of these courts was a carryover from the Soviet period, with trial courts, appellate courts, and a supreme court. An experiment with jury trials for serious crimes, begun in the 1990s, was institutionalized throughout Russia under Putin (Esakov 2012). In an effort to ease the burden on trial judges, justice-of-the-peace courts were authorized in 1998. Over the first decade of the 21st century, these courts were introduced across Russia (Hendley 2017). They handle simple cases, thereby freeing up judges at higher-level courts to devote more time to complicated cases.

As Figure 8.1 indicates, each court system has its own distinct hierarchy. But the Supreme Court serves as the court of last resort for both the *arbitrazh* courts and the courts of general jurisdiction. Its 170 judges are divided into five specialized divisions based on the nature of the underlying disputes. This court also handles electoral disputes and makes final decisions on the removal of judges. Like the Constitutional Court, the decisions of the Supreme Court serve as precedent, that is, they are binding on all citizens, not just on the parties to the case. Although the jurisdictions of the two courts are technically distinct, they sometimes end up ruling on the same issues. This can give rise to inconsistencies, when they decide differently on similar questions. They manage this problem by meeting periodically and issuing 'guiding explanations', aimed at smoothing out differences on particularly thorny areas of law.

Post-Soviet judges are no longer elected. They are now selected through a competitive process in which vacancies are advertised and those interested apply to their local qualification commission (Trochev 2006). The use of such commissions is common throughout continental Europe. Candidates are put through a battery of interviews and tests and, in theory, the most competent candidates prevail. But because the membership of these commissions is dominated by sitting judges, they tend to prefer candidates who have served as judicial clerks rather than practising lawyers. Prosecutors have an inside track for openings on the criminal bench. Women make up almost two-thirds of the judicial corps (Volkov et al. 2016).

The Russian courts have become increasingly transparent in recent years. All courts are required to have websites on which their decisions are published, along with their address and hours of operation. Some courts also post their schedule and provide a calculator that computes filing fees automatically. The quality of the websites varies by region. Several searchable databases are freely available (rospravosudie.com; sudact.ru), as well as subscription-based services, portions of which are open to the public (garant.ru; consultant.ru).

The Russian legal system in action

There is always a gap between the law on the book and the law in action. In Russia, this gap has sometimes seemed more like a chasm as political realities perverted well-intentioned institutional reforms. For example, the role of the Constitutional Court has shifted over time. Under Yeltsin, the Court heard cases that challenged some of his signature policies, including his conduct of the war in Chechnya. Its decisions tended to avoid direct confrontations with the Kremlin, a common tactic among high courts elsewhere. With the rise of Putin and United Russia, however, dissent among legislators has been effectively quashed. As a result, the Constitutional Court has become more quiescent.

More troubling has been the interference of political elites in the judicial process. Both the Kremlin and regional leaders have repeatedly brought trumped-up criminal charges against their enemies as a form of punishment. This harks back to the Soviet era, when selective prosecution was a favourite way to deal with dissenters. In those days, the law criminalized anti-Soviet behaviour and failed to define its prerequisites clearly, thereby giving maximum discretion to officials. The criminal code was stripped of these sections after the demise of the Soviet Union, though analogous provisions have crept back into the law in the guise of fighting terrorism and extremism. Creative officials can always find pretexts to indict their enemies, especially when prosecutors and judges are compliant and willing to accept proffered evidence without question. Much as during the Soviet era, the internal incentives for workers within the criminal justice system is to push cases forward. Though Russia has embraced the principle of adversarialism within the courts, which means that defence lawyers ought to be engaging in independent investigations, this rarely happens. Acquittals continue to be the exception in both politically motivated cases and in ordinary cases. Indeed, in a study of a Krasnoyarsk trial court from the late 1990s, one judge comments: 'There are judges that *take a risk* and render judgments of acquittal, but practically not even one of them is left to stand on appeal, they are reversed ... To acquit *is very scary*' (Pomorski 2001: 457).

Another troubling development is the growing criminalization of failed business transactions (Firestone 2009). When business partners grow disenchanted with one other, rather than taking their losses and moving on, they often accuse one another of criminal fraud or embezzlement. The accuser assembles documentary evidence, which frequently stretches the truth, and bribes the police to open a criminal case. His victim languishes in jail waiting for the trial because, despite introducing bail, it is rarely granted. In his absence, the accuser is able to solidify his control over the formerly joint assets (Pomerantsev 2014). This story has become so familiar that, in 2012, an ombudsman was appointed to protect the rights of entrepreneurs. Though this is a distinctly post-Soviet phenomenon, the remedy of having the legislature grant an amnesty to those victimized is familiar from the past (Pomeranz 2013).

As the descriptions of politicized justice and criminalized business deals suggest, corruption remains a nagging problem within the courts, just as for most Russian institutions. Top judicial officials, including the chairmen of the Russian Supreme Court and the Constitutional Court, have conceded that bribery persists. The same qualification commissions that select judges are also charged with reviewing complaints of ethical violations. Such charges tend to be difficult to prove.

An even bigger challenge to the integrity of the judicial corps is the deference given to court chairmen at all levels. At every stage in a judge's career, their relationship with the chairman of the court matters. Staying in their good graces is essential to career stability and advancement. Many commentators have criticized the influence of these chairmen as yet another source of dependence (Volkov et al. 2016; Solomon 2007; Pomorski 2001). Chairmen have multiple levers of influence. In many courts, they control case assignments and can direct politically sensitive cases to judges who will follow the unwritten rules (Anonymous 2010). Former judges have spoken out about their heavy hand and have argued that a determined chairman can always find a disciplinary pretext to get rid of a judge who refuses to go along. Yet even those who make these allegations concede that not all chairmen take this line. For example, Mariana Lukyanovskaya, a Volgograd oblast court judge who handled criminal cases who was removed from the bench in 2009 thanks to a disciplinary review initiated by the chairman of her court, is unforgiving when it comes to that chairman. She says that 'independence is only declaratory. In every case, the judge is dependent on his leadership'. She believes she was pushed out due to her refusal to accept the claims of the police and prosecutors without corroborating evidence. But she emphasizes that this sort of atmosphere had not always prevailed at her court. She quotes the previous chairman, whose mantra was: 'My boss is the law' (*Moi nachalnik – eto zakon*) (Eismont 2012). Thus, despite the common wisdom that chairmen treat their courts as their 'personal fiefdoms' (Anonymous 2010), whether a chairman exerts a positive or negative influence from the point of view of judicial independence depends on their own internal moral compass. Much depends on the character of the chairmen and their attitude towards the sanctity of law.

Many hoped that the return to jury trials in criminal cases (as was the practice in Tsarist Russia) heralded a new era. But juries are available only in cases involving the most serious crimes, such as murder, which originate in the regional courts, which inevitably mitigates their impact. For example, of the over 700,000 criminal cases decided in 2016, only about 200 involved juries (Otchet 2017). Russians' faith in juries has diminished. When surveyed in 2004, 34% were confident that juries were fairer than non-jury criminal processes. By 2013, such optimism was voiced by only 23%. On a more positive note, Russians' support for the idea that it is better to let a guilty person go free rather than risk jailing an innocent person grew from 51% to 61% between 2004 and 2013. Those who took the counter position were a small minority (around 12%), with the balance comprised of people who refused to take a position (Levada Center 2013d).

Russians' expectations of the legal system

This parade of horribles might lead one to believe that Russians are distrustful of their courts and unwilling to use them. The reality is more complicated. Survey data confirm that a majority of Russians (60%) are sceptical of the fairness of courts (Levada Center 2016). At the same time, they are using them in record numbers, albeit only as a last resort when all other options have been exhausted. This suggests that trust is not necessary for use; litigants can have a variety of motivations for initiating a lawsuit (Hendley 2012). Over the 15 years from 1995 to 2010, the annual number of cases grew almost fourfold, from 6.2 million to 23.4 million (Rassmotrenie 2013; Svodnye 2015). Given the coercive reputation of the Russian state, it might be assumed that criminal prosecutions account for this increase. But criminal cases, as a percentage of the total caseload, have actually decreased over time from 17.4% in 1995 to 4% in 2015. The number of cases that go through the *arbitrazh* courts is much smaller, but it grew over seven-fold between 1995 and 2015, from less than 250,000 in 1995 to 1.9 million in 2015 (Sudebno 2006; Rassmotrenie 2016).

More surprising is that Russians are generally satisfied with their experiences in the courts. A 2010 survey fielded by the Levada Center in 2010 included 638 court veterans (the 'Levada Survey'). When asked to assess the decision in their case, over 40% said it was completely fair and another 30% said it was mostly fair. Only 13% believed their decisions were completely unfair. These respondents were then asked a battery of 10 questions about various aspects of their courthouse experiences, beginning with the filing of their complaints and continuing through the enforcement of the outcomes. Confounding the popular perception that Russian courts are unusable, these court veterans were generally pleased with their treatment. They felt supported when preparing and filing their complaints. Most viewed their judge as objective and believed they had been afforded a chance to present their arguments. They were confident that their decisions were grounded in law, which undermines the widespread assumption that judges routinely base their decisions on 'telephone law' (orders from bureaucratic superiors or political elites that determine case outcomes). Analysis confirmed that respondents who believed they were treated fairly by the judge were more likely to view the decision in their case as fair, regardless of whether they won or lost (Hendley 2016). To be sure, telephone law is a sad reality of Russian life, but tends to be limited to cases involving those with political or economic power.

One source for litigants' satisfaction with their experience is the speed and low cost of the courts. Filing fees are deliberately kept low in order to facilitate access to the courts. If the petitioner prevails, then the cost of filing the case is shifted to the defendant. A number of categories of cases likely to arise among ordinary Russians, most notably consumer claims, can be pursued at no charge. Each of the procedural codes lays out clear deadlines for resolving cases that range from several weeks to several months. Violations of these deadlines rarely exceed 5%. Russian judges' advancement in the system depends on their ability to manage their docket. Those within the judicial management structure have openly acknowledged that quantitative indicators such as delay rates and reversal rates are taken very seriously.

Criminal cases are generally heard in the district or regional courts rather than the JP courts (whose jurisdiction is limited to cases for which the maximum penalty is three years in jail or less). Criminal defendants are provided with defence counsel at no cost if they are unable to afford lawyers on their own. These lawyers are poorly paid, earning less than the equivalent of $20 for each instance. They tend to be overworked and are not always able to devote a great deal of attention to individual cases. In recent years, a form of plea bargaining has grown commonplace, according to which defendants admit their actions and give up the right to appeal their convictions, although they can appeal their sentence if dissatisfied.

Public opinion polling paints a less positive picture of the courts. Russians who have never been to court are more suspicious. In a 2016 survey by the Levada Center, only 22% said they fully trusted the courts (Levada Center 2016). When offered a choice about whether court decisions are mostly fair or unfair in a 2017 survey by the Foundation for Public Opinion, 43% said they were predominantly unfair. The silver lining to this dark cloud is that these negative feelings had dissipated over time. When surveyed in 2001, 58% believed court decisions tended to be unfair. A similar trend is visible as to corruption. In 2004, 67% of those surveyed agreed that a majority of judges take bribes, whereas this percentage had decreased to 56 by 2017. Not surprisingly, the primary source of information about courts and judges for these respondents was the popular media (Fond 2017a). The fact that such a significant percentage of ordinary Russians have doubts about the capacity of the courts to be evenhanded and believe judges can be swayed by extra-legal incentives is discouraging.

Most cases are of little interest to those not intimately involved; relatively few attract the attention of elites. The politically charged cases that generate headlines in Western newspapers are not featured in the Russian media. Ordinary Russians do not follow these cases and are not terribly sympathetic towards the defendants. For example, in a poll taken during the same month when Navalny was sentenced, less than five percent of those polled in a national survey admitted to following the case carefully (Levada Center 2013b). Even in 2017, 46% of surveyed Russians claimed not to know who Navalny was (Levada Center 2017). Along similar lines, when queried about Khodorkovsky, a plurality (38%) were convinced that his conviction had been ordered by the Kremlin, but few (less than 5%) felt any sympathy for him (Levada Center 2013a). Over time, support for his early release increased. In 2007, only 19% supported favoured it; by 2012, this had increased to 31% (Levada Center 2012); it eventually took place when a presidential pardon was issued in December 2013. As to Pussy Riot, a majority (56%) felt their sentence had been appropriate (Levada Center 2013c). The release of Khodorkovsky and the members of Pussy Riot in December 2013 as part of an amnesty intended to commemorate the adoption of the Russian Constitution can be seen as compassionate, but cannot be seen as a reflection of a newfound devotion to the rule of law by the Kremlin. After all, amnesties are by their nature somewhat arbitrary and inconsistent with the mandate of due process that is at the heart of the rule of law.

More generally, periodic surveys from 1994 to 2014 reveal that a majority of Russians think that maintaining law and order is more important than protecting human rights (Levada Center 2014b). Along similar lines, Russians tend to place more value on social and economic rights than on civil and political rights. For example, about two-thirds of those surveyed from 1994 to 2013 consistently placed a high value on the right to free education and free medical care. By contrast, only 11% saw freedom of religion as critical in 1994, though this percentage had increased to 27 by 2013 (Levada Center 2014a). Perhaps this yearning for stability reflects a nostalgia for the Soviet past, which many now remember as a simpler time when jobs were guaranteed, conveniently forgetting the repressive nature of the regime. It may also be a reaction to the chaos of the 1990s in which a small group of Russians became very wealthy and many more Russians saw the social guarantees that they had come to rely on during the Soviet era disappear. Whatever the reasons, Russians remain comfortable with a strong state, even a state that encroaches on personal liberties. And they seem willing to tolerate censorship and other forms of political repression if the authorities promise social and economic stability.

Some argue that Russians have given up on law. Indeed, when gearing up for his successful 2008 presidential campaign, Dmitry Medvedev famously commented that '[w]ithout exaggeration, Russia is a country of legal nihilism. ... [N]o other European country can boast of such a level of disregard for law' (Polnyi tekst 2008). Such sentiments are not a post-Soviet phenomenon: they have endured through Russia's many political upheavals. Alexander Herzen, a prominent political philosopher of the nineteenth century, wrote: '[w]hatever his station, the Russian evades or violates the law wherever he can do so with impunity; the government does exactly the same thing' (quoted in Huskey 1991). In the present-day context, claims of widespread legal nihilism turn out to be hyperbole. Analysis of survey data shows that, in general, Russians are not significantly more prepared to ignore the law than their counterparts elsewhere. All the same, it did reveal some troubling trends. Those most disillusioned with law are not the elderly who survived the blatantly instrumental use of law by the Communist Party, but those now in their forties and fifties who were victimized by the economic turmoil of the 1990s. Younger generations are also more likely to embrace legal nihilism than their elderly relatives (but less likely than their parents). These demographic realities suggest that legal nihilism may be on the upswing (Hendley 2016).

Russians who want to challenge abuses of their rights by state officials now have more avenues open to them than did their parents and grandparents in the Soviet era. As in the past, Russians can direct complaints to prosecutors or to the president. But all Russian courts are now open to such petitions, at least in theory. When surveyed in 2017, over 40% viewed the courts as the most appropriate venue, though few relished the prospect of litigation (Fond 2017b). Those dissatisfied with their treatment by the courts can pursue their claims to the European Court of Human Rights. Indeed, Russian petitions have dominated the docket in Strasbourg for many years (Trochev 2009). Russians who are uncomfortable with the courts can turn to the ombudsman's office for help (Gilligan 2010). As elsewhere, they can also make use of informal tools, such as social media, to seek redress.

Prospects for the rule of law in Russia

Where does this leave Russia in terms of the rule of law? Defining what is meant by the rule of law is the first step. At its heart, the concept captures the goal of having a legal system in which all are treated equally and judged by law regardless of their wealth or political connections. Packed within this seemingly simple definition are a myriad of institutional goals, such as independent, accessible and non-corrupt courts, clarity and transparency in the written law, and the availability of due process for all (Fuller 1964). This is the definition that will be used in this chapter. Because it focuses mostly on procedural indicators, it is sometimes referred to as a 'thin' definition. Others have argued that the rule of law should actively embrace certain substantive goals, such as a full complement of human rights and guarantees of property rights (for instance Møller and Skaaning 2012). But this sort of 'thick' definition of the rule of law assumes that all countries share the Western commitment to civil and property rights. The failure to distinguish between these two concepts of the rule of law has led to a remarkable lack of clarity in the public debate over how to encourage transition countries to move towards this goal.

Without doubt, the keystone of the rule of law is equal treatment for all before the law. As the foregoing has documented, Russia has a spotty record on this critical issue. Opponents of the Kremlin live with the very real fear that they may be prosecuted on trumped-up charges as a way of discrediting them and their views. Businessmen who toil in obscurity have likewise been subjected to criminal prosecution due to the willingness of the police to accept bribes to open an investigation. The institutional incentives against acquittals have landed many such businessmen in jail for extended periods. The written law has been largely irrelevant in these cases. The spectre of corruption in all state institutions has likewise undermined the power of the law on the books. These realities help explain why Russia is typically seen as being at the lower end of the spectrum in terms of the rule of law.

But if the Russian courts were completely incapable of acting as honest brokers, then few would use them voluntarily. Just the opposite is happening in Russia. Individuals and firms are turning to the courts in ever-increasing numbers. Moreover, as the results of the Levada Survey suggest, they are mostly satisfied with their treatment by the courts. This should not be taken to mean that there is deep societal trust of the courts. Rather it may indicate a grudging willingness to use the courts when efforts to settle break down. In-depth interviews with ordinary Russians have at least convinced this author that they understand when the courts are reliable and when they may be compromised. My respondents were uniformly prepared to take their quarrels with neighbours or local governmental agencies to court, if necessary. But if they stumbled into a dispute with someone of higher status or with a powerful state office, they studiously avoided the courts, fearing that the other side would be able to dictate the outcome through informal extra-legal mechanisms (Hendley 2017).

Russia presents a paradoxical case. The vast majority of cases respect the rule-of-law principle of equality before the law, but a small well-publicized minority do not. In some ways, the Russian legal system is not so different from Western legal systems in which one's ability to retain competent lawyers has a profound influence on the chances for victory. In Russia, the currency is less likely to be money and more likely to be political connections, but the impact is the same. Where Russia parts company from its Western counterparts is in the lack of predictability as to when 'telephone law' will trump the law that is set out in statutes, and in its willingness to use criminal prosecutions as a weapon against opponents. These features raise the stakes considerably and help explain why Russia consistently languishes near the bottom of all indexes that purport to measure the rule of law.

Having a legal system that treats everyone equally means little if it is difficult to access. On this criterion, Russia's performance is more impressive. Going to court, in fact, is a relatively quick and inexpensive way to resolve problems. This does not mean that Russians are eager to do so. As in other countries, going to court in Russia is a last resort exercised only when efforts to resolve difficulties informally have failed. Once in court, cases are generally resolved within several months, if not more quickly. The filing fees have deliberately been kept low and the procedural rules are sufficiently straightforward that many litigants in non-criminal cases are able to represent themselves. The weakness of the adversarial system means that parties who oppose one another in court need not emerge as mortal enemies, as is so often the case in purer adversarial systems like those in the US and the UK. In comparison to Western legal systems, the Russian courts are easier for non-legal specialists to access. For the most part, however, the indexes that track levels of the rule of law around the world do not take account of this more positive aspect of the Russian legal system.

9 A FEDERAL STATE?

Darrell Slider

Federalism in Russia has always been a contested concept. Regional elites and 'democrats' or liberal politicians have seen the division of power and decentralisation of some policy making as a precondition for effective governance and further democratisation of the political system. Communists and Russian nationalists have viewed regional autonomy or a genuine sharing of powers with the regions as first steps towards the disintegration of the country. For many it conjures up memories of the collapse of the Soviet Union, as Soviet republic leaders took power through elections and forced concessions from Mikhail Gorbachev that set in motion the weakening of central power. The ethnic identity of republics has led some Russian nationalists to urge the redrawing of administrative boundaries to eliminate republics, perhaps by restoring administrative boundaries of the *guberniyas* that existed in the Tsarist era.

Under Yeltsin, Russia for the first time in its history adopted federalism as a basis for organizing the relationship between the centre and the regions. The historic pattern of governance had always been highly centralised, despite the formal label in Soviet times which designated Russia as the 'Russian Soviet Federated Socialist Republic'. Yeltsin's adoption of federalism was in part making a virtue out of necessity: the Russian government was too weak and divided to exert control over the provinces, and allowing regions some political and economic autonomy overcame separatist pressures. The exception was Chechnya, where Yeltsin launched a brutal war in late 1994 in an unsuccessful effort to bring the republic back under Russian control (see James Hughes (2007) who analyses Russia's wars to defeat first separatists, and then Islamists in Chechnya).

Tax revenues under Yeltsin were allocated in ways that helped to buy off regions that were 'most likely to secede'. Redistribution of revenues is essential in a state like Russia where oil and natural gas are the biggest sources of tax revenue, since only a few, sparsely populated regions account for the bulk of these revenues. Precise data on the relative share of centre/region revenue sharing are impossible to come by because regions were using non-monetary barter deals to collect taxes from enterprises at that time. Overall, both the federal centre and regions suffered from the lack of revenues due to economic disruption and low resource prices through the 1990s.

Yeltsin's 1993 Constitution provided the broad outlines of a division of powers between centre and regions, though much was left to be done through subsequent legislation. At the time the constitution was adopted there were 89 'subjects of the federation', which included different types of entities which in large part were a legacy of the Soviet-era administrative divisions. Republics (as well as smaller entities called 'autonomous oblasts') had been created to reflect historic homelands of non-Russian ethnicities. There are currently 85 federal entities, including Crimea, annexed from Ukraine in 2014. Three cities have federal status – Moscow, St Petersburg, and (since 2014) Sevastopol. The most numerous regional administrative entities which contain most of the population are ethnically Russian oblasts and larger krais, and Russians comprise around 81% of the total population of the country.

From the beginning of the Yeltsin period, the realities of the distribution of political power and the role of nationalism among several key non-Russian ethnic groups meant that the Russian model of federalism was 'asymmetric': some regions were given more powers than others. Yeltsin in August 1990 famously urged ethnic republics to 'take as much sovereignty as they could swallow'. Bilateral treaties and agreements were negotiated separately with regions, sometimes with provisions that took the form of secret protocols. Special provisions gave regions such as Tatarstan and Bashkortostan the right to keep natural resource revenues that normally would go to the centre.

Initially Yeltsin appointed governors of regions. Popular elections of republic presidents and later oblast governors at first took place without central approval, but by 1995 Yeltsin had accepted the principle of elected regional leaders. Konitzer (2005) shows that elections held between 1995 and 2001 had real contestation; on average there were three viable candidates competing for the top regional post. He also argues that voters often rewarded or punished sitting governors based on the economic performance of their regions. Voters often elected candidates whom the Kremlin opposed. 'Red governors' from the communist party managed to win elections in many of the more conservative, rural regions (by 1999 there were 14 communist governors), and candidates from other political movements also won in a few cases. New regional legislatures were also elected regularly starting in 1994. At first, political parties were hardly represented at all in these bodies, but over time party groups developed, and assemblies in some regions played an active and independent role in governance.

The constitution provided for an upper house of parliament to represent regional interests, the Federation Council. It consists of two representatives from each region who were initially elected, but later the top executive and legislative official in each region became 'senators'. In the Yeltsin years the Federation Council played a major role in the legislative process, and it often vetoed laws submitted to it from the State Duma that were perceived to threaten regional interests. According to Tom Remington (2003), from 1996 through 1999 the Federation Council vetoed approximately 23% of the draft laws submitted to it.

Putin's vertical of power

When Vladimir Putin became president at the end of 1999 the first issue he confronted was the relationship between the regions of Russia and the centre (the federal government). In Putin's narrative of the 1990s, one which he has retold over and over again, the regions became too powerful at the expense of the centre and threatened the continued existence of the Russian state. Putin himself was a regional official, first deputy mayor of St Petersburg from 1994 until 1996, and in 1997–98 he held the Kremlin post that oversaw the regions. Once he became president, Putin set about to establish a 'vertical of power' [in Russian, *vertikal vlasti*] that would subordinate regions to the centre in a hierarchical chain of command. This began what turned out to be a frontal attack on the principles of federalism as the model for centre-region relations. Since regional executives – governors or republic presidents – were the key political actors in the regions, he began by creating a system that would allow him to better monitor their performance without depending on information from governors themselves.

One of the very first changes introduced by Putin was a new division of Russia into seven macroregions – 'federal districts' comprising the Northwest, Central, Southern, Volga, Urals, Siberian, and Far Eastern territories. In 2011, while Dmitry Medvedev was president, an eighth federal district, the North Caucasus district, was carved out of the Southern district. In 2016 the two new regions of Crimea and Sevastopol' were added to the Southern District after initially comprising a separate, ninth federal district. A new official outside the constitutional structure was appointed to oversee these districts, called the 'authorised representative' of the president (*polpred* in Russian). The calibre and experience of those appointed to the post varied greatly, which reflected the fact that presidential priorities differed from region to region. Initially, most of the officials were not political figures or even government bureaucrats. They were drawn from the *siloviki*, with military or police backgrounds.

Perhaps as a reflection of Putin's higher education in law, one of the first assignments he gave to his representatives was to bring regional legislation in line with federal legislation. While the polpreds were supposed to oversee regional leaders, they had few powers of their own and no funds of their own to distribute. Their strength lies in their role as Putin's emissaries and their line of communications to the Kremlin. Over time, appointments to the post of polpred have become quite varied. In crisis situations, Putin has turned to some of his closest and most trusted associates such as Dmitry Kozak (sent to the Southern district in 2004), Aleksandr Khloponin (sent by Medvedev to the North Caucasus in 2010), and Yuri Trutnev (appointed to the Far East in 2013). Yet in 2012, Putin's first staffing appointment upon returning as president was the Urals polpred, Igor Kholmanskikh, a foreman from a Nizhny Tagil tank factory with no political or administrative experience. Kholmanskikh had come to Putin's attention during a live, televised question and answer session with the president in December 2011, just after massive anti-Putin demonstrations had been held in Moscow. Kholmanskikh offered to bring 'his boys' to Moscow to help subdue the protesters, if the police were not up to the task.

One of the purposes of 'restoring' the vertical of power was to reduce the degree to which Russian regions had asymmetric powers. Yeltsin's bilateral agreements were either phased out or scrapped entirely. This affected most of all ethnic republics such as Tatarstan, Bashkortostan, and the North Caucasus republics. The implicit deal offered by Putin allowed the most popular and powerful regional leaders to remain in office, even if they initially resisted his strategy. More recently, even symbolic aspects of regional autonomy have been targeted – for example, the practice adopted in the early 1990s of calling the heads of republics 'presidents'. By 2013, all except for Tatarstan had dispensed with that title and leaders are now called simply the 'head' of a republic. Tatarstan, which is home to part of Russia's largest ethnic minority (Tatars make up about 3.7% of the total population) retained some elements of its special status in a treaty signed by Putin in 2007, but the new treaty effectively eliminated most of the privileges Tatarstan had been awarded in its 1994 treaty. The treaty formally expired in 2017 and was not renewed. Excessive centralisation has led to disputes with ethnic regions, for example on the republics' attempts to require schooling in the native language. Federal prosecutors and federal education officials forced the leaders of ethnic republics, including Tatarstan, to drop mandatory courses in non-Russian local languages.

A critical development in the strengthening of the vertical was the decision in late 2004 to end popular elections of regional executives. The pretext for this was the terrorist takeover of a school in Beslan, North Ossetia. The authorities' confusion and disputes over who was in charge at Beslan led Putin to conclude that Russia was not ready for democratic governance at the regional level. Ending elections gave Putin the ability to appoint his own choice as governor, though formally the procedure involved regional assemblies. Putin was given the power to remove governors who had 'lost his trust,' though he was reluctant to exercise it until 2017. Many of the Yeltsin-era regional 'heavyweights' continued to run their regions until they were removed by President Medvedev in 2010–11.

Another element of tightened central control was the rise of the ruling party United Russia. Almost all governors were forced to give up any previous party affiliations and join the ruling party. The Kremlin set as its goal a United Russia majority in every regional assembly. As a result of elections held between 2004 and 2010 United Russia went from a majority in 20 regions to a clear majority in 82 of 83 regional assemblies (all but St Petersburg). In 62 of these regions, United Russia held two-thirds or more of the seats, which allowed it to adopt any law without the support of other legislators. The declining popularity of the United Russia party in the aftermath of the December 2011 elections presented a dilemma for the Kremlin that still sought to maintain a political monopoly in the regions. Most regions had mixed electoral systems, with at least one-half chosen by party list and one-half of the seats chosen from individual races in legislative districts. United Russia always dominated district contests to a much greater extent than proportional party list voting, and this is what allowed the party to achieve a super-majority in most Russian regions.

The speed with which Putin was able to transform an emerging federal system into a centrally controlled state was shocking. Why did powerful regional leaders succumb to the new relationship with the centre virtually without a fight? In social science terminology, what regional leaders faced was a collective action dilemma. To stand up to the Kremlin individually would mean political suicide for even the strongest of regional leaders.

The Kremlin was rapidly consolidating power – the 1999 Duma elections and subsequent defections to the ruling party (then called Unity) combined with Putin's convincing election victory in 2000 created a new political reality. Meanwhile, Putin was demonstrating at this time how brutally the regime could act to bring a rebellious region under control – Putin had launched the second Chechen war when serving as prime minister and acting president in autumn 1999.

Part of the explanation for the shift in relative power from regions to the centre was the result of what Putin did to the Federation Council. Putin moved quickly to dismantle the principal mechanism for collective action by the regional elite that had been established in the Yeltsin years. He transformed the upper house by first removing governors and speakers of regional assemblies as senators. They were replaced with appointees that were technically nominated from the regions (one each from the executive and legislative branches of regional government) but who were candidates 'suggested' by the Kremlin. At least one-third had no ties to the region they supposedly represented, and almost all were subject to manipulation by the Kremlin by the fact that they spent almost all of their time in Moscow. They understood that their well-being did not depend on representing their regions, but on maintaining good relations with the office in the Presidential Administration tasked with supervising them. As a result, the Federation Council quickly ceased to act as a defender of regions' rights and federal principles. A Federation Council veto of a Kremlin-sponsored law, even if it was designed to undermine the rights of regions, came to be a virtually unthinkable action (Slider 2005).

Scholars who have sought to explain the rapid change of centre-regional relations have offered alternative explanations. Paul Goode (2011) makes the case that an important reason for region leaders' compliance with the new order was an implicit bargain that they would be allowed to impose the same hierarchical control over sub-regional political actors such as mayors and city councils. Gulnaz Sharafutdinova (2013), drawing on the experience of the non-ethnic Russian republics that had most aggressively asserted their sovereignty in the 1990s, argues that a radical shift in the political discourse under Putin left regional leaders with little choice. The public statements by leaders of Tatarstan could no longer tout federalism and democracy as a way of defending the republic's special status. Putin had changed the rhetorical frame of reference to one of strengthening the state and overcoming disunity. John Reuter (2017) emphasises the role of United Russia in this process. He argues that regional elites were offered a bargain: they could gain a stable place in a new system, with access to 'the spoils' of power, so long as they were willing to give up most of their autonomy by joining the newly formed dominant party.

There were also powerful economic and budgetary factors that enhanced central control over the regions. Economically, thanks to rising oil prices and the recovery of the Russian economy in the period after the August 1998 default, the centre had access to greater resources with which to fund federal programmes and buy cooperation in the regions. Philip Hanson (2005) has shown that federal revenues as a share of GDP increased dramatically at the same time that Putin was strengthening the vertical. Most regions lacked sufficient revenue sources of their own and were therefore increasingly dependent on the Kremlin and the ministry of finance for budgetary subventions. In recent years, the budgetary problems of regions have worsened. Election campaign promises by Putin in 2012, notably the so-called May Directives (*ukazy*), required regions to raise wages for state employees in education and health care, but regional budgets were not correspondingly increased. In part because of these directives, in recent years two-thirds of regions typically experience serious budget deficits that have forced a reduction in government spending in other areas, such as infrastructure investment. As of November 2017, 57 regions lacked the resources to meet their obligations and of these 24 could not do so even after receiving additional 'equalisation' subsidies from the centre (*Kommersant*, 30 November 2017).

In response to demands expressed by opposition demonstrators after the December 2011 State Duma elections, the Kremlin formally reinstated popular elections of regional leaders. Restrictions on competition and built-in advantages to the sitting governor, though, meant that the change did nothing to change the place of governors in the system. Governors, elected or not, serve only if they are acceptable to Putin. They will still be evaluated by the Kremlin, and the process of elections is tightly controlled to prevent 'accidental' candidates from winning. When legislation for the return to elected governors was passed, it included a 'municipal filter' at the candidate registration stage which, when combined with other legal and extralegal measures, effectively restricted political contestation. The municipal filter requires signatures of 5–10% of local council members in the region; some regions further stipulated that the total would have to include at least one signature from 75% of the councils. Viable opposition candidates in several regions were removed from the ballot or prevented from registering; in other cases candidates that the Kremlin wanted in the race were helped to pass registration barriers. Many regions adopted election laws that require all candidates to be nominated by a registered political party, thus precluding self-nomination.

Candidates favoured by the Kremlin had enormous advantages and typically won by large margins. Incumbent governors have enormous advantages, which have become known over the years as 'administrative resources.' In 106 gubernatorial elections held between October 2012 and September 2017, only once did the candidate not chosen by Putin win. This was in 2015, in Irkutsk oblast, where the sitting governor, a United Russia candidate, got the most votes but failed to win outright in the first round of voting. The opposition consolidated around the communist candidate, Sergei Levchenko, who won the second round. Levchenko met with Putin, who agreed not to use his 'presidential filter' to remove the newly elected governor.

The only other candidate who even came close to forcing an incumbent governor into a second round of voting was the opposition leader Alexei Navalny, in the September 2013 Moscow mayoral election. The incumbent, Sergei Sobyanin, won 51% according to the official results. Sobyanin (and the Kremlin) allowed Navalny to run to increase the legitimacy of his presumed landslide victory. The municipal filter was manipulated to give Navalny the needed signatures, which otherwise could have prevented all candidates except Sobyanin from running, since almost all neighbourhood municipal councils were dominated by United Russia at that time. (In 2017 local elections, the opposition was able to win control over many district councils in Moscow, though still not enough to surmount the municipal filter.) The election campaign was outrageously unfair. The two national government television channels which are viewed by the largest number of Muscovites ran repeated and lengthy reports on Sobyanin's 'achievements', including the ceremonial opening of a suspiciously large number of road-ways, bridges, and metro stations in the days before the election. The same channels mentioned Navalny on the day he was registered as a candidate in July and then did not mention his name again until after the voting was over on 8 September. Navalny's attempts to purchase advertising spots on major radio stations were denied, apparently after pressure was placed on the stations from the mayor's office. Supporters of Navalny who hung banners for their candidate from their balconies saw city workers descend from the roofs on ropes to cut them down. 'Debates,' without Sobyanin's participation, were limited to local channels with low ratings at inconvenient times of the day. That Navalny was still able to win, in the official vote totals, over 27% of the vote was testimony to a vigorous campaign conducted mostly through face-to-face meetings with voters and aided by a small army of young volunteers.

Irkutsk is the only region in Russia where the ruling party acts as a political opposition to the governor, but it is not the only region with governors not from United Russia. Putin allowed each of the parliamentary parties to have its own governor. Thus, there is a communist governor in Orel, a member of the Just Russia party is governor in Omsk, and the LDPR has its own governor in Smolensk (appointed by Medvedev in 2012), and after the September 2018 regional elections the LDPR took control of Khabarovsk krai and Vladimir oblast. The token representation of 'within-system' opposition parties among the governor corps does not mean that the opposition controls these regions. Governors are still expected to work for United Russia and Putin when they are on the ballot.

In recent years, Putin has made it clear that popular elections and the term to which they were elected were less important than his personal will. In the last months of 2017, 11 governors resigned at Putin's request. Of these, several had been elected with resounding majorities only two to three years earlier and still had two to three years left in their term. It was widely assumed that the changes were designed above all to help Putin's campaign for the presidency in March 2018. Those governors who were targeted had been seen as weak or incompetent, or had been plagued by intra-elite conflict within their regions.

Another change in recent years is that governors are no longer beyond the reach of law enforcement, and it is widely assumed that Putin personally signed off on the orders to arrest governors accused of corruption or abuse of office. At the end of 2017, five former governors were in jail, either on trial or awaiting trial. The FSB generally took charge of these investigations, and their culmination was often a video-taped scene showing the handoff of what was purported to be a bribe. In fact, though, governors often engage in semi-legal, cash-based fundraising for regional projects or for campaign funds which can then be presented in court as a crime. Among those arrested in 2016 was the one 'outside-of-the-system' liberal, Nikita Belykh. Formerly head of the Union of Right Forces (SPS), Belykh was appointed governor of Kirov by Dmitry Medvedev at the end of 2008. A few weeks before the 2018 presidential election Belykh was found guilty and sentenced to eight years in prison.

To provide an extra margin of control in 'difficult' regions – designed in particular for use in the North Caucasus – Putin pushed for a new law at the beginning of 2013 that allowed regions to dispense entirely with popular elections for governor. Instead, the regional legislature can select the head of the region, based on a short list of Putin's nominees. The new provision was implemented in both Ingushetia and Dagestan in September 2013. Later the same procedure was used to choose governors in the regions of Adygeya, Kabardino-Balkaria, Khanty-Mansi, Yamalo-Nenets, Nenets, North Ossetia, and – initially – in newly annexed Crimea and Sevastopol. In 2017 Sevastopol held its first popular election for governor.

At the sub-regional level, the main officials are mayors of cities and municipalities. Until relatively recently, they continued to be popularly elected – a fact which left them outside the Kremlin's vertical of power. The 1993 Russian Constitution intended this to be the case, as local government institutions were called 'organs of local self-management.' Notwithstanding the constitution, Putin's Kremlin has pursued multiple strategies over the years to bring mayors under central control. First, the United Russia party was active in recruiting sitting mayors and played a major role in local elections of both mayors and city councils. As a result, the vast majority of Russian mayors are at least formally members. This has not, however, precluded conflicts between mayors and regional governors from the same party. Second, in many cities elected mayors have either been replaced or forced to share their powers with 'city managers' who have been chosen directly by city councils. Usually city managers have the power to determine how the local budget is allocated. Third, a suspiciously large number of city leaders – particularly those who were political independents or members of opposition parties – have been removed from office on charges of corruption or of misallocating city funds. Two of the most spectacular removals of Russian officials from their posts were the 2013 arrests (shown widely on Russian television) of the mayors of Makhachkala (the capital of Dagestan) and Yaroslavl. Both mayors were viewed as threats to the power of regional leaders who had close ties to the Kremlin, and were arrested by federal law enforcement agencies and immediately transferred to pre-trial detention facilities in Moscow. Finally, financial centralisation has hit cities especially hard, and cities and municipalities became increasingly dependent on allocations from regional budgets and federal agencies.

Interactions between governors and the president

The direct personal interaction between governors and the federal executive is one key indicator of the relationship between these institutions and how it has changed over time. These meetings took place in a variety of settings. Many occurred in the course of visits to the regions by Putin or Medvedev, during which the president and governor would meet alone for discussions. In late summer, both Putin and Medvedev followed a practice of inviting governors to meet with them at the summer presidential residence in Sochi. The pattern of meetings (illustrated in the graph) shows several changes over time. Initially, Putin was reluctant to spend his time meeting with governors or republic presidents. In his first full year as president, Putin went a full nine months (from February to November 2000) without meeting a single regional leader face to face. This appears to have been part of a strategy to preclude regional lobbying as he tightened central control. After Putin had more or less established the terms of the 'vertical,' meetings with governors became more frequent from 2001 to 2004. There was another major increase in the number of meetings between 2004 and 2005. This marked the beginning of presidential appointments of governors and a change in their status to component parts of the 'power vertical'. Henceforth, there was much clearer dependent relationship between governors and the president. Putin's return to the presidency in 2012 corresponded with the return of elections for governors, and while the number of these contacts continued to be higher than during Putin's first term, they began to return to the norm he established in the mid-2000s. When Putin nominated an appointed governor for election, this meant the governor had to formally resign his or her post. The now 'temporarily acting governor' would meet once or twice with Putin prior to the ballot. This was a transparent attempt to influence the outcome of the elections by demonstrating Putin's personal support.

Meetings with governors came to be routinely scheduled to conduct a periodic evaluation of performance. Face-to-face encounters provided an opportunity for governors to report on their regions, and sometimes they were subjected to an uncomfortable grilling when confronted by contrary evidence that the president had obtained from his own sources.

Despite the fact that regional leaders have very little time with the president, the issues discussed – at least in the part of the meetings that is made public – usually are drawn from recent initiatives or promises made by the Kremlin. A significant portion of the interaction could be categorised as an attempt to verify policy implementation. For example, Putin would ask why is Kurgan region not yet paying teachers at a rate equal to or higher than the average pay in the region (as Putin had promised would happen)? In 2017, a new wrinkle was added after one of the president's annual 'direct line' televised response to questions from the public. Thousands of complaints gathered in the days leading up to the broadcast were used by Putin in his one-on-one meetings with governors to indicate unresolved problems in the region. For several months, televised reports of Putin's meetings with individual governors would show a neon green folder on his desk with 50–100 pages of text that he would read from and then hand to the governor for further action.

Group meetings with the complete contingent of regional leaders were also a significant forum for Putin to hear views from the regions while announcing the goals and priorities that he had established. Particularly important were meetings with the State Council (*Gossovet*), an institution formed in 2000 with the purpose of providing a regular forum for discussions – led by Putin personally – on major issues of policy. In July 2012 the membership of the State Council was expanded to include the speakers of both houses of parliament and the heads of the party factions in the Duma. The group meets quarterly, sometimes in one of the regions, to consider a specific problem faced by regions. Several months prior to the session a working group is normally formed, headed by a governor, which prepares reports and recommendations. Several months after the session Putin typically issues a set of detailed instructions to the Council of Ministers or specific agencies on preparing reports or draft laws, with deadlines for completion. A working body called the presidium is formed by choosing one regional leader from each of the federal districts and then rotating the membership every six months. The presidium meets separately with the president four times per year and has an agenda that is different from that of the State Council. The State Council and its presidium allow for input by governors on important policy questions, but everything is advisory in nature and must pass through the Presidential Administration. No one who has observed a meeting of the State Council would be under the illusion that governors are treated as the political equals of the president. On several notable occasions Putin has scolded members for poorly preparing for the session or for not paying attention (talking among themselves or sending tweets, for example). In one widely reported exchange, Valery Shantsev, long-serving governor of the important industrial region of Nizhny Novgorod, was warned by Putin to 'never interrupt me again' during a State Council session in May 2013. (Putin replaced Shantsev in September 2017.)

In the absence of elections, the Kremlin developed a supposedly objective system for evaluating the performance of appointed governors. Soon it took on the appearance of micromanagement. The first such indicators, issued in 2007, included 43 criteria. By the end of the Medvedev presidency in 2012, the number of indicators had reached 460, with 260 'basic' and 200 'supplementary' indicators. The ratings were not only part of a personnel evaluation system; some budget allocations are made to reward regional performance in key indicators.

In August 2012 Putin signed a decree changing the basis for evaluating governors, which greatly simplified the system. It reduced the indicators to 11, and governors were required to present reports based on the previous year's performance to the government by 1 April of each year. Indicators included many basic economic, social, and demographic factors such as the unemployment rate, volume of investment, new housing built, average income, role of small business, life span and death rates, and tax and non-tax revenues. In November 2017 Putin more than doubled the number of indicators, to 24, and he dropped all but four used since 2012. Among the new indicators were the region's crime rate, quality and accessibility of housing and housing-related services (gas, electricity, heat, water), rating of the business climate compared to other regions, percent of population employed in small and medium-sized businesses, density of the regional road network, and end of year regional budget debts compared to annual revenues.

Many of the indicators from both 2012 and 2017 are outside the ability of governors to influence in any significant way. Demographic factors such as the size of the population and the death rate, for example, are less dependent on policy or policy implementation than on trends that were set years ago. The birth rate is heavily dependent on the number of women of child-bearing age, and nothing can overcome the massive drop in the birth rate of the 1990s. Economic conditions such as regional unemployment are heavily dependent on the state of the overall economy. Growth of small business and outside investment is a function not just of regional policies but the policies of federal ministries, which are implemented by federal agencies in the regions – businesses large and small are subject to tax audits, visits by police, fire and health inspections, and federal migration service raids.

Given that gubernatorial elections lost their value as contests between truly competitive candidates, the system of evaluation incorporated new measures of public opinion from the region. The 2012 indicators included survey data on how people viewed the effectiveness of the governor and his team. New survey items added in 2017 focused more specifically on the quality of health care and education in the region, along with culture and social services. Residents will also be questioned about the overall potential in the region for 'self-realisation,' including for one's children. One interesting addition was an indicator of the percent of the population in the region reporting that they had personally encountered corruption.

For those indicators over which governors can have an impact, the process sometimes encourages a perverse manipulation of the outcomes. Governors maintain a strong hold on local media, thus helping to shape the public opinion being measured. Despite periodic attempts from the Kremlin to restrict the practice, governors spend significant sums on public relations efforts to tout their own achievements. When regions were judged based on test scores on the university entrance examinations (the Unified State Examination, or *YeGE*), the desire to help students get better scores than they deserve – by cheating – was shared by not just students and their parents but also by teachers, principals, city education officials, regional education ministers, and governors themselves. (Several scandals – including a rash of perfect scores in regions not known for their educational achievements – led to new security procedures, including live webcasts of test-takers.) A similar set of incentives helps explain the temptation to commit vote fraud in national and regional elections, which it turns out are also often overseen by school teachers who serve on precinct election commissions.

In the past, changes in regional leaders were virtually never connected to regional evaluations, no matter what the number of criteria. The formal list is supplemented with an informal list that is constantly being revised as new problems emerge.

One major unlisted indicator is the ability of governors to deliver votes for national presidential or Duma elections. One of the largest waves of resignations came in the aftermath of the December 2011 Duma elections, mostly in regions where United Russia received a share of the vote lower than the national average, and just before the new law on electing governors came into force. The message to regional officials is clear: failure to use their control over regional election commissions to squeeze out a higher vote for United Russia or for Putin could cost them their jobs. Reuter and Robertson (2012) showed that election results in the regions were the best predictor of whether a governor was removed or reappointed, and this factor was far more important to Russia's authoritarian leadership than 'good governance' as measured in economic performance. Reisinger and Moraski (2017) have further demonstrated that over the entire Putin period, regional electoral fraud and manipulation of the outcomes, which is most prevalent in ethnic republics, was an important factor contributing to the development and consolidation of the authoritarian political system at the national level.

Federal agencies in the regions and the problem of decentralisation

The concept of 'vertical of power' is misleading in that it implies that there is one channel from top to bottom, from the Kremlin to the regions. The reality is that there are dozens of channels, with each federal ministry and agency overseeing its own chain of command. Since 2000 hypercentralisation has produced an explosion in the numbers of regionally based officials of federal agencies. There are now roughly 2.5 times as many federal administrative employees in the regions as there are regional government employees. These federal officials in the regions are paid by, and report to, their headquarters in Moscow. They are not subordinate to regional officials, and yet the activities of these federal agencies in the regions greatly affect how regions are in fact governed.

It is not unusual in federal systems for there to be such national-level agencies (the FBI, for example, in the US) with offices in the regions. This reflects the division of powers and responsibilities that defines federalism. As the system has developed under Putin, however, the number of these agencies and the scope of their activities is far from normal. Federal agencies include not just law enforcement (the prosecutor's office, Ministry of Internal Affairs [police], FSB, the drug enforcement agency, and Investigative Committee) and tax inspectors. A partial list would include the anti-monopoly agency, the office for registering property, the youth affairs agency, conservation officials, the migration service, technical standards enforcers, emergency services and fire inspectors, the federal roads agency, and many more.

The same complexity applies to the allocation of budget revenues from the centre to the regions. The actual practice of the Russian financial redistribution to the regions is most often not through regional governments, but through regional branches of federal ministries and agencies. In theory this gives the central government more control over how funds from the centre are spent. In practice distribution of much of this money is highly non-transparent. Rather than formula-based allocations (say, based on population or economic conditions) funds are distributed in response to behind-the-scenes lobbying. Regions vary significantly in their lobbying abilities, and the overall result is to distort the budget process. As budgetary resources have declined since the 2000s, the relative share of revenues that are distributed opaquely and subject to lobbying has increased (Sharafutdinova and Turovsky 2016).

The pattern of numerous vertical channels of control and finance creates massive monitoring and coordination problems, which contributes to corruption and misallocation of resources. Rather than attempting reforms, Putin treats corruption as a problem that can be solved by a more aggressive, though selective, use of law enforcement. In Russia it is widely assumed that the most corrupt regions are the republics of the North Caucasus. Here 'normal' corruption is multiplied by the impact of tightly knit clans that have taken over entire sectors of government activity. Putin unleashed an unprecedented operation designed to clean up Dagestan less than two months before the 2018 presidential election, and he visited the republic himself five days before the election to highlight his role in the effort. Teams of investigators and prosecutors from Moscow combed through the records of the region's government agencies at all levels in search of evidence of abuse of power. Those arrested included the republic's prime minister and two deputy prime ministers, the mayor of Makhachkala, the city's chief architect, the head of MVD criminal investigations, a former education minister, director of the Federal Anti-Monopoly Service, the head of the Derbent region, and others.

An obvious solution to improving regional governance would be to roll back the excessive centralisation of the Putin years and shift decision-making authority – and accountability – to governors. During the Medvedev presidency, in June 2011, two of Russia's most important regional administrators, Dmitry Kozak and Aleksandr Khloponin, were assigned to head working groups to prepare proposals for decentralisation of administration and finance. They reported their conclusions at a meeting of the State Council in December 2011. Kozak presented the most radical proposal. He called for a reorganisation that would transfer to regions over 100 functions then carried out by federal agencies. Over 220,000 federal employees in the regions, around 38% of the total, would be reassigned to new regional agencies. Governors would also have greater say over who should head the federal agencies that remained in the region. Khloponin proposed budgetary reforms that would replace the multiple funding streams with a single subvention or block grant to the region, so that governors could make their own choices about how to allocate the money. He also proposed increasing incentives for innovation and development by allowing regions to keep more of the taxes generated by these activities. As one would expect, governors were enthusiastic in their support of these proposals, while federal ministers found them 'problematic'. Minister of Finance Anton Siluanov argued that regional inequality would sky-rocket, while macroeconomic stability would be undermined. Putin, still prime minister at the time, raised doubts that his budgetary priorities (for the military, security agencies, pensions) could be satisfied under the new scheme. He also doubted that 'national standards' could be maintained if regions took over federal functions. (The State Council session transcript from 26 December 2011 is at president. kremlin.ru/news/14139.)

Once Vladimir Putin returned to the presidency, there was a noticeable shift in tone. Very few new powers would be given to the regions, and the process would take place slowly to avoid any negative consequences. At a second State Council meeting on this question in July 2012, Putin emphasised the accountability of governors if they did not effectively carry out any transferred responsibilities, thus setting the stage for dismissing governors if federal ministers complain about their performance. At a December 2012 meeting with regional legislators Putin admitted that he was bored with the whole process of redistributing powers: 'It all comes down to one thing – to the interests of specific agencies, unfortunately. As soon as you begin to talk about something being transferred to the regional level, this or that, immediately arises a whole mass of arguments from federal agencies on why that would be wrong to do.' (13 December 2012; president.kremlin. ru/news/17125.) While Putin promised some decentralisation, it was clear that his heart is with federal ministers. As one Russian analyst of the regions with close Kremlin ties, Yevgeny Minchenko, put it, 'The federal authorities, having announced a process of decentralisation, really don't want to give money to the regions' (quoted in *Kommersant-vlast'*, 9 July 2012).

To summarise, it is difficult to describe Russia today as a federal state, since so many of the elements that constitute federalism have been consciously undermined by Putin's Kremlin. Regional politics has been de-politicised by predetermining the outcome of elections or eliminating them altogether. Putin has frequently stated that the ideal governor is not a politician, but an effective manager – which explains why he frequently appoints governors with no previous connection to the region. Of 11 acting governors named at the end of 2017, only three had significant regional ties. Institutions that are supposed to represent regional interests in the centre have been reconstituted for other purposes. New institutions such as the State Council are designed to control and channel the efforts of regional leaders, rather than seek their input. The division of powers and budgetary resources has become both highly centralised and yet compartmentalised, making coordination within a region nearly impossible. Finally, and symbolically significant, protestors who have called for 'federalisation' of their regions have been imprisoned on charges of extremism.

10 MANAGING THE ECONOMY

Philip Hanson

For the past few years Russian economic policy has been dominated by two concerns. The first is the country's deteriorating economic performance. The second is the falling out with the United States and Europe. The first concern has prompted a search for a new economic 'strategy' that would enable the nation's output to grow faster than the world average. The slowing growth of 2013–14, the decline of 2015–16 and the prospect of growth at less than 2% a year into the 2020s are lumped together, in current Russian political parlance, as 'stagnation'. The worry underlying this use of the word is not that Russia is literally standing still but that the nation's share of world output has been falling and is expected to fall further. That is a politically unwelcome outcome. The question is whether the policymakers can change it in ways that are compatible with the established social and political order and with their second concern. That second concern has led to a different policy search: for greater national economic invulnerability. This takes many forms: import substitution policies; minimising external public debt; austerity policies to counter inflation; budget rules to make the public finances less sensitive to the price of oil. A preoccupation with notions of national economic sovereignty goes back a long way, but the Ukraine crisis and the 2014 fall in oil prices have made it a real driver of policy.

In this chapter recent Russian economic policy is viewed in the light of these two dominant concerns. First we review the performance of the economy in recent years. Next the factors influencing that performance are discussed. Then the development of policies is outlined, with particular reference to budgetary policy and the winners and losers from fiscal decisions. Finally, there is a look at the future: what policy changes and institutional reforms might attain the policymakers' goals of acceleration and enhanced independence? To what extent are the two goals compatible? Can the existing Russian political order adapt in ways that allow these goals to be met?

Russia's recent economic performance

In autumn 2017 Russia was emerging from a recession. This was not a new experience. In the 26 years of its post-Soviet existence the Russian economy has been through three crises, one sustained boom and a great deal of uncertainty. Most analysts failed to foresee these ups and downs. The crisis years were 1992–99, 2008–09 and 2014–16. The depth and duration of the first of these, the 'transition recession' of the Yeltsin years, were not widely foreseen either in the West or in Russia. That fall in economic activity was deeper and lasted longer than the corresponding declines in Central Europe. The boom of 2000–08, triggered by the devaluation of 1998 and then driven by rising oil prices, was also, for most analysts, unexpected. The sharp fall in output (7.8%) in 2009, the steepest decline experienced by any G-20 nation, was a delayed effect of the global financial crisis, pushing down oil prices. Most countries found that recovery from that crisis was slow and unsteady, and Russia was no exception. But the Russian crisis of 2014–16 was different again: it was not part of a renewed global decline, and it had nothing to do with 'transition'.

After 2009 the economy resumed growth but at rates that were subdued by the standards of the earlier boom. Then in 2012–13 there was a further slowdown to a GDP growth rate of 1.8%. This slowdown can be ascribed chiefly to domestic factors. Then in 2014 Russia encountered a perfect storm: weak domestic conditions, warfare in Ukraine, economic sanctions on Russia by the West, and in the autumn a steep fall in oil prices.

Output: falling behind

The outcome in 2013–16 was painful for Russian national pride and for the ambitions of Russia's leaders. In the medium term Russia was no longer narrowing the per capita output gap between itself and the leading rich countries. They were also experiencing slow growth, but not as slow as Russia's in 2014 and not negative, like Russia in 2015 and 2016. Moreover, Russia was widely judged to be facing the prospect of further sluggish development. In summer 2017 the bullish Ministry of Economic Development (MinEkon) was daring to hope for growth slightly over 2% in the full year (Shapovalov 2017), but the Central Bank of Russia (CBR) was sticking to a forecast of less than 2%. In the event, the final figure was growth of just 1.5%. The official government projection through 2019 was also for an average rate below 2%. Medium-term projections in general clustered around 1.5%. (For example, the August 2017 poll of 24 independent forecasters by the Development Center of Moscow's Higher School of Economics produced a median forecast of 1.4% GDP growth in 2017 rising to 1.8% in 2023, https://dcenter.hse.ru/prog2/). This did not augur well for 'catching up' with the West (Figure 10.1).

Another result of this slow growth is that since 2012, Russia's share of global economic activity has been edging downwards. It is widely projected to go on doing so. This is a situation it shares with Brazil, of the original four BRIC countries; the other two, India and China, continue to increase their shares of world output. So Russia has been failing to consolidate its global economic position, as well as lagging behind the most highly developed economies.

From late 2014 to late 2016 slowing growth turned into outright decline. The fall in output is very largely attributable to the fall in oil prices. An early projection of these losses by Gurvich and Prilepskiy puts them at not far

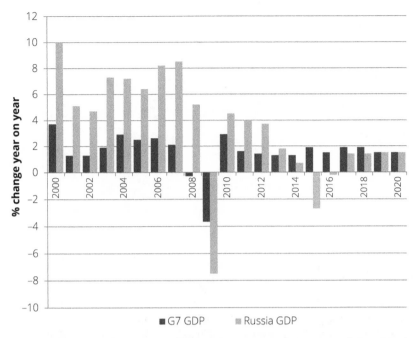

Figure 10.1 Ceasing to catch up, Year-on-year growth in the GDP of Russia and of the Group of 7 countries, 2000–16 actual and 2017–20 projected (% p.a.)

Sources: Created using http://www.imf.org/external/pubs/ft/weo/2017/01/weodata/index.aspx and http:// www.gks.ru/wps/wcm/connect/rosstat_main/rosstat/ru/statistics/accounts/ [Accessed 15 August 2017]

short of 3% a year on average from 2014 to 2017 inclusive. The same authors put the likely losses due to financial sanctions over the same period at about 0.6% per annum (Gurvich and Prilepskiy 2015). These numbers are quite robust, as such estimates go, and they suggest that even in the absence of the oil price shock and Western sanctions, Russian output growth would have continued to be sluggish, as it was in 2013.

Adjustment

In the face of the steep fall in oil prices in late 2014 the CBR took an important decision: rather than accept a big decline in foreign exchange reserves in order to defend the previous exchange rate, it let the rouble float. Floating in this case meant sinking: from somewhat over 30 roubles to the dollar briefly to 80 and subsequently to around 60. The close correspondence between the oil price and a freely floating rouble is illustrated in Figure 10.2.

The population at large bore the burden of adjustment. The tumbling rouble meant rising import prices, and imports loom large in Russian household consumption. The rise in the consumer price index peaked at an annual rate of 17% in early 2015 and ended the year (the December 2015 index over that of December 2014) at 12.9%. Money wages did not keep pace, as Figure 10.3 shows.

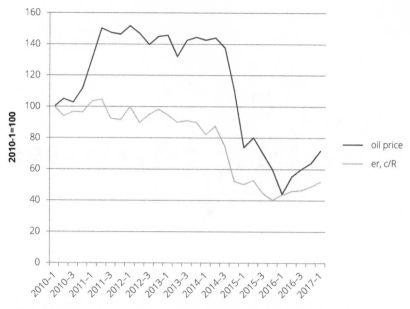

Figure 10.2 The price of Urals oil ($ per barrel) and the rouble–dollar exchange rate (cents per rouble), quarterly data 2010–17 (indices, 2010 Q1 = 100)

Source: Created using data from Central Bank of Russia (http://cbr.ru/statistics/) [Accessed 15 August 2017]

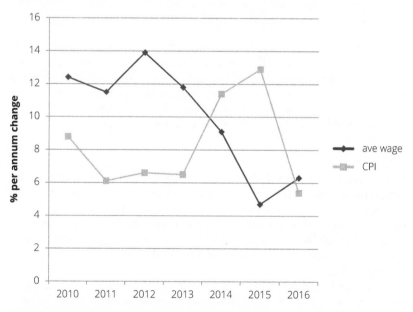

Figure 10.3 Money wages and the consumer price index, annual data, 2010–16 (end-year inflation) (% annual change)

Source: Created using data from Rossat (http://www.gks.ru/wps/wcm/connect/rosstat_main/ross-tat/ru/statistics/accounts/ [Accessed 17 August 2017]

Thus real wages fell in 2015 by almost 8%. Retail sales fell by 10% that year and by 5% in 2016 and began to revive only in mid-2017. This was unlike the pattern in 2008–09, when GDP fell far more steeply but the population suffered less.

Unemployment remained low. In a downturn Russian companies tend to cut earnings rather than numbers employed (Gimpelson and Kapeliush-nikov 2015). Unemployment edged up from 5.2% at end-2014 to 5.6% one year later and then eased down to 5.1% at mid-2017. There appears to have been some shifting from the registered to the 'grey' (unregistered) economy, but overall the labour market in the big cities remained tight.

The impact of the recession was felt by lower-income households in particular. The government programme of budgetary austerity extended to real-terms cuts to pensioners. In 2016 nominal pensions were raised by only 4% (the CBR inflation target) and not, as usual, by the percentage increase in the consumer price index of the previous year. Pensioners recorded as still working received no indexation at all. The overall loss to real-terms pension incomes was about 10%. (See the section on policy below.) In addition Russia's own 2014 'counter-sanctions', an embargo on food imports from countries that had imposed sanctions on Russia, contributed to the rise in food prices, which was proportionally more of a burden on lower-income households.

Effects on the budget

The fall in oil prices affected the budget, forcing policymakers to choose between austerity and stimulus. For reasons to be discussed later, they chose austerity, cutting federal expenditure to keep the deficit low, as Figure 10.4

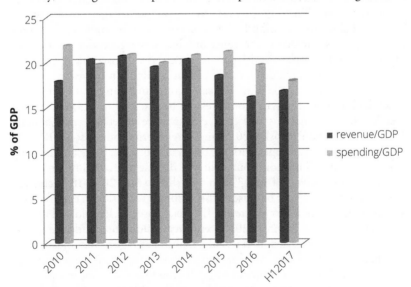

Figure 10.4 Federal budget revenue and expenditure, 2010–17 (% of GDP)

Source: Created using data from Bank of Finland (https://www.bofit.fi/en/monitoring/statistics/russia-statistics/) [Accessed 17 August 2017]

illustrates. The federal budget, it should be noted, is by no means the whole of state revenue and spending in Russia. There are also regional and local budgets and extra-budgetary funds, most notably the state Pension Fund. But the regions have little autonomy so far as tax bases and tax rates are concerned, have limited borrowing options and in aggregate depend on federal transfers, as does the Pension Fund. The federal budget is therefore the key instrument of policy.

Before the 2014 oil-price fall, federal revenues from oil and gas were close to half of total revenue. This crucial budgetary prop was abruptly reduced in size. There was some compensation from the fall in the rouble: each petro-dollar was now worth more roubles and budgetary spending is very largely in roubles. But as a mitigating factor this was limited. The budget was in difficulties.

External finances and the impact of sanctions

The lower oil price, of course, also meant lower export revenues, since crude oil, oil products and natural gas had accounted for about two-thirds of the value of merchandise exports. However, imports also fell precipitously in 2015 and 2016 as domestic economic activity declined. Russia's habitual surplus in the current account of the balance of payments fell quite sharply in 2016 but the balance remained positive.

Western economic sanctions, imposed mainly in 2014 but with some later additions, also affected Russia's external finances. The visa bans and asset freezes on targeted individuals probably had no direct effects observable at a macroeconomic level, but the so-called sectoral sanctions, particularly those blocking the provision of finance to an array of Russian banks and companies, certainly did. The effect was not only on the banks and companies named in the sanctions but more generally on Russian entities, as US, European and Japanese lenders saw 'Russia risk' increasing. There was an associated decline, not just in lending but in inward foreign direct investment as well. Most Russian banks and non-bank companies, which had borrowed heavily from Western banks, now had trouble rolling over loans. (On sanctions and their effects more generally, see Connolly 2015, Gurvich and Prilepskiy 2015, and Oxenstierna and Olsson 2015.)

Russian companies coped with the financial blockade, in part by delaying capital spending. This contributed to the decline in fixed investment in Russia, a cumulative fall of 13% in the three years 2014–16 inclusive.[1] Russia continued, in part because of this enforced reduction in external borrowing, to maintain a strong external financial position. Its gold and foreign exchange reserves in summer 2017 were over $400 billion and its external assets continued to exceed its external liabilities, as Figure 10.5 illustrates.

Thus, in 2017 Russia was emerging slowly from recession and was widely believed to face a future of sluggish growth but was not in a position of financial dependence on the outside world – with much of which it was at odds. Economic independence was in this respect preserved.

---

1 http://www.gks.ru/wps/wcm/connect/rosstat_main/rosstat/ru/statistics/accounts/#.

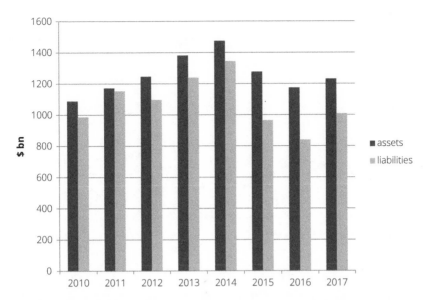

Figure 10.5 Russia's international assets and international liabilities, 2010–17, at the start of each year ($ billion)

Source: Created using data from Central Bank of Russia (http://cbr.ru/statistics/) [Accessed 17 August 2017]

The domestic sources of stagnation

Part of Russia's economic enfeeblement, and possibly all of the 2015–16 fall in Russian output, can be attributed to two external factors: the oil-price decline and Western sanctions. These sources of economic difficulty lie outside the reach of Moscow's economic policymakers (though the sanctions problem might be ameliorated by Russian foreign policy). It is likely that before 2014 sluggish growth in Europe did Russia no favours. Europe after all takes more than 40% of Russia's exports. But with that qualification, the main sources of Russian 'stagnation' are domestic.

Two influences are immediately apparent: employment has lately been almost stationary, and fixed investment has been in decline. See Figure 10.6.

Therefore labour and capital inputs into production have been making little or no contribution to economic growth. In the case of labour, this is due to demographic problems: a rapidly falling cohort of young Russian labour-force entrants, offset by immigrant labour from the poorer CIS countries, mainly from Central Asia and the Caucasus. This pattern is expected to last into the mid-2020s.

Two questions arise: Why has investment been so low? And what else might contribute to increased production when capital and labour inputs are lagging? The outright fall in fixed investment over three years was the product of crisis: rapid inflation, falling consumer demand, the effect of sanctions on inward foreign investment and very high uncertainty. That fall did not continue in the first half of 2017, as inflation was brought down and real wages and demand increased again. The difficult question

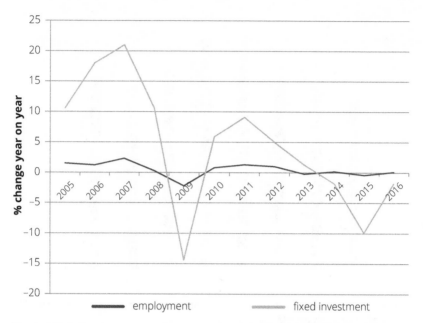

Figure 10.6 Employment and investment in Russia, 2010–16 (% per annum change)

Note: In calculating the percentage change in employment between 2014 and 2015, employment in Crimea in 2015 (included in the official figures for the first time) was excluded so as to compare like with like. The change from 2015 to 2016 includes Crimea.

Source: Created using data from Rossat (http://www.gks.ru/wps/wcm/connect/rosstat_main/ross-tat/ru/statistics/accounts/) [Accessed 17 August 2017]

is why investment grew so sluggishly already in 2012–13 and why it is not expected to rise strongly in the current recovery. Indeed there is a longer-term problem: the share of fixed investment in Russian GDP has long been modest by the standards of middle-income countries: around 20%. That longer-term phenomenon can probably be attributed to a generally unfavourable national 'ecosystem' for private business in Russia, on which more will be said below. The slowdown in investment growth after 2011, however, is hard to account for; it is perhaps the product of increased uncertainty about future taxation and about the informal rules of the business-state game.

If labour and capital inputs grow slowly, how might the productivity of labour and capital be raised to offset the effects of their slow growth? The list is not a long one: improvements in human capital, an accelerated rate of introduction and diffusion of new products and processes, and shifts in the allocation of resources from less productive to more productive lines of economic activity. The changing composition of the labour force, with fewer young labour-market entrants and mostly low-skilled immigrants, makes it unlikely that increased skills and knowledge (enhanced human capital) will be the answer. One policy response to the labour shortage – raising the pension age – would in this respect be unhelpful, though it would ease fiscal problems.

Technological innovation will play some part. However, like investment in plant and machinery, innovation is often discouraged by 'pressure' on business by the state. The real possibility of losing your business to the illicit machinations of rival firms in league with corrupt law enforcement is a deterrent to both investment and innovation. (For a survey of asset-grabbing in Russia, see Hanson 2014; for a vivid example of problems for an innovator, see Higgins 2017.) Moreover, Western sanctions have narrowed the channel of imported innovation.

The influence of weak property rights on rates of investment and innovation in Russia cannot be quantified, but some evidence on the comparatively slow development of a business class and the relative paucity of small firms is suggestive. The business class, in the sense of owners of businesses, is relatively small. According to the surveys conducted by the Global Entrepreneurship Monitor (GEM) consortium, Russia in 2014 was 71st out of 73 countries in the proportion of the working-age population owning an established business.[2] Below Russia were Kosovo and Puerto Rico.

The role of small firms in the economy is correspondingly modest. Russian official data on small firms in 2016 (defined as firms with up to 100 people working in them) show small-firm employment at 15% of total employment.[3] That does not include the shadow economy of firms not registered for tax purposes. A more comprehensive estimate, that of the small-business association, Opora, works out at about 28% of total employment.[4] Typical figures for Central and West European economies are of the order of 40% or more. The figure for the UK in 2016, for firms with up to 99 people engaged in them, is 43%.[5]

The remaining source of productivity growth is change in the allocation of resources. The productivity of labour and capital in Russia has been increased by the movement of these inputs out of low-productivity (and sometimes even value-subtracting) manufacturing inherited from Soviet times and into hitherto-underdeveloped services. This process may not yet be completed but it has slowed down. Meanwhile there has also been a less helpful resource transfer, of labour out of formal (registered and incorporated) businesses into the grey economy of unregistered and unincorporated business activity. Labour productivity is lower in the grey economy. On the whole, it does not look as though resource shifts will be the source of strong growth in productivity.

These are the reasons why baseline scenarios of future Russian growth are so modest and why 'stagnation' is so widely acknowledged. We turn next to the ways in which economic policies have developed during the crisis, before finally looking at how policy and reforms might develop in the near future.

2   http://www.gemconsortium.org/docs/download/3616.
3   http://www.gks.ru/free_doc/new_site/business/inst-preob/tab-mal_pr_m.htm.
4   http://www.opora.ru/upload/iblock/c5a/c5a6de1c92f3d930b033159991eb29d2.pdf.
5   https://www.gov.uk/government/statistics/business-population-estimates-2016.

Recent economic policy in Russia

The Russian leadership has so far responded to the deterioration of the country's economic performance by means of policy, rather than reform. We can take reform, in this context, to mean major changes in institutional arrangements, such as the establishment of an independent judiciary or a large-scale programme of privatisation. Policy measures, on the other hand, include the adjustment of monetary controls and signals such as the CBR's key interest rate; alterations in taxes and spending and *ad hoc* interventions such as the introduction of subsidies to support domestic telecoms production. The effects of policy changes can often be judged fairly well in advance; reforms are more likely to have unintended consequences. It is understandable that Putin and those close to him, especially as the 2018 presidential election approached, stuck to existing policy while speaking of the possibility of reform later.

Guiding policy ideas

In May 2017 a document was published that sets out the concerns behind recent and prospective economic policy. This is the official Strategy of the Economic Security of the Russian Federation for the period to 2030 ('O strategii' 2017). It is the work of an interdepartmental group and it shows different interests each putting in something from their own agenda. Economic security is said to be the preservation of national sovereignty by defence against external and internal threats (p. 4). Present risks to it are listed. The natural-resource-export model [for Russia] has had its day (p. 6). Investment is too low in Russia and the business climate needs to be improved; at present property rights are not protected (p. 7). The system of strategic economic planning must be improved. So must the vetting of foreign investment in strategically important industries (p. 9). A sufficient level of technological independence must be achieved (p. 10). Strategic reserves of capacity must be created. Critical dependence on imported technology must be reduced. (p. 11). The risks [to business] of asset-grabbing must be lowered (p. 15). A list of indicators of national economic security (p. 17) includes, among many others, per capita GDP at purchasing power parity, Russia's share of global output, the investment share of GDP, the rate of inflation, the level of external debt and the size of the federal budget deficit.

The desiderata plainly come from both technocratic liberal insiders and statists. There is probably agreement among them that Russia should grow faster, whether for reasons of security or for the sake of social welfare. On the need for greater technological independence and better planning there is probably less agreement. Another declared need, for better protection of property rights, is one that statists can perhaps pay lip service to, without striving to make it a reality.

So far as actual policies are concerned, there have been three major developments in recent years: in monetary policy, which is managed by the CBR; in the government's fiscal policies, in which the Ministry of Finance plays the lead role; and in industrial policy, where the Ministry of Economic Development (MinEkon) and the Ministry of Industry and Trade (Minpromtorg) are the leading players. In each case President Putin's approval has probably been necessary.

Monetary policy

The November 2014 change by the CBR to a floating rouble has already been mentioned. Previously the central bank had based its monetary policies on targeting a closely managed exchange rate for the rouble. No central bank can simultaneously target the exchange rate and the rate of inflation. The CBR had since 2010 announced its intention to move to inflation targeting. It took the late-2014 rouble crisis, however, finally to force such a move. The bank could sell a lot of foreign exchange from the reserves in a probably vain attempt to prop up the rouble against the US dollar and the euro. Or it could save a big draw-down of reserves by letting the rouble decline as the market dictated. Having done that, it switched its efforts to inflation targeting.

The immediate effect of the rouble's massive depreciation was a steep rise in the rouble price of imports and therefore in the domestic price level. The bank set its key interest rate above the rate of inflation. That meant the key rate itself was high and bank interest rates to customers even higher. The growth of credit and therefore of the broad money supply slowed down. Business complained but the inflation rate came down to 5.4% in December 2016 and to less than the target level of 4% (for the consumer price index) in summer 2017.

This tough monetary policy was combined, under Elvira Nabiullina's leadership of the CBR, with numerous closures of weak commercial banks by the central bank. Nabiullina faced some critics but had one rather important supporter: President Vladimir Putin. He praised her strong monetary stance on several occasions, and in March 2017 re-appointed her for a new five-year term (Tanas and Kravchenko 2017). Putin is, it seems, a monetarist.

Budgetary policy

A tough, orthodox monetary policy was complemented by fiscal austerity. The Ministry of Finance has pushed, so far with some success, for what is euphemistically called 'fiscal consolidation' – that is, spending cuts. These policies have evidently been accepted by President Putin. They have elicited approval from Western credit rating agencies and the IMF.

First, some background to recent developments. For reasons set out above, we focus on the federal budget. During the boom years 2000–07, that budget ran surpluses as oil revenues grew fast. Oil export duties and the mineral extraction tax generated up to half of federal budget revenue. A stabilisation fund, later split into the Reserve Fund and National Welfare Fund, was set up; sovereign debt was paid down. When the global financial crisis sent the oil price and oil and gas revenues down in 2008–09, the federal budget went into deficit. The subsequent limping recovery in the

Russian economy saw the beginning of a new phenomenon: a federal budget deficit while the nominal oil price was back to historically high levels.

Developments after 2009 are illustrated in Figure 10.4 above. The most visible achievement in the way of spending cuts is the fall in federal-budget spending as a percentage of a marginally reduced GDP in 2016. The battles fought on the way to this achievement will be summarised below. But there is a question to be addressed first: could the Russian state have avoided or at any rate minimised spending cuts by borrowing more?

Despite the recent deficits, Russian public debt is small by Western standards, like that of many other oil-exporting nations. This is part of the legacy of the fat years. Western sanctions on finance for Russia have helped to preserve that legacy. There is on the face of it plenty of room for the Russian state to borrow more. In fact, the constraints are formidable. They include the shallowness of Russian domestic financial markets and the current difficulty of borrowing abroad because of sanctions. Modest international borrowing ($3 bn in 2016), some domestic borrowing and a drawing down of the Reserve Fund saw the deficit financed in 2016. The plans for the following three years' budgets aim at reducing the deficit, mainly by continued spending restraint. They are based on the cautious assumption that the Urals oil price will average $40 per barrel.

The Ministry of Finance's caution is also embodied in a new 'budget rule' designed to lock in limits on spending. On 5 July 2017 the Duma approved at first reading a rule that oil and gas budget revenues accruing from an oil price above $40 a barrel must be channelled into the Reserve Fund and not into current spending – $40/b being the cut-off point in 2017, rising by an annual 2% in subsequent years.[6] This is not just a measure taken in the cause of fiscal prudence. It also serves the cause of economic 'security' by limiting the economy's sensitivity to the ups and downs of the oil price.

A striking feature of budgetary policymaking in 2016 was the absence of visible resistance to cuts in some areas that might have been expected to be contentious. Two sets of cuts will make the point: to pensions and to defence spending.

Social policy excluding health care and education has generally been treated as sacrosanct. Yet in 2016 there were some cuts, actual or planned, in sensitive places. These included, as mentioned above, suspending the payment of pension increments to some nine million pensioners who were still working (36% of the total). Another decision was to index state pensions in 2016 by only 4%. The normal rule is to index by the rate of consumer price inflation in the previous year – which in this case was 12.9% – so the cut overall, compared to what pensioners would routinely have expected, was about 10%. In the event, Russian pensioners did not storm the Kremlin, inflation came down substantially and indexing by the past year's inflation was promised for 2017, together with a modest one-off payment.

Similarly, defence spending was cut in 2016. This is not obvious from the headline figures but once a R800bn repayment of earlier defence-industry

---

6   Report by Vadim Visloguzov, https://www.kommersant.ru/doc/3344061.

debt is stripped out so that the comparison with 2015 is on a like-for-like basis, it becomes clear. Reported clashes on the subject are few. They concern not the 2016 or 2017 budgets but the draft programme for military modernization for 2018–25. Pavel Felgenhauer, in a Western publication, says that the Minister of Defence, Sergei Shoigu, was moved to 'shout' at the Finance Minister, Anton Siluanov, accusing him of undermining efforts to modernise the military and threatening national security (Felgenhauer 2016). That would have been in September, when the decision on the scale of the programme was postponed. But military spending was trimmed in 2016 and was planned to be held down in 2017–19, and there was no other sign of this creating a split within the elite.

One side-effect of budgetary policy did create a sort of political discord. It was agreed that some ambitious privatisations would be carried out to help finance the federal budget. In particular the state stake in the oil company Bashneft and 19.5% of the leading oil company, Rosneft, leaving a majority stake still in the hands of the state, were to be sold off. After much public debate, Rosneft was allowed, despite its being a state company, to buy the Bashneft stake. Then Igor Sechin, the boss of Rosneft and a political heavyweight, performed a characteristic conjuring trick. He secured a sale of the Rosneft stake to the Qatari sovereign wealth fund and the trading company Glencore for an amount equivalent to about 0.8% of GDP.[7]

In the aftermath of these transactions came the Ulyukaev affair. Aleksei Ulyukaev, the then-Minister of Economic Development, along with several other senior officials, had initially opposed the Rosneft takeover of Bashneft but eventually accepted the idea and gave his approval. (Putin reportedly had been against the purchase in early August but came round to it in September; that would have determined the outcome.)

In November Ulyukaev was arrested on a charge of attempting to extort a $2mn bribe from Sechin for approving the purchase of Bashneft. According to one report, nobody in the government believed in Ulyukaev's guilt (https://www/kommersant.ru/doc/3181641, accessed 30 December 2016). In such matters, however, the views of the government do not count for much.

Apart from the Ulyukaev affair and perhaps some shouting by Shoigu, the Russian elite handled the shift to fiscal austerity smoothly and with apparent unity. The lack of division was almost certainly made possible by President Putin's clear preference for financial caution. That preference seems to be based on a sense that Russia has to retain its economic sovereignty by all possible means, including the minimisation of public debt.

Industrial policy

The Russian government's recent industrial policies have been focused on reducing the country's vulnerability to external influences. In the recent context of sanctions this is hardly surprising, but often these policies can

---

7   http://www.vedomosti.ru/economics/articles/2016/11/10/660198-minfin-konserviruet-rashodi.

be traced back several years. For instance, in 2006 Vladislav Surkov, then a deputy head of Putin's Presidential Administration, introducing his notion of 'sovereign democracy', stressed the importance of not being 'managed from outside' (Connolly and Hanson 2016, p. 2).

One of the most obvious ways in which Russia is particularly vulnerable to external developments is its economic sensitivity to fluctuations in the oil price. One response to this has been the channelling of oil and gas revenue into reserve funds when the oil price is high, to be drawn on to support economic activity when the oil price is low. This defence has been severely tested since 2014, and the new budget rule, described above, is one way in which that defence has been reinforced.

Another defence frequently invoked over the years is economic diversification. If that is pursued as a matter of policy, it means state support for production other than oil and gas. The comparatively heavy taxation of the hydrocarbons sector is one form this policy has taken. In May 2014, however, a more interventionist set of measures was launched: an import substitution campaign. This includes investment subsidies for certain lines of production in Russia and restrictions on state-sector purchases of an array of items for which domestic 'analogues' are deemed to be available. The emphasis here is on machinery and equipment, including information technology. Critics, including some senior officials, claim that these restrictions and subsidies result in higher equipment prices and lower quality, and there have been calls for moderation in this policy (for an overview, see Connolly and Hanson 2016).

Separately, the 'counter-sanctions' blocking food imports from nations imposing sanctions on Russia served a similar purpose. Introduced in 2014, explicitly as a response to Western sanctions, they have served to protect Russian agri-business and have been extended several times, most recently to end-2018. Here too, critics claim the main result is higher prices. However, the food-import embargo is welcomed by the Russian farm sector and may well outlast the sanctions war – even as that war itself looks set to persist (Kostyrev 2017).

The import-substitution campaign and counter-sanctions tend to reduce competition in an economy that already favours incumbent companies and political connections. They also go against Russia's potentially beneficial integration into the wider world economy. The liberal view would be that in the longer term, on balance, they compound the damage done to the Russian economy by the sanctions themselves. The statist view would be that if there are any economic costs, they are outweighed by the gains in economic security.

The future: reform for the sake of faster growth?

The consensus view, as we have seen, is that in the absence of any significant change in circumstances the Russian economy will grow at between 1 and 2% per annum over the next few years. If we assume – perhaps rashly – that the consensus is right, what might change this scenario?

Russia's economic prospects depend in part on 'stuff happening', and in part on the actions of the authorities. The most obvious 'stuff' that could happen is that the oil price departs substantially and for a lengthy period from the generally assumed range of $40–$60 per barrel. The direct, short-term effect would be that the economy would move in the same direction as the oil price. In the medium term, other things equal, the economy would probably revert to its previous growth path. This is because it is the change in the oil price, not its level, that prompts changes in the growth rate of Russian GDP.

Other eventualities are easy to imagine, but their consequences may be less obvious. If Russia's political confrontation with the West tipped into a new military conflict, the economic effects would probably be negative. If Putin for whatever reason ceased to be President, the resulting increase in uncertainty would most likely have negative effects, but those effects might dissipate over time. And so on.

The actions of the authorities and their likely impact are more open to assessment. That Putin and those close to him are unhappy about Russia's economic performance is clear. What they are prepared to do about it is not, but the available options are limited. There is much talk about a change of 'strategy'. The word could denote some combination of policy changes and reforms. Several schemes are on offer, and we review them briefly below.

Three main packages of measures have been put forward for consideration by the President. The expectation is that a 'strategy' will be drawn up from them for the newly elected President to put in place as official policy from 2018. All are supposed to provide antidotes to stagnation, ensuring at least 4% GDP growth by 2025 at the latest.

The best-known of these schemes, though it has not been made public in full, is that drawn up by the Centre for Strategic Research under former finance minister Aleksei Kudrin. It includes continued macroeconomic restraint but with some increase in spending on health care and education, raising the pension age, substantial privatisation, reform of state adminis-tration, and measures to improve the business climate including judicial reform to make the courts more independent (CSR 2017).

The Stolypin Club proposal is fronted by the presidential ombudsman for business, Boris Titov. This also espouses improving the business environment, where Titov's track record is encouraging. Its main emphasis, however, is on macroeconomic policy. Here it is diametrically opposed both to current policy and to the CSR recommendations: it calls for a surge in spending financed by monetary emission and a loosening of restrictions on the federal budget deficit to allow it to be up to 3% of GDP – still a moder-ate level by Western standards.[8]

Also in play is an in-house strategy from the government, led by MinEkon. In an early version, this stressed holding down wage levels to facilitate the growth of profits and thus, it was hoped, investment. Whether

---

8   Aleksandra Prokopenko in *Vedomosti*, 1 March 2017, http://www.vedomosti.ru/economics/articles/2017/03/01/679501-stolipinskii-klub.

this is still part of the MinEkon plan is not clear. MinEkon favours stimulus but a more modest stimulus than that advocated by the Stolypinists.

Could some of these measures make a substantial difference to the country's economic prospects? Plans for stimulus are unlikely to get a hearing from the present leadership. Putin's preference for austerity, rooted in 'economic security' concerns, is clear. Some proposals, such as a shift in state spending to human capital needs (education and health care) would probably be beneficial in the long term. This is a measure that could be adopted, though at the expense of some other part of the budget.

Raising the age at which state pensions are paid might not do a great deal for output, since many younger Russian pensioners continue to work anyway. But present pension ages of 55 for women and 60 for men are low by international standards, and a step-by-step raising of those ages would reduce the Pension Fund's drain on the federal budget. This is why in September 2018 the Duma finally adopted a reform which raised the retirement age of women to 60 and men to 65.

Large-scale privatisation would tend, other things equal, to make the economy more dynamic. Kudrin has spoken of the desirability of privatising the likes of Gazprom and Rosneft within seven or eight years. So long as the bosses of these companies prefer the status quo, that looks difficult, to put it mildly. Insofar as Putin has a detectable view on the subject, there is no sign that it includes a distaste for state enterprise. Direct state control in 'strategic' sectors, at least on some views, can help to ensure economic security. For that reason, and because of the lobbying power of big state companies, substantial privatisation looks unlikely.

The most fundamental reform ambitions are to do with the environment for private business. If property rights were protected against asset-grabbing, and entrepreneurs could rely on protecting their businesses through independent courts, the business environment would change fundamentally. Even the big-business tycoons, with their private aircraft, houses in London, yachts and other possessions, hold their Russian assets at the state's discretion. Incumbent firms, large and small, need to cultivate their ties with officials to fend off competition from rivals. The ecosystem for business is not a favourable one.

A radical improvement of that ecosystem is probably the most substantial of the possible sources of improvement in the Russian economy. It is certainly the most politically sensitive of the reforms and policy measures that are on offer. It goes to the heart of contemporary Russia's political economy.

Courts that were independent of the local and national authorities would be incompatible with the everyday working of the present system because they would allow citizens, including businesspeople, to mount genuine challenges to officials. This would have consequences that would threaten the interests of the political elite, including those members of the elite who are economic liberals and aware of the costs of the present business climate. Lower-level officials would lose their ability to 'feed off' those they regulate. That would undermine their loyalty. At the same time, the leadership would lose the means of selectively applying the formal laws and the informal rules of the game to keep those lower-level officials in a state of suspended punishment and therefore biddable. Finally, independent courts would pose risks for the leaders themselves, since they, too, live beyond their salaries and have questions to answer.

The barriers, therefore, to a radical improvement in the protection of property rights are formidable. It is hard to see them being removed except as part of a profound change in the social order. On the other hand, the leadership's concerns about both stagnation and economic security are acute. Some move to make the courts somewhat more independent, or at least to reduce the coverage of 'economic crimes' under criminal law, cannot be ruled out. In the longer term more radical change, perhaps unintended, might come about. Meanwhile, the measures that look more likely to be taken also look likely to have only a marginal effect on Russia's economic performance.

11 INEQUALITY AND SOCIAL POLICY IN RUSSIA

Thomas F. Remington

In early 2012, a team of policy experts from several Moscow think tanks issued a report on the economic and social challenges facing Russia, called 'Strategy-2020' (Strategiya-2020). The report called for a new model of economic growth and a fundamental reorientation of social policy. The report was produced by a team of some 1,500 experts convened by Vladimir Putin to advise the government on policies through 2020 and beyond. It concluded that the country's current economic system was close to exhausting its potential for further growth and that a new model of growth was required based on entrepreneurship and competition; that inequality in incomes and access to benefits was excessive; that the shrinking of the workforce and aging of the population threatened the pension and health care systems; that high economic growth was needed to finance increased social spending and increase investment in human capital, but that such reforms could in turn fuel growth; and that, in order to alleviate redistributive tensions, the groups on whom the tax burden fell most heavily must have greater institutional opportunities for participation and representation in policy-making.

The challenge of social policy

The report appeared at a time when the deep decline in economic performance triggered by the 2008 global economic crisis seemed to be ending, and President Putin was preparing to return to the presidency. It reflected the views of one wing of Putin's advisors who favoured reforms that would generate long-term, sustained growth by encouraging innovation, improving the investment climate, and reducing dependence on natural resource exploitation. The report called for investing more in human capital and infrastructure; widening the pooling of risk, cost, and gain from growth; finding a more efficient balance between state and private provision; and raising the quality of social services. Tacitly it urged democratisation, to encourage the public to contribute more to social policy by having more say over taxing and spending.

The proposal had little impact on policy. Like many previous strategic planning documents, its recommendations were soon overtaken by events – the crisis in Ukraine, the annexation of Crimea, the resulting sanctions imposed by Western countries on Russian financial institutions, and a steep fall in world oil prices beginning in autumn 2014. A new slowdown in growth starting at the end of 2013 further dulled the regime's appetite for significant reform.

A few years later, finance minister Aleksei Kudrin convened another group of policy experts to issue another strategic planning proposal in 2017 (Kudrin and Sokolov 2017). Its recommendations paralleled those of the earlier ones: Russia should cut its budget spending on defence and security as a share of GDP, but increase its spending on human capital (education and health care) and other productive investments (transportation and communications) in order to raise growth. Without major shifts in budget priorities, they concluded, Russia would inevitably spend an ever rising share of its budget and its national income on pensions and medical expenses associated with the aging of the population. What combination of exogenous shocks and leadership changes would be needed for Russia's leaders to heed these warnings and carry out a major overhaul of policy priorities? Adopting Kudrin's plan, however, would be politically difficult; it would strike a blow at powerful bureaucratic and social constituencies, requiring the president to expend a considerable amount of political capital.

Russia's social policies continue to reflect the legacy of the Soviet social welfare system, which were adopted at a time when income inequality was low and there was no private wealth. The Soviet social welfare system offered a relatively high implicit level of social protection – a system often called the 'Soviet social contract' because it provided comprehensive social welfare but demanded political fealty. The problem was that the state's social policy commitments were not adequately funded. Indeed, their actual cost was unknown, because prices of goods and services were arbitrarily set by the planners and distortions in relative prices accumulated over time. Many benefits were in the form of subsidised prices for housing, transportation, utilities, medications, health care, recreation, and other goods and services. Some came in the form of cash (such as pensions) but were provided in an economy where many goods and services could not be purchased for cash and wages were administratively controlled. Many benefits were free to the consumer, such as education and health care. The point is that in the socialist planned economy, prices were secondary to the planners' decisions on how to balance consumption and production across the economy. Accordingly, neither state planners nor beneficiaries had more than the haziest idea how much the social welfare system cost relative to GDP. This meant that when Russia dismantled central control over planning of production and prices, goods and services began to be shaped by considerations of cost and demand. Provision of an adequate social safety net and system of public services strained the capacity of the post-communist Russian government to finance the obligations it inherited. Then, once the shift to a market-oriented economy began, the old social welfare system was poorly suited to providing a social safety net for those who lost out from the transition.

A crucial feature of the Soviet-type social contract was the central role of the workplace in delivering benefits. In Russia, 'enterprise paternalism' reflected the fact that in addition to guaranteed lifetime employment, workers also received their housing and many other benefits through their enterprises. The fact that the state enterprise itself served as a kind of welfare state allowed enterprises to retain a continuing hold over both workers and government well into the transition era.

As a result, the shift of the economy onto a market footing created an enormous practical dilemma: how to finance social policy? In Russia, as in most post-communist countries, the principal response was to retain a fairly extensive set of entitlements but to reduce their strain on the state budget by converting much of the burden of state spending for pensions, health care, and other forms of social assistance into new social insurance pools using defined contributions rather than defined-benefits schemes. Some benefits continued to be paid directly from the state budget (such as public education), while others were largely moved into the private marketplace (most housing, some education, some health care). Payroll taxes generally continued to be relatively high, which led to a large amount of evasion and informal employment. Less apparent was the continuing default control by state enterprises over a great deal of social provision. The central government also sought to decentralise much of the financial burden for social benefits to lower levels of government. The large role for the private sector in housing, education, health care, child care, and other services contributed to high and cumulative inequality of income, wealth, and opportunity. Finally, the attempt to create a combination of mandatory and voluntary insurance mechanisms for pension, health care, disability, maternity, and unemployment protection has led to severe financing problems. The social insurance schemes are expensive for employers and employees but payroll tax revenues are increasingly unable to meet current obligations. As a result, the government has had to subsidise pension and other social fund deficits out of the state budget. Russia has also diverted the mandatory individual pension contributions to cover current pension commitments. Moreover, many private and some public enterprises find ways to evade their obligations by relying on illegal wage schemes. Informal employment – employment not covered by social insurance schemes – is extensive and growing. These trends help explain why the government experts consider the current system to be unsustainable.

Russia has largely privatised housing and introduced market elements into both education and health care. But in those areas of social policy where formerly budget-financed entitlements were placed on a mandatory social insurance basis – pensions, health care, unemployment, disability, and maternity benefits – the current system imposes and high and growing strain on the state budget, encourages tax evasion and informal employment, perpetuates the dualism between insiders and outsiders, and deepens inequality.

Russia's government seeks to use social policy to serve two competing objectives: stimulating economic development while preserving a social safety net. It has had some success. The pension system has largely succeeded in preventing dire poverty among the elderly. Unemployment has stayed relatively low even during periods of recession. However, social protection is highly inefficient in that most social spending goes to categorical programmes – programmes where eligibility is determined by a social status rather than by material need – rather than being progressively scaled. For example, people in various veterans' categories or who have been recognised for special service to the state receive numerous benefits regardless of need. Mandating discounted and cost-free goods and services is a politically easy way for governments to distribute largesse to their populations without actually having to levy taxes to pay for them. As a result, Russia, like many governments that use generous discounts and subsidies on everyday goods and services, faces serious unfunded mandates in its social obligations.

One consequence of underfunded social commitments is the flourishing of black and gray markets in services such as education and health care. This means that as income inequality has grown, those who can pay for private education, health care, and the like are able to enjoy better quality services. Often this drains resources from the public sector. Therefore although the government has made some effort to bring the obligations of the social support system into line with its financial resources, the publicly funded services available to many people are of low quality. The rich, on the other hand, can turn to the marketplace to ensure that they receive good services. In this respect, Russia bears many similarities to the US, where inequality is similarly high, redistribution of income through taxes and social policy minimal, and public goods increasingly subject to being privatised.

Rising inequality

Russia's overall level of income inequality is comparable to the level in the US and China. In its level of wealth inequality, according to some estimates, Russia leads the world. As in most countries today, poverty and inequality trends in Russia tend to move independently of each other. Often inequality rises even when poverty falls, and falls when poverty rises. As in the US and China, most of the growth in income inequality in Russia is driven by the rising concentration of earnings at the upper end of the distribution, rather than by falling incomes at the bottom. Periods of economic recovery tend to increase inequality by raising high-end earnings first. When wages stagnate, income inequality tends to level off until the next period of economic growth.

The World Wealth and Income Database (WID.world) compiles and analyzes figures on the distribution of income and wealth for many countries, using a variety of sources – income tax records, household surveys, national accounts, and records of financial flows. This is the most up-to-date and statistically sophisticated set of estimates on inequality of income and wealth and has the advantage of using the same methodology for all countries covered.

Figures 11.1 and 11.2 present the most recent available WID data for income and wealth inequality in Russia, the US and China. They indicate that the three countries are quite comparable in their high levels of inequality. However, the bottom half of the income distribution in China is somewhat better off than in the other two countries (net wealth in fact is slightly negative in the US, due to the excess of liabilities over assets for this group). Russia's level of wealth concentration in the top 1% of wealth holders is higher than either the US or China, and its level of concentration of income in the top 1% is the same as that of the US.

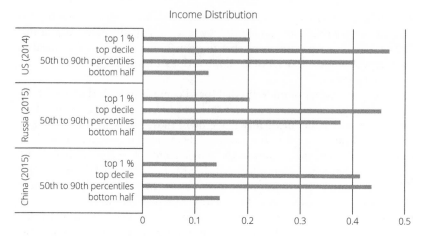

Figure 11.1 Distribution of pretax income by percentile group

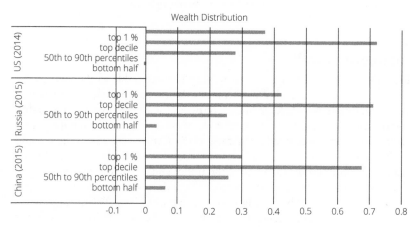

Figure 11.2 Distribution of national wealth by percentile group

Sources: Both figures created using data from WID World (https://wid.world/data) [Accessed 18 July 2018]

Other measures of inequality are available as well and provide similar results. Using household surveys, Russia's own statistical service reports two measures of total income inequality, the Gini index and the 'funds coefficient.' The Gini index is a widely used measure of the distribution of total national income across households at different income levels. If in some hypothetical economy, one household received all the income, the Gini index would be 1 (or 100%). If every household received exactly the same share of total income, the Gini index would be 0. The US has a Gini index of about 48 for pre-tax income, according to the Census Bureau; Russia's is at 41, according to the Russian Statistical Agency (Rosstat). The 'funds coefficient' measure reported by Rosstat is a ratio of the average income of those above the 90th percentile in the income distribution (that is, the richest 10% of the population) to the average income of the bottom 10%. Russia's ratio is close to 16. A similar measure, more widely used around the world, compares the income of the 90th percentile – that is the income dividing the top 10% from the bottom 90% – to the 10th percentile. (Because the 90:10 ratio compares percentiles, while the 'funds coefficient' measure reports averages for the incomes of the top and bottom deciles, the latter will be higher than the former.) In any case, the 90:10 ratio for the United States is around 12.2.

By both standards, the US is the highest in inequality in the developed capitalist world, just as Russia has the highest inequality among the former East European communist states. Of course, we should not take these figures too literally, particularly in Russia's case. One reason is that they rely on household surveys. Not only do household surveys tend to under-represent people in the highest income brackets, high-income people also have strong incentives to understate their actual incomes. In a country with a very substantial share of 'gray' – hidden – income, household surveys are likely to understate the actual level of income inequality. This is one reason that economists prefer to use data drawn from income tax records, as Emmanuel Saez, Gabriel Zucman and Thomas Piketty have done in the 'World Wealth and Income Database' project.

Based on official Russian survey figures, Figure 11.3 tracks the rise and fall of incomes, inequality, and poverty in Russia from 1995 to 2016. It shows that when growth falls, inequality tends to fall and poverty to rise. When the economy recovers, those at the high end are the first to benefit from rising wages.

Related to the concentration of wage gains at the highest end of the distribution is the stagnation of wages at the lower end. Research by Vladimir Gimpel'son at the Higher School of Economics and by Sberbank has shown

Figure 11.3 Incomes, poverty and inequality, 1995–2016

Source: Created using data from Rossat (www.gks.ru) [Accessed 18 July 2018]
Mean income figure is a multiple of the national subsistence minimum
Decile ratio is the ratio of the average income of the top decile to the average income of the bottom decile

that the share of labour in the informal sector has risen over the last decade. Estimates of the informal labour share range from around one-fifth to one-third, and observers agree that it has steadily increased (Tseplyaeva and Sonina 2014; Gimpel'son and Kapelyushnikov 2013, 2014). Wages in the informal sector are considerably lower than in the formal sector, averaging roughly 55% of formal sector wages. Since informal workers pay less than (or none of) the full share of their required contributions to the social insurance funds, the shortfall is considerable: If informal workers were to pay their full share, the Pension Fund would receive another 700 billion rubles per year (Tseplyaeva and Sonina 2014). Informal workers are therefore doubly disadvantaged: They are paid lower wages and also have lower pension entitlements upon retiring.

The most distinctive feature of the rise of economic inequality in Russia is the growing concentration of wealth. Wealth in all societies is more unequally distributed than incomes. Wealth refers to assets that can be converted into income, whether those be stock shares, real estate, or other types of assets. The Credit Suisse Bank produces an annual report on the distribution of wealth globally and within countries, based on an exhaustive examination of public records. Credit Suisse compared Russia with the rest of the world and concluded that 'inequality in Russia is so far above the others that it deserves to be placed in a separate category' (Credit Suisse Research Institute 104, p. 31). Tables 11.1a and 11.1b indicate how Russia compares with the US and China in the concentration of wealth in 2016 (Credit Suisse Global Wealth Databook 2015, p. 149):

Table 11.1a Shares of wealth owned by top strata of households, 2016

	Top decile	Top 5%	Top 1%
Russia	89	84.8	74.5
China	73.2	63.2	43.8
US	77.6	66.5	42.1

Table 11.1b Top decile's share of national wealth

	2000	2007	2014	2015	2016
Russia	77.1	75.4	84.8	87	89
China	48.6	56.1	64	66	73.2
US	75.6	74.8	74.6	76	77.6

Source: Created using data from Credit Suisse Global Wealth Databook, 2016; Credit Suisse Global Wealth Report, 2016. (https://www.credit-suisse.com/corporate/en/articles/news-and-expertise/the-global-wealth-report-2016-201611.html) [Accessed 18 July 2018]

The Credit Suisse analysts also sought to estimate the wealth holdings among the middle class, where middle class was defined in terms of wealth holding. Noting the melting away of the assets of those in the middle after the 2008 world financial crisis, the report concluded that, 'After trebling in size by 2007, Russia has lost more middle-class members since 2008 than any other country. Like Greece and Turkey, the middle class in Russia is only a little smaller now than in 2000' (Credit Suisse Research Institute 2015, p. 37). Yet in the same period, those at the top of the pyramid increased their wealth.

The reasons for the rising inequality of income and wealth are similar in some ways to those seen in the US, but different in other ways. The rents accruing to the natural resource sector enable employees in that sector – particularly upper-level managers – to enjoy very high salaries and benefits. Likewise, the financial sector, as in the US, has seen steady increases in average wages and concentration of wage gains at the top. High-ranking state officials also receive extremely high salaries, bonuses, and benefits. These sectors benefit from being able to extract rents from society (Stiglitz 2013). Those at the top of these sectors are also able to convert their income streams into off-shore financial accounts and real estate assets, which contribute nothing to national economic productivity. One consequence of the rising share of rent-extraction in the economy is the steady fall in the share of household incomes derived from entrepreneurship, which has fallen by more than half since the mid-1990s (from 16.4% in 1995 to 7.8% in 2016).

Evolution of the social welfare system

There have been four kinds of change to the social support system since the fall of the communist system: *conversion* of state services into social insurance pools; *decentralisation* of administrative and financial responsibility for many services from central to lower levels of government; *commercialisation* of services as public providers find ways to charge fees for services; and *privatisation* as assets are turned over to the marketplace.

Pension insurance

Russia began to reform its pension system even before the Soviet Union broke up. Russia's government created the Pension Fund in 1990, funding it by a 26% pension tax on the wage fund. Along with the other off-budget funds covering medical care and social insurance (disability, unemployment, maternity and so on), the Pension Fund was to operate as a social insurance fund that would alleviate the strain on the state budget of meeting current social obligations. Reforming social policy was an extremely contentious area of policy in the 1990s. Even apart from the inter-branch deadlock that paralyzed adoption of a more comprehensive pension reform, actual benefits suffered from high inflation, the implosion of the state's capacity to deliver benefits, and high and mounting pension arrears (Cook 2007; Chandler 2004).

With his majority of support in parliament following the December 1999 Duma election and convincing victory in the 2000 presidential election, Vladimir Putin had the leverage to enact the reforms that Yeltsin's advisors had proposed. In addition to adopting the mandatory defined-contributions system with individual accounts, the new plan lowered payroll tax rates. At the same time Putin replaced the progressive income tax with a flat 13% rate and lowered profits tax levels. Benefiting from rising global oil prices also enabled the Putin government to increase state spending on health care, education, and infrastructure. Over the decade, real wages more than tripled but pension benefits in real terms rose even faster, reaching about 35% of the average wage by 2010. Poverty among pensioners fell significantly, and overall mortality rates declined.

By the end of the first decade of the 2000s, however, the unsustainability of the pension system became apparent. The deficit in Pension Fund was rising. The continuing tug of war between the pro-growth and pro-social spending wings of the government resulted in a constant flux in the level of payroll taxes and structure of benefits. The base payroll tax rate was changed from 35.6% in 2000, to 26% in 2005, 34% in 2011, and 30% as of 2012.

Because the pension insurance system runs a deficit, the government began in 2013 diverting contributions made to the mandatory insurance contributions into the social insurance fund and subsidising pension insurance through large transfers from the budget. In effect, the system is still funded on a pay-as-you-go (PAYG) basis. Almost half the budget of the Pension Fund consists of direct transfers from the federal budget (Pensionnyi fond 2012). Former Russian Finance Minister Aleksei Kudrin flatly calls the current pension system a pyramid scheme: each generation is paying more in taxes than the previous generation, and getting more than it paid in (Kuvshinova 2012). The 'social bloc' of the government – i.e. the coalition of labour and social welfare ministries that tend to support more redistributive social policies – has staunchly opposed using a private pension savings system. It has argued that investing individual retirement savings in the financial market shifts the burden of risk onto individual pensioners, and that the state has an obligation to provide a secure old-age income through a PAYG system backed by the state budget. The 'liberal bloc' of the government (the ministries concerned with stimulating economic growth) responds that the state simply cannot afford to finance the pension system out of current pension contributions and budget transfers. Such a system, the liberal bloc argues, will leave pension benefits grossly inadequate to maintain an adequate stream of income for pensioners given the aging of the population and the shrinking share of working-age people in the population.

The basic problem is that the three-tier pension system was built on top of the old Soviet model that was based on state control over labour and capital. That system could offer generous pension benefits to all state employees because wages were low and budget constraints soft. Unlike many other benefits, wages and pensions were paid in cash, but because of pervasive shortages, cash could only make limited claims on goods and services. When the economy was put on a market footing, and budget constraints hardened, the government needed to finance its social spending obligations through new taxes that required substantial administrative capacity to collect. Wages became an important regulator of the labour market, so employers wanted to raise wages but minimise the taxes paid on the wage fund. Employees had little trust in the system and often preferred to receive the full amount of wages in cash. Of course, many workers, especially in the informal sector, had no choice in the matter. Tax evasion and labour market dualism followed. Meantime Russia's financial markets are shallow, volatile, and inefficient.

They are prone to regular crises, so cannot guarantee a steady long-term return. Russia in effect is stuck between an unsustainable Soviet-era socialist model and an immature market-based model of retirement insurance.

If Social Security reform is the 'third rail' of American politics – in the sense that it is dangerous for elected politicians to try to put the system on a more sustainable footing – it is equally so in Russia. For example, Russia (at the time of writing) still allows women to retire at 55 and men at 60 and begin collecting pension benefits. These ages were set in 1932 under Stalin, when life expectancy was far shorter (not even taking into account the effect of mass terror). Yet the issue of raising the pension age is highly sensitive, and the Putin regime has been reluctant to embrace the idea. The aging of the population means that the pension-age population is increasing both in absolute and relative terms. In Russia, the labour force has been shrinking since the mid-2000s, and more and more people are both receiving pensions and employed – over half of women between the ages of 55 and 59 are employed, as are 29% of men between 60 and 72. Pension benefits are too low in most cases to cover living expenses, so combining a pension and a salary is increasingly common. This is particularly true in the low-paying public sector (teachers, health care providers, and scientific workers). In the private sector, employers are quicker to cut pay for older workers. They often do this by cutting bonuses, which often make up one-third or more of monthly earnings (Lomskaya 2017).

Starting in 2015, the government replaced the 'defined benefits' pension scheme with a points system. A pensioner's benefits would depend on the number of points he or she had accumulated, using a complex formula that included the number of years worked, the amount contributed, and the financial situation of the Pension Fund as of the time of retirement. As a result, it is very difficult for pensioners to calculate how much exactly they will receive in retirement. The problem is compounded by the pension reform of September 2018, raising the pension age of men to 65 and women to 60, adopted after considerable controversy and Putin's personal intervention to modify the government's original proposals announced in June.

Inefficient and regressive taxation

Russia's tax system complicates its ability to implement redistributive social policy. The payroll tax (i.e. the mandatory wage-based contributions to pension, health, disability, and unemployment insurance) rate is relatively high, but is capped at a relatively low ceiling. This imposes a proportionately greater tax burden on low- and middle-income individuals in the formal sector. Income tax revenues are not a large share of state revenues; consumption taxes including the VAT form are a much larger part of total revenues. The individual income tax yields only about 21% in Russia (compared to over 40% of federal revenues in the US), and in any case it is principally a source of revenue for provincial governments rather than the federal government (Russian State Tax Service). The income tax rate is a flat 13%. The payroll tax, as noted, was lowered to 30% in 2012, with a 10% surtax for incomes above 512,000 rubles a year (about $17,000). About half the federal budget revenues come from various mineral resource-related taxes, meaning that the government is highly vulnerable to fluctuations in the world price of energy (Strategiya-2020, pp. 144–45). The relatively low thresholds on payroll taxes mean that high-end earners pay a much lower share of their total earnings into the social insurance system, while informal labour is not paying in at all. This fact imposes a substantial burden on middle-income earners in the formal sector, and on state enterprises, where compliance with payroll taxes tends to be higher.

Wages and poverty

Although the average wage throughout the economy is 36,700 rubles per month – about $611 – a large segment of the labour force receive wages at or below the poverty line. Currently, the poverty line for a working-age person is 10,524 rubles per month ($175), and some 5 million people, or about 7% of the workforce, are earning wages at that level. Wages for many more people are only slightly above the poverty line, so if prices go up faster than wages, and the government-set poverty line is not adjusted, real poverty goes up whereas the official estimate of poverty declines ('Snizhenie' 2017). Officially, 13.3% of the population receives an income below the subsistence minimum. In the US, a person working full-time at the federal minimum wage would receive an annual income of $15,080, well below what a household with one dependant would need to live above the poverty line. In both countries, incomes at the low end of the distribution are very low: in the US, the bottom quintile of the population receives about 3.1% of total income; in Russia, the figure is 5.3%. In both countries, by the same token, high-end incomes are very high. Moreover, there is reason to suspect that the official figures on high-end incomes understate the actual extent of income concentration.

Many of the poor, both employed and not, qualify for social assistance and social benefits that have the effect of reducing poverty and inequality. However, neither taxation nor social policies have much of a redistributive effect. Nearly all of the inequality generated in the labour market is carried over into the post-tax and transfer distribution of income.

Fiscal burden-shifting

Related to the inefficient and regressive structure of the tax system in Russia is the effort by the central government to shift the fiscal burden for social welfare. Once market reforms began, Russia moved to decentralise much of the responsibility for administering and financing social benefits to sub-national governments. It also privatised some formerly state-funded benefits, particularly housing. Decentralisation, commercialisation, and privatisation have had a number of undesirable consequences. Regional governments have resorted to illegal or informal schemes to meet their budget responsibilities. In many cases local governments have colluded with local enterprises in winking at non-payment of taxes, or resorted to revenue-raising schemes not authorised by the central government.

Creeping commercialisation

As Russia has rebalanced public and private financing for other formerly state-funded services, such as transportation, housing, medications, education, and health care, elements of commercialisation have gradually spread into nominally free state services, a tendency Vladimir Putin has termed 'creeping forced commercialisation' (*raspolzanie prinuditel'noi platnosti*) (Putin 2012). Commercial elements have crept into the education and health care systems, opening the door for semi-legal ways for providers to charge fees for services. Both have attempted to privatise in whole or in part other formerly free public services as well.

In the sphere of education, while most education continues to be state funded, opportunities for the establishment of private schools have opened up, particularly in the tertiary sphere. In Russia, the number of students enrolled in institutions of higher education has almost doubled in the 2000s, almost all of them private tuition-paying students (Strategiya-2020, pp. 250–51). State schools now often levy fees for formerly free services, such as supplementary classes to prepare pupils for the university entrance exams. Almost half the families whose children are enrolled in extra-curricular programmes in public schools must pay extra fees (Strategiya-2020, p. 278). Three-fourths of families also have to pay for textbooks (Shishkin and Popovich 2009). The introduction of private fees into public education has had some undesirable consequences, among them an increase in corruption among school instructors and administrators and an increase in inequality of access to education. Education is not reducing inequality. Income inequality as a function of differences in levels of education is declining, while inequality among individuals with the same level of education is rising (Strategiya-2020, p. 323).

Similarly, private fee-for-service provision of medical services has supplemented funding through the mandatory health insurance system, again resulting in corruption and inequality of access. About 40% of spending on medical care is out of pocket (Shishkin and Popovich 2009, pp. 7–10). This private spending pays for medications, private insurance, and gratuities to providers. This is consistent with the estimate in the Strategy-2020 report that in Russia, as of 2009–10, state health care spending accounted for 3.2% of GDP, private spending another 2.1% (Strategiya-2020, p. 401).

Income inequality and access to social services

These processes – conversion, decentralisation, commercialisation, and privatisation of formerly state-provided benefits – under the conditions of growing economic inequality mean that there is growing inequality in access to what had formerly been public goods. The rich can enjoy the benefits of good private education, private health care, retirement income and housing, while the poor depend on low-quality public services. The same holds for differences between poor and rich regions. The cumulative effect is to compound advantages for those well-off enough to benefit from access to better services. And as in the United States, the entrenchment of privilege also increases the ability of the rich and powerful to block moves towards more redistributive taxation or spending or towards broader pooling of risks and benefits. For example, whenever Russian reformers propose to make the personal income tax progressive – i.e. individuals earning higher incomes would pay a higher rate – or to impose a surtax on luxury goods, the proposal is defeated on the grounds that the effect would be counter-productive: the tax authorities would be unable to administer it due to massive tax evasion. In a society where there is an ever-higher concentration of wealth and income in the highest strata, those selling goods and services to the ultra-rich do very well.

Russian leaders have expressed concern about the socially destabilis-ing implications of high inequality. Putin characterised the current level of income inequality in Russia as 'unacceptable, outrageously high' in a pre-election article in February 2012, and repeated the point in a speech to the State Council in July 2012 (Putin 2012). A report by the Higher School of Economics in 2011 concluded that 'the principal issue for the Russian econ-omy and society is the current level of inequality.... High level of inequality, the more increasing, can be the source of distrust in society, and therefore a threat to the stability [sic]' (Andrushchak 2011, p. 72). The Strategy-2020 report argues that inequality's growth is creating growing social dissatisfac-tion and blocking upward mobility. Rather than expanding in size, it claims, the middle class has grown richer (Strategiya-2020, p. 317).

The principal policy response has focused on raising incomes at the bot-tom rather than increasing redistribution. Putin has focused on reducing poverty and increasing income security, raising pension levels, and improv-ing pay for public sector employees. His government has also taken steps to redistribute resources from the shrinking number of rich regions to the growing number of poor regions. Many regions run budget deficits, count-ing on federal budget credits and subsidies for basic operating expenses. The federal government tries to rein in their spending and encourage them to raise their own revenues but is fearful of the social consequences of overly drastic cuts. Some regions depend for 80% and more of their budgets on federal transfers.

Reformers often point out that, as a legacy of the Soviet welfare system, most spending on social benefits is categorical rather than targeted to the most needy. That is, people qualify for assistance based on the fact that their eligibility is based on belonging to some particular designated category, such as war veteran, having a disability, or being a victim of Stalin-era political repression. Very little of social spending (even excluding pension benefits, which are also categorical) explicitly targets the needy. As a result, three-quarters of all social payments go to people who are not needy (Kudrin and Sokolov, p. 23). Social policy therefore is not particularly redistributive.

The challenge of policy reform

Throughout the world, reforming social policy is politically contentious. This is as true of democracies and dictatorships, developed and developing states, communist and post-communist states. Exacerbating the redistribu-tive conflict inherent in choosing how much to balance social and private provision of social services are the forces of globalisation, population aging, and slowing economic growth.

Authoritarian regimes are generally no more effective at reaching solutions to these problems than are democratic regimes, and usually are less effective. Democracies rely on a wider social pooling of risk and reward from economic growth through bargaining across parties, employer associations and labour unions. In contrast, social policy choices are made in Russia through a process of bargaining and deliberation within the government. Policy-makers recognise that too radical a move towards reducing benefits could result in widespread popular protest. Alternatively, too drastic an increase in tax rates is likely to result in large-scale non-compliance and labour force dualism. These constraints tend to make policy more incremental than might be expected in an authoritarian regime. More far-reaching policy reforms tend to be implemented gradually.

Currently the liberal wing of Russia's policy community is proposing another plan for pension reform. Under the new scheme – called 'Individual Pension Capital' – employers would automatically enroll employees in individual retirement savings plans. An individual would be allowed to opt out of the system. By default, an individual's contributions would start at 0% of earnings in the first year, then rise 1% per year until reaching 6% per year. The funds would be managed by a central administrator and placed in a private pension savings plan that the employee could choose. The contribution would come out of the employee's pay rather than from the enterprise's funds. The objective would be to rebuild the country's private pension fund assets, which could then be used both for long-term infrastructure development projects yielding a steady higher-than-inflation return. This would supplement the basic state-funded, PAYG pension insurance system. Whether the government ultimately adopts this plan or not, the government will be forced to make some other painful choices that include raising the age of eligibility for pensions, and possibly reducing benefits, and ending early retirement. These are inevitable because the size of the working age population is shrinking relative to the pension-age population, and because economic growth is close to zero. Whether the government can take these steps without provoking major social unrest remains to be seen.

In Russia's bureaucratic authoritarian regime, policy-making on these major social issues takes place within the bureaucracy rather than in parliament or at a corporatist roundtable. To some extent the process does accommodate the interests of organised interests (big business has a voice, labour almost not at all), but broader latent interests in society generally lack the institutional resources to pool their demands and influence policy-making. Since business and labour have not had to bargain with one another, they have not had to acquire the capacity to seek mutually acceptable solutions to thorny redistributive problems. Studies of advanced Western democracies suggest that the capacity of business to unite around common interests is greater in settings where organised labour's bargaining power is greater. The ability of peak associations to constrain their own members and enforce agreements depends in part on the strength of their opponents in the bargaining arena. Where business and labour featured higher levels of centralisation, they were also able reach agreements that alleviated redistributive conflict, for example by coordinating investment in human capital formation. This helps account for the lower levels of income inequality observed in coordinated market economies compared with liberal market economies (Iversen and Soskice 2006).

The Russian system of social welfare exhibits a level of inequality in access to social services and public goods characteristic of liberal market economies such as the US, but its levels of social insurance contributions are similar to those of social democratic welfare states. I have argued that this reflects the enduring influence of institutional deficits inherited from the Soviet social contract. Greater associational capacity on the part of business, labour and other broad social sectors would enable the state to alleviate some of the conflict between growth and redistribution by raising the productivity of labour and investing in skill formation. Businesses and workers would be more willing to report the full value of their wages and pay their full tax bill if they believe that the state is providing public goods such as order, contract enforcement, political stability, and efficient administration. Strong institutions for consultation and coordination between the state, business, and labour would help overcome many of these dilemmas.

A transitional state where administrative control has been weakened, whether by decentralisation or the loss of traditional centralised monitoring mechanisms, faces a trade-off between distributional equality and autonomy for firms and social organisations. Russia has given firms a great deal of autonomy to pursue their economic strategies, but has relinquished much of its power to supply public goods and services impartially, let alone to carry out a redistributive policy. Expanding the participatory arena for business and labour, and eventually for competitive political parties, would be one way to recapture control over the broader environment of economic reform. Russia has a well-articulated system of business associations, but they are not forced to deal with labour or other organised interests as equals. Moreover, Russia's growth rate has slowed to a crawl, and the natural resources which fuel much of its development are unequally distributed across its vast territory.

Institutional arrangements inherited from the communist era have hampered the state's capacity to achieve its larger strategic objectives. Some core features of the old welfare regime have continued to exert their influence long after the state had sought to place the system of social benefits on a sound and market-based financial foundation. Society lacks the institutional means to influence social policy and the absence of mutual coordination by business and labour over the distribution of the costs and benefits of economic growth. The result is a sub-optimal level of social investment in human capital formation and the increase of economic inequality across social groups, regions and generations.

12 RUSSIAN FOREIGN POLICY

Valentina Feklyunina

Russian foreign policy has undergone tremendous transformation over the post-Soviet period. While Moscow initially sought closer cooperation with its former Cold War enemies, especially with the US, a quarter of the century later Russia's relationship with the West has dramatically deteriorated, with a large number of analysts on both sides describing the tensions as a new Cold War. To understand this major change, this chapter will begin by examining how Russian foreign policy works. It will then proceed to look at how Russia's understandings of the international environment and of its foreign policy priorities have evolved since 1991. The third part will focus on major shifts in Russia's foreign policy. The chapter will then discuss Russia's dilemmas in its relations with key international actors. Finally, the chapter will conclude by considering possible explanations of change and continuity in Russia's foreign policy.

The making of Russian foreign policy

Similar to other areas of Russian politics, Russian foreign policy is overwhelmingly dominated by the president. According to Article 80 of the Constitution, the president shall 'determine the basic objectives' of Russian foreign policy, and 'as the Head of State, shall represent the Russian Federation within the country and in international relations'. Article 86 further clarifies that the president 'shall hold negotiations and sign international treaties', 'sign instruments of ratification' and 'receive letters of credence and letters of recall of diplomatic representatives accredited to his (her) office'.

While the role of the president is exceptionally important, a number of other bodies are also involved in foreign policy-making. The Foreign Policy Department of the Presidential Administration assists the president in both developing a foreign policy strategy and overseeing its implementation. Another important body is the Security Council of the Russian Federation. Its responsibilities include 'formulat[ing] the State's foreign and military policy guidelines, and forecast[ing], identif[ying], analys[ing] and assess[ing] threats to Russia's national security' (Foreign Policy Concept 2016). The Security Council is headed by the president, who also appoints its members. Since the constitution does not prescribe the details of the membership, it is up to the president to decide who should be there at any particular time. During Putin's third presidential term, the role of the secretary of the Security Council was performed by Putin's long-standing ally Nikolai

Patrushev, while the permanent members included the head of the Presidential Administration, the prime minister, the defence minister, the foreign affairs minister, the internal affairs minister, the chairmen of both chambers of the Parliament, the head of the FSB (Federal Security Service), the head of the Foreign Intelligence Service, and the presidential envoy for environment and transport (another Putin long-standing ally, Sergei Ivanov).

The role of the Parliament in both developing a foreign policy strategy and overseeing its implementation is fairly limited. According to the constitution, both chambers of the Parliament shall pass legislation on ratification and denunciation of international treaties, and on war and peace (Article 106). Moreover, the Federation Council has the power of 'deciding on the possibility of using the Armed Forces of the Russian Federation outside the territory of the Russian Federation' (Article 102). Yet, these formal powers have been increasingly limited by President Putin's dominance in Russia's political system. During Boris Yeltsin's presidency in the 1990s, the Duma often challenged the president, including in matters of foreign policy. For example, Yeltsin struggled to secure the ratification by the Duma of the START II (Strategic Arms Reduction Treaty). Signed by President Yeltsin and US President Bush in 1993, the treaty was finally ratified by the Duma only in 2000. Such challenges became impossible during Putin's presidency. Indeed, when Putin asked the Federation Council to authorise the deployment of Russian troops abroad in March 2014, he received unanimous support.

The implementation of Russian foreign policy is the remit of the Ministry of Foreign Affairs. In the 1990s, Russian foreign ministers played an important role in shaping Russia's foreign policy. Foreign Minister Andrei Kozyrev, who headed the Ministry in the early 1990s, for example, was an ardent advocate of a pro-Western policy. Yevgeny Primakov, who headed the Ministry in 1996–98, on the other hand, was instrumental in shifting Moscow's behaviour towards closer relations with China and India and a more proactive foreign policy in the post-Soviet area. During Putin's era, Russian foreign ministers became noticeably less independent, with the role of the Ministry largely confined to implementing the decisions taken elsewhere. The president's dominance is further reinforced by the fact that the Ministry of Foreign Affairs alongside other 'power' ministries is accountable to the president rather than to the prime minister. Another body that is directly involved in foreign policy implementation and which operates under the jurisdiction of the Foreign Ministry is the Federal Agency for the Commonwealth of Independent States, Compatriots Living Abroad, and International Cultural Cooperation (also known as Rossotrudnichestvo). Established in 2008, it focuses on Russia's humanitarian cooperation with other states, with a particular focus on the post-Soviet area. Rossotrudnichestvo is primarily tasked with enhancing Russia's soft power by strengthening Russia's influence among ethnic Russians and Russian speakers beyond Russia's borders.

While all these bodies either assist the president in his decision-making or are responsible for the implementation of the president's directions, President Putin is unquestionably the sole decision-maker in matters of foreign policy (Trenin 2015: 34).

Russia's foreign policy priorities

Russia's foreign policy priorities have been shaped by its changing understandings of the international environment and of its position. We can trace these changes by examining Russia's key foreign policy documents, such as official 'Foreign Policy Concepts', and major statements by the Russian presidents. Over the post-Soviet period, Russia adopted five 'Foreign Policy Concepts' – in 1993, 2000, 2008, 2013 and 2016.

Following the Soviet Union's collapse, Russian political elites and citizens struggled to adjust to the dramatic change in Russia's international position. The USSR had been one of two most powerful states, and the Russian Empire before that had played a major role in European politics. This legacy of greatness, or as some refer to it, of great power-ness, made it exceptionally difficult for most Russians to come to terms with Russia's diminished international status. Another factor that contributed to this difficulty was the ambiguity of Russia's international position in the 1990s. On the one hand, Russia possessed some formal attributes of a great power. It inherited the Soviet Union's seat as a permanent member of the United Nations (UN) Security Council, and, following several years of negotiations with newly independent Belarus, Ukraine and Kazakhstan, kept the Soviet Union's nuclear arsenal. On the other hand, as a result of the Soviet Union's break-up, the Russian state became significantly smaller in terms of its territory and population. The economic turmoil of the 1990s also significantly reduced Russia's capabilities and undermined Moscow's status. These dramatic changes led to an acute identity crisis.

This ambiguity was evident in Russia's first post-Soviet 'Foreign Policy Concept', which was signed by President Yeltsin in April 1993 (Kontseptsiya vneshnei politiki 1993). On the one hand, the document reaffirmed Russia's pro-Western foreign policy. In particular, it stressed the need to develop a closer relationship with the US with an aim of building a 'strategic partnership'. On the other hand, it expressed concerns that Washington could start acting as 'the only super-power' and that it could attempt to squeeze Russia out of the area of its 'traditional influence'. The 1993 Concept emphasised that one of Russia's key foreign policy priorities was to ensure that its international role was appropriate for its great power status (ibid).

The pro-Western focus of Russian foreign policy did not last long. Already by the mid-1990s Russia was increasingly critical of what it saw as Western expansionism. A particularly important turning point was a bitter disagreement between Moscow and the North Atlantic Treaty Organisation (NATO) over the conflict in former Yugoslavia. NATO bombing of Serbia in 1999 despite Moscow's attempts to prevent a military intervention was exceptionally painful for Russia. It demonstrated that NATO, and the US in particular, were willing to disregard Russia's views. Given that Serbia had been Russia's traditional ally, Moscow's inability to prevent the NATO bombing underscored Russia's diminished international status. Additionally, since the mid-1990s Russia was increasingly criticised by Western states for its handling of the conflict in Chechnya. Thus, the hopes of the early 1990s for Russia's closer cooperation with the West were increasingly replaced with mutual disappointment.

This major change was reflected in the second 'Foreign Policy Concept', which was approved by Putin in July 2000 (Kontseptsiya vneshnei politiki 2000). The document acknowledged that Russia's aspirations to establish equal and mutually beneficial relations with the West had not materialised. On the contrary, Russia faced increasingly serious challenges in its relations with the West, especially with the US and NATO. The document was critical of NATO eastern enlargement, and it was suspicious of Washington's intentions to withdraw from the 1972 Anti-Ballistic Missile Treaty (ABM Treaty) – an arms control treaty between the USSR and the US. In Moscow's eyes, this treaty was 'a cornerstone of strategic stability' because it limited Russia's and US's defences against each other's nuclear weapons. Russian policy-makers feared that Washington's withdrawal would allow the US to build an anti-missile defence that would make it practically invincible. This, Moscow feared, would undermine the existing nuclear parity. The 'Concept' expressed Russia's concerns about an emerging unipolarity – an international order dominated by the US (Kontseptsiya vneshnei politiki 2000).

Thus, compared to the early 1990s, Russia was noticeably unhappy with the way in which the international environment was changing, and it was dissatisfied with its position. Apprehensive of the emerging unipolarity, Russia declared its intention to 'seek the formation of a multipolar international system', and it repeatedly emphasised the importance of sovereignty and the central role of the UN. The 2000 'Concept' reiterated Russia's insistence on 'equality' in its relations with other states and organisations. It also reiterated that Russia was seeking an international position that was appropriate for its great power status. Russia's regional priorities, according to the document, included developing closer relations with members of the Commonwealth of Independent States (CIS). Russia was also interested in deepening its cooperation with European states and with the European Union, which the 'Concept' described as one of Russia's 'most important political and economic partners'. The relationship with the US, on the other hand, moved down the list of Russia's priorities. Yet, even though the document acknowledged some 'fundamental' disagreements between Moscow and Washington, it nevertheless emphasised the importance of cooperation with the US (Kontseptsiya vneshnei politiki 2000).

During the first years of Putin's presidency, Moscow's bitter disappointment with the West gave way to some renewed hopes that Russia could build an equal relationship with the US. Russia expressed its unreserved support of Washington in the wake of 9/11 and provided assistance to the NATO campaign in Afghanistan. Yet, Moscow's hopes that its contribution to the 'war on terror' would be rewarded with a recognition of its equal status proved short-lived. In Moscow's eyes, the West continued to ignore its concerns. Russia was critical of the 2003 invasion of Iraq by the US-led coalition. It was also increasingly suspicious of the continuing NATO enlargement, of Washington's plans to build an anti-missile defence system, and of the US's and the EU's democracy promotion in the former USSR. As seen from Moscow, the Western support of the Orange Revolution in Ukraine in 2004–05 in particular indicated that the West aimed to diminish Russia's influence. As interpreted by Moscow, it also indicated that the West could potentially support a pro-democracy movement in Russia.

These suspicions, coupled with the growth of authoritarianism in Russia, contributed to Moscow's increasingly critical stance towards the West. Putin's speech at the Security Conference in Munich in February 2007 summarised Russia's grievances. It contained a scathing critique of Washington's attempts to build a unipolar international order and accused the US of making the world more dangerous by undermining international law. Putin described NATO enlargement as 'a serious provocation that reduces the level of mutual trust'. Putin accused the US and NATO of violating their own promises regarding NATO enlargement that had been given to the Soviet leadership. He also argued that 'the fall of the Berlin Wall was possible thanks to a historic choice (…) that was also made by (…) the people of Russia' (Putin 2007). Putin's words struck a chord with many members of the Russian political elite who believed that Russia was humiliated by a triumphalist West instead of being treated as an equal partner.

By the end of Putin's second presidential term, Russia became not only increasingly critical of the West, but also more confident about its ability to pursue a more assertive foreign policy. Following nearly a decade of impressive economic growth, Russia recovered much of its international strength. The new 'Foreign Policy Concept', adopted in January 2008, repeatedly underscored Russia's 'increased role (…) in international affairs' (Foreign Policy Concept 2008). This emphasis on Russia's growing strength, as opposed to the weakness of the 1990s, remained central to Russia's vision of itself even despite several serious crises that hit Russia's economy in subsequent years. At the same time, in Russia's eyes, the global financial crisis of 2007–08 demonstrated that power was shifting away from the West towards the Asia-Pacific (Foreign Policy Concept 2013). As Russia's relations with the West experienced major tensions – starting from the 2008 Russian-Georgian war to bitter disagreements about the Arab spring – Moscow began to prioritise its relationship with China, as well as to pursue more active participation in various non-Western multi-lateral fora and organisations, including the Shanghai Cooperation Organisation (SCO) and the BRICS (Brazil, Russia, India, China and South Africa).

During Dmitry Medvedev's presidency in 2008–12, Moscow's understandings of Russia's priorities appeared to shift towards a more constructive relationship with the West. Medvedev's agenda, as he formulated it in his newspaper article 'Go Russia!', focused on modernising Russia's economy. In Medvedev's view, this task could be facilitated through Russia's closer cooperation with technologically advanced states (Medvedev 2009). Although during Medvedev's presidency Moscow was noticeably more open towards engaging with the EU and the US, Medvedev predictably struggled to implement his security agenda. In particular, he failed in his attempts to persuade NATO members to develop a new security mechanism that would make Russia an equal partner. Moscow's disappointment with this short, mildly pro-Western experiment in Russia's foreign policy was further reinforced in 2011–12 when Russia witnessed a wave of public protests unprecedented for the post-Soviet period. The protests fed into the Kremlin's fears of another Orange Revolution supported by the West. Moscow responded by cracking down on the protests and by adopting an openly anti-Western stance.

Following Putin's 2012 re-election, Moscow's understanding of Russia's foreign policy priorities was increasingly affected by Putin's domestic agenda of mobilising the electorate in order to strengthen the regime. While previously Putin had distanced himself from any explicit ideological programme, since 2012 he openly resorted to socially conservative rhetoric in his vision of Russia and its place in the world. This understanding underscored Russia's civilisational distinctness from the West, and praised Russia's spirituality and moral integrity based on its continuing adherence to Christian values. In his appeal to nationalist sentiments, Putin articulated a romantic vision of a 'Russian world' – a multi-national civilisational space that extended beyond Russia's borders and that was united by the Russian language, culture and common history. While the idea of a 'Russia world' was certainly not new, it became particularly prominent in Moscow's vision of Russia and of its neighbourhood in the run up to the crisis in and around Ukraine.

Russia's annexation of Crimea in March 2014 and its covert involvement in the conflict in eastern Ukraine was accompanied by a further rise in Moscow's nationalist and anti-Western rhetoric. In his major speech devoted to Crimea on 18 March, Putin accused the West of continuing attempts to contain Russia 'because we have an independent position, because we maintain it and because we call things like they are and do not engage in hypocrisy'. He proceeded to blame the West for provoking the conflict. To quote Putin, 'with Ukraine, our western partners have crossed the line, playing the bear and acting irresponsibly and unprofessionally' (Putin 2014). While Russia's annexation of Crimea and its support of separatists in eastern Ukraine triggered an unprecedented, for the post-Soviet period, diplomatic crisis, Moscow successfully employed an escalating anti-Western rhetoric to mobilise the Russian electorate.

Putin's third presidential term saw the publication of two 'Foreign Policy Concepts' – in 2013 and 2016 respectively – that reiterated Russia's long-lasting concerns about NATO enlargement and Washington's anti-missile defence. They also reiterated Moscow's negative attitude towards any form of humanitarian intervention. According to the 2016 'Concept', Russia will aim 'to prevent military interventions or other forms of outside interference contrary to international law, specifically the principle of sovereign equality of States, under the pretext of implementing the "responsibility to protect" concept' (Foreign Policy Concept 2016). In particular, Moscow was deeply critical of Western intervention in the Middle East. In Moscow's eyes, Russia's intervention in Syria, which began in September 2015, was fundamentally different as Russian troops entered the conflict at the request of the Syrian government. Russia's campaign in Syria represented a major turning point in Moscow's vision of Russia's foreign policy priorities. As Russia's first military campaign outside its immediate neighbourhood, it signalled that Russia was no longer satisfied with being a regional power but that it had more far-reaching international ambitions.

At the end of Putin's third presidential term, Russia's understanding of its international position centred on the idea of strength. As seen from Moscow, this strength had been demonstrated by Russia's ability to 'return' Crimea and by its projection of military power in Syria. In a major speech only two weeks before the 2018 presidential elections, Putin praised Russia's scientists for what he described as a major breakthrough in military technology, particularly in nuclear weapons. To quote Putin (2018), 'no other country has developed anything like this'. According to Putin, Russia's newly developed weapons would allow Russia to penetrate any anti-missile defence, including Washington's. Putin's words signalled a radical transformation of Moscow's understanding of its international position, as compared to the early 1990s. They signalled Russia's confidence that it had successfully reclaimed a great power status, and that its voice would no longer be ignored by the West. In Putin's words, 'nobody really wanted to talk to us about the core of the problem, and nobody wanted to listen to us. So listen now' (Putin 2018).

Russian foreign policy: from integration to confrontation with the West

Moscow's evolving understandings of the international environment shaped Russia's international behaviour. At the same time, profound changes in Russia's capabilities allowed Moscow to pursue an increasingly independent and assertive foreign policy. While at times Russia oscillated between seeking closer cooperation with Western states and organisations, competing against them and challenging them, we can identify four distinct phases in Russia's foreign policy when a particular pattern of engagement was dominant:

1. Seeking integration with the West, 1991–95;

2. Balancing the West, 1996–99;

3. Competing with the West, 2000–12;

4. Challenging the West, since 2012.

Although this periodisation emphasises Russia's relationship with the West, it does not suggest that Russia's relations with other actors were not important. On the contrary, as the chapter will demonstrate, at certain points Moscow prioritised its policy in the post-Soviet area or towards China. However, even at times of Russia's confrontation with the West and its rejection of Western development as a suitable example for Russia, Russia continued to use the West as a reference point in its understandings of identity and foreign policy priorities. With this in mind, let us examine these phases in more detail.

Seeking integration with the West, 1991–95

Following the dissolution of the USSR, Yeltsin's Russia initially pursued an openly pro-Western foreign policy. Although Russia's first 'Foreign Policy Concept' prioritised Russia's relations with its neighbours in the newly established Commonwealth of Independent States, Moscow did not invest any significant effort or resources to transform the CIS into a viable regional organisation. As mentioned earlier, Russia's Foreign Ministry at the time was led by Andrei Kozyrev, who was an ardent advocate of an Atlanticist agenda, i.e. of prioritising closer relations with the US.

Hoping that the West would assist Russia in its transformation into a market economy, Moscow sought to join Western economic and political organisations. In 1993 Russia submitted an application to join the General Agreement on Tariffs and Trade (GATT) – the predecessor of the World Trade Organisation (WTO). It also sought to become a member of the Group of Seven (G7) – a prestigious political and economic forum of the advanced economies. In the European direction, Russia sought membership in the Council of Europe, which it finally achieved in February 1996. Russia even appeared to entertain a hope that it could potentially become a NATO member. As Yeltsin wrote in a letter to NATO in December 1991, Moscow 'wish[ed] to develop [a] dialogue in each and every direction, both on the political and military levels', and it was 'raising a question of Russia's membership in NATO, however regarding it as a long-term political aim' (Friedman 1991).

Russia's somewhat romantic Atlanticism began to wane already in the early 1990s. Western financial assistance to support Russia's economic reforms was far below Moscow's expectations, and was certainly incomparable to the Marshall Plan that had prevented an economic collapse in the post-World War II Europe. On the contrary, Russia was increasingly burdened with international debt. The rising poverty and inequality that accompanied Russia's 'shock therapy' approach to the economic transformation emboldened critics of the pro-Western foreign policy. Yeltsin's domestic opponents, particularly communists and nationalists, accused the government of abandoning Russia's interests and of accepting a subordinate position towards the West. In their view, this was incompatible with Russia's great-power identity. By the mid-1990s, even supporters of the pro-Western policy were increasingly disillusioned with Russia's attempts to develop an equal and mutually beneficial partnership with the West. As Foreign Minister Kozyrev wrote in 1994, the 'partnership between Russia and the United States faces problems or fails altogether in some areas' (Kozyrev 1994).

Balancing the West, 1996–99

Russia's growing disappointment with its subordinate position led to a noticeable shift in its foreign policy which became particularly apparent with the appointment of Yevgeny Primakov as Russia's new foreign minister in January 1996. As Russia's current Foreign Minister Sergei Lavrov described it, 'the moment he took over, the Russian Foreign Ministry heralded a dramatic turn of Russia's foreign policy. Russia left the path our western partners had tried to make it follow after the breakup of the Soviet Union and embarked on a track of its own' (TASS 2014). Primakov rejected the prioritisation of Russia's relationship with the West. Instead he attempted to strengthen Russia's international position through reinvigorating Russia's engagement with the CIS members, pursuing a more active policy in the Middle East and seeking closer cooperation with India and China. In particular, Primakov viewed a Russia-India-China triangle as a counterbalance to Washington and as a building block of a multi-polar international order as opposed to a unipolar order dominated by the US.

This shift in Russian foreign policy was supported by many in Russia as it was consistent with the dominant great-power identity. Primakov's criticism of NATO enlargement and his opposition to NATO intervention in former Yugoslavia also struck a chord with many in Russian society. However, Russia's attempts to counterbalance the US were hampered by its continuing economic problems and diminished military power. The 1998 partial default of the Russian currency, when Russia postponed payments to its international creditors, demonstrated a wide gap between Russia's great-power ambitions and its capabilities. As discussed, Moscow's inability to prevent the NATO bombing of Serbia in 1999 also underscored Russia's weakness and strengthened anti-American and anti-Western attitudes in the country.

Despite Moscow's attempts to counterbalance Washington and despite the growth of anti-Western sentiments, Russian foreign policy in the late 1990s was not inherently anti-Western. While seeking to build closer ties with non-Western actors, Moscow nevertheless continued to develop constructive relations with Western states and organisations. In 1997 Russia finally joined the political forum of the G7 which, as a result, became known as the G8. In May 1998 Russia ratified the Council of Europe's Convention for the Protection of Human Rights and Fundamental Freedoms. Thus, it accepted the jurisdiction of the European Court of Human Rights, which gave Russian citizens an opportunity to seek protection of their rights in Strasbourg. At the same time, Russia's relationship with the West was increasingly burdened with mounting tensions. As discussed earlier, Russia was unhappy with its international status and its exclusion from the Western security framework. Western states, on the other hand, were increasingly critical of Russia's internal developments, particularly its handling of the Chechen conflict and rampant corruption.

Competing with the West, 2000–12

While in the late 1990s Russia had insufficient capabilities to balance the West, in the 2000s it benefitted from an impressive economic growth, which allowed Moscow to conduct an increasingly assertive foreign policy. Upon his election as President in March 2000, Putin initially sought to repair Russia's relationship with the West by supporting Washington in the 'war on terror' and by boosting economic ties with the EU. Pragmatism and predictability became a leitmotif of Moscow's foreign policy rhetoric as Russia sought to position itself as a reliable business partner (Feklyunina 2008). At the same time, Putin sought to strengthen Russia's position in the post-Soviet area by using a range of means from economic leverage, particularly in energy trade, to support of pro-Russian elites.

Yet, already by the end of Putin's first presidential term Russia's relationship with the West began to deteriorate. As discussed earlier, Moscow was critical of the 2003 US-led invasion of Iraq, and it was apprehensive of NATO enlargement and of Washington's intentions to build an anti-missile defence. On the other hand, Western states were increasingly critical of Putin's growing authoritarianism and of Russia's attempts to reassert its dominance in the post-Soviet space. These tensions intensified in the aftermath of the colour revolutions in Russia's immediate neighbourhood – the

Rose Revolution in Georgia in 2003, the Orange Revolution in Ukraine in 2004–05 and the Tulip Revolution in Kyrgyzstan in 2005. Moscow interpreted these events as orchestrated by the US and the EU in their attempt to undermine Russia's influence in the post-Soviet area. The Russian authorities were particularly sensitive to Georgia's and Ukraine's intentions to seek NATO membership. While Moscow had already been concerned about NATO enlargement to the Baltic States, it saw the possibility of Georgia's and Ukraine's membership as an existential threat to Russia's security.

Thus, on the one hand, Russia's economic recovery, albeit fuelled by high oil prices, strengthened Moscow's already salient great power aspirations. On the other hand, Russia's dissatisfaction with its exclusion from the European security framework, its fears of a further NATO expansion to its immediate neighbourhood and suspicions of Western democracy promotion contributed to the rise of a 'besieged fortress' narrative (Feklyunina 2012). Putin responded to these challenges by engaging in a multi-faceted competition with the West. This competition focused on three areas that Russia saw as particularly important for its aim to reclaim a great-power status. First, Russia intensified its efforts to consolidate its dominant position in the post-Soviet space in order to prevent the West from encroaching on what it perceived as an area of its 'privileged interests' (Medvedev 2008). Second, Russia stepped up its attempts to solidify its dominant position as an energy supplier in Europe. At the same time, it used energy prices to apply economic pressure on its neighbours in the post-Soviet area. Third, it engaged in a fierce media competition with the West by launching an English-language TV channel 'Russia Today'.

As discussed earlier, Russia's growing dissatisfaction with its international position became particularly apparent when Putin voiced Russia's grievances at the 2007 Security Conference in Munich. The Russo-Georgian war a year later demonstrated that Moscow was willing to protect its position in the post-Soviet area by military means. The war was accompanied by an intense information campaign. While Russia's military incursion into the Georgian territory triggered a profound diplomatic crisis (Wivel and Mouritzen 2012), its consequences for Russia's relations with the West proved fairly short-lived. Already the following year the Obama administration attempted to repair the US-Russian relationship by introducing a policy of 'reset'. In the eyes of Western leaders, Medvedev's presidency in 2008–12 provided an opportunity to decrease the tensions that had accumulated during Putin's presidency. The reset had a number of significant successes, including the signing of the New Strategic Arms Reduction Treaty (New START) in 2010 and cooperation between Moscow and Washington towards Iran. Yet, it did not address the issue that was at the heart of Moscow's dissatisfaction with its international position, namely Russia's exclusion from the European security framework (Deyermond 2013).

Challenging the West, since 2012

Following Putin's return to the presidency in May 2012, Russian foreign policy underwent further transformation – from competing against the West to challenging the West. The beginning of Putin's third presidential term witnessed Moscow's turn to cultivating nationalist sentiments and appealing to socially conservative values. While Putin's agenda of 'traditional values' was primarily used to mobilise the Russian electorate, it was also promoted in Russia's immediate neighbourhood and in the West with the help of an increasingly sophisticated propaganda and support of various political actors in the far right.

As discussed earlier, the wave of public protests in Russia's major cities during and after the 2011 parliamentary and 2012 presidential elections strengthened Moscow's fears of an Orange Revolution and contributed to the dramatic rise of anti-Western rhetoric. As summarised by Trenin (2015: 33), Russia embarked on three 'pivots' – 'to itself (…), to Eurasia (…) and to Asia'. The pivot to itself entailed an even stronger emphasis on sovereignty and insulation from any outside influence on Russia's domestic or foreign policies. The pivot to Eurasia heralded Moscow's renewed focus on integration in the post-Soviet area in the form of the proposed Eurasian Union. Finally, the pivot to Asia included prioritisation of Russia's relations with states and organisations in Asia, particularly with China (ibid).

Yet, Putin's efforts to consolidate Russia's position in the post-Soviet space encountered a major obstacle in Ukraine. While Moscow hoped to include Ukraine in the Eurasian Economic Union (EEU), Kyiv sought closer ties with the EU. To prevent Ukraine from signing an association agreement with the EU, Russia resorted to economic and political pressure. Although Moscow succeeded in influencing President Viktor Yanukovych's decision to postpone the signing of the agreement in November 2013, it certainly did not anticipate the extent of public protests in Ukraine triggered by Yanukovych's withdrawal. Putin's aggressive response to the events in Ukraine – Russia's annexation of Crimea in March 2014 and covert support of pro-Russian separatists in eastern Ukraine – took most Western policy-makers and experts by surprise. Moscow's actions marked a major turning point in Russia's post-Soviet foreign policy. As argued by Trenin (2017), 'during the 2014 Ukraine crisis, Russia broke from the post–Cold War system and openly challenged US dominance'.

The resulting crisis was unprecedented for the post-Soviet period. The Russian membership in the G8 was suspended. Russian delegation in the Parliamentary Assembly of the Council of Europe (PACE) was denied voting rights. The US, the EU and some other states and organisations introduced a series of sanctions that aimed to hurt Russia's economy and undermine Putin's support. As Russia's relationship with the West was badly damaged, Moscow prioritised its pivot to Asia by pursuing an even closer cooperation with China. At the same time, the Russian authorities responded by introducing counter-sanctions and by intensifying information pressure on the West. In addition to justifying Moscow's actions, Russian media outlets, such as RT (formerly Russia Today) and Sputnik, increasingly sought to cultivate divisions among Western states and to shape domestic debates in individual Western countries. Moscow's apparent success in amplifying existing divisions in Western societies exacerbated fears of Russian propaganda and hybrid warfare (Giles 2016).

Russia's entry in the Syrian conflict in September 2015 marked another milestone in Russian foreign policy. By supporting the Syrian President Bashar al-Assad militarily, Russia challenged 'a post–Cold War U.S. monopoly on the global use of force' (Trenin 2017). Russia's use of its military outside the post-Soviet area demonstrated its dissatisfaction with the status of a regional power and its ambition to reclaim the status of a world power. Thus, by the beginning of Putin's fourth presidential term in 2018, Russia challenged the West on multiple fronts – from a normative challenge of 'traditional values' to the media challenge of RT to the military and diplomatic challenges in Ukraine and Syria.

Russia's foreign policy dilemmas

Russia faces a number of difficult dilemmas in its relationships with individual states and organisations. Some of them have been on Moscow's agenda throughout the post-Soviet period. Others have become particularly salient fairly recently. One of Russia's major concerns that has consistently dominated its foreign policy agenda is its exclusion from the European security framework. Russia initially hoped that NATO lost its relevance after the end of the Cold War and the dissolution of the Warsaw Pact. As these hopes did not materialise, Russia was increasingly frustrated with NATO's eastern enlargement to the states of the former Soviet bloc, with the Czech Republic, Hungary and Poland joining NATO in 1999, and Bulgaria, Romania, Slovakia, Slovenia and three Baltic States of Estonia, Latvia and Lithuania following suit in 2004. More recent rounds of enlargement included Albania and Croatia in 2009 and Montenegro in 2017. Russia remains particularly concerned with a possibility of Georgia's or Ukraine's accession, which it has repeatedly described as a red line.

Despite the tensions related to NATO enlargement and to the conflict in former Yugoslavia, Russia cooperated with NATO on a number of issues. In 1994 Russia joined NATO's Partnership for Peace. In 1997 Russia and NATO signed the NATO-Russia Founding Act on Mutual Relations, Cooperation and Security, and established a Permanent Joint Council which was later replaced with a NATO-Russia Council. Moscow's cooperation with NATO was particularly intense in the wake of 9/11 when Russia allowed the US-led coalition in Afghanistan to use its airspace. Yet, following Russia's annexation of Crimea, Russia's relationship with NATO has been at the lowest level in the post-Soviet period. In response to Russia's actions towards Ukraine, NATO suspended military and civilian cooperation with Moscow and increased its presence in the Baltic States and Poland. Thus, while Russia's actions in Ukraine may have potentially undermined Ukraine's ambitions to join NATO, they have also intensified an already acute security dilemma.

Russia's security concerns have also dominated its relationship with the US. As demonstrated earlier, Moscow has been consistently critical of Washington's plans to build the anti-missile defence shield. Despite recurrent tensions, particularly those related to Washington's democracy promotion and its opposition to Russia's attempts to reassert its dominance in the post-Soviet space, Russia has at times cooperated with the US on important international issues, such as disarmament or the fight against terrorism. However, the Russian-US relationship remains severely hindered by a lack of strong economic ties, and, more importantly, by divergent views on the desirable international order and on Russia's international status. During Putin's third presidential term Russia became increasingly willing to challenge Washington, from its opposition to the US-backed resolutions in the UN Security Council to an alleged interference in the US presidential elections. Donald Trump's victory in the 2016 elections exacerbated the tensions, with a special-counsel investigation in the US looking into possible collusion between Trump's presidential campaign and the Russian government.

Russia's relationship with the EU has also dramatically deteriorated. The EU remains Russia's biggest trading partner. However, the volume of trade has significantly decreased, partly because of the sanctions and counter-sanctions introduced by both sides in 2014. Although Russia continues to see the EU as an important economic partner, particularly as a destination for Russia's energy exports, it also sees it as a geopolitical rival in the post-Soviet area. Russia's traditionally strong relations with some individual EU member states, particularly with Germany, have also suffered as a result of the Ukraine crisis. At the same time, the EU has been increasingly concerned with Russia's growing influence in some of its member states due to Moscow's support of nationalist and Eurosceptic political forces and its skilful use of propaganda. Russia's 2018 presidential elections were marked by a severe diplomatic crisis in the Russia-UK relationship following the poisoning of a former Russian double agent with a nerve agent which the UK government identified as developed in Russia.

The unprecedented crisis in Russia's relations with the West contributed to Russia's shift to a closer relationship with China. Moscow sees economic cooperation with China, especially in energy trade, as a way to both limit Russia's dependence on the EU and benefit from the growth of the Chinese economy. Moscow also sees China as an important diplomatic partner in the UN Security Council where Moscow and Beijing can use their veto power to block Western-backed resolutions. However, Russia's policy towards China is complicated by the highly asymmetric nature of their relationship and by Russia's reluctance to be China's junior partner.

Russia's military campaign in Syria also poses some difficult dilemmas for Moscow. Its support of the Syrian government is consistent with Russia's long-standing opposition to external regime change. At the same time, Russia aims to secure a long-term presence in the Middle East by using the Khmeimim air base and the Tartus naval base in Syria as a foothold for its more active role in the region. While Russia's campaign has led to new tensions in Moscow's relations with the West, it clearly has helped Russia to enhance its international status by forcing the West to take into account Russia's interests in the region. However, Moscow's interference in the conflict on President Assad's side risks to alienate Russia's Muslim population.

Russia's biggest dilemmas are, however, in the post-Soviet area. Russia's annexation of Crimea and its continuing support of pro-Russian separatists in eastern Ukraine have arguably undermined any prospect of Ukraine's participation in the Eurasian Economic Union. Russia's actions have also contributed to strengthening Ukraine's pro-European foreign and security policy preferences. Yet, Putin's handling of the crisis in and around Ukraine continues to enjoy an exceptionally high level of support in Russian public opinion.

Conclusion: explaining Russian foreign policy

Changes and continuity in Russian foreign policy may be explained by different factors, ranging from domestic considerations to the structural constraints of Russia's geography and economy. Russia's authoritarianism at home, for example, may explain Moscow's increasing concerns with the spread of pro-democracy and pro-Western movements in its immediate neighbourhood. As argued by Mendras (2015: 81), Russian 'authoritarian' foreign policy under Putin has been 'first and foremost concerned with regime consolidation at home'. Putin's anti-Western rhetoric and Moscow's assertiveness have helped the Russian authorities to convert nationalist sentiments into a valuable source of domestic legitimacy. Russia's annexation of Crimea in particular gave an enormous boost to Putin's domestic approval ratings. Another important factor is Putin's role as a sole decision-maker in matters of foreign policy. Putin's personal background, including his past work in security services, may explain his deep-seated suspicions of the West (Hill and Gaddy 2015). Russian foreign policy has also been shaped, albeit to a lesser extent, by economic interests of various elite groups, particularly in relation to Russia's energy exports.

Another explanation prioritises geopolitical considerations. As argued by Lo (2015: xv), 'geopolitics has returned as the main organising principle of Putin's foreign policy'. Russia's exclusion from the European security framework and the enlargement of Western integration projects – NATO and the EU – to Russia's borders contributed to an acute security dilemma. This explanation interprets Russia's actions towards Ukraine as stemming from its security concerns: 'great powers are always sensitive to potential threats near their home territory' (Mearsheimer 2014: 5–6).

Finally, Russia's international behaviour may be explained by the evolution of its dominant identity (Morozov 2015; Tsygankov 2016; White and Feklyunina 2014). Russia's ambiguous position in Europe – being part of Europe geographically and culturally, but often diverging from the European experiences politically and economically – gave rise to Russia's long-standing identity debate. Different understandings of identity produce often incompatible understandings of Russia's interests and foreign policy preferences, ranging from cooperation with the West to expansionism and confrontation with the West. Yet, despite their disagreement regarding Russia's European-ness or Eurasian-ness, most variants of Russian identity share a vision of Russia as a great power (Mankoff 2009). As Foreign Minister Kozyrev wrote in 1994, 'the only policy with any chance of success is one that recognizes the equal rights and mutual benefit of partnership for both Russia and the West, as well as the status and significance of Russia as a world power'. Kozyrev's conclusion appears somewhat prophetic: 'If Russian democrats fail to achieve it, they will be swept away by a wave of aggressive nationalism …' (Kozyrev 1994).

What do the recent changes in Russian foreign policy – its annexation of Crimea, its covert involvement in the conflict in eastern Ukraine and its military campaign in Syria – tell us about Russia as an international actor? Most western analysts argue that Russia has become a revisionist power that seeks to undermine the existing international order (Light 2012: 27). An alternative explanation suggests that Russia's revisionism aims to challenge the initial revisionism of the West that had occurred after the end of the Cold War when Western states began to reinterpret international norms. As argued by Sakwa (2015a: 66), by challenging the West Russia attempts to force 'the Western powers to obey their own rules'. Furthermore, these changes in Russian foreign policy signal that the Russian government views Russia as sufficiently strong to challenge the West and to withstand the consequences of the confrontation. They also signal that Moscow is not willing to compromise on those issues that it sees crucial for its international status, great-power identity and security. At the same time, Russia's demonstration of strength masks significant domestic weaknesses that have the potential to undermine Russia's international position in the future.

13 SECURITY, THE MILITARY AND POLITICS

Bettina Renz

For more than two decades following the collapse of the Soviet Union, Russia's status as an important actor in global security affairs appeared to be in terminal decline. As a country that could barely muster enough military power to suppress an insurgency within its own borders, as the troublesome wars in the Chechen republic had demonstrated, it seemed that its influence had been reduced at best to the immediate neighbourhood. As a result, throughout much of the 1990s and 2000s, little attention was paid in the West to developments in Russian security and military affairs. During the presidency of Boris Yeltsin, if the subject was addressed at all, analyses were largely limited to the study of failed military reforms and the continuing decay of the armed forces. When Vladimir Putin was elected president in spring 2000, the attention of observers was drawn to developments in the country's force structures – quasi-military organisations other than the regular armed forces tasked predominantly with internal security – and in particular to the role of the Federal Security Service (FSB). Putin's close ties to this service and the rising numbers of officials with a background in the FSB, the so-called *siloviki*, became a popular subject of inquiry.

Although Putin also made military reforms a priority from the outset, developments in this area evoked little interest in the West during his first two terms in office, because it was assumed that the significance of his security policies was limited largely to the domestic realm. Western interest in Russian military and security affairs rose dramatically when Moscow launched a military operation in Ukraine in spring 2014, which resulted in the annexation of the Crimean peninsula. When the Russian armed forces were sent to intervene in the Syrian civil war in 2015 – their first expeditionary operation beyond the borders of the former Soviet Union – it seemed clear that the world was witnessing a fundamental shift in Moscow's security and defence policies with grave implications for the post-Cold War global order. Within a matter of a couple of years, Russia seemingly had turned from a power in decline into the top threat to global stability, as a strategy paper published by the US European Command described it (Breedlove 2015).

This chapter puts into historical and political context the perception of a sudden shift in Russian security and military affairs. It will show that, rather than adequately reflecting developments since 1991, the perception of dramatic change has been vastly distorted by the subject's previous neglect. Although Russian security and military affairs were not considered an important object of inquiry in the West throughout much of the 1990s and 2000s, this did not mean that significant developments in the sector did not occur. A more contextualised understanding of contemporary Russian security and military affairs is important for putting into perspective the reasons for and implications of recent developments. A side effect of the abrupt return of Western attention to Russian security and military affairs has been the tendency to focus almost entirely on their external aspects, that is, their potential implications for international security. Whilst this aspect is important, there is yet again a danger of neglecting other, crucial aspects and developments. Russian security and military affairs are not only about foreign policy and the West, but also have an important domestic dimension. Both aspects need to be considered for a balanced assessment of recent developments.

The chapter provides an overview of developments in Russian security and military affairs since the end of the Cold War. Outlining the political drivers for continuity and change in these areas, it will show that the idea of a sudden turnaround in the direction of the Kremlin's policies does not reflect the complexity of developments during the first two decades of the post-Soviet era. The force structures have been an important power resource of the Russian executive since the end of the Cold War. The ambitions for rebuilding a strong military also date back to Yeltsin's first term in office, but they did not turn into reality for a variety of political, societal and economic factors until later. Concerns over domestic order and regime stability have been a significant determinant in the direction of reforms of both the force structures and the armed forces throughout the post-Soviet years. The idea that recent changes in Russian security and military affairs were pursued, above all, to confront the West represents a one-sided interpretation of events.

Yeltsin, security and the military

The security sector – defined here as all those institutions tasked with the provision of state security, including the armed forces, security organs and law enforcement agencies – always has been an important actor in Russian governance and society. During the Cold War, the Soviet security sector was made up of three powerful force structures. The KGB and Interior Ministry (MVD) were maintained to enforce order and regime stability internally. The Ministry of Defence was in command of the armed forces. These had manpower levels of up to four million men and were tasked with deterring and dealing with external threats to the state's security and national interests. The Soviet armed forces also had an important symbolic function: arguably, it was the Soviet Union's military might, rivalled only by that of the US, which gave the country superpower recognition. A military career was considered a prestigious profession and the Red Army's victory over Nazi Germany was a source of pride for citizens then as it is today. During the Cold War, the security sector was prioritised over all other state institutions. It is well known that excessive spending on security and defence, which exceeded 10% of GDP, was at least one of the reasons for the Soviet Union's collapse.

When the Russian Federation emerged as a newly independent state, the security sector lost its position of absolute privilege. This did not mean, however, that the force structures and military did not continue to play an important role in the Russian state and society. President Boris Yeltsin was suspicious of the Soviet force structures, and especially of the KGB, because of the involvement its leadership had had in the August 1991 coup attempt. Rather than dismantling it outright, however, he split the KGB into several smaller agencies in order to diffuse its potential power. The FSB, which was created in 1995, emerged as the KGB's major successor organisation. Yeltsin's policies led to a proliferation in the number of force structures. These organisations today employ around 500,000 military personnel in addition to the approximately 800,000 soldiers under the command of the Ministry of Defence (*The Military Balance* 2016).

The maintenance of a powerful and sizeable security sector in Russia after the end of the Cold War occurred for a number of reasons. The inability to make hundreds of thousands of former Soviet security personnel redundant certainly was a factor. Some of the force structures also were needed to make up for shortcomings in the military's capabilities for dealing with the various 'new' security challenges and smaller-scale contingencies facing the Russian Federation during the early 1990s. The armed forces, which had been trained throughout the Cold War to fight conventional state-on-state wars in a European theatre, were ill-prepared to cope with the demands of the ethnic conflicts and separatist insurgencies erupting around and within Russia's borders. Especially in Chechnya, military personnel from other force structures with relevant expertise, such as the civil defence troops of the Ministry of Emergency Situations (MChS) and the counterterrorism units of the FSB, served to support the military. Political factors, however, were the most important reason a strong security sector was maintained. In Yeltsin's eyes, the major threat to his nascent regime were revisionist elements in the political and military elite, who sought to put a stop to or reverse the ongoing process of transition.

Splitting up the force structures into several smaller entities permitted the pursuit of a 'divide-and-rule' strategy that prevented any one organisation from becoming too powerful. It also allowed for fostering forces loyal to the president and that he could rely on in the eventuality of challenges to his leadership. Yeltsin's most favoured force structure, which he reportedly called 'the president's own KGB', was the Presidential Security Service (SBP) (Nikolsky 2013). This existed as a separate service from 1993 until it was subsumed into the Federal Guard Service (FSO) in 1996. The SBP was headed by a close confidant of the president, Aleksandr Korzhakov, who had been involved in Yeltsin's personal protection since 1985. Korzhakov exerted significant influence on executive decision-making until he fell from grace and was dismissed when he controversially called for the postponement of the presidential elections in 1996. The MChS, headed by Sergei Shoigu from its creation in 1994 until his appointment as defence minister in 2012, was another force structure close to Yeltsin. Shoigu had been supportive of Yeltsin since the August 1991 coup attempt and his appointment to the helm of the powerful new ministry, created in part as a counterbalance to the other force structures, was seen as a reward for his loyalty (Dobrolyubov 2013). Yeltsin's divide-and-rule strategy vis-à-vis the security sector paid off when during the violent 1993 constitutional crisis, force structures loyal to him resolved the situation in his favour.

During the early post-Soviet years, potential challenges to the stability of Russia, in Yeltsin's eyes, came predominantly from 'within' – in the form of revisionist political forces, but also separatist tendencies, such as the unfolding crisis in Chechnya, and 'new' security challenges, such as organised crime. The prioritisation of the force structures over the regular armed forces, which focused on external threats that seemed at the time largely diminished, therefore made sense (Taylor 2007). Having said this, even during the 1990s, the political leadership did not lack awareness that reforming the remnants of the Soviet military into a more modern force was an urgent necessity. Throughout his time in office, Yeltsin faced considerable pressure from the military leadership and patriotic elements in the political elite to put a stop to the decay of the country's army, air force and navy. Their dismal performance and humiliating defeat by a technologically and numerically vastly inferior opponent during the Chechen war put into question the country's ability to defend its security and territorial integrity. Poor service conditions, low pay, rampant corruption and vast casualty numbers in the Chechen campaign had also led to a sharp deterioration in the prestige of the military profession and a crisis in the recruitment and retention of military personnel.

Although the Russian military continued enjoying a high degree of popular trust compared to other state institutions even during the 1990s, this was mostly symbolic and based on historical perceptions and pride. Few Russian citizens were prepared to serve in the armed forces, and most families did anything in their power to prevent their sons from having to complete conscript service (Renz 2012). The need for military reforms was also underlined by the growing recognition that the deterioration of Russia's conventional military was restricting the country's freedom of international action. Moscow's inability to influence the course of events in the former Yugoslavia in the run-up to NATO's Operation Allied Force over Kosovo in 1999, which it vehemently opposed, was seen by many in the Russian military and political elite as a humiliation and as evidence of the country's diminished international clout as a result of its decaying military power. Several attempts at military reforms were pursued during the Yeltsin years in order to deal with these problems, but these never led to systematic change (Arbatov 1998, 2000). Reforms during the 1990s were limited for the most part to the reduction to more realistic levels of the 2.3 million strong armed forces the Russian Federation had inherited.

Even during the early 1990s, the need for systematic military reforms was acknowledged in official Russian documents and political rhetoric. For example, the 1993 military doctrine already outlined vast ambitions in the realm of conventional military capabilities. Many aspects of the reforms leading to Russia's military revival under Putin, such as increasing professionalisation, improvements in permanent readiness and technological modernisation, already had been discussed at length during the Yeltsin years. From this point of view, there has been significant continuity in Moscow's ambitions and views on the importance of having a powerful military. It was not Yeltsin's fundamentally different views on the utility of military force, or just the lack of political willingness to push through systematic reforms, that prevented these ambitions from turning into reality. Given the country's economic weakness in the 1990s, the realisation of these ambitions was simply not affordable. In fact, although Russian spending on defence vastly diminished after the collapse of the Soviet Union and decreased consistently until the economic collapse in 1998, spending was always relatively sizeable even during the Yeltsin years. Average defence spending as a percentage of GDP from 1992 until 1999 was 4.15%, which does not differ considerably from the average of 4.16% under Putin's and Dmitry Medvedev's presidencies from 2000 to 2015 (SIPRI Military Expenditure Database). Given Russia's economic weakness during the 1990s, however, even 4% of the GDP was insufficient to sustain the existing armed forces at a reasonable level, let alone to pursue a costly programme of reforms.

Putin, security and politics

During Yeltsin's presidency, little attention had been paid in the West to developments in the Russian force structures. Instead, the necessity of military reforms and Moscow's ongoing failure to pursue systematic change in this respect dominated what little there was in analysis of Russian security. Putin's election to the presidency in 2000 led to a partial reversal of this trend. As is well known, Putin has a career background in the KGB and also acted as the director of its main successor organisation, the FSB, from 1998 to 1999. It was the rapid rise under Putin in the number of politicians and state officials with career backgrounds in the force structures – the so-called *siloviki* – that caught the attention of Western observers. Many suspected that this development indicated Putin's intention to turn the country in a more authoritarian direction, reversing the democratic trend in favour of a 'militocracy' (Kryshtanovskaya and White 2003). These fears seemed to be confirmed when Putin implemented wide-ranging reforms of the force structures during his first years in office, which strengthened the power of the FSB. Although the authoritarian turn in many areas of Russian politics since Putin's accession to power is beyond doubt, the abruptness of the change in the two presidents' leadership styles was not as pronounced as often implied. Rather than dismantling the powerful Soviet security sector in pursuit of a democratic course, Yeltsin had put into place a system where sizeable force structures were available to the president as an important instrument of personal power. Moreover, Yeltsin had fostered a highly personalised regime, where institutionalised channels of elite recruitment characteristic of democratic systems of governance were never developed. Putin's reliance, at least in part, on former colleagues from the security services was therefore almost inevitable (Renz 2006).

During Putin's first two terms in office, the 'militarisation', or more specifically 'FSB-isation', of domestic politics under the growing influence of the *siloviki* dominated Western analyses of Russian security trends. As Ian Bremmer and Samuel Charap put it at the time, 'practically every Kremlin policy change … from Iran policy to back-tax claims, has been credited to this mythologized [*siloviki*] clan' (2006–07: 83). Under Putin, as had been the case during the Yeltsin years, however, the significance of the force structures has been about more than the appointment of individuals to political posts. During several reforms of the security sector, Putin amended the force structures he had inherited by disbanding and merging a few of them. In part, these reforms were carried out to do away with overlapping functions and to strengthen capabilities in areas that seemed particularly important at the time. Under Putin, too, reforms of the sector took the form of reorganisation, rather than reductions in its overall size and personnel. For example, in 2003 the Federal Tax Police Service was brought under the control of the MVD and the Federal Border Guard Service was subsumed into the FSB. The Federal Agency for Government Communication and Information (FAPSI) was disbanded, but its functions and assets were distributed between the FSB, the Federal Guard Service (FSO) and the foreign intelligence service (SVR).

An entirely new force structure, the Federal Service for the Control of the Drugs Trade (FSKN), was also created in 2003. This was a sizeable outfit with around 40,000 personnel, manned partly on the personnel basis of the disbanded Federal Tax Police Service. The official explanations for these reforms at the time were the country's growing need for capacity in fighting terrorism – a major area of responsibility of the FSB – and to stem the growing flow of drugs into the country. Another significant round of security reforms took place in 2016. This time, the FSKN was abolished again as a separate service and brought under the control of the MVD. At the same time, Russia's up to 200,000 interior troops, which until then had been left largely unreformed and were notorious for their inefficiency, were removed from the MVD. Along with the latter's riot police and rapid reaction units, they were turned into a new force structure, the Federal National Guards Service (FSNG), with the remit of ensuring the security of the state and of society.

As was the case for Yeltsin, political factors have been the major reason for Putin's maintenance of powerful force structures, which remain in many ways bloated and inefficient. The president's handling of the sector continues being characterised by a divide-and-rule strategy, where the fortunes of individual force structures are determined by their perceived loyalty to the president and utility for upholding the regime in power, rather than by their competence and efficiency. The FSB has been Putin's favoured force structure, not least because he can rely on trusted personal ties within it. The FSB was headed by Nikolai Patrushev, a central and influential member of Putin's 'team', from 1999 until 2008, when he was appointed to the powerful position of secretary of the Russian Security Council. Even though the FSB's loyalty to Putin has never been in doubt, other powerful force structures were fostered as a counterbalance. When the FSB's size and authority grew considerably as a result of the 2003 reforms, the FSKN was created with another trusted Putin ally – Viktor Cherkesov – as its director. When the FSNG was established in 2016, at the same time as the FSKN was dismantled, Russian security experts, such as Nikolai Petrov, suspected that this decision was a 'corrective to the power imbalance in the *siloviki*, where, in recent years, the Federal Security Service (FSB) and the Army have tremendously increased in power' (2016).

The perceived threat to regime stability from revisionist forces in the political and security elite, which had influenced Yeltsin's approach to the force structures, quickly dissipated when Putin was elected to the presidency. His turn towards an explicitly pragmatic political course, which emphasised stability rather than political change and democratisation, co-opted large swathes of the communist and nationalist opposition and their electorate. His promise not only to bring stability domestically, but also to restore what he called 'Russia's prestige and leading role in the world' (Putin 2000a), including strong and proud armed forces, raised his popularity with the military and security establishment, which had never trusted Yeltsin. Nevertheless, it is clear that Putin has used the force structures throughout his presidency to enhance the power of his own regime and to protect it against real or perceived forces of instability. During his first term in office, the force structures were heavily involved in dispersing the power of the oligarchs, which had amassed vast wealth and political influence as central figures of Yeltsin's personalised regime. A prominent example of this was the investigation into the Russian private oil company Yukos and the arrests of a number of its top executives, including Mikhail Khodorkovsky, in autumn 2003.

More recently, it has become evident that Putin views domestic instability caused by outside and specifically Western influence over the Russian population as a major potential threat to his regime. Although such fears date back to the late 1990s (Bacon et al. 2006), they grew with what the Putin leadership has perceived as instances of Western meddling in the 'colour revolutions' in Georgia and Ukraine and in the Arab Spring in 2011. Fears over outside meddling are behind the growing centralisation and state control of all aspects of society under Putin, often with involvement of the force structures. Such fears have driven developments, such as restrictions to media freedom, the adoption of registration laws for civil society organisations, instances of 'spy mania' – the accusation and arrest of certain individuals and groups on treason charges – and crackdowns on opposition rallies and public protests. When the FSNG was created in April 2016, Russian security experts evaluated this mostly as the result of sharpening fears over public unrest and disorder following the protest cycles of 2011–12 (Galeotti 2016). As discussed below, fears over internal instability and Western meddling have also been a factor in the military reforms pursued by Putin.

Putin, the military and politics

Owing to the preoccupation with the president's FSB background and the *siloviki*, little attention was paid in the West to the Russian armed forces during Putin's first two terms in office. This was despite the fact that he made these reforms a priority from the very beginning. As mentioned above, shortly before his election in March 2000, he asserted in a televised address that, as President of the Russian Federation, he would restore the country to its rightful place in the world and that the restoration of a strong military would play a major role in this process (Putin 2000a). The urgent need for military reforms was discussed at several meetings of the Russian Security Council shortly after his election. Summarising these meetings in a speech to top military brass, Putin promised to address shortcomings that had previously been identified in the areas of combat readiness, discipline and available technology. Referring to Chechnya, he confirmed that the Russian military was not sufficiently prepared 'to neutralize and rebuff any armed conflict and aggression', which could come from 'all strategic directions'. He also highlighted the need to improve the image of the military as an essential component of reforms and promised to 'put an end to the humiliating situation of servicemen'. Having a military that trusted the state and took pride in its work, in his words, was 'directly linked with national security interests' (Putin 2000b).

Putin's commitment to military reform was not just rhetorical. In order to create the conditions required for the implementation of change, he broke with the Soviet tradition of appointing career army officers as ministers of defence, which had continued during the Yeltsin years. This had always been seen as problematic, because it was assumed that an insider would be less willing and able to push through changes unpopular with the military leadership. In 2001, a close Putin ally and fellow former KGB officer, Sergei Ivanov, was appointed as civilian minister of defence. He was replaced in 2007 with an economist, Anatoly Serdyukov, whose experience working in the Federal Tax Service was to be applied to increase cost-efficiency and root out corruption. Amendments to the Russian Federal Law 'On Defence' in 2004 also removed many of the ambiguities regarding the division of labour between the defence ministry and the General Staff of the armed forces. Overlapping functions and competencies had previously led to disagreements between defence ministers and chiefs of the General Staff over plans for reforms. The amendments placed the direction of reforms firmly in the hands of the defence minister (Renz 2012). Ultimately, it was improvements in the Russian Federation's economic situation that enabled the successful pursuit of reforms. As Putin had also noted in his above-mentioned speech to military leaders, although the need for military reforms was urgent, it would not be pursued at any cost. In his words, Russia 'should not just plan what we need, but plan proceeding from what we can afford' (2000b). As the economy recovered, not least owing to rising gas and oil prices, the country's GDP grew consistently from 1999 until the global economic crisis hit in 2008. This had positive implications for the defence budget, which rose almost five-fold between its low point in 1998 and 2015. The growth in defence spending was achieved without significantly raising the percentage of GDP spent during the Yeltsin years, at least until 2015, when as a result of the contracting economy, military spending started exceeding 5% of GDP.

By the time of Russia's war against Georgia in August 2008, military reforms and better funding had improved the performance of the Russian armed forces in comparison to the Chechen wars. Although significant shortcomings were still evident, especially when it came to equipment and tactical command and control, the apparent equation by some Western analysts of operational problems with a strategic failure for Russia overlooked the fact that Moscow easily defeated the Western-trained Georgian forces and achieved its objectives in a mere five days. Lessons learned from the war in Georgia provided the impetus for accelerated military reforms. In autumn

2008, an extensive programme of modernisation was revealed. Continuing the gist of previous reform efforts, this programme set out to turn the Russian military into a force fit for a twenty-first-century global power. It aimed to make the armed forces more useable in different conflict scenarios by improving its cost-effectiveness, streamlining central command bodies, decreasing the size of the top-heavy officer corps, cutting the overall number of units with more emphasis on permanent readiness, and increasing the number of professional soldiers. The programme included changes to military education and training in order to enhance mobility and combat readiness of troops. Better funding meant that large-scale exercises, which had not taken place for almost two decades, were reintroduced and inter-service exercises preparing the armed forces for joint operations were held. A central element of the modernisation programme was the updating of equipment and technology available to the armed forces, which had received barely any new kit throughout the 1990s. This took the form of an ambitious and costly state armaments programme with a view to increasing the figure of 10% of hardware classed as 'modern' in 2008 to 70% by 2020. The military's image problem was also tackled with improvements to the financial rewards and welfare of both professional soldiers and conscripts (McDermott et al. 2012).

Backed up by political will and solid financing, the 2008 reform programme was implemented with impressive speed. It transformed the Russian military into a force that is unrecognisable when compared to the demoralised and underfunded organisation that it was during the 1990s. Although military reforms had been gathering momentum since 2000 and seriously accelerated from 2008 onwards, the West's attention was only caught when Russia launched its military operations in Crimea. Although the operation was of limited scale, it demonstrated vast improvements in tactical command and control. The special forces that were mostly involved in the takeover of government buildings and military installations in Crimea also showed an array of new equipment, such as modern 'webbing' and personal radios, which had been unavailable at the time of the Georgian conflict. A large-scale snap exercise conducted on Russian soil near the theatre of operations signalled Moscow's ability to dominate in the case of outside interference or escalation. The conflict in Syria offered Moscow an opportunity to show to the world that the modernisation programme had led to improvements much bigger than enhanced capabilities for successful special forces operations in its immediate neighbourhood. Russia had regained the sea and airlift capabilities required for expeditionary operations on a global scale and command and control issues, which had led to the loss of several aircraft in friendly fire incidents during the Georgia war, had been overcome.

A Russian military resurgence?

The impressive achievements of Russian military modernisation are not in doubt. However, it is clear that the complete turnaround in Western interest in Russian security and military affairs, from almost complete ignorance to top concern, has contributed to skewed interpretations of both the reasons for, and implications of, these reforms. Russian plans and ambitions for rebuilding a strong conventional military date back to the 1990s. The reasons reforms have been seen as a requirement are numerous and cannot be reduced to the desire to confront the West. On the most fundamental level, the decay of the Russian armed forces during the 1990s had led to a situation where the country's ability to defend its territorial integrity was in doubt. Such a state of affairs would be a significant security concern for any country, including for Russia, which is located in a difficult geopolitical position, adjacent to many areas of instability, and has long borders that are difficult to defend. Deteriorating service conditions, corruption, and high casualty rates incurred in Chechnya had serious implications for the image of the military profession. The armed forces were increasingly unable to recruit and retain staff at sufficient levels.

Extensive military reforms were needed in order to attract the quality and quantity of soldiers required to deal with the country's various security challenges and interests. Moreover, a disgruntled military feeling increasingly betrayed by the political leadership, and with access to an arsenal of lethal weapons, was a potential source of insecurity not only for Russia. Finally, it became increasingly evident that without a strong conventional military, the country would be unable to uphold its status as a global power, to which it has always aspired. Although the end of the Cold War raised expectations that military power would be less relevant as an indicator of a country's international status, these expectations did not come to pass. Other powerful states, such as the US and China, continued enhancing their conventional capabilities, and it is clear that military strength and mass remains an important, if not essential, symbol of a great power.

In addition to the historical context of Russian military reforms, comparative context is also essential for assessing the implications for international security. Although Moscow's armed forces are bigger and better than they were during the 1990s in every way, they are still no match for the much more advanced militaries of the West, of the US in particular, and also increasingly those of China. Russian law sets the maximum size of the armed forces at one million personnel. Although exact numbers are not known, it is widely assumed that in reality it comprises no more than 800,000 soldiers. Around 350,000 personnel are serving on a contract basis, the rest are conscripts. Increasing the number of professional servicemen and servicewomen is too costly and, owing to Russia's demographic problems, the recruitment of more conscripts to make up an army of one million is simply impossible. Compared to the 1.4 and 2.3 million professional soldiers, respectively, serving in the US and Chinese armed forces, Russian manpower does not look all that impressive. In comparative perspective, Russian defence spending, too, still has a lot of catching up to do. Although the defence budget has risen consistently since 2000, Moscow's spending of around 70 billion dollars in 2016 was still dwarfed by the budgets of the US and China, which amounted to over 600 billion and 225 billion, respectively (SIPRI Military Expenditure Database). Although by 2016 Russia had the world's third largest defence budget, its spending in real terms remained much closer to that of the mid-top-10 ranking countries, such as Saudi Arabia (60 billion), France (55 billion) and the UK (52 billion). Ongoing economic stagnation is making further growth in the Russian defence budget increasingly unaffordable.

Comparative shortcomings also remain in the realm of military technology. The Russian military, and especially the air force, has received a lot of new equipment over the past decade, but only a fraction of this is 'modern' in the sense of cutting-edge, twenty-first-century technology. The country's defence industry remains strong in the production of legacy systems, such as fighter jets, air defence systems and tanks. It has been unable to catch up with the West, however, in the development of the latest high-tech equipment, such as sophisticated precision-guided munitions and long-range unmanned aerial vehicles (UAVs). Shortcomings remain, above all, in Russia's ability to project global maritime power. Lacking the experience and facilities required for the equipment of a blue-water fleet, naval modernisation plans were based on the expectation that the required skills and components would be imported from the West. The economic sanctions imposed on Russia in the aftermath of the annexation of Crimea have precluded this option (Connolly and Sendstad 2016).

Finally, the annexation of Crimea led to fears that, even if Russia's conventional military continued lagging behind those of the West, Moscow could overcome these shortcomings with the use of 'hybrid warfare'. This concept has gained vast popularity since 2014 and, not unlike the *siloviki* debate during the 2000s, it has developed into an umbrella term used to explain almost any policy move by the Kremlin. The term 'hybrid warfare' does not originate in Russian military thinking and was imposed with hindsight by Western analysts to explain the success of the operations in Crimea. The term 'hybrid' in this sense refers to the use of non-military instruments in warfare, such as information and psychological operations, decreasing the need for physical force and destruction. Whereas Russian military operations in the past had relied on the use of overwhelming firepower, Crimea was conquered without almost a single shot fired. From this point of view, 'hybrid warfare' seemed an adequate description. It is far from guaranteed, however, that what worked in Crimea would be equally successful in a different context. After all, it is obvious that the use of extensive military power simply was not necessary in Crimea, given that the circumstances were so favourable for Russia. The Ukrainian leadership was severely weakened, the Ukrainian military did not offer any kind of resistance, there was little chance of outside interference and, most importantly, a large portion of the population in Crimea supported Russia's objectives. When Moscow intervened in Syria a year later, it clearly did not see a hybrid warfare approach as sufficient and opted instead for a conventional air campaign. It is highly unlikely that the Kremlin would fancy its chances of defeating the West in a campaign of 'hybrid war'.

The merits of hybrid warfare as a concept describing an approach to military conflict can be debated. However, since 2014 the concept has developed into a quasi-theory of Russian foreign policy that is much broader and vaguer than this (Renz 2018). Fears of Russian 'hybrid threats' against the West, in the form of 'information warfare', 'cyber warfare' and 'fake news', have becoming increasingly prominent. These fears are not without basis, especially since evidence of alleged Russian meddling in the domestic affairs and elections of various countries has come to light. It is important, however, to disentangle military action and political interference in this respect. There is nothing hybrid in the use of information or propaganda on its own. Presenting these issues and actions in the language of warfare unhelpfully suggests that Russia already is at war with the West and that such hybrid threats are just one step removed from military action. It is also important to bear in mind that Russia's hybrid warfare approach is often traced back by Western analysts to an article written by the Chief of General Staff, Valerii Gerasimov, in 2013, the so-called Gerasimov Doctrine. As various security experts have since explained, the interpretation of his article as a new Russian way of war is mistaken. Gerasimov discussed the growing importance of non-military instruments in warfare, including information, propaganda and psychological operations, but he described this as a general trend characterising, above all, a Western approach. As Charles Bartles put it, rather than outlining a future Russian way of war, the article highlighted Gerasimov's view of 'the primary threats to Russian sovereignty as stemming from US-funded social and political movements, such as color revolutions, the Arab Spring, and the Maidan movement' (2016: 36). The threat of external information influence over the population was also listed as a domestic military danger in the Russian military doctrine published in 2014 for the first time. As such, Western fears of hybrid threats mirror Russian concerns over domestic instability and external meddling, which have been driving Putin's security policies for many years.

Conclusion

Western views of a sudden shift in Russian security and military affairs do not reflect the complex developments in this area since the early 1990s which, until the annexation of Crimea in 2014, had been largely ignored. The force structures have always played an important role in Russian politics and the recognition that a strong military is essential dates back to the early 1990s. Reforms of the Russian security sector have always been about more than just the West. The perceived need to protect domestic order and regime stability has always been an important factor in efforts to secure the Russian Federation with strong force structures and a powerful military. The Russian armed forces' much-improved capabilities pose certain challenges to Russia's neighbours and to the West. However, fears that Putin has been pursuing military reforms above all with the intention to launch offensive operations and to challenge the West in a military confrontation can be allayed if the historical context of Moscow's security and military policies are taken into account. Better military capabilities alone do not effect substantial changes in a country's views on the utility of force. The Kremlin has used military force for the achievement of various policy objectives in the past, and it is likely to do so in certain situations in the future. The use of military force, however, will remain closely linked to Moscow's domestic and foreign policy priorities. For the time being at least, these appear still to be centred on the stability of Putin's regime and the achievement of great power recognition, rather than on the wish for global domination.

14 RUSSIA AND ITS NEIGHBOURS

Samuel Charap

From the moment the Soviet Union legally ceased to exist on 25 December 1991 the issue of how the new post-Soviet Russia would relate to its freshly independent neighbours has been highly fraught, within the region, in Russian domestic politics, and in Moscow's relations with the West. Three decades later, particularly following Russia's 2014 annexation of Crimea and subsequent intervention in eastern Ukraine, the issue is more contested than ever. Despite the passage of time and the cementing of a number of trends, the future of the region, referred to here as post-Soviet Eurasia (i.e. the former-Soviet republics minus the three Baltic states), remains highly uncertain, with a number of scenarios possible.

This chapter begins by providing a brief history of the key developments in the region from 1991 to 2014. It then describes the immediate causes and consequences of the 2014 Ukraine crisis. Finally, it concludes with some analysis of new dynamics in the region and potential future trajectories.

A diverse region

In 1991, Russia found itself in historically unique circumstances. Unlike other former imperial metropoles, which had ruled over lands farther afield, the post-Soviet states are arrayed around Russia's borders. Russia's central location has given it significant leverage in dealing with its neighbours. But that same centrality creates a degree of insecurity as well. A revolution in India or a shift in Kenya's foreign policy would have limited direct consequences for the UK's security. Similar events in Belarus or Azerbaijan have a far greater import for Russia. It should not be surprising, then, that Russia has claimed 'vital interests' in its post-Soviet Eurasian neighbourhood.

But that neighbourhood is anything but uniform. The 11 post-Soviet Eurasian states vary on a wide array of characteristics: location and climate, size, economic conditions, language, religious tradition, and past association with Russia. Yet they share much history, remote and recent; Russian as a lingua franca; a multitude of informal practices and norms; and a visceral reaction to policies emanating from Moscow. This in part stems from power asymmetries: regardless of its intentions or policies, Russia is the regional hegemon by dint of its relative demographic and economic heft. Using 2015 data, Russia's population ranged from about three to one (for Ukraine) to more than 50 to one (for Armenia). In terms of economic output as of 2013, the variation is much greater, from 10 to one (for Kazakhstan) to more than 100 to one (Kyrgyzstan, Moldova and Tajikistan).

Pushing and pulling

Geopolitical dynamics in the region have been dominated by three key trends since 1991. The first has been Moscow's drive – in fits and starts – to reassert some degree of control. The second has been the involvement of other external actors, particularly the West – and its institutions, the EU and NATO – and China. And the third is the geopolitical balancing act performed by the ruling elites of the region's states while they have simultaneously sought to reinforce their countries' statehood while maximizing international freedom of manoeuvre, rents, and political control at home through their dealings with the outside powers. These three trends produced explosive outcomes, first in 2008 and then again in 2014.

From the start, Russia has asserted special rights in the region. This began long before Vladimir Putin rose to national power in 1999. His predecessor, Boris Yeltsin, described the approach in a decree on 'The Strategic Course of the Russian Federation with Respect to the Member States of the Commonwealth of Independent States' or CIS, signed in September 1995. (The CIS, as we describe below, was a loosely knit organization that incorporated all 11 post-Soviet Eurasian states.) The document stated that '[o]n the territory of the CIS are concentrated Russia's most vital interests in the domains of economics, defence, security, and defence of [its citizens'] rights. [Russia will be the] leading force in forming a new system of international ... relations in the post-USSR space [and will] foster integrative processes in the CIS'. The decree states that Moscow will 'obtain from the CIS states performance of their obligations to desist from alliances and blocs directed against any of these states'. Cooperation with international organizations in managing regional conflicts was permissible, but it is necessary 'to get them to understand that this region is first of all Russia's zone of influence' (President of the Russian Federation 1995). In short, the West and its organizations must keep out, except to the extent permitted by Moscow, and the other states in the region must join Russia in rejecting their presence. The decree remains in force through to the present.

As far as actions were concerned, in the 1990s Russia was consistently coercive but with no apparent master plan. Moscow meddled in the domestic politics of the region's states, providing media backing and funding for parties and personalities friendly to Russia, but lacked a broader strategy. In Ukraine, for example, Russia supported Yuri Meshkov, the head of the Crimean provincial government, who was pushing for secession of the peninsula from the rest of the country. When he was ousted in 1995, he fled to Moscow and was given asylum. Russia kept Soviet-era military outposts in all 11 states of the region for at least some of the years after 1991; in several cases, these installations remain to the present day. Initially, some of the garrisons resulted from Moscow's role as peacekeeper in the ethnic and political conflicts that broke out as the Soviet Union splintered. In Moldova, the Soviet and then Russian 14th Army defended the rebel province of Transnistria in its conflict with Chisinau in 1990–92. As of this writing, Russian peacekeepers and remnants of the 14th Army are still in place, and Transnistria remains an unrecognized but autonomous entity. In Georgia, Moscow brokered ceasefires in two ethnic conflicts between Georgians and South Ossetians (1991–92) and Abkhaz (1992–94), which had eponymous self-governing regions within the Georgian Soviet republic. The ceasefire agreements created Russian-dominated peacekeeping forces in both areas. Moscow also deployed its military to end the 1992–97 civil war in Tajikistan, which resulted in over 50,000 deaths. While Russia did not directly intervene in Nagorno-Karabakh, the breakaway province of Azerbaijan populated by ethnic Armenians that saw a six-year conflict, it brokered a 1994 armistice. It maintained a base in Gyumri, Armenia, and offered Yerevan security guarantees.

In the 1990s, Moscow played a needed role in these crises, as no other power was prepared to step in, and it was successful in putting an end to the bloodshed. Despite some misgivings, the West was generally supportive of Russia's interventions, since Western governments had no intention of getting involved themselves. However, essentially all of the post-conflict arrangements Moscow brokered became mired in stalemate and thus came to be called 'frozen conflicts'. The lack of settlements provided a convenient excuse for keeping Russian peacekeepers in Abkhazia, South Ossetia and Transnistria, along with the bases in Armenia and Tajikistan. In Transnistria, South Ossetia and Abkhazia, Russia began issuing passports to locals. Russian citizens often served in the separatist governments.

Russia has also used its economic advantages to coerce its neighbours. Russia's natural resource endowment and the legacy of the Soviet planned economy – assets were strewn across the Union with no regard for what were then purely administrative boundaries – gave Moscow substantial advantages. Generally, Moscow used these levers simply to gain concessions or commercial advantage for Russian companies. The energy sector was a major source of influence. Russia was the supplier of natural gas to all but Azerbaijan, Kazakhstan, Turkmenistan and, to a lesser extent, Uzbekistan, which had their own hydrocarbons; it regularly sold at below-market prices and on credit, making for a dependent relationship with the buyers. Until the construction of new pipelines that came online in the early 2000s, Moscow also controlled all of the former USSR's export pipelines, including those leading to Western Europe and its lucrative gas market, which gave it bargaining advantage over its four fellow energy exporters. At various times, Russia has bullied uncooperative partners by raising energy prices or suspending deliveries, calling in debts, increasing tariffs on imports or excise taxes on exports, and cutting off access for non-Russian oil and gas exporters to its pipelines. By resorting to such blunt tactics whenever one of its neighbours did not behave to its liking, Russia made threat perceptions throughout the region more acute and came to be feared and mistrusted by local elites. The bullying also convinced many in the West that the independence of Russia's neighbours was under threat.

Moscow has sought to integrate the region through a plethora of multilateral institutions, of which the CIS was the oldest and the broadest in mandate and membership. The CIS established an executive secretariat, an inter-parliamentary assembly, 12 coordinating bodies (for heads of state, heads of government and ministers), and over 50 specialized bodies, dedicated to everything from patents to meteorology, civil aviation and phytosanitary standards. By 2004, the CIS Council of Heads of State had adopted 500 documents and the Council of Heads of Government more than 900; few had any impact on the centrifugal forces unleashed by the disintegration of the USSR.

Russia was the driving force behind all of these endeavours. But Moscow was too distracted with troubles at home in the 1990s to counteract the entropy rampant throughout the region. Protectionism and cumbersome national rules set in, leading intra-regional trade to collapse by two-thirds. The centrality of the CIS accord was undercut by the decision of Russia, Belarus and Kazakhstan in 1995 to forge a trilateral customs union, to which Kyrgyzstan and Tajikistan later became party, called the Eurasian Economic Community (EurAsEC). This entity, too, accomplished little. Yet another framework, the Single Economic Space among Russia, Belarus, Kazakhstan and Ukraine, was announced in September 2003. As with the others, it proved largely to be a paper tiger.

In terms of security, the region remained equally fragmented. Six CIS members – Armenia, Kazakhstan, Kyrgyzstan, Russia, Tajikistan and Uzbekistan – signed the Collective Security Treaty, also known as the Tashkent Treaty, in 1992; Azerbaijan, Belarus and Georgia joined in 1993. The treaty had no practical impact, particularly given that several of its members were essentially at war with each other. An institution to carry out the treaty's provisions – the Collective Security Treaty Organization (CSTO) – was created in 2002. Membership had by that point been reduced to six: Russia, Belarus, Armenia, Kazakhstan, Kyrgyzstan and Tajikistan. Uzbekistan re-joined the CSTO in 2006 but pulled out again in 2012. The CSTO has a headquarters in Moscow and conducts joint exercises; on paper it has had a rapid-reaction force, but that has never been put to the test in practice. In effect, the CSTO is essentially a Russian security guarantee for the other members, all of which have very different security concerns. Belarus, for example, is unlikely to send its forces to protect Armenia, and vice versa.

Conflicts heat up and freeze

The conflicts in post-Soviet Eurasia that began in the late 1980s and early 1990s were driven by ethnic and political tensions. However, once NATO and the EU began to make an institutional push in the region in the mid- and the latter half of the 2000s, Russia transformed separatist conflicts into geopolitical levers, so that the territorial disputes serve as blocks to joining the Western clubs; neither institution wants to import unresolved conflicts that involve Russia. Thus, Russia is unlikely to allow Ukraine, Georgia and Moldova to restore their territorial integrity so long as doing so would facilitate their membership in Euro-Atlantic institutions. Azerbaijan is the exception that proves the rule; since Baku was never interested in NATO or EU membership or even integration, Russia has not stood in the way of a negotiated settlement in its conflict with Armenia over Nagorno-Karabakh (in that case, the conflict has been stuck for other reasons).

This 'geopoliticization' of separatist conflicts began in earnest with the Russia-Georgia war in 2008. The background for that clash was a dispute regarding the prospect of a NATO Membership Action Plan (MAP) for Ukraine and Georgia in the spring of 2008. MAP was a step towards NATO membership, setting down the conditions required to join. Russia was strongly opposed to NATO moving farther east and warned Brussels that granting Kyiv and Tbilisi a MAP would elicit a strong response. At a summit in Bucharest, Romania, in April 2008, NATO leaders, despite a strong push from the US, could not agree on granting the MAP, but as a compromise the summit communiqué declared that Ukraine and Georgia 'will become' members of NATO at some unspecified point in the future (NATO 2008). It became clear soon after that the decision was the worst of all worlds: while providing no increased security to Ukraine and Georgia, the Bucharest Declaration reinforced the view in Moscow that NATO was bent on bringing them into the organization.

In the months after the Bucharest summit, the security situation in Georgia deteriorated. Numerous skirmishes broke out between Georgian and South Ossetian separatist forces, and Russia conducted a 10,000-man military exercise just across the border, ending on 2 August. Following an intensification of fighting in South Ossetia, on the night of 7 August the Georgian government took the decision to begin an assault on Tskhinvali, the provincial capital. The Russian peacekeepers there also came under direct attack. Russia, after being caught off guard, responded with a massive counter-offensive, driving the Georgians (both the uniformed military and ethnic Georgian civilian residents) out of South Ossetia and invading deep into Tbilisi-controlled territory, wrecking much of the country's armed forces' matériel. Russian forces also pushed into Abkhazia, which Georgia had not attacked, and crossed the administrative boundary, destroying a number of military facilities. After five days, the war was over; Georgia had been routed. An estimated 500 people had been killed, and tens of thousands had been displaced. On 26 August, the Russian president, Dmitry Medvedev, recognized the independence of South Ossetia and Abkhazia, effectively putting the conflicts in a deep freeze (Independent International Fact-Finding Mission on the Conflict in Georgia 2009).

Since then, periodic talks on the conflict take place under the aegis of the 'Geneva International Discussions', but progress on humanitarian, security and other matters has been minimal. EU Monitors observe the situation on the Georgian government-controlled side of the administrative boundary lines, while Russian forces have built up permanent encampments in the two breakaway territories. One relative bright spot has been the partial restoration of bilateral Russia-Georgia ties, despite the continuing lack of formal diplomatic relations, which were cut off during the war. Russians can travel to Georgia visa-free, and trade restrictions have been lifted, leaving Russia Georgia's second-largest trading partner as of 2017.

Integration gets serious

Less than nine months after the guns fell silent in Georgia, Russia, Kazakhstan and Belarus agreed to form an institutionalised Customs Union, which entered into force on 1 January 2010. Unlike the previous paper tiger efforts at regional integration, the Customs Union was a significant departure from past regional habits of declarations far outpacing developments on the ground; in fact, the Customs Union's development was more akin to the early years of the EU than to the CIS. Under the terms of the agreement, the Customs Union Commission, headquartered in Moscow, served as a decision-making body for the bloc. It – not the national governments – now had the prerogative to set tariffs. Minsk, Astana and Moscow quickly moved to build on their initial success, creating a single market mechanism in 2012, and eventually a Eurasian Economic Union (EEU) in 2015, covering broader areas of economic policy. With the formation of the EEU, a Eurasian Economic Commission (EAEC), a genuine supranational institution with its own bureaucracy and decision-making bodies, took the place of the Customs Union Commission, while a court was created in Minsk to resolve trade disputes.

In its first years, the new Eurasian integration effort was a marked success, particularly by comparison to past attempts. Customs posts were removed on the borders between Russia and the two other members, and there was a significant increase in trade among the members in 2010–12. After Russia joined the World Trade Organization (WTO) in 2012, the Customs Union had to adopt a system of rules that comply with WTO standards, thus exporting international norms to the other members, which did not belong to the WTO. Political-level decisions are taken by consensus in the Council of the EAEC, which is made up of deputy prime ministers from all member states with a rotating presidency. While Russia has at times used political, economic and security levers to get its way, the requirement to obtain unanimous votes on major decisions has also forced Moscow to compromise with the other members. In effect, this gave the other members a voice on matters that Russia previously had decided without any external input.

The EEU was and formally remains a technocratic, economic endeavour, even though some experts have questioned the economic logic behind it (Dragneva and Wolczuk 2017). Soon after its creation, however, the EEU began to take on a geopolitical edge. In an October 2011 article in the daily *Izvestiya*, Putin laid out his vision for the future of the bloc. He envisioned a 'supranational association, capable of becoming one of the poles of the modern world.' He further claimed that joining the EEU need not contradict other countries' 'European choice', because in the future, there would be bloc-to-bloc talks. 'So joining the Eurasian Union … will allow each of its members to integrate with Europe faster and on more advantageous terms' (Putin 2011). The implicit message to the neighbours was clear: Moscow wanted a say on the pace and conditions of their integration with the EU.

As it happens, at the same time the EEU was taking shape, Brussels was getting more serious about its own engagement with the region. In May 2009, EU policies towards the six non-Central Asian post-Soviet Eurasian states (Belarus, Ukraine, Moldova, Armenia, Azerbaijan and Georgia) were branded the Eastern Partnership (EaP). The main event of the EaP was the

Association Agreements (AAs), documents that set out a framework for integration with the EU and a promise to liberalize trade and visa regimes. Rather than forging equal partnerships, AAs are meant to pave the way for countries to adopt the EU's technical and political norms. They set criteria for partners on economic and political matters, human rights and democratic principles; harmonise their domestic laws with EU directives on a wide range of economic regulations; and liberalize trading relations with the bloc. They are highly technical, voluminous documents negotiated over a number of years. Although the AAs had much in common with the initial stages of the EU accession process, they did not include any major funding from Brussels to ease the pain of reform and explicitly did not make any commitments regarding eventual membership.

The AA trade package, called Deep and Comprehensive Free Trade Area agreements (DCFTAs), eliminates most tariffs and quotas, allowing for free movement of goods, services and capital across borders. But these agreements are as much about legal approximation as they are about free trade; DCFTA signatories must adopt large portions of the EU's *acquis communautaire* (its rules and regulations) into their domestic law. In theory, successful implementation of the AAs would leave the EaP countries in a position similar to that of Norway: not in the EU, but fully integrated economically, and politically like-minded.

The theory behind the AAs rested on an assumption that Russia – as with EU enlargement in Central and Eastern Europe in the 1990s and early 2000s – might not like the initiative but had neither the will nor the means to stop it. In the event, both of these assumptions proved faulty.

Russia did push back, and push back hard. Beginning in the summer of 2013, it applied pressure to all four states that were in talks with the EU about the AAs. First, Armenian President Serzh Sargsyan during a visit to Moscow on 3 September 2013 made a shocking announcement: Yerevan now intended to join the Customs Union and eventually the EEU instead of signing the AA that it had been negotiating for over three years. Armenia's about-turn reflected its deep dependence on Russia for both its prosperity and its security. Russian firms control most strategic sectors of its economy and Armenia relies on the Russian military for support in its conflict with Azerbaijan over Nagorno-Karabakh. After a year of talks, Armenia signed the EEU treaty in October 2014. Kyrgyzstan, which shares borders with Kazakhstan (and China) but not with Russia, also began talks on membership in 2014, and joined the EEU in August 2015.

Moldova was also subjected to pressure to block its AA when Russia barred Moldovan wine, the country's staple export, in the summer of 2013. In the Georgian case, Moscow threatened to raise tariffs but never followed through. Both Chisinau and Tbilisi signed their AAs in June 2014.

The broader Ukraine crisis began in this context. In July 2013, Russia imposed trade sanctions on Ukraine, first by cutting off imports of key foodstuffs, and then by hitting steel manufacturers and other exporters with cumbersome new customs procedures. For several days the next month, the Russian authorities applied meticulous customs checks to all Ukrainian imports, all but blocking them.

Although normal trade soon resumed, Moscow's message was unequivocal: If Kyiv wanted to go ahead with the AA, its bilateral trade with Russia would be severely limited. To be more precise, Moscow threatened to end Ukraine's trade preferences under the CIS's free-trade agreement, which would have resulted in an effective increase in average tariffs of more than 10 percentage points.

The pressure had its desired effect, at least initially. In a dramatic reversal, on 21 November 2013, just a week before the planned signing ceremony for the AA, the Ukrainian government of President Viktor Yanukovych called off preparations to sign the document. In the following days, several thousand Ukrainians came out to protest Yanukovych's about-face on Kyiv's central Independence Square, *Maidan nezalezhnosti*. These peaceful, unarmed protests would likely have petered out had they been allowed to run their course. In the event, force was used against unarmed student protestors on 30 November. The next day, 1 December, upwards of 500,000 people came out where there had been only 10,000 before. Despite the EU flags on November's Maidan, the protests were now about overthrowing Yanukovych's corrupt authoritarian regime.

Beginning with that first use of force, the government and the radical avant-garde of the protestors (led by armed far-right nationalist groups) engaged in an escalatory spiral of violence that left the country on the brink of civil conflict. On 21 February Yanukovych and opposition leaders signed an agreement, brokered by three EU foreign ministers and a Russian presidential envoy, intended to end the political crisis, under which the country would return to the 2004 constitution limiting presidential powers, a government of national unity would be formed, and occupations of streets and buildings would end. However, the deal was refused that evening by the Maidan demonstrators and Yanukovych fled the capital the next day, rendering the agreement moot. In these extraordinary circumstances, the parliament took extra-constitutional action (the formal impeachment procedures were not followed) and voted on 22 February to remove him and install a new government. What came to be known as the Maidan Revolution dramatically shifted the balance of power away from the south and east (Yanukovych's electoral base), empowering political forces deeply opposed to closer ties with Russia.

At that point, what was an internal Ukrainian story began to morph into a major international crisis. Putin and his inner circle seemed to have believed that the Maidan Revolution resulted at least in part from a Western plot to install a loyal government in Kyiv that included far-right leaders who could revoke Russia's naval basing agreement in Crimea and quickly move Ukraine towards EU and NATO membership. In the final days of February, Putin decided to insert special forces, paratroopers and other servicemen into Crimea to boost the contingent already there as part of Russia's Black Sea Fleet. He was seeking to head off Russia's nightmare scenario of being completely pushed out of Ukraine by the West. His decision seemed aimed at securing the most important Russian physical assets in Ukraine, namely the Black Sea Fleet base, and to coerce the new Ukrainian authorities into accommodating Moscow's broader interests. It reflected the desperation that came after all other levers available to Russia had proven useless: During the previous few months, it had tried nearly all the tools it had – economic coercion (the summer trade sanctions), massive economic assistance (a \$15 billion aid package pledged to Yanukovych in mid-December) and diplomacy with the West (the 21 February agreement) – and all had failed to secure its interests.

The invasion had almost immediate knock-on effects on the ground. It emboldened pro-Russian politicians in Crimea, released latent separatist sentiment among the population, and hardened the position of the new government in Kyiv. The invasion thus foreclosed options other than annexation or capitulation, which was not really an option for Putin. In a deeply flawed plebiscite, held under the watchful eye of Russian servicemen in unmarked uniforms, 97% of Crimeans were reported to support a proposal to join Russia. US President Obama, reflecting widespread sentiment in the West, stated that the Crimea referendum will 'never be recognized by the United States and the international community' (Obama 2014). On 18 March Putin delivered a blistering speech to parliament and senior officials, both announcing what he called the 'reunification' with Crimea and launching into a diatribe against Western policies (Putin 2014). As many as two-thirds of the Ukrainian military units remaining in Crimea, including the commander of the Ukrainian fleet there, defected to Russia. By the end of March, Russian forces had ejected the rest from their bases.

Russia was clear about its objectives in the crisis from the beginning. In a document that Foreign Minister Sergei Lavrov gave US Secretary of State John Kerry and the Russian government subsequently published, Moscow set down its terms: Ukraine's neutrality, undisturbed economic ties with Russia and 'federalization' of Ukraine to ensure the pro-Russian regions have a veto over decision-making in Kyiv – all guaranteed by a UN Security Council resolution. Russia was seeking ironclad guarantees regarding Ukraine's future in a deal among the great powers (Ministry of Foreign Affairs of Russia 2014).

The West rejected these terms out of hand. Instead, its policy response had four main tracks: first, dramatically boosting financial, institutional, military and political support for Ukraine; second, sanctioning Russia for its actions and to deter further incursions; third, reassuring NATO allies in Central and Eastern Europe with further troop deployments; and fourth, pursuing a diplomatic solution. Yet as far as Ukraine was concerned, Western policy was largely about preventing Russia from achieving its objectives; there was no clear theory of victory emanating from Western capitals, particularly since none had the appetite to offer Kyiv a path to membership in the Euro-Atlantic institutions.

With the geopolitical clash intensifying, the crisis within Ukraine only deepened as unrest broke out in the eastern Donbas region of Ukraine. Russia conducted a no-notice snap exercise on the border and built up a 20,000–40,000-strong force there. Special forces, operatives, volunteers, and Russia's own nationalist extremists crossed the border to capitalise on eastern Ukraine's discontent with the new government. An insurgency against the post-Maidan government began to gather steam in April and May, particularly in Donetsk and Luhansk, where local rebellion leaders soon declared the (internationally unrecognized) 'Donetsk and Luhansk Peoples' Republics' (DNR and LNR, respectively). Rather than negotiate with the separatists in Donetsk and Luhansk, the Ukrainian government launched what it called an 'anti-terrorist operation' (ATO) and used the regular military and the newly created (and poorly trained) national guard, supported by pro-government paramilitaries, against the armed anti-Maidan rebel forces that were occupying official buildings.

Government forces began to achieve victories against the separatists, whom they outnumbered and outgunned by a wide margin. On 17 July, Malaysia Airlines flight MH17 was shot down over the Donetsk region as it flew from Amsterdam to Kuala Lumpur, killing all 298 passengers and crew on board. The incident further internationalized the conflict, as the majority of the civilians killed were from EU countries. Ukraine and the West blamed Russia, claiming a Russian SA-11 Buk surface-to-air missile system shot down the liner over rebel-held territory. Just as the separatist forces seemed on the verge of defeat in late August, Russia put its thumb on the scale. With the backing of regular Russian troops, the separatists launched a counteroffensive. The Ukrainian military suffered a stunning defeat in the town of Ilovaisk, when its forces were encircled. Over 360 Ukrainian servicemen were reportedly killed.

The late-August counteroffensive was meant to demonstrate to Kyiv that an outright military victory over the separatists would be impossible. Indeed, the setbacks did drive the Ukrainian government to the negotiating table. On 5 September, the representatives of Russia, Ukraine, the Organisation for Security and Cooperation in Europe (OSCE) and the DNR/LNR met in Minsk, where they signed a 12-point protocol for deescalating the conflict. It called for, among other stipulations, an immediate bilateral ceasefire; monitoring by the OSCE; the decentralisation of power within Ukraine, including a law on 'special status' for rebel-held areas of the Donetsk and Luhansk regions; the release of all hostages; an amnesty law for combatants; and the withdrawal of illegal armed groups and equipment.

Despite the agreement, fighting continued throughout the conflict zone, although it was greatly reduced compared to the period before the signing of the ceasefire. This decline in violence continued through to the end of the year and into early January 2015, but fighting escalated after the New Year holidays once again. Backed by a second direct Russian intervention, the separatists began pushing government forces into retreat. By February, the separatists had gained control over an additional 300 square kilometres. In an attempt to stop the renewed violence and prevent a broader war, German Chancellor Angela Merkel and French President François Hollande met with Putin and Ukrainian President Petro Poroshenko in Minsk on 11 February.

On 12 February, after 16 hours of negotiations, they finalized a set of 'implementing measures' intended to revive the principles of the original Minsk agreement. The new agreement – called 'Minsk II' – included provisions for a ceasefire; the removal of all heavy weaponry to create a buffer zone; negotiations to begin after the withdrawal on conducting local elections in separatist-controlled areas; amnesty for all combatants; the release of all hostages; free access for humanitarian aid; full restoration of Ukraine's social safety net, such as pension payments, and the banking system, in conflict regions; constitutional reform in Ukraine, of which the key element was decentralization agreed to in consultation with separatist representatives; the return of control of the Russia-Ukraine border to the Ukrainian government once the constitution is reformed; and the withdrawal of all foreign fighters. A footnote detailed exactly which authorities would be delegated to the administrations of the separatist-held areas; these included, among others, the right to appoint prosecutors and judges and to form a 'people's militia' to maintain public order.

If enacted as written, Minsk II essentially would transform Ukraine into an asymmetric confederation, requiring the central government to participate in a continuous bargaining process with the Russophile Donbas regions, which would have significant powers of self-rule, while the rest of the country would continue to be ruled by Kyiv. Russia would not have to cede control over the border until Ukraine reformed its constitution. In these respects, Minsk II locked in significant gains for Russia and major concessions from Ukraine.

By early 2018 the conflict in Ukraine had killed 10,500 people, leaving over 1.8 million Ukrainians displaced internally, while nearly 1.1 million had registered as refugees in Russia, although this number counts only formally registered refugees and not the hundreds of thousands who simply crossed the border and sought work and shelter. While Minsk II reduced the violence dramatically, little progress has been made on implementing its provisions. Many in Kyiv prefer a truly frozen conflict: avoiding the political commitments of Minsk II, but ending the bloodshed while severing the Russophile Donbas, allowing the rest of Ukraine to integrate with the West.

This outcome seems unacceptable to Moscow, and therefore Russia has kept up its support for the armed rebels in the Donbas. This has created a simmering rather than a frozen conflict, defined by continuous low-level fighting with regular upticks in violence. As a result, investment has been anaemic, and the Ukrainian economy and polity remain in disarray. But Moscow calibrated the conflict to avoid an all-out war or a more forceful Western policy response. And while it has made membership in Western institutions practically impossible for Kyiv, it has yet to obtain the great-power condominium it set out to achieve. In fact, the post-Maidan government accelerated military cooperation with NATO and its members and signed the AA with the EU. When the DCFTA component went into effect on 1 January 2016, Russia, as per earlier threats, ended the CIS trade preferences accorded to Ukraine. Moscow also placed an embargo on Ukrainian agricultural imports. In response, Kyiv banned a variety of Russian imports. Direct flights between the countries were also cut off, affecting up to 70,000 passengers per month. The economic relationship – once central for Ukraine and significant for Russia – had been reduced to a bare minimum.

Reverberations of developments in Ukraine dominated the strategic landscape throughout the region. Threat perceptions about Russia's intentions vis-à-vis its neighbours skyrocketed, particularly in the neighbouring states themselves. All states in question, even Russia's closest allies, have avoided directly and fully endorsing Moscow's line. The particular worries vary from state to state: Kazakhstan fears the rhetoric of protecting ethnic Russians, given its sizable Russian minority, while Azerbaijan objects to precedents of national self-determination affecting borders due to the Nagorno-Karabakh conflict. Even Russia's close ally Belarus has sought to diversify its foreign policy orientation following 2014.

The crisis also affected the development of the EEU. Russia had responded to Western sanctions by imposing counter-sanctions on agricultural imports in August 2014, but Moscow could not convince Minsk and Astana to go along, so it implemented them unilaterally, undermining the core principle of any customs union: a unified external tariff. A trade spat ensued, leading to the return of inspection points for a period at the Belarus–Russia border.

Conclusion

While the main geopolitical reference point for post-Soviet Eurasia has been the clash between Russia and the West, increasingly China is playing a more important role in the region's affairs. China's Belt and Road Initiative (BRI) has a number of planned infrastructure links tying its western provinces to European markets that go through Central Asia and Russia. Indeed, for many of the Central Asian countries, China, not Russia or the EU, is the most important economic partner. Beijing has joint military industrial development plans with Minsk and remains a major arms customer for Ukraine. However, unlike the West, China seems to have understood that Russia is willing to undermine other powers' initiatives in post-Soviet Eurasia if it feels threatened by them. In the case of the BRI, for example, Beijing headed off the kind of trouble that the EU's EaP faced but agreed to a significant political gesture, first proposed by Moscow during a summit in May 2015: a framework to coordinate BRI projects in EEU member states centrally through the EAEC. This gesture, though largely symbolic, was reassuring to Russia and headed off a clash between the two powers in the region, which many observers have long predicted.

China's increasing role in post-Soviet Eurasia underscores the extent to which an already complex region has grown even more diverse nearly 30 years after the USSR's collapse. Today, the states of the region defy black-and-white characterizations. None, even Moscow's close allies Belarus and Armenia, can be dismissed as Russian satellites or part of a Russian 'sphere of influence', a term largely devoid of meaning in the twenty-first century. For example, although Yerevan was forced to scrap its AA in 2013, it signed a comprehensive partnership with the EU in 2017. By the same measure, the self-declared 'pro-Western' governments in the region, Ukraine, Moldova, and Georgia, have little prospect of actually joining the institutional West and are unable and largely unwilling to cut themselves off fully from Russia; geography, after all, is a fact that cannot be ignored indefinitely. The region is likely to be short on geopolitical finality in the coming years. Major powers can either negotiate compromises to reflect that messy reality, or, as seems more probable for Russia and the West based on current trends, continue to compete in a game where no one – least of all the states of the region – will emerge the winner.

15 THE CONTINUING EVOLUTION OF RUSSIA'S POLITICAL SYSTEM

Henry E. Hale

Russia is clearly not a democracy. But Russian politics does not easily reduce to the alternative concepts Westerners most frequently use to describe it. Terms like dictatorship or kleptocracy all capture some element of the system, but miss the logic that actually drives its behaviour. For example, much like calling Putin a new 'tsar,' simply branding Russia 'authoritarian' puts too much emphasis on Putin's own role. He is clearly the most powerful figure in Russia today, but he cannot just do as he pleases. Studying his personality alone will yield only a poor guide to Russia's behaviour. Similarly, concepts like 'kleptocracy' or 'mafia state' do satisfy an urge to condemn bad practices while highlighting some consequential behaviours. But there is just too much going on that cannot adequately be described through the logic of stealing or criminality, such as the passage of far-reaching anti-smoking legislation and the introduction of jury trials.

Rather than identifying a negative feature of the regime and then reasoning backward to discern a logic that may have produced it, an alternative approach starts with some basic principles about the context in which politics happens as Russians themselves experience it. This begins with conceptualizing Russia's most important political actors and thinking about what drives their behaviour, and then looking at the implications without initially worrying about whether the result fits well with good or bad categories like, for example, 'democracy' or 'autocracy.' Such an approach might lead one to see Russian politics as a system in which powerful, loosely hierarchical networks compete with each other while penetrating both the economic and political worlds when the rule of law is weak and corruption is high – a form of politics that may at first seem exotic but is in fact very common throughout the world.

The story of contemporary Russian politics, then, is a dynamic one about how these networks arrange and rearrange themselves politically, proceeding from the chaotic competition of the 1990s to the tightly fit machine that produced Putin's 2018 re-election. It is also a tale of how Russia's leaders wrestle with the twin urges to create functioning institutions that can channel or even eliminate this network competition and help them rule effectively (as Russia has done with the Central Bank) and to wield state institutions flexibly and selectively so as to work through his own networks, using them to punish or strike useful deals with potential opposition (as Putin has done with prosecutorial organs). These processes come up in this book's chapters on specific themes, and the purpose of this chapter is to help tie many of these developments together into a larger picture of Russia's regime trajectory, one that is constantly in motion. Putin's longevity in office, then, masks an underlying dynamism, and the pressures he will face during his fourth term in office – first and foremost succession – surely portend still more surprises.

A social context of patronalism

Russia shares with much of the world a social context that I have called 'patronalism', the technical definition of which is a social equilibrium in which people primarily pursue their collective social and economic ends more through concrete, personalized rewards or punishments meted out through extended networks of actual acquaintance rather than by abstract principles that join people together without some concrete personal interaction connecting them (Hale 2015). In short, this is a context in which personal connections matter to a degree that would seem extreme to most people growing up in the US or Britain. In the latter countries, connections can matter for getting a job or obtaining tickets to a show but, for example, people usually do not feel they need a personal connection to the leadership of a highly rated charity organization before they are willing to donate money to it. Nor do they consider it common for bureaucrats to demand bribes to provide routine state services or for professors to take payments of some kind for good grades or recommendations.

Patronalism is an 'equilibrium' because its practice is self-reinforcing when it is widespread, and therefore it is very hard to root out. While not all patronalism is corruption, an example involving corruption shows how this is the case. Suppose you are a mayor and it is widely believed that you need to pay off various officials to get a new regional medical facility located in your town. You can decide to be honest and refuse to make the payments, but if you take the proverbial high road, some other ambitious mayor is likely to go ahead and make the payments and get the facility located in their region instead. The result is that your constituents will be deprived and may even blame you for not doing what was necessary. But if you make the payment and satisfy your voters by getting the facility in your town, you are contributing to the expectation that 'this is just how things work,' making others more likely to do the same when they have a chance.

At the level of national leadership, the practice is even more deeply rooted. Leaders tend to find it comfortable, convenient, and powerful to mete out individualized rewards and punishments through personal connections to get done whatever they want to get done. They thus have little incentive to do the very hard work necessary actually to change things fundamentally. Thus while all three of Russia's post-Soviet presidents have talked about the need to root out corruption and modernize the state, this has remained more talk than real action.

Power networks in Russian politics

One implication of the centrality of personal connections in Russia is that the key 'players' in the country's political arena are often not 'parties' or even formal institutions like the Duma, but extended networks of actual personal acquaintance led by powerful 'patrons'. At the very least, this is how many political insiders in Russia see it.

The most important power networks in Russia today fall into at least three main categories. One set of networks grew out of the economy, building vast business empires by gaming the post-Soviet privatization process and then translating this wealth into political clout. These networks, led by figures widely known as 'oligarchs', would get 'their' people into positions all across Russian political society and often controlled important mass media. In the 1990s, oligarchs like Boris Berezovsky, Mikhail Khodorkovsky and Vladimir Gusinsky were household names and thought to be among only a handful of men who essentially ran the country during President Boris Yeltsin's final term in office.

Another category might be called 'regional political machines', networks based in peripheral regions in which a strongman could use his (or, rarely, her) leverage as governor to gain control over local economic assets, media and legislatures. These assets could then be mobilized to deliver large shares of the province's votes to themselves or whoever they chose, leverage they could convert into influence in federal politics. Major political machines in regions like Tatarstan and Primorsky Krai were thus highly sought-after allies by national politicians, though the biggest and most famous of all political machines was the one led until 2010 by mayor Yuri Luzhkov in Russia's capital metropolis, Moscow.

A third type of network consists of those with home bases in the state itself. Perhaps the most prominent example today is that of Vladimir Putin, who turned a series of personal and professional acquaintances (many acquired during his days in the KGB or as a St Petersburg city official) into an extensive network that now occupies key posts in the state (most obviously, Putin himself serving as president), the economy (e.g. Igor Sechin controlling the oil company Rosneft), mass media (e.g. Yuri Kovalchuk founding the National Media Group), and multiple political parties with diverse ideologies (e.g. Putin's St Petersburg associates Dmitry Medvedev atop the United Russia party and Sergei Mironov leading the Just Russia party). This network started to come together as a coherent power network of national importance in the late 1990s, as Putin was finally reaching the pinnacle of Russian power, and it now represents the country's dominant network.

The emergence of Russia's single-pyramid system

The process through which nearly all major power networks came to be arranged into a single 'pyramid' of power, recognizing the primary authority of a single patron, began in the 1990s under Yeltsin. The USSR's collapse had left that country's most powerful networks in a state of disarray, leaving myriad emerging regional political machines and budding oligarchs to compete intensely with each other – and with the Kremlin – for power with only a weak institutional framework to govern this contestation. While Putin supporters today often exaggerate the degree to which the 1990s were a period of chaos and economic collapse, there certainly was a much higher rate of disorder than any fully functioning state would tolerate. By one count, as many as half of all regional acts were found to be inconsistent with the federal constitution as provincial networks and oligarchs often colluded to pursue their own interests without paying much heed to 'the centre' (Stoner-Weiss 2001, p. 121).

It was in this context that Yeltsin took moves that ultimately helped unify the country more through informal than formal means. Yeltsin laid the cornerstone in late 1993 when he defeated the Congress of People's Deputies in a dispute over the constitution that turned violent, putting before voters a referendum question that effectively had them choose between a new basic law that strongly favoured the president or no constitution at all. He then employed a variety of methods to win over (or coerce) at least some major regional political machines to his side and to strike deals with key oligarchs. The most infamous deal, 'loans-for-shares', allowed figures like Khodorkovsky and Berezovsky to obtain some of Russia's most valuable assets, including oil, in return for providing the cash-strapped Kremlin with badly needed funds (Johnson 2000, pp. 185–87). With a presidential election looming in 1996 and Yeltsin trailing badly in the polls, the Russian president opted against cancelling elections and instead (for the first time in post-Soviet Russia) successfully mobilized a broad coalition of regional political machines and newly enriched oligarchs to win a national election. Rallying against the candidate who had been favoured by many to win at the start of the year, Communist Party leader Gennady Zyuganov, the regional machines in Yeltsin's corner delivered huge numbers of votes his way (sometimes reversing outcomes between the first and second rounds of voting); at the same time oligarch-controlled media warned of a dark communist restoration while burnishing Yeltsin's own image in their news and other programming.

Yeltsin eked out a victory, convincing many that the money, media and machines he controlled could elect anyone president of Russia. These included some key people who ultimately helped Yeltsin pick Putin as prime minister and hence designated successor in August 1999, and one reason is that he was steeped in the 'hardball' methods that Yeltsin and many around him thought were needed to bring Russia's independent-minded oligarchs and political machines to heel. The seeds of Putinism in the 2000s were thus sown in the 1990s.

The problem of presidential succession

Before the hastily assembled machine from 1996 could be kicked into gear again, however, it nearly fell apart due to one of the central problems single-pyramid systems face: succession. With Yeltsin physically ailing and running up against a constitutional term limit, many of the political machines and oligarchic networks that had backed Yeltsin's re-election in 1996 now started to think ahead to a future without him, seizing the opportunity to try and proactively shape that future in ways that suited them. The most dramatic event was the emergence of a major new challenger to Kremlin power, the Fatherland-All Russia bloc, reflecting a coalition of some of Russia's mightiest political machines (including Moscow, St Petersburg, Tatarstan, Bashkortostan) and powerful oligarchic networks (including Gusinsky's 'Most' network and even the state-owned Lukoil) under the leadership of popular former Prime Minister Yevgeny Primakov. As of summer 1999, the opposition was the odds-on favourite to win the December 1999 parliamentary elections and after that the 2000 presidential race.

This challenge forced the Kremlin to scramble, ultimately winning only after an absolutely wild set of events took place in the second half of 1999. After a series of mysterious explosions killed hundreds of people in ordinary residential buildings in different regions of Russia and terrorized the nation, Putin responded by sending the Russian military into Chechnya, a small restive region that he identified as the source of the problems. This move proved highly popular. Demonstrating strong leadership after years of seeming chaos and incapacity at the top, Putin quickly shot up the presidential standings until by December 1999 he was already well above 50% in the presidential race, more than double that of his closest competitor. In parliamentary elections that same month, a brand-new Unity bloc created just three months earlier surged to a surprisingly strong second place after backing Putin unequivocally, demonstrating Putin's electoral appeal. Yeltsin sealed Putin's status as favourite by resigning on New Year's Eve, making Putin acting president and moving presidential elections up to March 2000. Seeing the writing on the wall, some of the key networks in the opposition coalition started to withdraw or even lend their support to Putin in the presidential race.

Tightening the political machine

One of the things Putin clearly learned from the 1999–2000 succession crisis was that one of the most serious potential threats to Kremlin power is the 'defection' of a coalition of regional political machines and oligarchs, especially those controlling mass media, to the opposition. Some of his very first moves, therefore, were to attack sources of gubernatorial and oligarchic power.

Targeting governors, he removed them from the upper house of parliament (the Federation Council), carved the country up into seven new 'federal districts' led by presidential envoys who could undercut gubernatorial power, and, starting in 2005, replaced direct elections for governor with a system that analysts generally treat as a form of presidential appointment. While the Kremlin restored direct elections in response to a wave of pro-democracy protests in 2011–12, they came with a big catch: To get on the ballot, a candidate had to get the signatures of a large share of deputies in lower-level councils, which were usually dominated by Putin supporters. This system, which came to be known as the 'municipal filter', was designed to ensure that no unwanted candidates could challenge the Kremlin's choice for governors, and indeed, in only one instance as of mid-2018 has its choice lost (Irkutsk, whose winner in 2015 hailed from the Communist Party) (see Chapter 9). To ensure that these Kremlin-friendly governors faced little challenge at home, mayoral elections have been steadily eliminated, to the point at which direct elections for mayor remained in place in only seven regional capitals as of April 2018 (Kara-Murza 2018). At the same time, to make sure that governors do not wield local power bases strong enough to challenge the Kremlin, frequently governors are installed who have little connection to the region.

As for the oligarchs, Putin quickly forced the two with the biggest media assets (Berezovsky and Gusinsky) into de facto exile and offered a deal to the rest by which they could keep their property so long as they did not go against the Kremlin's political interests and economic priorities, a proposal punctuated by an emphatic 'or else'. What 'else' meant became clear in 2003 with the arrest of Yukos chief Mikhail Khodorkovsky, at the time Russia's richest man, who appeared to be flouting Putin's preferred arrangement. As Putin's power grew, it also became evident that he could send a company's stock price plummeting merely by mentioning its owner's disloyalty and hinting at a new Yukos scenario, as the firm Mechel painfully discovered in 2008 (*The Economist* 2008). Additionally, oligarchs were increasingly enlisted to perform certain social functions aimed at preventing social explosions, as illustrated when Putin personally scolded oligarch Oleg Deripaska for neglecting his firm's obligations to the local population of the town of Pikalevo in 2009 (Barry 2009). Especially in the 2010s, figures with deep roots in Putin's own personal network rose to new economic heights, controlling massive economic assets ranging from the oil giant Rosneft to private trading companies like Gunvor and reputedly siphoning off billions for their (and potentially Putin's) personal use (Dawisha 2014). Throughout the latter 2000s and the 2010s so far, then, oligarchic networks were no source of challenge for the regime, and many of them were in fact quite eager to demonstrate willingness to play ball. Inequality in Russia, therefore, remains high, with little emphasis on redistribution (see Chapter 11). This appears to not to have changed despite the fact that Western sanctions have explicitly tried to impose costs on them for their support of Putin as the latter presided over the annexation of Crimea and backed an insurgency in eastern Ukraine (Chapter 14).

Sealing these moves against oligarchs and governors was another key move: the formation of a dominant party (Chapter 3). By 2002, a new United Russia party was founded that included not only core Putin supporters, but former opponents like Moscow Mayor Luzhkov acting on the old maxim 'if you can't beat 'em, join 'em'. Governors soon rushed to join the party, which served a crucial purpose of helping bind elites to the regime. With the 2007–08 election cycle, credible reports emerged that the Kremlin was effectively directing even the financing of opposition parties, telling specific oligarchs which opposition or systemic parties they should fund (Morar' 2007). Of course, it almost goes without saying that close Putin network associates have been in firm control of the 'force agencies' throughout his period in power (Chapter 13). Even there, though, he has kept them divided in ways that would seem to ensure that no one figure could orchestrate a major challenge by himself even if such an unlikely idea happened to enter into his head.

Finally, and perhaps even most importantly, Putin also learned from his rise to power that one of the surest ways to navigate a succession crisis and more generally to stay in power is to maintain popular support. Yeltsin lost public support during his time in office, incentivising former allies to break with him and join the opposition, while Putin won popular support and thereby was able to put the coalition back together. Indeed, if a leader is genuinely popular, then calls by opposition leaders for 'democracy' lose their sting and hence their attractiveness since this opposition would likely lose even if it were granted. When you have popular support, it is harder for opposition leaders to rally people to the streets against you and less costly for you to counter-mobilize or suppress. And a truly popular president like Putin – one with demonstrated 'political coattails' – can alter balances of potential electoral power by his mere verbal endorsement, as when he sent his associate Dmitry Medvedev's standing in presidential ratings soaring when endorsing him to succeed him as president in the 2007–08 election cycle. The Kremlin has thus paid a great deal of attention to Putin's public standing at the same time that it has sought to narrow the channels through which opposition could translate into regime vulnerability.

Dilemmas of governance facing Putin

These lessons that Putin learned from his rocky rise to power and the actions he took in response, however, are fraught with dilemmas, and these are a constant source of dynamism in the regime (Petrov, Lipman, and Hale 2014). On one hand, popularity has been the crucial underpinning of stability in the system he established, enabling him to rise to power in the first place and also to move in and out of the presidency while still maintaining control. The best way to be popular is to give people what they want (and not to give them what they explicitly do not want). This, in turn, requires governing effectively and democratically, or at least appearing to do so, as well as undertaking sometimes-painful reforms that can lead to long-run economic prosperity.

On the other hand, governing effectively and democratically (and even appearing to do so) typically involves creating strong, transparent institutions and democratic practices that can limit the discretion of the ruler and possibly even produce challenges to their hold on power. Many of Putin's actions in office can be understood as his wrestling with just such dilemmas. This can involve attempts to strengthen certain institutions and constitutional regularities at the same time as others are weakened in favour of the flexibility that working through personal connections and individualized rewards and punishments can bring, a phenomenon that Richard Sakwa has characterized as Russia's 'dual state' (Sakwa 2010).

Putin's appeal

Indeed, as several chapters in this volume show, along with all of the moves discussed above to stifle political competition and negate potential sources of opposition, Putin and his supporters have presided over a number of positive changes in the way average Russians live (Chapter 2). First and foremost is the rapid economic growth of the 2000s, which proved a major boon to many Russians throughout the country, even though a wealthy few benefited disproportionately. Research has consistently shown that Putin has benefited politically from this economic progress (McAllister and White 2008). In part, Putin was lucky that his early years in power largely coincided with a surge in world oil prices, and he also benefited from a rouble devaluation in 1998 that had led the economy to return to growth shortly before he arrived in office.

At the same time, at the very least it can be said that he did not mess things up, including making moves like cutting off the internet, which would undoubtedly have been extremely damaging, and in fact he oversaw a number of economic reforms that are hard to explain through a logic of kleptocracy and that have been widely recognized as making positive contributions to economic growth (Chapter 10). These include the institution of a 13% flat tax and the creation of stabilization and investment funds to manage Russia's incoming oil wealth, funds that arguably helped Russia weather the 2008–09 global financial crisis relatively successfully. It was under Putin's watch that Elvira Nabiullina was named best central bank governor of 2015 by *Euromoney*, reflecting the strong performance of the Central Bank of Russia despite its corrupt surroundings and the economic challenges coming from Western sanctions over Russia's military interventions in Ukraine (Reuters 2015). Russia's judiciary has also continued to improve, becoming more and more frequently used by individuals and businesses alike in cases that are not seen to involve major political actors (Gans-Morse 2017) (and see Chapter 8).

Putin's public appeal has not been limited to economic performance, however, as was made clear when his popularity did not collapse after the period of rapid growth ended in the major economic contraction of 2009. First and foremost, Putin wins support for his in-command, dynamic leadership style. Indeed, his surge in popularity in 1999 owed not so much to any rise in nationalism as to a nearly euphoric sense that Russia was finally getting a take-charge, tough-talking, evidently competent, can-do leader determined to end what seemed to be Russia's ongoing decline and collapse after decades (in their view) of a doddering Leonid Brezhnev, a bumbling Mikhail Gorbachev, and an erratic, ill, or drunk Boris Yeltsin who was widely seen as better at destroying the USSR than building anything new in Russia. Putin is also widely associated with broad policy positions that have at least plurality support in Russia, including favouring a deepening of market reform over returning to socialism (Colton and Hale 2014). At the same time, he has been quick to back down from reforms that, once announced, have generated too much opposition (Petrov, Lipman, and Hale 2014), as with a partially abortive 2005 effort to replace many state-supplied benefits going to the elderly and veterans (among others) with monetary payments, a move that sparked massive street protests (Chapter 6). And when his support seemed to be slipping in the early 2010s, Putin delivered a kind of coup de grace with the 2014 annexation of Crimea, a move that proved wildly popular and sent his approval ratings skyward, where they remained until a dip became noticeable by fall 2018.

Putin's strong-hand rule: more subtle than brutal

Putin has also recognized that he does not have to ban opponents in order to defeat them. Instead, more subtle mechanisms usually suffice, instruments that are less costly or risky than attempting to establish a Soviet-style totalitarian state or practicing ballot-box fraud on a truly massive scale. With economic actors understanding that their economic fortunes hinge on not 'crossing' Putin and his allies politically, it can be very hard for opposition politicians to raise money, get coverage in media, or even find premises in which to campaign – even without explicit repressive orders from the top. Similarly, state employees can be mobilized to vote for the regime by communicating to them that their firms could be in peril if the precincts in which they are located do not produce strong votes for the desired candidates or parties (Frye, Reuter, and Szakonyi 2014).

Buttressing such practices, the most influential media skilfully deliver messaging that the Kremlin calculates works in its political favour, led by the trio of state-controlled national television channels on which the large majority of potential voters continue to rely for political information: First Channel, Rossiya-1 and NTV (Chapter 7). With television so dominant, feisty independent sources of information like the hard-hitting *The New Times* or the free-wheeling Ekho Moskvy radio station can be tolerated even when they report on egregious regime corruption or voice harsh opposition narratives, so long as they remain in certain 'ghettos' where funding is scarce and the effective audience minimal. Since most Russians (like ordinary people everywhere) gravitate to the kind of highly professional and attractive entertainment programming that can be found in Russia primarily on the country's main television channels, they are likely to stay there for their news as well, at least so long as news shows retain their good ear in spinning or amplifying those pro-Kremlin narratives that resonate with the public or undercut the most promising opposition narratives (Chapter 5).

In fact, Russia's leadership has had little need to institute the most brutal forms of repression found elsewhere in the world. Unlike China and Saudi Arabia, prisoners (not to mention political ones) are not executed, and in fact the number of political prisoners has long been very low, arguably rising significantly only since 2012 (Gel'man 2015). But even the more recent wave of repressions – even if one counts the 2015 murder of the liberal opposition figure Boris Nemtsov just outside the Kremlin and a few other extrajudicial killings and assaults that some suspect are Kremlin-linked – does not compare with the scale of the crackdowns in Turkey after the anti-Erdoğan coup attempt in July 2016 or in Egypt following the Arab uprising and the ouster of President Mohamed Morsi in July 2013, not to mention routine repression in China and many other hard-core autocracies.

Moreover, when it comes to elections, Putin's regime has actually taken care *not* to strip them of all meaning by eliminating opposition. Instead, some kind of real opposition has been on the ballot in almost every major national election in Russia, including at least a candidate from the Communist Party, which while having reached a comfortable arrangement with the Kremlin that retains its status as the second-largest bloc in parliament, does represent something genuinely different for which people can vote. This does not mean the Kremlin allows every opposition candidate on the ballot who goes for it. The 'weeding out' of candidates through various judicial decisions and technicalities remains an important tactic for shaping electoral outcomes. Most recently, would-be contender Aleksei Navalny was kept off the presidential ballot of March 2018 after what strongly appear to be trumped-up criminal convictions were hung on him. But it does mean that voters almost always are given the appearance of at least *some* choice. And while independent (especially Western) media frequently report credible instances of fraud in Russian elections, perhaps most egregiously some turnout figures over 100% in occasional localities, in reality the scale has rarely been high enough to dramatically shape electoral outcomes. The really important manipulation occurs before people ever get to the ballot box, where it reinforces regime efforts to win genuinely heartfelt votes.

On the strength of all this, the share of Russians who think that Russia is a democratic country has actually risen under Putin, hitting the 50% mark for the first time in 2016 by one measure, as can be seen in Figure 15.1. While Russians are aware of many of their system's shortcomings, they generally feel that the outcome is nevertheless democratic since the candidate with the most popular support (consistently Putin) consistently wins. And they do support democracy. Indeed, while Russians can be found to support a leader who rules with a 'strong hand', a response that is often used as a measure of Russian support for authoritarianism, if one probes deeper one can find that Russians still want the right to choose whose hand gets to be the strong one in free and fair elections (Hale 2011). This gives the Kremlin extra incentive to avoid the worst forms of repression and to work in the more subtle ways described above.

Finally, the Kremlin has been quite willing to change course politically when this has been needed to ensure control without having to resort to the

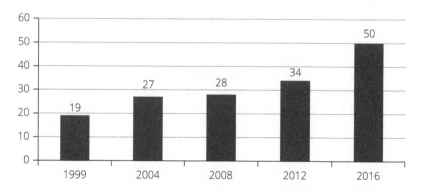

Figure 15.1 Percentage of the Russian population believing Russia is a democratic country, by year

Source: Russian Election Studies (RES) surveys, each representing a nationally representative sample of Russia's adult population, calculations by the author using appropriate weights. On the RES series, see Colton and Hale (2014)

most brutal forms of repression. For example, when United Russia's popularity was at a peak in 2007, the Kremlin replaced the district-based first-past-the-post component of elections for the State Duma with party-list voting that would weaken the regional political machines it was still undercutting at the time, but after United Russia's popularity dropped in the early 2010s the Kremlin restored district-based elections so that the Kremlin could compensate for a lower United Russia party-list result with pro-Kremlin candidates whose district victories could be engineered by regional political machines that were now more firmly under Putin's control (Chapter 4). Putin's own ceding of the presidency to Medvedev during the tandem period can also be understood as a successful regime recalibration, reaching a peak in the balance of people thinking the country is going in the right as opposed to the wrong direction that has not been surpassed, even with the annexation of Crimea (Colton 2017, pp. 14–15). When Putin announced his return to the presidency in 2011 as his popularity was starting to slip and massive protests erupted after the Kremlin tried to compensate with more evident fraud than usual, the Kremlin recalibrated again. First, it liberalized, among other things relaxing a very strict law that had reduced the number of officially recognised political parties to just seven. But shortly afterwards, it shifted focus by mobilising support on the basis of 'conservative values' and branding big-city protesters as supporters of supposedly anti-Russian positions on homosexuality and religion. This move was soon followed by an uptick in repression, including the increasingly frequent arrest and imprisonment of the types of people who earlier could usually count on remaining free or at least being released from police detention shortly after being arrested at an illegal opposition rally. And last but certainly not least, the annexation of Crimea produced one of the most consequential regime recalibrations of all, sending Putin's standing into the realm of 'historic figure' for many ordinary Russians.

So, what kind of regime is Russia and what lies ahead?

Overall, building on roots emerging already in the Yeltsin era, Putin has managed to establish a tight single-pyramid system in Russia. Crucially, this is a political system in which opposition is not so much directly repressed as starved of resources (material, organizational, and even virtual) thanks to the Kremlin's control over the elite wielders of these resources. Central to this control is the leader's ability to coordinate the activities of the powerful, rival political-economic networks that are the 'wielders' in question. Repression occurs, but its forms are far more subtle and less direct than what most notions of 'dictatorship' or 'authoritarianism' typically connote. Ordinary life can feel very free to ordinary Russians, especially those who do not care much about politics. This general 'single-pyramid' state of affairs is what has remained constant under Putin, with the Kremlin being willing to flexibly 'recalibrate' almost everything else as needed in order to sustain it, with the uptick in repression and the patriotic surge over Crimea being only the most recent recalibrations.

So while Russia is clearly not a democracy, whether it qualifies as fully 'authoritarian' depends on one's definition. If the latter label simply refers to any non-democratic regime, as can be useful for certain scholarly or policymaking purposes, then Russia is authoritarian. But political science has relatively recently developed other important concepts, such as the notion of 'hybrid regimes' that are meant to capture some of the peculiar patterns that distinguish politics in places like Russia from politics in, say, Saudi Arabia or China, where elections for the country's top posts are either nonexistent or single-party, unlike the case in Russia. Hybrid regimes combine elements of democracy with their authoritarian elements, and it has been argued here that the holding of at least somewhat contested elections for a country's highest offices matters politically even when the outcome often seems foreordained, making the regime more attentive to public opinion than it would otherwise be while also making it more vulnerable to succession crises. There is a strong argument made that this concept is more promising than many others for answering the question of what kind of regime Russia has (Colton 2018).

That said, what categories are most useful depends on the goals of the analysis. And the whole idea of seeking a single label for Russia's regime – placing it in a category like democracy, autocracy, or even hybrid regime – would seem to underemphasize the nearly constant change that has been such an important feature of Russian politics. Static categories tend to lead us to expect continuity, whereas Russia has continually surprised us. In 1981, few expected the USSR's complete collapse within the decade. In 1999, few anticipated that any new leader could radically reverse the disorder that seemingly pervaded Russian politics within a decade. In 2012, few thought that a war between Russia and Ukraine was in the realm of the possible within two years. A careful look at Russian political history, then, should lead us to be open-eyed about the possibility that we may be surprised yet again, with Russian politics taking us in directions that at the moment may seem unthinkable.

At the same time, an understanding of the network dynamics that lie at the heart of Russian's single-pyramid system should give us some tools for making the unthinkable at least a little bit more thinkable. At a minimum, it suggests that we need to pay close attention to the politics of succession, and to expect Putin during this period to pay particularly close attention to public opinion as a key resource influencing how much control he will be able to exercise over the succession process, whether it occurs in 2024 as constitutionally scheduled, or sometime before or after. We should also expect him to be highly concerned about the relationship among different networks that are now integrated into his political system but could, with possible succession looming, quickly go their own ways should the country's chief patron make a false move. These are likely to be among the crucial questions for students of Russian politics in the years ahead.

GUIDE TO FURTHER READING

Current information on the institutions, personalities, and politics of the Russian presidency, federal executive, and political system is most readily found on the internet, with many valuable sites in Russia offering their information in English. Especially notable are the official internet site of the Russian presidency (http://eng.kremlin.ru/) and Russian government (http://government.ru/en/). In-depth presentations of President Putin's views are available in his annual question-and-answer sessions, 'Direct Line with Vladimir Putin' (since 2001), and his occasional appearances before the Moscow-based Valdai Discussion Club (since 2004); many of these can be found online, and some are subtitled in English. Oliver Stone's four-part television series *The Putin Interviews* (filmed 2015–17) are available for viewing online and the narratives may be read in Stone (2017). Russian news sites with up-to-date information include the news agency, RIA Novosti (http://en.rian.ru/); Russia's leading English-language newspaper, *The Moscow Times* (http://www.themoscowtimes.com/); and the government-funded news channel, Russia Today (http://rt.com/). The Valdai Club website carries important analytical and policy-related papers: http://valdaiclub.com/. Especially useful Western sites include the compendium news website, Russian News Online (http://russiannewsonline.com/), and the daily listserv of Russian news, Johnson's Russia List (http://www.russialist.org/). Survey data, including barometers of public approval levels of Russian politicians and institutions, are to be found at the Levada Centre (http://www.levada.ru/eng/) and VTsIOM (http://www.wciom.com/).

Chapter 1 Politics in Russia

There are a number of good overviews of the Soviet system. These include Gooding (2001), Keep (1996), Kenez (1999), Malia (1994), Marples (2010), Sakwa (1998, 2010), Sandle (1997), Service (2005), Suny (1998) and Westwood (2002). The Gorbachev period is covered by Aron (2012), Brown (1996, 2007), Taubman (2017) and by Gorbachev himself (1987), Sakwa (1990) and White (1994). Arnason provides a fine analysis of the overall failure of the Soviet system, while Cox's edited book (1998) presents debates about the academic study of the fall. More detailed analyses can be found in Kotkin (2001) and Kotz and Weir (1997) and an overview in White (2000). General analyses of contemporary Russian politics can be found in Bacon (2017), Brown, ed. (2001), Dutkiewicz and Trenin, eds (2011), Lane, ed. (2002), Ledeneva (2013), Lynch (2011), McFaul, Petrov and Ryabov (2004), Monaghan (2016, 2017), Remington (2004) Ross (2004), Sakwa (2008, 2011, 2014, 2017), Treisman (2011), Wegren (2013) and White (2011). Fine biographies of Yeltsin are provided by Aron (2000) and Colton (2008), and his leadership is compared with Gorbachev's by Breslauer (2002), while the Putin period is analyzed by Herspring, ed. (2003), Judah (2013) and Sakwa (2008, 2011), with his own views presented in Putin (2000).

Chapter 2 Presidency and Executive

For contrasting discussions of the Putin presidency and legacy, see Dawisha (2014), Gel'man (2015), Myers (2015), and Treisman (2012). Willerton (2016 and 2017) analyzes the Putin programme and Russian public assessments. Among the various texts on Putin, Hill and Gaddy (2013), Hutchins with Korobko (2012), and Solovyov (2008, in Russian) set out alternative perspectives. Regarding Putin's leadership style, see Petersson (2014 and 2017). For a stimulating analysis surrounding Putin's popularity, see Frye, Gehlach, Marquardt and Reuter (2016). For an overview of the groups and personalities making up the Putin team, see Zygar (2016). Robert's book on United Russia is definitive (2011). Urban (2010) provides a thoughtful analysis of Russian elite political culture and communication. For a look back at Soviet period institutions and policies, see Hough (1979).

Chapter 3 Political Parties

For analysis of the overall evolution of Russia's parties through Putin, see Gel'man (2005) and Hale (2006). Comprehensive discussions of Russia's parties in individual election cycles can be found for 1993 in White, Rose, and McAllister (1997) and Colton and Hough (1998), for 1995–96 in Colton (2000) and Belin and Orttung (1997), for 1999–2000 in Colton and McFaul (2003), Hesli and Reisinger (2003), and Rose and Munro (2002) and for 2003–04 in Hale (2006). For more theoretical treatments of parties in the 1990s, see Smyth (2006) and Hale (2006). For additional discussion of parties in the Duma, see Remington (2001) and Smith and Remington (2001). For more on United Russia and its emergence, see Reuter (2017), Roberts (2011), and Smyth, Wilkening, and Urasova (2007). For more discussion of opposition parties, see March (2009), Reuter and Robertson (2015) and the collection of essays in Ross (2015).

Chapter 4 Parliamentary Politics in Russia

An English-language version of the 1993 Russian Constitution is available here: http://www.constitution.ru/en/10003000-01.htm. For an interactive infographic that allows the user to trace individual deputies from the first through to the sixth convocations, see https://ria.ru/infografika/20131212/983608028.html. There are a number of book-length treatments of the Federal Assembly, including Chaisty (2006), Ostrow (2000), Remington (2001), and Troxel (2003). For very good analyses of the shift to executive dominance of the Federal Assembly, see Chaisty (2005, 2008) and Remington (2007, 2008). For an analysis of the Federation Council, see Ross and Turovsky (2013). For a more recent take on legislative politics at the federal level, see Noble and Schulmann (2018). It is important not to forget that parliamentary politics take place below the national level in Russia, too. Although this chapter focuses on the federal-level legislature, see, for example, Reuter (2018), and Panov and Ross (2013, 2016) for recent analyses of legislative activities in the federal subjects.

Chapter 5 National Identity and the Contested Nation

On Russian nationalism, its diverse currents and its ongoing transformations, see Kolstø and Blakkisrud (2016 and 2018) and Laruelle (2018). On the new forms of geopolitical imagination, see Suslov and Bassin (2016). On the concept of Eurasianism, see Bassin and Gonzo (2017) and Laruelle (2008). On Russia's evolving relationship to ethnic issues and the rise of xenophobia towards migrants, and the role of television in it, see Hutchings and Tolz (2015). On the role of Orthodox and of Orthodox presence on the web, see Suslov (2016). On the place of the semantics of fascism in Russia and in its neighbours, see Laruelle (2018).

Chapter 6 Protest, Civil Society and Informal Politics

On protest and contention in the USSR see Viola (2002) and Kozlov (2002). For the role of protest in the collapse of the USSR, Beissinger (2002) is essential reading. Those interested in civil society in the Gorbachev era should see Brovkin (1990). On the difficulties of organizing in the 1990s, read Ashwin (1999). On the first Chechen war, Lieven (1998) makes interesting reading. For protest politics in post-Communist era, see Robertson (2011) and Greene (2014). For a fascinating set of articles on how Putin's system works, see Treisman (2018).

Chapter 7 Russia, Media and Audiences

See *Private Truths, Public Lies: The Social Consequences of Preference Falsification*, Kuran (1995), for analysis of a widespread phenomenon affecting evaluation of opinion polls, timing of dissidence, and the social/political context of support, loyalty, prejudice, and other societal processes with examples from a number of countries and issues. Because studying media effects on a large scale is rarely possible, Enikolopov, Petrova, and Zhuravskaya (2011) is essential reading for an exceptionally informative and methodologically sound study of the effect of NTV on electoral voting in Russia. For an invaluable source, see Andrei Richter's past and current reports for the OSCE containing data and expert evaluation of regulations relating to freedom of the press in the relevant countries. Additionally, specific, timely, well-sourced, and documented publications of the European Audiovisual Observatory provide essential reading on laws and their application in important cases, Richter and Richter (2015). See Mickiewicz (2008) for an analysis of Russian television audiences at the individual level in four cities through focus groups expressing attitudes towards trust in news, salience of issues, and the confusion of election news coverage. For a study of the media, especially the internet, and Russia's highest elite university students and attitudes towards the United States, Russia, other countries and methods determining trust or distrust of websites, see Mickiewicz (2014). For an informed study combining computer science and political science to analyse the initial attempt by Soviet mathematicians to network the entire country and the political and bureaucratic obstacles that ended it, see Peters (2016). For important and original parallel studies of great-power use of mass media when conflict policy has failed, as in Vietnam for the US and Afghanistan for the USSR, see Roselle (2006). For a history of Soviet state television that documents and speculates on the interplay between television audiences and entertainment programming, see Evans (2016). For a cyberpessimist's analysis of the internet and its speculative and contested likely evolution, see Morozov (2011).

Chapter 8 Assessing the Rule of Law in Russia

For a comprehensive overview of the Russian law and legal system, see Maggs, Schwartz, and Burnham (2015). See Henderson (2011) and Sharlet (1992) on the constitution. For an assessment of ongoing legal reform, see Kahn (2008), Solomon (2007), and Kurkchiyan (2003). For more information on the Russian courts, see Solomon and Fogelsong (2000) on the courts of general jurisdiction; Hendley (2017) on the justice-of-the-peace courts; Trochev (2008) on the constitutional court; Hendley (2004) on the *arbitrazh* courts; Trochev (2006) on selecting judges; and Esakov (2012) on jury trials. For more on criminal justice, see Moiseeva (2016), Firestone (2009), Pomorski (2001), and Solomon (1987). On Russians' attitudes towards law, see Hendley (2017) and Ledeneva (2013).

Chapter 9 A Federal State?

For a sophisticated analysis of how Russian regions, through elections at both the federal and regional level, set the stage for Putin's authoritarian regime, see Reisinger and Moraski (2017). The earlier, more democratic period of gubernatorial elections, in which governors were often defeated or reelected based on economic performance, is well treated in Konitzer (2005). Reuter (2017) explores the role played by the party United Russia in regional politics. On the acute problems facing Russian authorities in the North Caucasus, see Ware (2013), and one of the best studies on the conflicts in Chechnya remains Hughes (2007).

Chapter 10 Managing the Economy

The Oxford Handbook of the Russian Economy, Alexeev and Weber (2015), is a compendium of authoritative articles on just about every sector and theme that is important for an understanding of the Russian economy, There are, for example, chapters on the legacy of the command economy, growth trends, institutional performance, the tax system, oil and gas, the labour market and financial markets. The contributors are leading specialists, Russian and non-Russian, and the level is post-graduate. *The Challenges for Russia's Politicized Economic System*, Oxenstierna (2015), understandably has some overlap with *The Oxford Handbook* in coverage and contributors but is more policy oriented and more readily accessible to undergraduates. The most useful all-round guide to the content of Western sanctions against Russia and issues related to them is Oxenstierna and Olsson's *The Economic Sanctions Against Russia. Impact and Prospects of Success* (2015). It is not up to date but is strong on the content of the 2014 sanctions and the issues to do with them, which remain important.

Chapter 11 Inequality and Social Policy in Russia

Linda Cook (2007) provides an overview of the reform of welfare policies in Russia and Eastern Europe along with an account of the bureaucratic battles behind the reforms. Novokmet, Piketty and Zucman (2017) estimate top income shares and wealth shares in Russia using a combination of tax and survey data. Remington (2011) explores the political and economic factors accounting for differences in levels of inequality across Russian regions. Remington (forthcoming in *Problems of Post-Communism*) compares the bureaucratic policymaking processes in Russia and China with respect to pension policy, and Remington (forthcoming in *Comparative Politics*) discusses some of the ways in which inequality trends in Russia are similar to and different from those in the United States.

Chapter 12 Russian Foreign Policy

Various aspects of Russian foreign policy are explored in Cadier and Light (2015), Donaldson and Nogee (2014), Kanet and Piet (2016), Morozov (2015), Mankoff (2009), Lo (2015), Rumer (2017), Trenin (2016) and Tsygankov (2017, 2018). Russia-US relations are analyzed in Legvold (2016) and Stent (2015). White and Feklyunina (2014) focus on Russia's relationship with Europe, while Kaczmarski (2015) examines Russia's policy towards China. Russia's engagement with its immediate neighbours in the post-Soviet area is covered in Grigas (2016) and Molchanov (2016). Russia's role in the Ukraine crisis and the consequences of the conflict for Russia's relations with the West are examined in Birchfield and Young (2017), Black and Johns (2016), Menon and Rumer (2015), Rosefielde (2016), Sakwa (2015b) and Wilson (2014). Russia's use of energy in its external relations is explored in Balmaceda (2013), Kandiyoti (2015) and Sotiriou (2015). Various aspects of Russia's influence and soft power are studied in Van Herpen (2015), Sherr (2013) and Shekhovtsov (2017). Russia's engagement with the idea of military intervention is analyzed in Allison (2013).

Chapter 13 Security, the Military and Politics

For more details on the Russian force structures, see Taylor (2007). For the *siloviki* debate and security under Putin, read Kryshtanovskaya and White (2003), Renz (2006) and Bacon et al. (2006). A good outline of military reforms under Boris Yeltsin can be found in Arbatov (1998, 2000). For military reforms under Putin, see McDermott et al. (2012). Connolly and Senstad (2016) provide a particularly perceptive account of ongoing problems in the Russian defence industry. For a contextualized analysis of developments in Russian security and military affairs, including the 'hybrid warfare' discussion, see Renz (2018).

Chapter 14 Russia and its Neighbours

For an excellent overview of the region and Russia's role, see Trenin (2011). For an examination of Russia–West dynamics in the region, see Hill (2012), Charap and Colton (2017), and Charap and Troitskiy (2013–14). Cooley (2010) is the definitive work on great-power dynamics in Central Asia; see also Malashenko (2013) specifically on Russia's policy. On the 2008 Russia-Georgia war, see Asmus (2010) for an insider's account, and Pukhov (2010) for an analysis of the military dynamics. On the Ukraine crisis, Charap and Colton (2017), Menon and Rumer (2015), Sakwa (2014) and Wilson (2014) offer competing perspectives. Howard and Pukhov (2015) cover the military aspects of the crisis. Hampson and Troitskiy (2018) contains a range of views on security and conflict in post-Soviet Eurasia; King (2001) covers the origins of many of the protracted conflicts. The collection of Russian-language essays in Timofeev, Makhmutov and Khaspekova (2017) provides a wide-ranging view on the region, largely as seen from Moscow. On the Eurasian Economic Union, see Dragneva and Wolczuk (2017) and Dragneva and Wolczuk (2013).

Chapter 15 The Continuing Evolution of Russia's Political System

Debates on how to characterise (and explain) Russia's regime under Putin are legion, with competing perspectives to be found, for example, in Colton (2018), Dawisha (2014), Fish (2005, 2018), Hale (2010, 2015), Levitsky and Way (2010), McFaul (2018), Rivera and Rivera (2014), Robertson (2011), and Sakwa (2014b). Among works examining political-economic networks and informal politics more generally in Russia are Dawisha (2014), Hale (2015), Ledeneva (1998, 2006, 2013), Markus (2015), Sakwa (2011, 2014a), Sharafutdinova (2010), Wilson (2005), and Zygar' (2016). Stimulating exercises in anticipating Russia's future trajectory can be found in Lipman and Petrov (2011, 2013) and the Spring 2017 special issue of the journal *Daedalus*, the introductory essay to which is by Colton (2017).

GLOSSARY

advokat	lawyer
apparat	party bureaucracy
arbitrazh	arbitration (commercial) courts
demokratizatsiya	democratisation
Duma	lower house of Federal Assembly (parliament)
federal'nyi zakon	federal law
glasnost	openness
Gossovet	State Council
guberniya	province (in Tsarist era)
komsomol	communist youth league
krai	province
natsional'nost	ethnic origin of an individual
neformaly	unofficial social associations
nomenklatura	list of party-controlled posts
oblast	region
obshchestvennye	social or public organisation
perestroika	restructuring
polpred	presidential envoy
poslanie	address, speech
pravovoe gosudarstvo	legal state
pravovoe upravlenie	legal department
preemstvennost	continuity
reglament	standing orders
Rossiiskaya Federatsiya	Russian Federation
rossiiskii	Russian (civic)
rossiyan	Russian (civic)
russkii	Russian (ethnic and civic)
russkoe gosudarstvo	Russian state
Shchetnaya Palata	Audit Chamber
siloviki	security and intelligence officials
sovet	council
ukazy	presidential decrees
uskorenie	acceleration
vertikal vlasti	power vertical
zastoi	stagnation

REFERENCES

Allison, Roy (2013), *Russia, the West, and Military Intervention*. Oxford: Oxford University Press.

Andrews, Josephine T. (2002), *When Majorities Fail: The Russian Parliament, 1990–1993*. Cambridge: Cambridge University Press.

Andrushchak, G. et al. (2011), *Mode of Life and Living Standards of Russian Population in 1989–2009*. Moscow, Higher School of Economics and Ekspert Magazine. XII International Academic Conference on Economic and Social Development, 5–7 April, p. 72.

Anonymous (2010), Repressivno-truslivoe pravosudie, *Novaia advokatskaia gazeta* (July). Available at http://www.advgazeta.ru/arch/72/442.

Antonova, Natalia (2014), Russian State Duma: 'Possessed printer' or executor of the people's will?, *The Moscow News*, 29 January. Available at: http://russialist.org/russian-state-duma-possessed-printer-or-executor-of-the-peoples-will/.

Arbatov, Aleksei G. (1998), Military reform in Russia: dilemmas, obstacles and prospects, *International Security, 22*(4), pp. 83–134.

Arbatov, Aleksei G. (2000), The transformation of Russian military doctrine. Lessons learned from Kosovo and Chechnya, The Marshal Centre Papers, 2.

Arnold, Richard (2016), *Russian Nationalism and Ethnic Violence: Symbolic Violence, Lynching, Pogrom and Massacre*. London: Routledge.

Aron, Leon (2000), *Boris Yeltsin: A Revolutionary Life*. London: HarperCollins.

Ashwin, Sarah (1999), *Russian Workers: The Anatomy of Patience*. Manchester: Manchester University Press.

Bacon, Edwin, Bettina Renz, and Julian Cooper (2006), *Securitising Russia: The Domestic Politics of Vladimir Putin*. Manchester: Manchester University Press.

Balmaceda, Margarita Mercedes (2013), *The Politics of Energy Dependency: Ukraine, Belarus, and Lithuania between Domestic Oligarchs and Russian Pressure*. Toronto: University of Toronto Press.

Barry, Ellen (2009), Putin plays sheriff for cowboy capitalists, *The New York Times*, June 4, sec. Europe. Available at: https://www.nytimes.com/2009/06/05/world/europe/05russia.html.

Bassin, Mark, and Gonzalo Ponzo (2017), *The Politics of Eurasianism: Identity, Popular Culture and Russia's Foreign Policy*. London: Rowman & Littlefield.

Bartles, Charles K. (2016), Getting Gerasimov right, *Military Review*, Jan.–Feb., pp. 30–38.

Beissinger, Mark R. (2002), *Nationalist Mobilization and the Collapse of the Soviet State*. Cambridge: Cambridge University Press.

Belin, Laura and Robert Orttung (1997), *The Russian Parliamentary Elections of 1995: The Battle for the Duma*. Armonk, NY: ME Sharpe.

Birchfield, Vicki L. and Alasdair R. Young (eds.) (2017), *Triangular Diplomacy among the United States, the European Union, and the Russian Federation: Responses to the Crisis in Ukraine*. Basingstoke: Palgrave Macmillan.

Black, Joseph Laurence and Michael Johns (eds.) (2016), *The Return of the Cold War: Ukraine, the West and Russia*. London and New York, NY: Routledge.

Breedlove, P. (2015), Theater strategy, United States European Command, October, http://www.eucom.mil/media-library/document/35147/useucom-theater-strategy.

Bremmer, Ian and Samuel Charap (2006–07), The *Siloviki* in Putin's Russia: Who they are and what they want, *The Washington Quarterly, 30*(1), pp. 83–92.

Brovkin, Vladimir (1990), Revolution from below: Informal political associations in Russia 1988–89, *Europe-Asia Studies, 42*(2), pp. 233–257.

Brown, Archie (1996), *The Gorbachev Factor*. Oxford: Oxford University Press.

Brudny, Yitzhak M. (2000), *Reinventing Russia: Russian Nationalism and the Soviet State, 1953–1991*. Cambridge, MA: Harvard University Press.

Cadier, David and Margot Light (eds.) (2015), *Russia's Foreign Policy: Ideas, Domestic Politics and External Relations*. Basingstoke: Palgrave Macmillan.

Carothers, Thomas (2002), The end of the transition paradigm, *Journal of Democracy, 13*(1), pp. 5–21.

Chaisty, Paul (2005), Majority control and executive dominance: Parliament-president relations in Putin's Russia, in Alex Pravda (ed.), *Leading Russia: Putin in Perspective*, pp. 119–137. Oxford: Oxford University Press.

Chaisty, Paul (2006), *Legislative Politics and Economic Power in Russia*. Basingstoke; New York, NY: Palgrave Macmillan.

Chaisty, Paul (2008), The legislative effects of presidential partisan powers in postcommunist Russia, *Government and Opposition, 43*(3), pp. 424–453.

Chaisty, Paul (2012), The Federal Assembly and the power vertical, in Graeme Gill and James Young (eds.), *Routledge Handbook of Russian Politics and Society*, pp. 92–101. Abingdon; New York, NY: Routledge.

Chaisty, Paul (2013), The preponderance and effects of sectoral ties in the State Duma, *Europe-Asia Studies, 65*(4), pp. 717–736.

Chandler, Andrea (2004), *Shocking Mother Russia: Democratization, Social Rights, and Pension Reform in Russia, 1990–2001*. Toronto: University of Toronto Press.

Churakova, Ol'ga (2017), 'Rossiya pouchit deputatov dialogu [Russia will teach deputies dialogue]', *Vedomosti*, 15 October, https://www.vedomosti.ru/newspaper/articles/2017/10/15/737916-rossiya-deputatov.

Colton, Timothy J. (2000), *Transitional Citizens: Voters and What Influences Them in the New Russia*. Cambridge, MA: Harvard University Press.

Colton, Timothy J. (2008), *Yeltsin: A Life*. New York, NY: Basic Books.

Colton, Timothy J. (2017), Paradoxes of Putinism, *Daedalus, 146*(2): pp. 8–18. https://doi.org/10.1162/DAED_a_00430.

Colton, Timothy J. (2018), Regimeness, hybridity, and Russian system building as an educative project, *Comparative Politics, 50*(3), pp. 455–473. https://doi.org/10.5129/001041518822704935.

Colton, Timothy J. and Henry E. Hale (2014), Putin's uneasy return and hybrid regime stability: The 2012 Russian Election Studies Survey, *Problems of Post-Communism, 61*(2), pp. 3–22.

Colton, Timothy J. and Jerry Hough (eds.) (1998), *Growing Pains: Russian Democracy and the Election of 1993*. Washington, DC: Brookings Institution Press.

Colton, Timothy J. and Michael McFaul (2003), *Popular Choice and Managed Democracy: The Russian Elections of 1999 and 2000*. Washington, DC: Brookings Institution Press.

Connolly, Richard (2015), Troubled times: Stagnation, sanctions and the prospects for economic reform in Russia, Chatham House paper, February, https://www.chathamhouse.org/publication/troubled-times-stagnation-sanctions-and-prospects-economic-reform-russia.

Connolly, Richard and Philip Hanson (2016), Import substitution and economic sovereignty in Russia, Chatham House Research Paper, June, https://www.chathamhouse.org/publication/import-substitution-and-economic-sovereignty-russia.

Connolly, Richard and Cecilie Sendstad (2016), Russian rearmament: an assessment of defence-industrial performance, *Problems of Post-Communism*, doi: 10.1080/10758216.2016.1236668.

Cook, Linda J. (2007), *Postcommunist Welfare States: Reform Politics in Russia and Eastern Europe*. Ithaca, NY: Cornell University Press.

Credit Suisse Research Institute, *Global Wealth Report 2014*.

Credit Suisse Research Institute, *Global Wealth Databook 2015*.

Credit Suisse Research Institute, *Global Wealth Report 2015*.

CSR (2017), Centre for Strategic Research presentation on reform, http://csr.ru/wp-content/2017/01/GF4.pdf.

Dale, Hellie C. (2015), Russia's 'weaponization' of information. Testimony Presented to the House Foreign Affairs Committee, Washington, DC, quoted in Ellen Mickiewicz (2017), *No Illusions: The Voices of Russia's Future Leaders*, pp. 1–2. Oxford: Oxford University Press., paperback edn.

Dalton, Russell J. and Martin P. Wattenberg (2002), *Parties without Partisans: Political Change in Advanced Industrial Democracies*. Oxford: Oxford University Press.

Dannreuther, Roland and Luke March (eds.) (2011), *Russia and Islam: State, Society and Nationalism*. London: Routledge.

Dawisha, Karen (2014), *Putin's Kleptocracy: Who Owns Russia?* New York, NY: Simon & Schuster.

Deyermond, Ruth (2013), Assessing the reset: Successes and failures in the Obama administration's Russia policy, 2009–2012, *European Security, 22*(4), pp. 500–523.

Dobrolyubov, N. (2013), Emergency at the defense ministry, *Moscow Defense Brief, 34*(2).

Donaldson, Robert H. and Joseph L. Nogee (2014), *The Foreign Policy of Russia: Changing Systems, Enduring Interests, 2014*. London and New York, NY: Routledge.

Dragneva, Rilka and Kataryna Wolczuk (2017), *The Eurasian Economic Union Deals, Rules and the Exercise of Power*, Chatham House Research Paper, May, https://www.chathamhouse.org/sites/files/chathamhouse/publications/research/2017-05-02-eurasian-economic-union-dragneva-wolczuk.pdf.

Eismont, Mariya (2012), My dolzhny verit ne dokazatel'stvam, a silovikam na slovo, *PublicPost*, 25 May. Available at: http://www.publicpost.ru/theme/id/1495/my_dolzhny_verit_ne_dokazatelstvam_a_silovikam_na_slovo/.

Engström, Maria (2014), Contemporary Russian messianism and new Russian foreign policy, *Contemporary Security Policy, 35*(3), pp. 356–379.

Engström, Maria (2017), The new Russian Renaissance: Why the Kremlin is fascinated by classical antiquity, *Intersection* (4 April). Available at: http://intersectionproject.eu/article/russia-europe/new-russian-renaissance.

Enikolopov, Ruben, Maria Petrova, and Ekaterina Zhuravskaya (2011), Media and political persuasion: Evidence from Russia, *American Economic Review, 101*(17), pp. 3253–3285.

Esakov, Gennady (2012), The Russian criminal jury: Recent developments, practice, and current problems, *American Journal of Comparative Law, 60*(3), pp. 665–702.

Evans, Alfred B., Laura A. Henry, and Lisa McIntosh Sundstrom (eds.) (2006), *Russian Civil Society: A Critical Assessment.* Armonk, NY: M.E. Sharpe.

Evans, Christine E. (2016), *Between Truth and Time: A History of Soviet Central Television.* New Haven, CT: Yale University Press.

Feifer, Gregory (2010), Opposition legislators say Russia's parliament is no parliament, *RFE/RL*, 18 October, https://www.rferl.org/a/Opposition_Legislators_Say_Russias_Parliament_Is_No_Parliament/2193979.html.

Feklyunina, Valentina (2008), Battle for perceptions: Projecting Russia in the West, *Europe-Asia Studies, 60*(4), pp. 605–629.

Feklyunina, Valentina (2012), Constructing Russophobia, in Raymond Taras (ed.), *Russia's Identity in International Relations: Images, Perceptions, Misperceptions*, pp. 91–109. London: Routledge.

Felgenhauer, Pavel (2016), Russia's relations with the West deteriorate as military prepares for "resource wars", *Eurasia Daily Monitor, 13*(177) (3 November).

Firestone, Thomas (2009), Armed injustice: Abuse of the law and complex crime in post-Soviet Russia, *Denver Journal of International Law & Policy, 38*(4), pp. 555–580.

Fish, M. Steven (2001), Conclusion: Democracy and Russian politics, in Zoltan Barany and Robert G. Moser (eds.), *Russian Politics: Challenges of Democratization*, pp. 215–251. Cambridge: Cambridge University Press.

Fish, M. Steven (2005), *Democracy Derailed in Russia: The Failure of Open Politics.* Cambridge: Cambridge University Press.

FOM (2012), Gosudarstvennaya duma: Otsenka raboty Gosdumy i itnoshenie k deyatel'nosti deputatov [The State Duma: An assessment of the work of the State Duma and the relationship to activities of deputies], 25 October, http://fom.ru/politika/10669.

Fond obshchestvennogo mneniie (2017a), Reputatsiya sudov i sudei. Available at: http://fom.ru/bezopasnost-i-pravo/13239.

Fond obshchestvennogo mneniie (2017b) Zashchita prav i obrashchenie v sud. Available at: http://fom.ru/Bezopasnost-i-pravo/13252.

Foreign policy concept of the Russian Federation (2008). Available at: http://en.kremlin.ru/supplement/4116, accessed 25 March 2018.

Foreign policy concept of the Russian Federation (2013). Available at: http://www.mid.ru/en/foreign_policy/official_documents/-/asset_publisher/CptICkB6BZ29/content/id/122186 (accessed 25 March 2018).

Foreign policy concept of the Russian Federation (2016). Available at: http://www.mid.ru/en/foreign_policy/official_documents/-/asset_publisher/CptICkB6BZ29/content/id/2542248 (accessed 25 March 2018).

Fortescue, Stephen (2006), *Russia's Oil Barons and Metal Magnates: Oligarchs and the State in Transition.* Basingstoke: Palgrave Macmillan.

Friedman, Thomas L. (1991), Soviet disarray: Yeltsin says Russia seeks to join NATO, *New York Times*, 21 December. Available at: https://www.nytimes.com/1991/12/21/world/soviet-disarray-yeltsin-says-russia-seeks-to-join-nato.html (accessed 24 March 2018).

Frye, Timothy, Ora John Reuter, and David Szakonyi (2014), Political machines at work: Voter mobilization and electoral subversion in the workplace, *World Politics, 66*(2), pp. 195–228.

Frye, Timothy, Scott Gehlach, Kyle L. Marquardt, and Ora John Reuter (2016), Is Putin's popularity real?, *Post-Soviet Affairs, 33*(1), pp. 1–15.

Fuller, Lon L. (1964), *The Morality of Law*, rev. ed. New Haven, CT: Yale University Press.

Galeotti, Mark (2016), Putin's new National Guard – what does it say if you need your own personal army?, Moscow's Shadows blog, 5 April, https://inmoscowsshadows. wordpress.com/2016/04/05/putins-new-national-guard-what-does-it-say-when-you-need-your-own-personal-army/.

Gandhi, Jennifer (2008), *Political Institutions under Dictatorship*. Cambridge: Cambridge University Press.

Gans-Morse, Jordan (2017), *Property Rights in Post-Soviet Russia: Violence, Corruption, and the Demand for Law*. Cambridge: Cambridge University Press.

Gel'man, Vladimir (2005), Political opposition in Russia: A dying species?, *Post-Soviet Affairs*, *21*(3) (July–Sept.), pp. 226–246.

Gel'man, Vladimir (2015), *Authoritarian Russia: Analyzing Post-Soviet Regime Changes*. Pittsburgh, PA: University of Pittsburgh Press.

Gerber, Ted and Zavisca, Jane (2017), Political and social attitudes of Russia's Muslims: Caliphate, kadyrovism, or kasha? *PONARS Eurasia Policy Memo*, no. 468 (April). http://www.ponarseurasia.org/memo/political-and-social-attitudes-russias-muslims-caliphate-kadyrovism-or-kasha.

Giles, Keir (2016), *Russia's New Tools for Confronting the West: Continuity and Innovation in Moscow's Exercise of Power*. London: Royal Institute of International Affairs Chatham House.

Gilligan, Emma (2010), The human rights ombudsman in Russia: The evolution of horizontal accountability, *Human Rights Quarterly*, *32*(3), pp. 575–610.

Gimpel'son, Vladimir and Rostislav Kapeliushnikov (2013), Zhit' 'v teni' ili umeret' 'na svetu': neformal'nost' na rossiiskom rynke truda, *Voprosy ekonomiki*, November, pp. 65–88.

Gimpel'son, Vladimir and Rostislav Kapeliushnikov (eds.) (2014), *V teni regulirovanyia*. Moscow: Vysshaia shkola ekonomiki.

Gimpel'son, Vladimir and Rostislav Kapeliushnikov (2015), Labor market adjustment: Is Russia different? in Michael Alexeev and Shlomo Weber (eds.), *The Oxford Handbook of the Russian Economy*, pp. 693–725. Oxford: Oxford University Press.

Golosov, Grigorii (2011), Russia's regional legislative elections, 2003–2007: Authoritarianism incorporated, *Europe-Asia Studies*, *63*(3), pp. 397–414.

Goode, James Paul (2011), *The Decline of Regionalism in Putin's Russia: Boundary Issues*. London and New York, NY: Routledge.

Goode, James Paul (2018), Everyday patriotism and ethnicity in today's Russia, in Helge Blakkisrud and Pål Kolstø (eds.), *Russia Before and After Crimea: Nationalism and Identity, 2010–2017*, pp. 258–281. Edinburgh: Edinburgh University Press.

Gorbachev, Mikhail (1987), *Perestroika: New Thinking for Our Country and the World*. London: Collins.

Greene, Samuel A. (2014), *Moscow in Movement: Power and Opposition in Putin's Russia*. Stanford, CA: Stanford University Press.

Grigas, Agnia (2016), *Beyond Crimea: The New Russian Empire*. New Haven, CT: Yale University Press.

Gurvich, Evsey and Ilya Prilepskiy (2015), The impact of financial sanctions on Russia's economy, *Russian Journal of Economics*, I, pp. 359–385.

Haggard, Stephan and Matthew D. McCubbins (2001), Introduction: Political institutions and the determinants of public policy, in Stephan Haggard and Matthew D. McCubbins (eds.), *Presidents, Parliaments, and Policy*. Cambridge: Cambridge University Press.

Hahn, Gordon M. (2002), *Russia's Revolution from Above, 1985–2000: Reform, Transition, and Revolution in the Fall of the Soviet Communist Regime*. New Brunswick, NJ: Transaction Publishers.

Hale, Henry E. (2006), *Why Not Parties in Russia: Democracy, Federalism, and the State*. New York, NY: Cambridge University Press.

Hale, Henry E. (2011), The myth of mass Russian support for autocracy: The public opinion foundations of a hybrid regime, *Europe-Asia Studies*, *63*(8), pp. 1357–1375. https://doi.org/10.1080/09668136.2011.601106.

Hale, Henry E. (2015), *Patronal Politics: Eurasian Regime Dynamics in Comparative Perspective*. New York, NY: Cambridge University Press.

Hanson, Philip (2005), Federalism with a Russian face: Regional inequality and regional budgets in Russia,' in Peter Reddaway and Robert Orttung (eds.), II *The Dynamics of Russian Politics: Putin's Reform of Federal-Regional Relations*, pp. 295–318. London, Boulder, CO, and New York, NY: Rowman & Littlefield.

Hanson, Philip (2014), *Reiderstvo*: Asset-grabbing in Russia, Chatham House paper, https://www.chathamhouse.org/publications/papers/view/198133.

Hanson, Philip (2017), Western sanctions: Helping the Russian leadership ride out recession, Chatham House Expert Comment, 10 March, https://www.chathamhouse.org/expert/comment/western-sanctions-helping-russian-leadership-ride-out-recession.

Henderson, Jane (2011), *The Constitution of the Russian Federation: A Contextual Analysis*. Oxford: Hart Publishing.

Hendley, Kathryn (2004), Business litigation in the transition: A portrait of debt collection in Russia, *Law & Society Review*, *31*(1), pp. 305–347.

Hendley, Kathryn (2012), The puzzling non-consequences of societal distrust of courts: Explaining the use of Russian courts, *Cornell International Law Journal*, *45*(3), pp. 517–567.

Hendley, Kathryn (2016), Justice in Moscow?, *Post-Soviet Affairs*, *32*(6), pp. 491–511.

Hendley, Kathryn (2017), *Everyday Law in Russia*. Ithaca, NY: Cornell University Press.

Hesli, Vicki L. and William M. Reisinger (eds.) (2003), *The 1999–2000 Elections in Russia: Their Impact and Legacy*. New York, NY: Cambridge University Press.

Higgins, Andrew (2017), Russia wants innovation, but it's arresting its innovators, *New York Times*, 9 August. Available at: https://www.nytimes.com/2017/08/09/world/europe/vladimir-putin-russia-siberia.html.

Hill, Fiona and Clifford G. Gaddy (2015), *Mr. Putin: Operative in the Kremlin*. Washington, DC: Brookings Institution Press.

Holmes, Stephen (1993/1994), Superpresidentialism and its problems, *East European Constitutional Review*, *2*(4), *3*(1), pp. 123–126.

Hough, Jerry (1998), The failure of party formation and the future of Russian democracy, in Timothy J. Colton and Jerry F. Hough (eds.), *Growing Pains: Russian Democracy and the Election of 1993*. Washington, DC: Brookings Institution Press, pp. 669–712.

Hough, Jerry F. and Merle Fainsod (1979), *How the Soviet Union Is Governed*. Cambridge, MA: Harvard University Press.

Hughes, James (2007), *Chechnya: From Nationalism to Jihad*. Philadelphia, PA: University of Pennsylvania Press.

Huntington, Samuel P. (1968), *Political Order in Changing Societies*. New Haven, CT: Yale University Press.

Huntington, Samuel (1991), *The Third Wave: Democratization in the Late Twentieth Century*. Norman, OK: University of Oklahoma Press.

Huskey, Eugene (1991), A framework for the analysis of Soviet law, *Russian Review*, 50(1), pp. 53–70.

Hutchings, Stephen and Vera Tolz (eds.) (2015), *Nation, Ethnicity and Race on Russian Television: Mediating Post-Soviet Difference*. London: Routledge.

Hutchins, Chris, with Alexander Korobko (2012), *Putin*. Leicester: Troubador Publishing Ltd.

Independent International Fact-Finding Mission on the Conflict in Georgia (2009), Independent International Fact-Finding Mission on the Conflict in Georgia Report, September, http://echr.coe.int/Documents/HUDOC_38263_08_Annexes_ENG. pdf.

Ishiyama, John T. (1999), Political integration and political parties in post-Soviet Russian politics, *Demokratizatsiya*, 7(2), pp. 188–203.

Iversen, Torben and David Soskice (2006), Electoral institutions and the politics of coalitions: Why some democracies redistribute more than others, *American Political Science Review, 100*(2), pp. 165–181.

Johnson, Juliet (2000), *A Fistful of Rubles: The Rise and Fall of the Russian Banking System*. Ithaca, NY: Cornell University Press.

Kaczmarski, Marcin (2015), *Russia-China Relations in the Post-Crisis International Order*. London and New York, NY: Routledge.

Kahn, Jeffrey (2008), Vladimir Putin and the rule of law in Russia, *Georgia Journal of International and Comparative Law, 36*(5), pp. 511–557.

Kalinina, Ekaterina (2014), Mediated Post-Soviet Nostalgia, PhD dissertation, Sodertorn University.

Kandiyoti, Rafael (2015), *Powering Europe: Russia, Ukraine, and the Energy Squeeze*. New York, NY: Palgrave Macmillan.

Kanet, Roger and Rémi Piet (eds.) (2016), *Shifting Priorities in Russia's Foreign and Security Policy*. London and New York, NY: Routledge.

Kara-Murza, Vladimir (2018), In Russia, a democratically elected mayor finally succumbs to Putinism, *Washington Post*, 5 April. Available at: https://www.washingtonpost. com/news/democracy-post/wp/2018/04/05/in-russia-a-democratically-elected-mayor-finally-succumbs-to-putinism/?utm_term=.c8deeac0f5fe.

Kolstø, Pål (2014), Russia's nationalists flirt with democracy, *Journal of Democracy*, 25(3), pp. 120–134.

Kolstø, Pål (2016), Marriage of convenience? Collaboration between nationalists and liberals in the Russian opposition 2011–12, *The Russian Review*, 75(4), pp. 645–663.

Kolstø, Pål and Helge Blakkisrud (eds.) (2016), *The New Russian Nationalism: Between Imperial and Ethnic*. Edinburgh: Edinburgh University Press.

Kolstø, Pål and Helge Blakkisrud (eds.) (2018), *Russia Before and After Crimea. Nationalism and Identity, 2010–17*. Edinburgh: Edinburgh University Press.

Konitzer, Andrew (2005), *Voting for Russia's Governors* Washington, DC: Woodrow Wilson Center Press.

Kontseptsiya vneshnei politiki Rossiiskoi Federatsii (1993), in Tatiana Shakleina (ed.) *Vneshnyaya politika i bezopasnost' sovremennoi Rossii 1991–2002*, vol. 4, pp. 109–121. Moscow.

Kontseptsiya vneshnei politiki Rossiiskoi Federatsii (2000), in Tatiana Shakleina (ed.) *Vneshnyaya politika i bezopasnost' sovremennoi Rossii 1991–2002*, vol. 4. Moscow, pp. 109–121.

Kostyrev, Anatolii (2017), Plody zapreshcheniya, *Kommersant*, 7 August, https://www. kommersant.ru/doc/3374177.

Kozenko, Andrei and Maria Krasovskaia (2008), Natsionalisty stroiat evro-peiskoe litso, *Kommersant*, no. 120 (14 July). http://www.kommersant.ru/doc.aspx?DocsID¼912162&NodesID¼2.

Kozlov, Vladimir (2002), *Mass Uprisings in the USSR: Protest and Rebellion in the Post-Stalin Years*. Armonk, NY: M.E. Sharpe.

Kozyrev, Andrei (1994), The lagging partnership, *Foreign Affairs, 73*(3), pp. 59–71.

Kreppel, Amie (2014), Typologies and classifications, in Shane Martin, Thomas Saal-feld, and Kaare Strøm (eds.), *The Oxford Handbook of Legislative Studies*. Oxford: Oxford University Press.

Kryshtanovskaya, O. and S. White (2003), Putin's militocracy, *Post-Soviet Affairs, 19*(4), 289–306.

Kudrin, A. I. Sokolov (2017), Budzhetnyi manevr i strukturnaya perestroika rossiiskoi ekonomiki,' *Voprosy ekonomiki* no. 9, pp. 5–27.

Kuvshinova, Ol'ga (2012), Lovushka starosti, *Vedomosti*, 13 March.

Kuran, Timur (1995), *Private Truths, Public Lies: The Social Consequences of Preference Falsification*. Cambridge, MA: Harvard University Press.

Kurkchiyan, Marina (2003), The illegitimacy of law in post-Soviet societies, in Denis J. Galligan and Marina Kurkchiyan (eds.), *Law and Informal Practices: The Post-Communist Experience*. Oxford: Oxford University Press.

Laruelle, Marlene (2009), *In the Name of the Nation: Nationalism and Politics in Con-temporary Russia*. New York, NY: Palgrave Macmillan.

Laruelle, Marlene (2014), Alexei Navalny and challenges in reconciling 'nationalism' and 'liberalism', *Post-Soviet Affairs, 30*(4), pp. 276–297.

Laruelle, Marlene (2015a), Eurasia, Eurasianism, Eurasian Union: Terminological gaps and overlaps, *PONARS Eurasia Policy Memo*, no. 366 (July). http://www.ponarseurasia.org/memo/eurasia-eurasianism-eurasian-union-terminological-gaps-and-overlaps.

Laruelle, Marlene (2015b), The three colors of Novorossiya, or the Russian nationalist mythmaking of the Ukrainian crisis, *Post-Soviet Affairs, 32*(1), pp. 55–74.

Laruelle, Marlene (2016), The Izborsky club, or the new conservative avant-garde in Russia, *The Russian Review, 75*(4), pp. 626–644.

Laruelle, Marlene (2017), The Kremlin's ideological ecosystems: Equilibrium and compe-tition, *PONARS Eurasia Policy Memo*, no. 493 (November). http://www.ponarseurasia.org/memo/kremlins-ideological-ecosystems-equilibrium-and-competition.

Laruelle, Marlene (forthcoming), Commemorating 1917 in Russia: State ambiv-alent history policy and church's conquest of the history market, *Europe-Asia Studies*.

Laruelle, Marlene (forthcoming), *Russia and the Symbolic Landscape of Fascism*. Pitts-burgh, PA: Pittsburgh University Press.

Laruelle, Marlene (2018), *Russian Nationalism, Foreign Policy and Identity Debates in Putin's Russia*. New York, NY: Columbia University Press.

Ledeneva, Alena (2013), *Can Russia Modernise? Sistema, Power Networks and Informal Governance*. New York, NY: Cambridge University Press.

Legvold, Robert (2016), *Return to Cold War*. Hoboken, NJ: John Wiley & Sons.

Lenta.ru (2017), Snizhenie bednosti v Rossii ob'iasnili 'zamerzaniem' prozhitochnogo minimuma, https://lenta.ru/news/2017/07/27/freezepoverty/.

Levada Center (2010), Kakie iz prav cheloveka, po Vashemu mneniyu, naibolee vazhny? Available at: http://www.levada.ru/archive/prava-cheloveka/kakie-iz-prav-cheloveka-po-vashemu-mneniyu-naibolee-vazhny-otvety-ranzhirova.

Levada Center (2012), Okolo treti rossiyan – za docrochnoe osvobozhdenie Mikhaila Khodorkovskogo. Available at: http://www.levada.ru/25-10-2012/okolo-treti-rossiyan-za-dosrochnoe-osvobozhdenie-mikhaila-khodorkovskogo.

Levada Center (2013a), Obshchestvennoe mnenie o Khodokovskom. Available at: http://www.levada.ru/25-06-2013/obshchestvennoe-mnenie-o-khodorkovskom.

Levada Center (2013b), Pervoe vpechatlenie rossiyan ot prigovora po delu Kirovlesa. Available at: http://www.levada.ru/2013/09/12/lev-gudkov-ob-itogah-vyborov-mera-moskvy/.

Levada Center (2013c), Rossiyane o Pussy Riot i tserkvi. Available at: http://www.levada.ru/20-05-2013/rossiyane-o-pussy-riot-i-tserkvi.

Levada Center (2013d), Rossiyane o sude prisyazhnykh. Available at: http://www.levada.ru/31-07-2013/rossiyane-o-sude-prisyazhnykh.

Levada Center (2014a), Rossiyane o svoikh pravakh. Available at: https://www.levada.ru/2014/01/27/rossiyane-o-svoih-pravah/.

Levada Center (2014b), 'Zakony i poryadok v gosudarstve'. Available at: http://www.levada.ru/2014/12/22/zakony-i-poryadok-v-gosudarstve/.

Levada Center (2016), Institutsional'noe doverie. Available at: http://www.levada.ru/2016/10/13/institutsionalnoe-doverie-2/.

Levada Center (2017), Protesty i Naval'nyi. Available at: https://www.levada.ru/2017/07/17/protesty-i-navalnyj/.

Lewin, Moshe (1988), *The Gorbachev Phenomenon: A Historical Interpretation.* Berkeley, CA: University of California Press.

Lieven, Anatol (1998), *Chechnya: Tombstone of Russian Power.* New Haven, CT: Yale University Press.

Light, Margot (2015), Russian foreign policy themes in official documents and speeches: Tracing continuity and change, in David Cadier and Margot Light (eds.), *Russia's Foreign Policy: Ideas, Domestic Politics and External Relations*, pp. 13–29. Basingstoke: Palgrave Macmillan.

Likhachev, Viacheslav and Vladimir Pribylovskii (eds.) (1997), *Russkoe Natsional'noe Edinstvo: Istoriia, politika, ideologiia.* Moscow: Panorama.

Lipman, Maria (forthcoming), Putin's 'besieged fortress' and its ideological arms, in Maria Lipman and Nikolay Petrov (eds.), *Russia Before and After Crimea: Nationalism and Identity, 2010–2017.* New York, NY and London: Palgrave Macmillan.

Lo, Bobo (2015), *Russia and the New World Disorder.* Washington, DC: Brookings Institution Press.

Lomskaya, Tat'yana (2017), Zarabotki rossiyan nachinayut padat' zadolgo do vykhoda no pensiyu, *Vedomosti*, 27 July.

Maggs, Peter B., Olga Schwartz and William Burnham (2015), *Law and Legal System of the Russian Federation*, 6th edn. Huntington, NY: Juris Publishing.

Malaev, Mikhail and Ol'ga Shkurenko (2017), Sravnitel'nyi parlamentarizm [Comparative parliamentarism], *Kommersant"*, 22 December, https://www.kommersant.ru/doc/3502058.

Malinova, Olga (2018), The embarrassing centenary: Reinterpretation of the 1917 Revolution in the official historical narrative of post-Soviet Russia (1991–2017), *Nationalities Papers*, 46(2), pp. 272–289.

Mankoff, Jeffrey (2015), *Russian Foreign Policy: The Return of Great Power Politics.* Lanham, MD: Rowman & Littlefield.

March, Luke (2002), *The Communist Party in Post-Soviet Russia.* Manchester: Manchester University Press.

March, Luke (2009), Managing opposition in a hybrid regime: Just Russia and parastatal opposition, *Slavic Review, 68*(3), pp. 504–527.

McAllister, Ian and Stephen White (2008), 'It's the economy, comrade!' Parties and voters in the 2007 Russian Duma election, *Europe-Asia Studies, 60*(6), pp. 931–57.

McDermott, R., B. Nygren, and C. Vendil Pallin (eds.) (2012), *The Russian Armed Forces in Transition: Economic, Geopolitical and Institutional Uncertainties*. London: Routledge.

McFaul, Michael (2001), *Russia's Unfinished Revolution: Political Change from Gorbachev to Putin*. Ithaca, NY: Cornell University Press.

Mearsheimer, John J. (2014), Why the Ukraine crisis is the West's fault: The liberal delusions that provoked Putin, *Foreign Affairs, 93*(5), pp. 77–89.

Medvedev, Dmitry (2008), Interview given by Dmitry Medvedev to Television Channels Channel One, Russia, NTV, 31 August. Available at: http://en.kremlin.ru/events/president/transcripts/48301 (accessed 25 March 2018).

Medvedev, Dmitry (2009), Dmitry Medvedev's Article, Go Russia! 10 September. Available at: http://en.kremlin.ru/events/president/news/5413 (accessed 5 March 2018).

Mendras, Marie (2015), The rising cost of Russia's authoritarian foreign policy, in David Cadier and Margot Light (eds.), *Russia's Foreign Policy: Ideas, Domestic Politics and External Relations*, pp. 80–96. Basingstoke: Palgrave Macmillan.

Menon, Rajan and Eugene Rumer (2015), *Conflict in Ukraine: The Unwinding of the Post-Cold War Order*. Cambridge, MA: MIT Press.

Mickiewicz, Ellen (2017), *No Illusions: The Voices of Russia's Future Leaders*. Oxford: Oxford University Press, paperback edn.

Mickiewicz, Ellen (2008), *Television, Power, and the Public in Russia*. Cambridge: Cambridge University Press.

Miller, Chris (2016), *The Struggle to Save the Soviet Economy: Mikhail Gorbachev and the Collapse of the USSR*. Chapel Hill, NC: University of North Carolina Press.

Ministry of Foreign Affairs of Russia (2014), Zayavlenie MID Rossii o Gruppe podderzhki dlya Ukrainy, 17 March, http://archive.mid.ru//brp_4.nsf/newsline/49766426492B6E9644257C9E0036B79A.

Mitrokhin, Nikolai (2003), *'Russkaia partiia': dvizhenie russkikh natsionalistov v SSSR 1953–1985 gg*. Moscow: NLO.

Moiseeva, Ekaterina (2017), Plea bargaining in Russia: The role of defence attorneys and the problem of asymmetry, *International Journal of Comparative and Applied Criminal Justice, 41*(3), pp. 163–185.

Molchanov, Mikhail A. (2016), *Eurasian Regionalisms and Russian Foreign Policy*. London and New York, NY: Routledge.

Møller, Jørgen and Svend-Erik Skaaning (2012), Systematizing thin and thick conceptions of the rule of law, *The Justice System Journal, 33*(2), pp. 136–153.

Morar', Natalia (2007), Chernaia Kassa Kremlia, *The New Times*, 10 December.

Morozov, Viatcheslav (2015), *Russia's Postcolonial Identity: A Subaltern Empire in a Eurocentric World*. Basingstoke: Palgrave Macmillan.

Morozov, Evgeny (2011), *The Net Delusion: The Dark Side of Internet Freedom*. New York, NY: Public Affairs Press.

Myers, Steven Lee (2015), *The New Tsar: The Rise and Reign of Vladimir Putin*. New York, NY: Vintage.

NATO (2008), Bucharest Summit Declaration, 3 April, http://www.nato.int/cps/en/natolive/official_texts_8443.htm.

Naumov, Igor' (2011), Vysokaya tsena besplatnoi shkoly, *Nezavisimaya gazeta*, 5 April.

Nefedova, Tatiana (2012), Szhatie i poliarizatsiia sel'skogo prostranstva Rossii, *Demoscop* no. 507–508 (April).

Neuman, Iver (2017), *Russia and the Idea of Europe*. London: Routledge.

Nikolsky, Aleksei (2013), Federal Protection Service – FSO, *Moscow Defense Brief, 36*(4).

Noble, Ben (2017a), The State Duma, the 'Crimean Consensus,' and Volodin's reforms, in Olga Irisova, Anton Barbashin, Fabian Burkhardt, and Ernest Wyciszkiewicz (eds.), *A Successful Failure: Russia after Crime(a)*. Warsaw: Centre Polish-Russian Dialogue and Understanding.

Noble, Ben (2017b), Amending budget bills in the Russian State Duma, *Post-Communist Economies, 29*(4), pp. 505–522.

Noble, Ben and Ekaterina Schulmann (2018), Not just a rubber stamp: Parliament and lawmaking, in Daniel Treisman (ed.), *The New Autocracy: Information, Politics, and Policy in Putin's Russia*. Washington, DC: Brookings Institution Press.

North, Douglass (1990), *Institutions, Institutional Changes and Economic Performance*. Cambridge: Cambridge University Press.

Novokmet, Filip, Thomas Piketty, and Gabriel Zucman (2017), From Soviets to Oligarchs: Inequality and Property in Russia, 1905–2016, NBER Working Paper Series, 23712, August.

Nygren, Bertil and Carolina Vendil Pallin (eds.), *The Russian Armed Forces in Transition: Economic, Geopolitical and Institutional Uncertainties*. London: Routledge.

O strategii (2017). O strategii ekonomicheskoi bezopasnosti Rossiiskoi Federatsii na period do 2030, http://publication,pravo.gov.ru/Documents/View/0001201705150001.

Obama, Barack (2014), Readout of the President's call with President Putin, 16 March, https://www.whitehouse.gov/the-press-office/2014/03/16/readout-president-s-call-president-putin.

O'Donnell, Guillermo (1993), On the state, democratization and some conceptual problems (a Latin American view with glances at some postcommunist countries), *World Development, 21*(8), pp. 1355–1369.

O'Loughlin, John, Gerard Toal, and Vladimir Kolosov (2016), Who identifies with the 'Russian world'? Geopolitical attitudes in southeastern Ukraine, Crimea, Abkhazia, South Ossetia, and Transnistria, *Eurasian Geography and Economics, 57*(6), pp. 745–778.

Omelicheva, Mariya (2017), A new Russian holiday has more behind it than national unity: The political functions of historical commemorations, *Australian Journal of Politics & History, 63*(3) (September), pp. 430–442.

Østbø, Jardar (2017), Securitizing 'spiritual-moral values' in Russia, *Post-Soviet Affairs, 33*(3), pp. 200–216.

Ostrow, Joel (2000), *Comparing Post-Soviet Legislatures: A Theory of Institutional Design and Political Conflict*. Columbus, OH: Ohio State University Press.

Otchet o rabote sudov obshchei yurisdiktsii po rassmotreniiu ugolovnykh del po pervoi instantsii za 12 mesyatsev 2016 g. (2016). Available at: http://www.cdep.ru/index.php?id=79&item=3832.

Oxenstierna, Susanne and Per Olsson (2015), *The Economic Sanctions against Russia. Impact and Prospects of Success*. Stockholm: FOI.

Panov, Petr and Cameron Ross (2013), Sub-national elections in Russia: Variations in United Russia's domination of regional assemblies, *Europe-Asia Studies, 65*(4), pp. 737–752.

Panov, Petr and Cameron Ross (2016), Levels of centralisation and autonomy in Russia's "party of power": Cross-regional variations, *Europe-Asia Studies, 68*(2), pp. 232–252.

Papkova, Irina (2011), Russian Orthodox concordat? Church and state under Medvedev, *Nationalities Papers*, *39*(5), pp. 667–683.

Pensionnyi Fond Rossiiskoi Federatsii (2012), *Godovoi otchet za 2011*. Moscow: Pensionnyi fond Rossiiskoi Federatsii.

Peters, Benjamin (2016), *How Not to Network a Nation: The Uneasy History of the Soviet Internet*. Cambridge, MA: MIT Press.

Petersson, Bo (2014), Still embodying the myth, *Problems of Post-Communism*, *61*(1), pp. 30–40.

Petersson, Bo (2017), Putin and the Russian mythscape: Dilemmas of charismatic legitimacy, *Demokratizatsiya*, *25*(3), pp. 235–254.

Petrov, Nikolay (2016), Changing of the guard: Putin's law enforcement reforms, ECPR commentary, 11 April, http://www.ecfr.eu/article/commentary_changing_of_the_guard_putins_law_enforcement_reforms_6084.

Petrov, Nikolay, Maria Lipman, and Henry E. Hale (2014), Three dilemmas of hybrid regime governance: Russia from Putin to Putin, *Post-Soviet Affairs*, *3*(1), pp. 1–26.

Polnyi tekst vystypleniya Dmitriia Medvedeva na II Grazhdanskom forume v Moskve 22 yanvariya 2008 goda (2008), *Rossiiskaya gazeta*. Available at: http://www.rg.ru/2008/01/24/tekst.html.

Pomerantsev, Peter (2014), *Nothing Is True and Everything Is Possible: The Surreal Heart of the New Russia*. New York, NY: Public Affairs.

Pomeranz, William E. (2013), How Russia puts business behind bars. Available at: http://blogs.reuters.com/great-debate/2013/07/05/how-russia-puts-business-behind-bars/.

Pomorski, Stanislaw (2001), 'Justice in Siberia: A case study of a lower criminal court in the city of Krasnoyarsk', *Communist and Post-Communist Studies*, *34*(4), pp. 447–478.

President of the Russian Federation (1995), Strategicheskii kurs Rossii s gosudarstvami – uchastnikami Sodruzhestva Nezavisimykh Gosudarstv, 14 September, http://archive.mid.ru/ns-osndoc.nsf/0e9272befa34209743256c630042d1aa/4e3d23b880479224c325707a00310fad.

Putin, Vladimir (2000a), *First Person: An Astonishingly Frank Self-Portrait by Russia's President Vladimir Putin*, with Nataliya Gevorkyan, Natalya Timakova, and Andrei Kolesnikov, translated by Catherine A. Fitzpatrick. London: Hutchinson.

Putin, Vladimir (2000b), TV address to the citizens of Russia, 24 March, http://en.special.kremlin.ru/events/president/transcripts/24201.

Putin, Vladimir (2000c), Excerpts from a speech at a meeting of top commanders of the Russian armed forces, 20 November, http://en.kremlin.ru/events/president/transcripts/21119.

Putin, Vladimir (2007), Speech and the following discussion at the Munich Conference on Security Policy, 10 February. Available at: http://en.kremlin.ru/events/president/transcripts/24034, accessed 14 March 2018.

Putin, Vladimir (2011), Novyi integratsionnyi proekt dlya Evrazii — budushchee, kotoroe rozhdaetsya segodnya, *Izvestiya*, 3 October.

Putin, Vladimir (2012), Spravedlivoe obustroistvo obshchestva, ekonomiki--glavnoe uslovie nashego ustoichevogo razvitiya v eti gody, *Komsomol'skaya pravda*, 13 February.

Putin, Vladimir (2014), 'Address by President of the Russian Federation', 18 March. Available at: http://en.kremlin.ru/events/president/news/20603, accessed 14 March 2018.

Putin, Vladimir (2018), Annual Address to the Federal Assembly of the Russian Federation, 1 March. Available at: http://en.kremlin.ru/events/president/news/56957, accessed 14 March 2018.

Radvanyi, Jean (2017), Quand Vladimir Poutine se fait géographe, *Herodote*, no. 166/167, pp. 113–132.

Rassmotreno del arbitrazhnymi sudami za 2011-2016 gody (2016). Available at: http://www.cdep.ru/index.php?id=79.

Rassmotrenie del i matrialov po I instantsii sudami obshchei yurisdiktsii za period s 1995 po 2012 gody (2013). Available at: http://www.cdep.ru/index.php?id=79&item=1627.

Reddaway, Peter and Dmitri Glinski (2001), *The Tragedy of Russia's Reforms: Market Bolshevism against Democracy*. Washington, DC: US Institute of Peace Press.

Reddaway, Peter and Robert Orttung (eds.) (2005), *The Dynamics of Russian Politics: Putin's Reform of Federal-Regional Relations* vol. II. London, Boulder, CO, and New York, NY: Rowman & Littlefield.

Reisinger, William M. and Bryon J. Moraski (2017), *The Regional Roots of Russia's Political Regime*. Ann Arbor, MI: University of Michigan Press.

Remington, Thomas (2001), *The Russian Parliament: Institutional Evolution in a Transitional Regime, 1989–1999*. New Haven, CT and London: Yale University Press.

Remington, Thomas F. (2003), Majorities without mandates: The Russian Federation Council since 2000, *Europe-Asia Studies*, 55(5), pp. 667–691.

Remington, Thomas F. (2007), The Russian Federal Assembly, 1994–2004, *Journal of Legislative Studies*, 13(1), pp. 121–141.

Remington, Thomas F. (2008), Patronage and the party of power: President-parliament relations under Vladimir Putin, *Europe-Asia Studies*, 60(6), pp. 959–987.

Remington, Thomas F. (2011), *The Politics of Inequality in Russia*. New York, NY: Cambridge University Press.

Remington, Thomas F. (forthcoming), Institutional change in authoritarian regimes: Pension reform in Russia and China, *Problems of Post-Communism*.

Remington, Thomas F. (forthcoming), Russian economic inequality in comparative perspective, *Comparative Politics*.

Renz, Bettina (2006), Putin's militocracy? An alternative interpretation of the role of the 'siloviki' in contemporary Russian politics, *Europe-Asia Studies*, 58(6), pp. 903–924.

Renz, Bettina (2012), Civil-military relations and Russian military modernization, in Roger N. McDermott, Bertil Nygren and Carolina Vendil Pallin (eds.) (2012), *The Russian Armed Forces in Transition: Economic, Geopolitical and Institutional Uncertainties*. London: Routledge.

Renz, Bettina (2018), *Russia's Military Revival*. Cambridge: Polity Press.

Reuter, Ora John (2013), Regional patrons and hegemonic party electoral performance in Russia, *Post-Soviet Affairs*, 29(2), pp. 101–135.

Reuter, Ora John (2015), Legislatures, cooptation, and social protest in contemporary authoritarian regimes, *Journal of Politics*, 77(1), pp. 235–248.

Reuter, Ora John (2017), *The Origins of Dominant Parties: Building Authoritarian Institutions in Post-Soviet Russia*. New York: Cambridge University Press.

Reuter, Ora John and Robertson, Graeme B. (2012), Subnational appointments in authoritarian regimes: Evidence from Russian gubernatorial appointments, *The Journal of Politics*, 74(4), pp. 1025–1037.

Reuters (2015), Russia's Nabiullina named Central Bank Governor of 2015 by Euromoney, 16 September, https://www.reuters.com/article/russia-cenbank-euromoney/russias-nabiullina-named-central-bank-governor-of-2015-by-euromoney-idUSL5N11M1X420150916.

RIA Novosti (2013), Deputat LDPR rasskazal, pochemu vnes zakonoproekt o zaprete chesnoka [LDPR deputy comments on why he introduced a bill on banning garlic], 1 April, https://ria.ru/politics/20130401/930378590.html.

Richter, Andrei and Anya Richter (2015), *Regulation of online content in the Russian Federation: Legislation and Case Law*. Strasbourg, France: European Audiovisual Observatory.

Richters, Katja (2012), *The Post-Soviet Russian Orthodox Church: Politics, Culture and Greater Russia*. London: Routledge.

Roberts, Sean (2011), *Putin's United Russia Party*. London: Routledge.

Robertson, Graeme B. (2011), *The Politics of Protest in Hybrid Regimes: Managing Discontent in Post-Communist Russia*. New York, NY: Cambridge University Press.

Rose, Richard and Neil Munro (2002), *Elections Without Order*. Cambridge: Cambridge University Press.

Rosefielde, Steven (2016), *The Kremlin Strikes Back: Russia and the West after Crimea's Annexation*. New York, NY: Cambridge University Press.

Roselle, Laura (2006), *Media and the Politics of Failure: Great Powers, Communications Strategies, and Military Defeats*. New York, NY: Palgrave Macmillan.

Ross, Cameron and Adrian Campbell (2009), *Federalism and Local Politics in Russia*. London and New York: Routledge.

Ross, Cameron (ed.) (2015), *Systemic and Non-Systemic Opposition in the Russian Federation*. London: Routledge.

Ross, Cameron and Rostislav Turovsky (2013), The representation of political and economic elites in the Russian Federation Council, *Demokratizatsiya: The Journal of Post-Soviet Democratization*, *21*(1), pp. 59–88.

Rosstat (2015), *Rossiiskii statisticheskii ezhegodnik—2015*. Moscow: Rosstat. Available at: www.gks.ru/free_doc/doc_2015/year/year15.rar.

Rosstat (2016), *Rossiia v tsifrakh—2016*. Moscow: Rosstat. Available at: http://www.gks.ru/free_doc/doc_2016/rusfig/rus16.pdf.

Rumer, Eugene B. (2017), *Russian Foreign Policy beyond Putin*. London and New York, NY: Routledge.

Russian State Tax Service, http://www.nalog.ru/fl/docs/3856626/print/.

Sakwa, Richard (2008a), *Russian Politics and Society*, 4th edn. London and New York, NY: Routledge.

Sakwa, Richard (2008b), *Putin: Russia's Choice*, 2nd edn. London: Routledge.

Sakwa, Richard (2010), The dual state in Russia, *Post-Soviet Affairs, 26*(3), pp. 185–206. https://doi.org/10.2747/1060-586X.26.3.185.

Sakwa, Richard (2011), *The Crisis of Russian Democracy: The Dual State, Factionalism and the Medvedev Succession*. Cambridge: Cambridge University Press.

Sakwa, Richard (2012), Modernisation, neo-modernisation and comparative democratisation in Russia, *East European Politics, 28*(1) (March), pp. 43–57.

Sakwa, Richard (2015a), Dualism at home and abroad: Russian foreign policy neo-revisionism and bicontinentalism, in David Cadier and Margot Light (eds.), *Russia's Foreign Policy: Ideas, Domestic Politics and External Relations*, pp. 65–79. Basingstoke: Palgrave Macmillan.

Sakwa, Richard (2015b), *Frontline Ukraine: Crisis in the Borderlands*. London and New York, NY: I.B. Tauris.

Samokhina, Sof'ya (2017), 'Tut vezde govoryat: napishi ob"yasnitel'nuyu, pochemu ty knopochku ne nazhal': V Gosdume posporili o printsipakh raboty parlamenta ['They are always saying: Write a letter of explanation regarding why you didn't press the voting button': Arguments in the State Duma about the principles of parliamentary work], *Kommersant"*, 24 November, https://www.kommersant.ru/doc/3475952.

Schenk, Caress (2010), Open borders, closed minds: Russia's changing migration policies: Liberalization or xenophobia?, *Demokratizatsiya: The Journal of Post-Soviet
Democratization, 18*(2) (April), pp. 101–121.

Schenk, Caress (2018), *Why Control Immigration?: Strategic Uses of Migration Management in Russia*. Toronto: University of Toronto Press.

Shapovalov, Aleksei (2017), VVP napolovinu polon, *Kommersant,* 27 July, https://www.
kommersant.ru/doc/3367785.

Sharafutdinova, Gulnaz (2014), The Pussy Riot affair and Putin's démarche from sovereign democracy to sovereign morality, *Nationalities Papers, 42*(4), pp. 615–621.

Sharafutdinova, Gulnaz (2013), Gestalt switch in Russian federalism: The decline in
regional power under Putin, *Comparative Politics,* April, pp. 357–376.

Sharafutdinova, Gulnaz and Rostislav Turovsky (2016), The politics of federal transfers
in Putin's Russia: Regional competition, lobbying, and federal priorities, *Post-Soviet
Affairs, 33*(2), pp. 161–175.

Sharlet, Robert (1992), *Soviet Constitutional Crisis: From De-Stalinization to Disintegration.* Armonk, NY: M.E. Sharpe.

Shekhovtsov, Anton (2017), *Russia and the Western Far Right: Tango Noir.* London:
Routledge.

Shenfield, Stephen D. (2001), *Russian Fascism: Traditions, Tendencies and Movements.*
New York, NY and London: M.E. Sharpe.

Sherr, James (2013), *Hard Diplomacy and Soft Coercion: Russia's Influence Abroad.*
Washington, DC: Brookings Institution Press.

Shevel, Oxana (2011), Russian nation-building from Yeltsin to Medvedev: Ethnic,
civic, or purposefully ambiguous? *Europe-Asia Studies, 63*(1), pp. 179–202.

Shishkin, Sergei and Laura Popovich (2009), Analiz perspektiv razvitiya chastnogo
finansirovaniia zdravookhraneniya, Institut ekonomiki perekhodnogo perioda,
Nauchnye trudy, no. 125P, Moscow: IEPP, pp. 7–10.

SIPRI Military Expenditure Database, https://www.sipri.org/databases/milex.

Slider, Darrell (2005), The regions' impact on federal policy: The Federation Coun-
cil, in Peter Reddaway and Robert Orttung (eds.) (2005), *The Dynamics of Russian
Politics: Putin's Reform of Federal-Regional Relations* vol. II, pp. 123–143. London,
Boulder, CO, and New York, NY: Rowman & Littlefield.

Slider, Darrell (2009), Putin and the election of regional governors, in Cameron Ross
and Adrian Campbell (eds.), *Federalism and Local Politics in Russia,* pp. 106–119.
London and New York, NY: Routledge.

Smith, Steven S. and Thomas F. Remington (2001), *The Politics of Institutional Choice:
Formation of the Russian State Duma.* Princeton, NJ: Princeton University Press.

Smyth, Regina (2006), *Candidate Strategies and Electoral Competition in the Russian
Federation: Democracy without Foundation.* New York, NY: Cambridge University
Press.

Smyth, Regina, Brandon Wilkening, and Anna Urasova (2007), Engineering victory: Institutional reform, informal institutions, and the formation of a hegemonic
party regime in the Russian Federation, *Post-Soviet Affairs, 23*(2) (April–June),
pp. 118–137.

Solomon, Peter H., Jr. (1987), The case of the vanishing acquittal: Informal norms and
the practice of Soviet criminal justice, *Soviet Studies, 39*(4), pp. 531–555.

Solomon, Peter H., Jr. (2007), Informal practices in Russian justice: Probing the limits
of post-Soviet reform, in Ferdinand Feldbrugge (ed.), *Russia, Europe, and the Rule of
Law,* pp. 79–92. Leiden, The Netherlands: Martinus Nijhoff.

Solomon, Peter H., Jr. and Todd Foglesong (2000), *Courts and Transition in Russia: The Challenge of Judicial Reform.* Boulder, CO: Westview Press.

Solovyov, Vladimir (2008), *Putin: putevoditel dlya neravnodushnykykh* (*Putin: guidebook for the not indifferent*). Moscow: Eksmo.

Sotiriou, Stylianos A. (ed.) (2015), *Russian Energy Strategy in the European Union, the Former Soviet Union Region, and China.* Lanham, MD: Lexington Books.

SOVA Centre's annual reports, available at http://www.sova-center.ru/.

Stent, Angela E. (2015), *The Limits of Partnership: US-Russian Relations in the Twenty-First Century.* Princeton, NJ and Oxford: Princeton University Press.

Stiglitz, Joseph E. (2013), *The Price of Inequality.* New York, NY: Norton.

Stone, Oliver (2017), *Oliver Stone Interviews Vladimir Putin.* New York, NY: Skyhorse Publishing.

Stoner-Weiss, Kathryn (2001), The Russian state in crisis: Center and periphery in the post-Soviet era, in Zoltan Barany and Robert G. Moser (eds.), *Russian Politics: Challenges of Democratization*, pp. 103–34. New York, NY: Cambridge University Press.

Strategiya-2020: Novaya model' rosta--novaia sotsial'naya politika: Itogovyi doklad o rezul'tatakh ekspertnoi raboty po aktual'nym problemam sotsial'no-ekonomicheskoi strategii Rossiii na period do 2020 g., http://2020strategy.ru/data/2012/03/14/1214585998/1itog.pdf.

Sudebno-arbitrazhnaya statistika o rassmotrennykh delakh arbitrazhnymi sudami Rossiiskoi Federatsii v 2002–2005 godakh (2006), *Vestnik Vysshego Arbitrazhnogo Suda Rossiiskoi Federatsii*, no. 5, pp. 22–23.

Sullivan, Charles (2014), Motherland: Soviet Nostalgia in Post-Soviet Russia. PhD dissertation, George Washington University.

Surkov, Vladislav (2006), Suverenitet – eto politicheskii sinonim konkurentosposobnosti, in Nikita Garadzha (ed.), *Suverinitet.* Moscow: Evropa.

Suslov, Mikhail D. (2014), 'Crimea is ours!' Russian Popular Geopolitics in the new media age, *Eurasian Geography and Economics*, 55(6,) pp. 588–609.

Suslov, Mikhail (2016), *Digital Orthodoxy in the Post-Soviet World: The Russian Orthodox Church and Web 2.0.* Stuttgart: Ibidem Verlag.

Suslov, Mikhail D. (2017), The Production of 'Novorossiya': A territorial brand in public debates, *Europe-Asia Studies*, 69(2), pp. 202–221.

Suslov, Mikhail and Mark Bassin (eds.) (2016), *Eurasia 2.0: Russian Geopolitics in the Age of New Media.* Lanham, MD: Lexington.

Svodnye statisticheskie svedeniya o deyatel'nosti federal'nykh sudov obshchei yurisdiktsii i mirovykh sudei za 2015 god (2015). Available at: http://www.cdep.ru/index.php?id=79&item=3417.

Svolik, Milan (2012), *The Politics of Authoritarian Rule.* Cambridge: Cambridge University Press.

Tanas, Olga and Stepan Kravchenko (2017). Putin nominates Bank of Russia head Nabiullina for new term, *Bloomberg*, 22 March, https://www.bloomberg.com/news/articles/2017-03-22/putin-nominates-bank-of-russia-head-nabiullina-for-new-term.

TASS (2014), Lavrov predicts historians may coin new term: The Primakov doctrine, 28 October, http://tass.com/russia/756973, accessed 14 March 2018.

Taubman, William (2017), *Gorbachev: His Life and Times.* New York, NY: Simon & Schuster.

Taylor, Brian D. (2007), *Russia's Power Ministries: Coercion and Commerce.* Syracuse, NY: Institute for National Security and Counterterrorism, Syracuse University.

Taylor, Brian D. (2011), *State Building in Putin's Russia: Policing and Coercion after Communism*. Cambridge: Cambridge University Press.

Teper, Yuri (2016), Official Russian identity discourse in light of the annexation of Crimea: National or imperial? *Post-Soviet Affairs*, *32*(4), pp. 378–396.

The Economist (2008), Mechel bashing, 31 July. Available at: https://www.economist.com/node/11848486.

The Military Balance (2016), Chapter ten: country comparisons – commitments, force levels and economics, *The Military Balance, 116*(1), pp. 481–92.

Tipaldou, Sofia and Katrin Uba (2014), The Russian radical right movement and immigration policy: Do they just make noise or have an impact as well? *Europe-Asia Studies*, *66*(7), pp. 1080–1101.

Tishkov, Valerii (2013), *Rossiiskii narod. Istoriia i smysl natsional'nogo samoznaniia*. Moscow: Nauka.

Tkachenko, Natalia (2017), Statistical analysis of federal legislation in Russia, *Statutes & Decisions*, *51*(4), pp. 518–564.

Tolz, Vera (2001), *Russia: Inventing the Nation*. London: Hodder Education.

Treisman, Daniel (2012), *The Return: Russia's Journey from Gorbachev to Medvedev*. New York, NY: The Free Press.

Treisman, Daniel (2018), *The New Autocracy: Information, Politics and Policy in Putin's Russia*. Washington, DC: Brookings Institution Press.

Trenin, Dmitry (2015), Russian foreign policy as exercise in nation building, in David Cadier and Margot Light (eds.), *Russia's Foreign Policy: Ideas, Domestic Politics and External Relations*, pp. 30–41. Basingstoke: Palgrave Macmillan.

Trenin, Dmitry (2016), *Should We Fear Russia?* Cambridge and Malden, MA: Polity.

Trenin, Dmitry (2017), Here's a breakdown of Russia's foreign policy goals, *Moscow Times*, 16 August. Available at: https://themoscowtimes.com/articles/heres-a-breakdown-of-russias-foreign-policy-goals-op-ed-58677, accessed 24 March 2018.

Trochev, Alexei (2006), Judicial selection in Russia: Toward accountability and centralization, in Kate Malleson and Peter H. Russell (eds.), *Appointing Judges in an Age of Judicial Power*. Toronto: University of Toronto Press.

Trochev, Alexei (2008), *Judging Russia: The Role of the Constitutional Court in Russian Politics 1990–2006*. Cambridge: Cambridge University Press.

Trochev, Alexei (2009), All appeals lead to Strasbourg? Unpacking the impact of the European Court of Human Rights on Russia, *Demokratizatsiya*, *17*(2), pp. 145–718.

Troxel, Tiffany (2003), *Parliamentary Power in Russia, 1994–2001: President vs. Parliament*. Basingstoke; New York, NY: Palgrave Macmillan.

Tseplyeva, Yuliya and Yuliya Sonina (2014), Sberbank Rossii. Tsentr makroekonomicheskikh issledovanii. 'Rossiia: neformal'naia zaniatost' kak novyi fenomen,' 27 February, http://pensionreform.ru/files/66660/27.02.2014.%20Центр%20макроэкономических%20исследований%20Сбербанка.%20Россия.%20неформальная%20занятость%20как%20новый%20феномен.pdf.

Tsygankov, Andrei P. (2016), *Russia's Foreign Policy: Change and Continuity in National Identity*. Lanham, MD: Rowman & Littlefield.

Tsygankov, Andrei P. (ed.) (2018), *Routledge Handbook of Russian Foreign Policy*. London and New York, NY: Routledge.

Umland, Andreas (2008), Zhirinovsky's 'last thrust to the south' and the definition of fascism, *Russian Politics and Law*, *46*(4), pp. 31–46.

Urban, Michael (2010), *Cultures of Power in Post-Communist Russia: An Analysis of Elite Political Discourse*. Cambridge: Cambridge University Press.

Van Herpen, Marcel H. (2015), *Putin's Propaganda Machine: Soft Power and Russian Foreign Policy*. Lanham, MD: Rowman & Littlefield.

Verkhovskii, Aleksandr (2014), Dinamika nasiliia v russkom natsionalizme, in Aleksandr Verkhovskii (ed.), *Rossiia—ne Ukraina: Sovremennye aspekty natsionalizma*, pp. 32–61. Moscow: SOVA.

Verkhovsky, Alexander (2008), Public interactions between Orthodox Christian and Muslim organisations at the federal level in Russia today, *Religion, State, and Society*, *36*(4), pp. 379–392.

Viola, Lynne (2002), *Contending with Stalinism: Soviet Power and Popular Resistance in the 1930s*. Ithaca, NY: Cornell University Press.

Volkov, Vadim, Arina Dmitrieva, Mikhail Pozdnyakov, and Kirill Titaev (2016), *Rossiiskie sud'i: sotsiologicheskoe issledovanie professii*. Moscow: Norma.

White, Stephen (2010), Soviet nostalgia and Russian politics, *Journal of Eurasian Studies*, *1*(1), pp. 1–9.

White, Stephen and Valentina Feklyunina (2014), *Identities and Foreign Policies in Russia, Ukraine and Belarus*. Basingstoke: Palgrave Macmillan.

White, Stephen, Richard Rose, and Ian McAllister (1997), *How Russia Votes*. Chatham, NJ: Chatham House.

Willerton, John P. (2007), The Putin legacy: Russian-style democratization confronts a 'failing state', *The Soviet and Post-Soviet Review*, *34*(1), pp. 33–54.

Willerton, John P. (2016), Russian public assessments of the Putin policy program: Achievements and challenges, *Russian Politics*, *1*(2), pp. 131–158.

Willerton, John P. (2017), Searching for a Russian national idea: Putin team efforts and public assessments, *Demokratizatsiya*, *25*(3), pp. 209–233.

Wilson, Andrew (2014), *Ukraine Crisis: What It Means for the West*. New Haven, CT: Yale University Press.

Wivel, Anders and Hans Mouritzen (2012), *Explaining Foreign Policy: International Diplomacy and the Russo-Georgian War*. Boulder, CO: Lynne Rienner Publishers.

Wood, Elizabeth (2011), Performing memory: Vladimir Putin and the celebration of World War II in Russia, *The Soviet and Post-Soviet Review*, *38*(2), pp. 172–200.

Yatsyk, Alexandra (2018), Visualizing Russia's enemies: Anti-American propaganda in the Euromaidan era, *PONARS Eurasia Policy Memo*, no. 514, March.

Zaionchkovskaya, Zhanna (ed.) (2009), *Migranty v Moskve*. Moscow: Tri kvadrata.

Zubarevich, Natalia (2014), Four Russias: Rethinking the post-Soviet map, in Gudrun M. Grabher and Ursula Mathis-Moser (eds.), *Regionalism(s): A Variety of Perspectives from Europe and the Americas*. Innsbruck: Institut fur Foderalismus, pp. 71–88.

Zygar, Mikhail (2016), *All the Kremlin's Men: Inside the Court of Vladimir Putin*, New York, NY: Public Affairs.

INDEX

A

Abkhazia, 73, 194, 196
Abramovich, Roman, 10
'acceleration' *(uskorenie),* 5
accountability, 11, 13, 16–17
activists
    backlash against, 89–92
    Communist Party of the Russian
        Federation (CPRF), 49–50
    under Putin, 86
    television coverage of, 97–98
    in 2011 protests, 88
    United Russia, 45
advertising, as propaganda, 105
advisory bodies, 29–30
Adygeya, 126
Afghanistan, 168, 176
Agrarian Party, 57
Albania, 176
All-Russian People's Front (ONF), 13, 19
amnesties, 115–116
Andropov, Yuri Vladimirovich, 3, 4
Anpilov, Viktor, 86
anti-alcohol campaign, 6
anti-Americanism, 73
Anti-Ballistic Missile Treaty
    (ABM Treaty), 168
anti-corruption protests, 80
apparatus, 6–7
Arab Spring, 17, 169, 186
arbitrazh courts, 110–111
Armenia, 194, 195, 196, 197, 198, 203
Asia-Pacific, foreign policy focus, 169
Association Agreements (AA), 197–198,
    202–203
'asymmetric' federalism, 120
audiences, 94–107. *See also* media; television
    cognitive processing by, 106–107
    demographics, 96
    for opposition media, 99, 213
    potential *vs.* actual, 103–104
    Russia Today influencing, 102–104
    and scale of media, 104–106

    scepticism of, 96–97
    television, 94, 95–96, 97
Audit Chamber, 57
austerity, 137, 143, 147–148
authoritarianism. *See also* democratisation;
    political system
    in hybrid regimes, 216
    party support for, 42–43
    preference for, 19–21
    under Putin, 13, 14, 25
    steering foreign policy, 168–169, 184
    and third-wave reforms, 15–16
'authoritarian modernisation,' 4, 5
Azerbaijan, 194, 195–196, 197, 198, 203

B

Barkashov, Alexander, 75
Bartles, Charles, 191
Bashkortostan, 69, 83, 120, 121, 209
Bashneft, 145
Belarus, 8, 12, 195, 197, 203
Belov, Aleksandr, 75
Belt and Road Initiative (BRI), 203–204
Belykh, Nikita, 126
Berezovsky, Boris, 10, 207, 208, 210
Berlin Wall, 7
'besieged fortress' narrative, 174
Beslan school massacre, 13
bills, 60–64. *See also* law and law-making;
    legislation; parliament
black markets, 153
blockades, 83
Bolotnaya Square, 88
Bolsheviks. *See* Communist Party of the
    Soviet Union (CPSU)
Bremmer, Ian, 184–185
Brezhnev, Leonid Il'ich, 3–4, 14, 72, 212
bribery, 113
BRICS (Brazil, Russia, India, China, and
    South Africa), 73, 134, 169
Bucharest Declaration, 196
Buddhism, 70
budgetary policy, 143–145

budgets. *See also* economic policies; economy
  military, 184, 187, 189
  oil prices affecting, 137–138, 143–144
  over time, 137, 144–145
  and privatisation, 145
  Putin stabilizing, 212
  regions *vs.* federal agencies, 130–131
  State Duma role, 62–63
Bulgaria, 176
bureaucracy, 1, 3, 6, 28, 163–164
Bush, George H.W., 166

C

Cabinet of Ministers, 31
Cabinet Presidium, 31
capitalism, 3, 6, 13–14
'castling' move, 15
cell phones, 100, 107
Central Bank of Russia (CBR), 34, 134,
    142–143, 212
  floating rouble, 135–137
Centre for Strategic Research, 147
centrism, 11, 46
chairmen (of courts), 113
Channel One (First Channel), 95, 102, 213
Charap, Samuel, 184–185, 192–204
Chechnya. *See also* Eurasian region; foreign
        policy; separatism
  conflicts in, 10, 75, 83–85, 119
  decrees to 'normalise,' 28
  invasion of, 84–85, 182
  Islam in, 69
  media coverage of, 84, 95
  and nationalism, 68, 74, 76
  under Putin, 123, 187, 209
  separatism in, 83–84, 119, 183
  Western perspective on, 167, 173
  under Yeltsin, 10, 83–84, 112, 183
'checks and balances,' 28
Cherkesov, Viktor, 185
Chernenko, Konstantin Ustinovich, 3, 4
chief of staff, 29
China, 169, 172, 213
  influencing Eurasian region, 193
  military strength of, 189
  relationship with, 177, 203–204
  wealth inequality in, 153–157
Chinese Communist Party, 44
Chisinau, 194
Chubais, Anatoly, 32
civil servants, 57

civil society, 80–93. *See also* social policy
  environmentalists and, 87
  government shaping, 85
  importance of, 85–86
Civil War, 2, 81
clientelism, 47
Clinton, Hillary, 102
cognitive processing of messages, 106–107
Cold War, 3–4, 5, 8, 181
Collective Security Treaty, 195
Collective Security Treaty Organization
    (CSTO), 195
'colour revolutions.' *See* revolutions
commercialisation, 'creeping forced,' 161
Committee for Protecting the People's
    Power and the Constitution, 55
Committee of State Security (KGB), 4, 21,
    181, 182, 184
Committee on Constitutional
    Supervision, 109
committees, for profiling laws, 60
Commonwealth of Independent States
    (CIS), 8, 168, 172, 195
communism. *See* Soviet system
Communist Party of the Russian Federation
    (CPRF), 41, 49–50, 57, 213. *See also*
    party system; political parties
  as CPSU successor, 9, 38
  and nationalist movements, 74, 75
  popular support for, 35, 46, 208, 210
  in regional politics, 125
  and 2011 protests, 88
Communist Party of the Soviet Union (CPSU),
    2, 4, 44. *See also* Soviet system
  apparatus, 6–7
  banning of, 8
  factions in, 6
  Komsomol, 45
  loss of 'leading role,' 7
  and rule of law, 109
compatriot repatriation program, 73
conflicts, freezing, 195–196, 202
Congress of People's Deputies of the Russian
    Federation (formerly RSFSR), 1, 7,
    9, 55
Congress of People's Deputies of the
    Russian Soviet Federative Socialist
    Republic (RSFSR), 55
Congress of People's Deputies of the
    USSR, 7, 55
Constituent Assembly, 2

Constitution (1993), 1, 9–10, 55–56. *See also* government; parliament; president
Articles
2, 54
31, 87
80, 26, 165
81.3, 11
86, 165
93, 26, 165
100.1, 56
104.1, 60
102, 166
106, 166
decrees, 28
federalist aspects of, 119–120
politics shaping, 82
and post-communist order, 16–17
role of mayors in, 126
Yeltsin amending, 11
Constitution (Soviet era), 108–109
Constitutional Court, 27, 110–111, 112
consumption, and floating rouble, 135–137
contentious politics, 80–81. *See also* activists; opposition parties; protests
and current issues, 92–93
environmentalism, 87
by ethnic groups, 83–84
history of, 81–85
Convention for the Protection of Human Rights and Fundamental Freedoms, 173
convocations, 57
Coordinating Council, 91
corporatism, 25
corruption, 4
in courts, 117
in legal system, 112–113, 115, 117
media investigations of, 99–100
and patronalism, 206
under Putin, 25
in regional financing, 131
Council of Europe, 172, 173
councils, 27
counter-parliament, 98
counter-sanctions, 146, 203
counterterrorism, 182, 185
court chairmen, 113
courts, 110–111. *See also* law and law-making; judges; legal system; rule of law
arbitrazh, 110–111

constitutional, 110–111
corruption in, 117
and economic reform, 148–149
improvement under Putin, 212
juries in, 111
justice of the peace, 111
protecting personal rights, 116–117
public perceptions of, 114, 115, 116
role of chairmen, 113
Supreme, 111
Credit Suisse Bank, 156
'creeping forced commercialisation,' 161
Crimea. *See also* Eurasian region; foreign policy; separatism
annexation, 73, 76, 91–92, 199–200
as federal entity, 68, 120, 121
hybrid warfare in, 190
influencing foreign policy, 24, 25, 175, 176, 179
legislature selecting leaders, 126
as macroregion, 121
media coverage of annexation, 97
public opinion of annexation, 97, 170, 177–178, 200, 212
and Putin's popularity, 20, 76, 79, 97, 178, 212, 215
supporting regime, 79, 170, 215
Ukraine crisis precipitating, 91–92, 180, 200
criminal trials, 108. *See also* courts; judges; legal system
Alexei Navalny, 91
for business disputes, 112
public attention to, 115
in Soviet Union, 109
as weapon, 112, 117, 210
Croatia, 15, 176
Cuban missile crisis, 3
cum hoc fallacies, 103
Customs Union Commission, 197
Czech Republic, 3–4, 176

D

Dagestan, 84, 126, 131
de-Russification, 69
debate, decline of, 62–63
Decembrist movement, 2
decentralisation, 131–132, 160
decrees, 28, 193
Deep and Comprehensive Free Trade Area agreements (DCTFA), 198

defence. *See* military; security
Democratic Union, 6
democratisation (*demokratizatsiya*), 5, 6, 55.
    See also authoritarianism; party system;
    political parties; political system
  challenges of, 15–17
  and federalism, 119
  guiding foreign policy, 178
  in hybrid regimes, 63, 216
  incomplete, 39–40
  and liberal parties, 50–52
  for long-term growth, 150
  'managed' democracy, 1, 14–15
  post-communism, 9, 16–17
  public perception of, 37, 214
  shaping national identity, 67–70
  'sovereign' democracy, 13–14, 146
  vs. stability, 13
  teleological *vs.* genealogical approach, 16
  United Russia's role in, 43
deputies, 56–59, 60–61, 64
Deripaska, Oleg, 210
'dictatorship of law,' 12
'Direct Line with Vladimir Putin,' 25
directorates, 27. *See also* Presidential
    Administration
districts, 29, 68
'divide-and-rule strategy,' 182–183, 185
Donbas, 200, 202
Donetsk, 201
dual state, 12–13, 14, 211
Duma. *See* State Duma
Dyumin, Aleksei, 32, 35

E
Eastern Partnership (EaP), 197–198
economic policies, 142–146. *See also*
    economy
  austerity, 143, 147–148
  budgetary, 143–145
  counter-sanctions as, 146
  diversification as, 146
  future reforms, 146–149
  guiding ideas, 142–143
  industrial, 145–146
  inflation targeting, 143
  interest rates, 143
  and international borrowing, 144
  monetary, 143
  for national sovereignty, 133, 142
  privatisation, 145, 148

'shock therapy' approach, 172
  stimulus *vs.* austerity, 147–148
economy, 10, 133–149. *See also* economic
    policies
  allocating resources, 141
  arbitrazh courts for, 110–111
  catalyzing protests, 83, 87
  differences across Russia, 69–70
  and Eurasian relations, 120, 194
  floating rouble, 135–137, 143
  growth rate, 133–135, 139–141
  importance of China, 203
  influencing media, 96
  macroeconomic changes to, 147–148
  market, 6, 8, 9, 32, 172
  and military spending, 184, 187, 189
  oil prices affecting, 133, 134
  periods of crisis, 133–134
  under Putin, 20, 21, 24, 25, 123, 212
  recent performance, 133–138
  sanctions affecting, 138–139
  St Petersburg influence, 32–33
  Western relations, 138–139, 174, 177
education, 36, 161
Egypt, 213
Ekho Moskvy, 98, 99, 100, 213
elections, 1, 6–7, 9, 15, 39–40. *See also* party
    system; political parties
  December 2011 protests, 88–89
  of deputies, 56–57
  eliminating mayoral, 210
  under Gorbachev, 5, 6, 7–8, 55
  liberal parties in, 50–52
  media coverage of regional, 125
  and political parties, 39–40
  of Putin, as paramount leader, 18–19
  of regional leaders, 120, 122, 124, 126,
    209–210
  scale of voting, 214
  of senators, 59
  shaping political system, 208, 213–214
  and Supreme Court, 111
  United Russia dominating, 42–47
elites
  access to diverse media, 99
  balancing Eurasian region, 193
  in Federation Council, 59
  interfering with legal system, 112
  shaping political system, 15, 19, 20
  supporting Putin, 24, 29, 34, 35, 36, 37
  in United Russia, 42–43, 44, 210

embezzlement, 112
Emergency Situations. *See* Ministry of
    Emergency Situations
emigration. *See* migration
employment. *See also* pensions; social policy;
    wages; workers
    informal *vs.* formal, 152, 155–156
    stationary rates of, 139, 140
energy prices, 20, 36, 194. *See also* oil prices
'enterprise paternalism,' 151
entrepreneurs, 78, 148
environmentalists, 87
Estonia, 8, 176
ethnic groups. *See also* Eurasian region;
    migration; national identity;
    nationalism
    regional privileges of, 121–122
    in Russian Federation, 67–68
    and Russian nationalism, 69
    Yeltsin-era conflicts, 83–84
Eurasian Economic Commission
    (EAEC), 197
Eurasian Economic Community
    (EurAsEC), 195
Eurasian Economic Union (EEU), 175,
    177–178, 197
Eurasian region, 192–193. *See also* ethnic
    groups; foreign policy; separatism;
    individual countries
    Association Agreements for, 197–198
    autonomy of, 119
    budgets, 124, 131
    China's role in, 203–204
    collective action dilemma, 122–123
    conflicts in, 83–84, 195–196, 203
    Customs Union, 197
    and Eastern Partnership (EaP), 197–198
    electing leaders, 120, 122, 124, 125,
        209–210
    federal agencies in, 130–132
    integration within, 197–203
    as macroregions, 121
    and national identity, 72–73, 77
    parliamentary representation,
        68, 120, 126
    political systems in, 128, 131–132, 208
    power networks in, 120–126, 207
    relationship with Russia, 127–128,
        192–204
    socioeconomic differences between, 69–70
    supranational institutions in, 128, 197

trade in, 194, 195
    and United Russia, 122
    Western influences in, 193–195, 198
Eurasian Union, 175
Euromaidan Revolution. *See* Maidan
    Revolution
European Court of Human Rights,
    116–117, 173
European Union (EU), 15, 173. *See also*
    foreign policy; United States; West
    Eastern Partnership (EaP), 197–198
    in Eurasian region, 193, 195, 199–200
    orchestrating revolutions, 174
    Russian relationship with, 168, 177
    and Ukraine, 175, 199–200, 202–203
executive. *See* president
extremism, 12, 100, 101, 132

F
Facebook, 52, 100, 104, 105
'failing state,' Russia as, 24
Fatherland-All Russia (FAR), 42, 209
Federal Agency for Government
    Communication and Information
    (FAPSI), 185
Federal Agency for the Commonwealth of
    Independent States, Compatriots
    Living Aboard, and International
    Cultural Cooperation, 166
Federal Assembly, 56–60. *See also* Federation
    Council; parliament; State Duma
    Federation Council, 59–60
    first elections, 55–56
    four roles of, 65
    recent developments in, 64–65
    as rubber stamp, 63
    State Duma, 56–59
Federal Border Guard Service, 185
federal executive, institutions of, 25–31.
    See also government; president;
    Presidential Administration; prime
    minister
Federal Guard Service (FSO), 182, 185
Federal National Guards Service (FSNG),
    185
Federal Security Service (FSB), 166, 180, 185
    counterterrorism units, 182
    creation of, 182
    and Putin, 180, 184, 185
Federal Service for the Control of the Drugs
    Trade (FSKN), 185

Federal Tax Police Service, 185
federalism, 119–132. *See also* Constitution;
        democratisation; Federal Assembly;
        parliament; political system
    'asymmetric,' 120
    and decentralisation, 130–132
    as form of extremism, 132
    and Navalny election, 124–125
    under Putin, 120–126
    shift away from, 123
    Yeltsin adopting, 119–120
Federation Council, 27, 59–60. *See also*
        Federal Assembly; parliament; State
        Duma
    Kremlin shaping, 59
    Putin changing, 123
    recent developments in, 64–65
    representing regions, 120
    role in foreign policy, 166
    role in law-making, 60, 61
federal agencies, and decentralisation,
        130–132
Feklyunina, Valentina, 165–179
Felgenhauer, Pavel, 145
First Channel (Channel One), 95, 102, 213
flash mobs, 87
Foreign Affairs ministry, 31
Foreign Agents Law, 90, 101
Foreign Intelligence Service (SVR),
        166, 185
foreign policy, 165–179. *See also* Eurasian
        region; European Union; military;
        security; United States; West;
        individual countries
    advisory bodies for, 29–30
    Asia-Pacific focus, 169, 172, 175
    authoritarianism steering, 168–169
    'besieged fortress' narrative, 174
    China, 177, 203–204
    conservatism guiding, 170, 175
    dilemmas, 176–178
    and Eurasian region, 192–204
    guiding principles, 170–171, 173,
        178–179
    implementing, 165–166
    international position and, 167
    under Medvedev, 169
    multi/unipolarity, 168
    nationalism shaping, 170, 175,
        178–179
    priorities, 167–171

    protests affecting, 175
    under Putin, 12, 24, 25, 170–171,
        174–176
    and revisionism, 179
    relationship with West, 167, 168–169,
        171–177
    St Petersburg influence, 33
    Syria, 176, 177
'Foreign Policy Concepts,' 167–171
Foreign Policy Department of Presidential
        Administration, 165–166
fraud, 112, 214, 215
FSB. *See* Federal Security Service
'funds coefficient' measure, 154–155
Fyodor Ivanovich (Tsar), 81

G
G7, 172, 173
G8 summit, 86
Gazprom, 30, 95, 148
GDP (Gross Domestic Product),
        134–135, 137
genealogical approach, 16
General Agreement on Tariffs and Trade
        (GATT), 172
'Geneva International Discussion,' 196
Georgia. *See also* Eurasian region; foreign
        policy; separatism
    Commonwealth of Independent States
        (CIS), 195
    'colour revolution' in, 186
    in Eastern Partnership, 197, 204
    ethnic conflicts, 194
    NATO membership, 176, 196, 204
    peacekeeping missions in, 196
    relations with Russia, 196, 198
    Russia-Georgia war, 169, 187–188, 196
Gerasimov, Valerii, 191
Gerasimov Doctrine, 191
Gimpel'son, Vladimir, 155–156
Gini index, 154
glasnost', 5, 6, 55
Global Entrepreneurship Monitor (GEM), 141
globalisation *vs.* nationalism, 71
Golos, 90
Goode, Paul, 123
Gorbachev, Mikhail Sergeevich
    and Cold War, 5
    reform socialism, 4, 5–8, 55
    use of television, 102
    weak leadership, 119, 212

Gossovet (State Council), 30, 128, 131–132

government, 27–31. *See also* Constitution;
  Federal Assembly; Federation
  Council; parliament; political parties;
  State Duma
  conflicts with Constitutional Court, 112
  consolidating power, 19, 121–123, 214
  controlling media, 94, 96, 98–100, 213
  co-opting nationalism, 76–78
  and Eurasian region, 120, 128–129
  vs. opposition leaders, 90–91
  power networks in, 207
  responding to public opinion, 214–215
  role in law-making, 60
  shaping national identity, 67–68, 70–74
  shaping parliament, 58, 59
  shaping social policy, 85, 163
  and United Russia, 42–43, 44

governors. *See also* Eurasian region; leaders
  controlling media, 129
  and decentralisation proposals, 131–132
  delivering national votes, 130
  Kremlin evaluating, 128–129
  as party substitutes, 40
  president interacting with, 127–130
  under Putin, 125–126, 209

Great Patriotic War, 3, 71, 78, 80

Great War, 2

grey markets, 153

Gromov, Aleksei, 29

Grudinin, Pavel, 35

Gryzlov, Boris Vyacheslavovich, 57, 58

gulag archipelago, 3

'guns and butter' policy, 18

Gunvor, 210

Gurvich, Evsey, 134

Gusinsky, Vladimir, 10, 207, 209, 210

Gyumri, 194

H

Hahn, Gordon, 17

Hale, Henry E, 40, 205–216

Hanson, Philip, 123–124

health care, 36, 161

hegemonic presidency, 18–19, 26–28, 36–37

Herzen, Alexander, 116

history, and national identity, 70–74

Hollande, François, 201–202

Holodomor, 3

Hughes, James, 119

Hungary, 176

Huntington, Samuel, 13, 15–16

'hybrid warfare,' 190–191

hybrid regimes, 216

hypodermic needle model, 94, 103

I

ideology. *See also* national identity;
  nationalism
  entrepreneurs shaping, 78
  and national identity, 71, 73–74
  shaping foreign policy, 170
  in State Duma, 58–59
  in United Russia, 46–47

Ilyukhin, Victor, 63

immigration. *See* migration

Immortal Regiment, 78

impeachment, 27

imports, affected by floating rouble, 135–137

India, 172

'Individual Pension Capital,' 163

industrial policies, 145–146

industrialisation, 3, 4, 6

inequality, 150–164. *See also* economic
    policies; social policy
  affecting social policy, 151–152
  creating black and grey markets, 153
  in education access, 161
  in health care, 161
  relative to growth, 152, 155
  rising, 153–157
  in social service access, 161–162
  and wealth concentration, 156–157

informal employment, 152

informal politics, 31–35, 80–93

informal power relations, 17

information warfare, 102–103, 190–191

Ingushetia, 126

Instagram, 52, 100

institutions. *See also* government; parliament
  democracies *vs.* regimes, 63
  government, 27–28
  integrating post-Soviet states, 195
  role in political system, 205–206

insurance, pension, 157–159

Inter-Parliamentary Union Assembly, 65

interest rates, 143

Interior Ministry (MVD), 26, 27, 31, 181, 185

international news, 97

internet, 97, 100–101. *See also* media;
    social media
  cognitive processing of messages, 106–107

legislation controlling, 100–101
  protesting via, 98, 100–101, 107
  scale of, 104–106
investment, 129, 138–140
Iraq, 168, 173
Irkutsk, 125, 209–210
Islam, 69, 70, 72–73, 177
Ivanov, Sergei, 29, 32, 64, 166, 187
Izborsky Club, 78

J

journalists, 100
judges, 109, 111, 112. *See also* courts;
    criminal trials; legal system
  and bribery, 113
    public perceptions of, 114, 115, 116
    relationship with chairmen, 113
jury trials, 111, 113
Just Russia, 41, 42, 48, 125, 207
Just Russia/Pensioners/Motherland, 46
justice-of-the-peace courts, 111

K

Kabardino-Balkaria, 126
Kadyrov, Ramzan, 76
Kasparov, Garri, 86
Kasyanov, Mikhail, 86
Kazakhstan, 194, 195, 197, 203
Kerry, John, 200
KGB, 4, 21, 181, 182, 184
Khakamada, Irina, 86
Khanty-Mansi, 126
Khasbulatov, Ruslan, 54
Khimki Forest, 87
Khloponin, Aleksandr, 121, 131
Khodorkovsky, Mikhail, 10, 207, 208
    fraud conviction, 108, 115, 186, 210
Kholmanskikh, Igor, 121
Khrushchev, Nikita, 3, 97
Kirienko, Sergei, 29
Kirovles, 91
Kolokoltsev, Vladimir, 34
Kommersant, 99
Komsomol, 45
Konitzer, Andrew, 120
Konovalov, Aleksandr, 34
Korzhakov, Aleksandr, 182
Kosovo, 183
Kosygin, Alexei, 3
Kovalchuk, Yuri, 207
Kozak, Dmitry, 32, 33, 121, 131

Kozyrev, Andrei, 166, 171, 172, 178–179
Krasnodar, 77
Kremlin. *See* government
Kudrin, Aleksei, 29, 34, 147, 148, 151, 158
Kyrgyzstan, 195, 198
    Tulip Revolution, 173–174

L

labour. *See* employment; pensions; wages;
    workers
labour camps, 3
labour discipline, 4
labour unions, 87
Lake Baikal, 87
Latvia, 8, 176
Laruelle, Marlene, 67–79
Lavrov, Sergei, 32, 34, 172, 200
law and law-making, 60–64, 90.
        See also courts; legal system;
        legislation; rule of law
    historical role of, 108–109
    vs. presidential decree, 28
    public disregard for, 116
'Law on the Protection of Children,' 101
leaders, 3. *See also* elections; governors;
        president; prime minister
    electing regional, 120, 122, 124, 126,
        209–210
    paramount, 18–19, 36–37
    and party affiliations, 40–43
    preference for strong, 19–21, 24, 25,
        116, 212
    Putin's popularity as, 24, 25, 209, 212
Left Front, 91
Legal Department of the Duma, 57
legal nihilism, 116
legal system, 108–118. *See also* courts;
        criminal trials; judges; law and law-
        making; rule of law
    in action, 112–113
    amnesties, 115–116
    corruption in, 112–113, 115, 117
    equality in, 117–118
    historical role of, 108–109
    improvement under Putin, 212
    jury trials in, 111, 113
    public using, 114–117
    regimes subverting, 16–17
    as state instrument, 108
    structure of, 110–111
    transparency, 111

legislation. *See also* government; parliament;
    rule of law
  aligning regional and federal, 121
  controlling speech, 100–101
  Kremlin shaping, 63
  and morality, 76
  president initiating, 27
  prohibiting extremism, 100
  rates of adoption, 61–62
  Russian Orthodox Church shaping, 76
  as vehicle for repression, 90
legitimacy, television conferring, 94–95
Lenin, Vladimir Il'ich, 2, 3
Leninism, 4, 6
Lenta.ru, 99–100
Levada Center, 20, 90, 114, 115
'Levada Survey,' 114
Levchenko, Sergei, 124
LGBT people, 90
Liberal Democratic Party of Russia (LDPR),
    39, 41, 46, 48–49, 125. *See also* party
    system; political parties
  nationalist movements, 74, 75
  as systemic opposition, 48
liberal parties, 50–52
liberalisation, 5, 15
liberalism, 16–17
Ligachev, Yegor, 102
Limonov, Eduard, 76, 86–87
LinkedIn, 101
Lithuania, 6, 7, 8, 176
Live Journal, 51–52
Lo, Bobo, 178
'loans-for-shares,' 208
lobbying, 63
long-haul truckers, 92–93, 98
'loyal opposition,' 48
Luhansk, 201
Lukoil, 209
Lukyanovskaya, Mariana, 113
Luzhkov, Yuri, 42, 77, 207, 210

M
Maidan Revolution, 199
Makhachkala, 126
Malaev, Mikhail, 62
Malofeev, Konstantin, 78
'managed democracy,' 14
market economy, 8, 9, 32, 172. *See also*
    economic policies; economy
Marxism, 2, 4

Masyuk, Elena, 95
Matvienko, Valentina, 35
May Directives (*ukazy*), 36, 124
mayors, 126, 210
Mechel, 210
media, 94–107. *See also* social media; *specific*
    forms of media
  audience scepticism of, 96–97
  cognitive processing of messages,
    106–107
  covering Chechen conflict, 84
  covering regional elections, 125
  cum hoc fallacies in, 103
  and Foreign Agents Law, 101
  hypodermic needle model, 94, 103
  international scope of, 97, 102–104
  internet, 100–101
  Live Journal, 51–52
  news aggregators, 101
  newspapers, 99–100
  and opposition voices, 51–52, 87,
    106–107, 213
  as propaganda, 71, 102–103, 129
  radio, 98–99
  Russia Today (RT), 102–104
  scale of, 104–106
  self-censorship in, 96
  supporting political system, 45, 96, 115,
    175, 213
  television, 94–98
Meduza project, 100
Medvedev, Dmitry Anatolevich, 3, 10, 11, 87
  creating macroregions, 121
  corruption, 65, 92, 126
  foreign policy under, 169
  and Georgian war, 196
  Presidential Administration under, 29
  as prime minister, 30–31, 32, 33
  and Russian political system, 14–15, 116
  tandem rule with Putin, 14–15
  and United Russia, 41, 207
Memorial, 90
Merkel, Angela, 201–202
Meshkov, Yuri, 193
Middle East, 170, 172
migrants, 70, 75, 76
migration, 70, 73
military, 180–191. *See also* foreign policy;
    security
  and Eurasian conflicts, 183, 187–188,
    199–200

maintaining Soviet garrisons, 193–194
modernisation of, 188–190
necessity of strong, 181, 189
under Putin, 186–188
resurgence, 183–184, 188–191
shifting objectives of, 182
spending on, 144–145, 181, 187, 189
technology, 190
using hybrid warfare, 190–191
West interpreting reforms, 188–189
under Yeltsin, 181–184
Miller, Aleksei, 32, 33
Minchenko, Yevgeny, 132
ministries, 27, 30, 31
Ministry of Defence, 31, 181, 182, 187
Ministry of Economic Development
    (MinEkon), 134, 142–143, 147–148
Ministry of Emergency Situations (MChS),
    27, 31, 34, 182
Ministry of Finance, 142–143, 144
Ministry of Foreign Affairs, 166
Ministry of Industry and Trade
    (Minpromtorg), 142–143
Ministry of Justice, 31
Minsk II, 201–202
Mironov, Sergei, 41, 48, 207
modernisation, 4, 5, 13, 14
Moldova, 193–194, 195, 197, 198, 204
Molodaya Gvardiya, 45
monetary policy, 143
Montenegro, 176
morality, 4
    of court chairmen, 113
    and legislation, 76
    necessity for reform, 183
    to repress opposition, 89–90
Moraski, Bryon, 130
Moscow, 77, 120, 209
mythology, and nationalism, 71–72

N
Nabiullina, Elvira, 32, 34, 143, 212
Nagorno-Karabakh, 194, 196, 198, 203
Naryshkin, Sergei, 32, 33
National Bolshevik Party, 86
national identity, 67–79, 214. *See also* ethnic
    groups; nationalism; nationalist
    movements
    vs. de-Russification, 69
    and Eurasian region, 71, 72–73
    as foreign policy, 178–179

media shaping, 71
migration affecting, 70
narratives of, 71–74, 78
post-Soviet crisis, 167
projected abroad, 72–73
religion and, 72–74
Russian World, 73
and Soviet era, 72
National Media Group, 207
national revolution, 77
National Welfare Fund, 143
National-Bolshevik Party, 76
nationalism, 67–79. *See also* Eurasian
    region; national identity; nationalist
    movements
    definition of, 67
    and economic security, 142
    entrepreneurs shaping, 78
    and Eurasian region, 71, 77
    guiding foreign policy, 170, 175
    Kremlin co-opting, 77, 78
    narratives of, 70–74, 78
    vs. Rossian identity, 69
    symbols of, 71–74
nationalist entrepreneurs, 78
nationalist movements, 74–77. *See also*
    national identity; nationalism
    anti-Yeltsin, 74–75
    Communist Party of the Russian
        Federation (CPRF), 49–50, 74, 75
    government connections, 77–78
    Liberal Democratic Party of Russia
        (LDPR), 48–49, 74, 75
    linked to Europe, 76
    Russian National Unity, 75
    Russian Orthodox Church, 74, 75,
        76–77
    skinheads, 75
'nationalities question,' 7
NATO (North Atlantic Treaty Organization),
    15, 168, 169. *See also* European
    Union; United States; West
    criticism of, 173
    enlargement of, 7
    frustrations with, 176, 183
    Georgia's membership, 174
    influencing Eurasian region, 174,
        193, 195
    Information Operations Groups, 103
    Ukraine's membership, 174
    and Yugoslavia, 167

NATO Membership Action Plan (MAP), 196
NATO-Russia Council, 176
NATO-Russia Founding Act on Mutual Relations, Cooperation and Security, 176
Navalny, Aleksei, 41, 76, 214
  campaigning by, 51–52, 91, 92, 124–125
  criticizing Putin, 35, 51–52
  detention of, 91, 108, 115
  on social media, 65, 92
  threat to party system, 52
neformaly, 6
Nemtsov, Boris, 51, 89, 213
Nenets, 126
New Economic Policy (NEP), 2, 6
'new political thinking' (NPT), 7
New Strategic Arms Reduction Treaty (New START), 174
New Times, The, 213
news. *See* media; newspapers; radio; television
news aggregators, 101, 107. *See also* media
newspapers, 99–100, 107. *See also* media
Nezavisimaya Gazeta, 99, 100
Nicholas II, 2, 3
Night Wolves, 77
9/11, 168, 176
Nineteenth Party Conference, 6
Noble, Ben, 54–66
non-governmental organisations (NGOs), 81, 85, 90, 101
non-system opposition, 48, 86. *See also* activists; party system; political parties; protests
  campaign to discredit, 89–92
  Progress Party as, 48
  protests as, 86
North Ossetia, 126
Novaya Gazeta, 99, 100
Novorossiya, 76, 77
NTV, 95, 213
nuclear capacity, 9, 170–171

O
oil prices, 150. *See also* energy prices
  affecting budget, 143–144, 159–160
  fall in output, 134–135
  future fluctuations in, 147
  over time, 134–135, 136
  shaping economic policy, 133, 134, 146

oligarchs, 10, 12, 207, 210
  dispersing powers, 186
  as party substitutes, 40
  in single-pyramid system, 208
opposition parties, 48, 213, 215. *See also* activists; party system; political parties; protests
Orange Revolution, 14, 168, 173–174, 175. *See also* Ukraine
'orange techniques,' 14
Organisation for Security and Cooperation in Europe (OSCE), 201
Organisation of Islamic Cooperation (OIC), 73
organized crime, 183
orthodoxy, 73–74
Other Russia, 86, 88
Our Home Is Russia, 50
output, declining, 134–135

P
pantheons, and national identity, 71–72
para-constitutional behaviour, 16
paramount leader, 18–19, 36–37
parliament, 6–7, 27, 54–66. *See also* Congress of People's Deputies; Federal Assembly; Federation Council; legislation; political system; State Duma
  committees, 57
  convocations, 57
  democracies *vs.* regimes, 63
  deputies, 56–59
  dissolving, 27, 82
  Federation Council, 59–60
  hierarchies, 57
  history of, 54–56
  law-making process, 60–64
  lobbying, 63
  1993 constitutional crisis, 55–56
  recent developments in, 64–65
  reforming, 64
  role in foreign policy, 166
  senators, 59
  State Duma, 56–59
  unworkable Soviet model, 9
  web-based counter-, 98
  yearly budget and, 62–63
Parliamentary Assembly of the Council of Europe (PACE), 175
parliamentary debate, 62–63

Partnership for Peace, 176
Party of Progress, 52
Party of Russia's Rebirth, 57
party system. *See also* democratisation;
    elections; opposition parties; political
    parties
    executive distance from, 40–41
    with incomplete democratisation, 39–40
    influence on law-making, 62
    liberal parties in, 50
    Navalny threatening, 52
    in *perestroika*, 38–41
    under Putin, 38, 41, 42–43
    in State Duma, 57–58
    United Russia dominating, 47
    volatility in, 39
    weaknesses of, 11
patriotism, 68, 73, 97
patronalism, 206
Patrushev, Nikolai, 165–166, 185
peacekeeping, 193–194, 196
Pension Fund, 157, 158
pension insurance, 157–159
pensions, 21, 24, 83. *See also* employment;
    social policy; wages; workers
    cuts to, 137, 144
    'Individual Pension Capital' scheme, 163
    as pyramid scheme, 158
    reforming, 148, 158, 159
    Soviet model for, 158–159
People's Deputies, 42
perestroika, 4, 5–8, 55
*Perestroika: New Thinking for Our Country
    and the World*, 6
Permanent Joint Council (NATO), 176
Petrov, Nikolai, 185
Pikalevo, 210
Piketty, Thomas, 155
Poland, 176
policy-making, 24, 25, 47. *See also* economic
    policies; foreign policy; social policy
    advisory bodies for, 29–30
    Putin's approach to, 21, 24, 35–36
political machines, 209–211
Political Order in Changing Societies, 13
political parties, 15, 38–41. *See also*
    Communist Party of the Russian
    Federation (CPRF); democratisation;
    elections; opposition parties; party
    system; protests; United Russia
    Agrarian Party, 57

All-Russian People's Front (ONF), 13, 19
All-Union Communist, 4
Bolshevik, 2, 4
Communist Party of the Soviet Union
    (CPSU), 2, 4, 6–7, 8, 44, 45
Fatherland-All Russia, 42, 209
Just Russia, 41, 42, 46, 48, 125, 207
Just Russia/Pensioners/Motherland, 46
liberal, 50–52
Liberal Democratic Party of Russia (LDPR),
    39, 41, 46, 48–49, 74, 75, 125
National-Bolshevik Party, 76, 86
opposition, 47–52
Our Home Is Russia, 50
Party of Progress, 52
Party of Russia's Rebirth, 57
Progress Party, 41, 46
and protest organizations, 86
Russian Party of Life, 48
Russian Pensioners Party, 48
Russian Popular Front (ONF), 13, 19
Socialist Revolutionary, 2
Solidarnost, 51
in State Duma, 39, 57–58
types of, 38–39
Union of Right Forces (SPS), 46, 51,
    86, 126
Unity, 42
VKP(b), 4
Yabloko, 41, 46, 51
political system, 26, 205–216. *See also*
    Constitution; democratisation;
    elections; federalisation; parliament;
    party system
    change as constant, 216
    fraud in, 214, 215
    media supporting, 213
    patronalism as context, 206
    political machines in, 209–211
    power networks in, 207
    under Putin, 213–215
    recent history of, 205–206
    as single-pyramid system, 207–208, 215
    St Petersburg influence, 32–33
    United Russia in, 43–45
politicians, as party alternatives, 40
politics. *See also* political system
    contentious, 81–85
    informal, 80–93
    shaping constitution, 82
    unconventional, 80–81

polpred, 121
pornography, 101
Poroshenko, Petro, 201–202
post hoc, ergo propter hoc fallacies, 103
post-communism, 8–11, 16
    conflicts between states, 195–196
    elite politics shaping, 18–19
    fate of countries, 15
    regional relationships, 192–204
    three waves of, 15–16
Potanin, Vladimir, 10
poverty. *See* inequality
power networks, 17, 207–208
pragmatism, as foreign policy, 173
Prague Spring, 3–4
Pravovoe upravlenie, 57
preemstvennost, 71
president, 7–11, 26–28, 213–215. *See also*
    government; leaders; parliament;
    political system
    creating stability, 20
    hegemonic, 18–19, 26–28, 36–37
    interacting with governors, 127–130
    ministries reporting to, 31
    role in law-making, 27, 60, 61, 62
    shaping policy, 26, 27, 165
    in single-pyramid system, 208–209
    term limits, 27–28
    Yeltsin creating dominant, 82–83
Presidential Administration, 28–30
presidential decrees, 28, 193
Presidential Security Service (SBP), 182
Prilepskiy, Ilya, 134
Primakov, Yevgeny, 166, 172, 209
prime ministers, 26, 27, 30–31
Primorsky Krai, 207
privatisation, 10, 32, 145, 207. *See also*
    economic policies
    in market economy, 152
    under Putin, 21, 24
    and social policy, 152, 160
    stimulating economy, 148
'profile' committee, 60
Progress Party, 41, 46, 48
Prokhanov, Aleksandr, 78
Prokhorov, Mikhail, 99
propaganda, 10, 102–103, 105, 190–191
property rights, 10, 30, 141, 148
proportional representation (PR) system, 56
Prospekt Sakharova, 88

protests, 80–93. *See also* activists; contentious
    politics; opposition parties
    backlash against, 89–92
    December 2011, 1, 88–89
    demographics of, 86
    and Eurasian region, 83–84, 124, 199
    and foreign policy, 175
    history of, 81–85
    and internet restrictions, 100–101
    issues inciting, 80, 86, 87, 92–93
    lack of, during Yeltsin era, 83
    modern tactics of, 87
    as non-system opposition, 86
    Other Russia, 86, 88
    under Putin, 85–92
    and rule of law, 108
    'Strategy 31,' 86–87
    television coverage, 97–98
Provisional Government, 2
Public Chambers, 85
public opinion, 22–23
    in political machines, 211
    of Putin, 18, 20–21, 22–23, 35, 37,
      211, 212
    of regional leaders, 129
    of rule of law, 116
    Russia as democracy, 37, 214
    shaping Kremlin behavior, 214–215
    of State Duma, 64
public suicides, 83
Pugachev Rebellion, 81
Pussy Riot, 108, 115
Putin, Vladimir Vladimirovich, 3, 11–15, 21,
    25, 41, 211–212
    authoritarianism under, 13, 14, 25
    criticizing West, 168–169, 199–200
    current position, 93, 205
    'divide-and-rule' strategy, 185
    economic policy, 13–14, 21, 24, 25,
      148, 157–158, 162
    and Eurasian region, 91–92, 122,
      125–128, 197
    foreign policy under, 12, 24, 25, 166,
      170–171, 173–176
    fourth term, 35–37
    informal politics under, 31–35
    leadership style, 12, 14, 18–21, 186,
      213–215
    meeting with State Council, 128
    military under, 186–188

and nationalism, 68, 75–77
negotiating Minsk II, 201–202
vs. NTV, 95
and oligarchs, 12, 210
opposition to, 35, 76, 85–87
policy-making, 11–12, 21, 24, 25,
   35–36, 85, 211
public opinion of, 18, 20–21, 22–23,
   35, 37, 211, 212
and reform, 13, 21, 24, 157–158
and regional leaders, 123, 209
repression under, 88–92, 213
Russian *vs.* Western assessments, 24, 25
and Russian Orthodox Church, 75
security policy, 180, 184–186
shaping political system, 12–13, 19, 27,
   38, 42–43, 120–126, 215
and *siloviki,* 33, 180
and St Petersburg elements, 32–33
tandem rule with Medvedev, 14–15
team, 31–35
ties to United Russia, 44, 45
wielding power, 12, 28, 120–126, 132,
   207, 213–215
'Putin fatigue,' 35

R
radio, 98–99, 102
raspolzanie prinuditel'noi platnosti, 161
RBC, 99
reform communism, 5, 6
'reform socialism,' 4
reforms. *See also* perestroika
   economic, 142–150
   under Gorbachev, 4, 5–8
   military, 180, 181, 186–188
   morality in, 183
   and national identity, 67–70
   of parliament, 64
   pension, 157–158
   under Putin, 13, 15, 21, 24, 212
   security, 185
   social, 162–164
   three waves of, 15–16
   under Yeltsin, 10
regimes, 16–17, 63. *See also* authoritarianism;
   government
   Crimea recalibrating, 215
   foreign policy consolidating, 178
   hybrid, 216

and national identity, 67, 72
para-constitutional behaviour by, 16
Putin, 12–14, 44, 186
trajectory of, 205–216
Regions of Russia, 42
Reisinger, William, 130
religion. *See also* Russian Orthodox Church
   influence of Islam, 69
   and national identity, 73–74
   in Russian Federation, 68–69
Remington, Thomas, 120, 150–164
Renz, Bettina, 180–191
representatives, 27
Republic of Chechnya. *See* Chechnya
Republic of Crimea. *See* Crimea
republics, 8, 68
Reserve Fund, 143, 144
Reuter, Ora John, 38–53, 123, 130
revenue, redistributing, 119
revisionism, 179
'revolution within the revolution,' 5
revolutions, 2, 186
   Maidan, 199
   and national identity, 72, 77
   Orange, 14, 168, 173–174, 175
   perestroika as, 6
   Putin repudiating, 12
   Rose, 173–174
   Tulip, 173–174
rights, 109, 116–117
Robertson, Graeme, 80–93, 130
Rodina, 48
Romania, 176
Romanovs, 2
Rose Revolution, 173–174
Roskomnadzor (Russian Committee for
   Oversight), 101
Rosneft, 145, 148, 207, 210
Rossian identity, 67–68, 69
Rossiiskaia Federatsiia. See Russian Federation
Rossiya (Channel Two), 95, 213
Rostov-on-Don, 77
rouble, 135–137, 143
rubber stamp, parliament as, 60, 63
rule of law, 108–118. *See also* law and
   law-making; legal system; legislation
   in action, 112–113
   amnesties, 115–116
   definition of, 117
   Gorbachev advocating for, 109

rule of law (*cont.*)
    public opinion of, 116, 118
    prospects for, 117–118
    and protests, 108
    public opinion of, 116, 118
    'telephone law,' 114, 118
Russia, 1–15, 192–193. *See also* government;
    parliament; political system; reforms;
    Russian Federation
    change as constant, 216
    and China, 203–204
    as consumer society, 14
    and continuity, 8–9, 71
    democratic *vs.* authoritarian, 216
    diaspora, 9
    and Eurasian region relationships,
    192–204
    and European Union, 176, 177, 198
    as 'failing state,' 24
    as federal state, 67–68
    global position, 9, 13–14, 72–73, 134,
    167, 176
    improvements under Putin, 211–212
    invasion of Chechnya, 84–85
    lack of redistributive power, 164
    national identity, 67–79
    oligarchy in, 10
    political characteristics of, 17, 31–35,
    82, 206, 215
    parliamentary politics, 54–66
    Putin as paramount leader, 18–19
    siloviki protecting interests, 33
    and United States, 176–177
    wealth inquality in, 153–157
Russia at the Turn of the Millennium, 12
'Russia, Forward!,' 14
Russia Today (RT), 102–104
Russian Federal Assembly. *See* Federal
    Assembly
Russian Federal Law 'On Defence,' 187
Russian Federation. *See also* democratisation;
    federalisation; government;
    parliament; political system
    affected by migration, 70
    components of, 68
    national identity, 67–74
    religion in, 68–69
    security prestige, 181–182
    as semi-presidential system, 26
    socioeconomic differences within,
    69–70

Russian Geographical Society, 71
Russian Marches, 77
Russian National Unity, 75
Russian Orthodox Church, 49. *See also*
    nationalism; religion
    formalisation of, 68–69
    as nationalist movement, 74, 75,
    76–77, 78
    shaping legislation, 76
    ties to Putin, 75
Russian Party of Life, 48
Russian Popular Front (ONF), 13, 19
Russian Revolution, 81
Russian Security Council. *See* Security
    Council
Russian World, 73, 170
'Russianess,' defining, 71–74
Rybkin, Ivan Petrovich, 57

S
Saez, Emmanuel, 155
Sajudis, 6
Sakha (Yakutia), 83
Sakwa, Richard, 1–17, 179, 211
salaries. *See* wages
Samokhina, Sofya, 65
sanctions, 24, 150, 175, 210. *See also*
    Crimea; economic policies; foreign
    policy; Ukraine; West
    vs. counter-sanctions, 146, 203
    economic effects of, 138–139
    influencing policy, 36
    shaping media, 96
Sanders, Bernie, 102
Sargsyan, Serzh, 198
Saudi Arabia, 213
Sberbank, 155–156
scale, in media, 104–106
Schetnaya palata, 57
Schulmann, Ekaterina, 64
Sechin, Igor, 32, 33, 145, 207
'Secret Speech' (Khrushchev), 3
security, 1, 15, 180–191. *See also* foreign
    policy; military; *individual agencies*
    advisory bodies for, 29–30
    agencies of, 182
    and counterterrorism, 182, 185
    vs. democracy, 13
    in Eurasian region, 183, 195, 196
    excessive Soviet spending, 181
    fostering loyalty in, 182

need for military reform, 189
and organized crime, 183
under Putin, 180, 181–182, 184–186
siloviki influence, 33
Western concerns, 180–181
under Yeltsin, 180, 181–184
Security Council of the Russian Federation, 29–30, 165–166, 185, 186
Seleznev, Genadii Nikolaevich, 57
self-censorship, 96
senators, 59, 123
separatism, 177–178, 183, 195–196, 201. *See also* Chechnya; Georgia
Serbia, 167, 173
Serdyukov, Anatoly, 34, 187
Sevastopol, 68, 120, 121, 126
Shaimiev, Mintimer, 42
Shanghai Cooperation Organization (SCO), 169
Shantsev, Valery, 128
Sharafutdinova, Gulnaz, 123
Shkurenko, Ol'ga, 62
'shock therapy,' economic policy, 172
Shoigu, Sergei, 32, 33, 34, 145, 182
siloviki, 33, 121, 180, 184–185
Siluanov, Anton, 34, 132, 145
Single Economic Space, 195
single-pyramid system, 207–209, 215. *See also* political system
skinheads, 75
slander, 101
Slider, Darrell, 119–132
Slovakia, 176
Slovenia, 176
Sobchak, Anatoly, 21, 30, 50
Sobchak, Ksenia, 97
Sobyanin, Sergei, 32, 34, 91, 124–125
social media, 92, 100–101, 104–106, 107
social policy, 150–164. *See also* employment; pensions; wages; workers
in black and grey markets, 153
bureaucracy shaping, 163–164
by category instead of need, 162
challenges, 150–153, 162–164
complicating taxation, 159–160
four changes to welfare system, 157–161
inequality affecting, 151–152
shift to insurance pools, 152, 157–159, 160
strategic planning for, 150–151

social welfare system, 157–162. *See also* inequality; social policy
socialism, 2, 6, 8, 34
Socialist Revolutionary party, 2
Solidarnost, 51
Solzhenitsyn, Alexander, 3
Sorok sorokov, 78
Soros, George, 86
South Ossetia, 73, 194, 196
'sovereign democracy,' 13–14, 146
Soviet system, 2–4, 5–8. *See also* Communist Party of the Soviet Union (CPSU); post-communism
excessive security spending, 181
legal system in, 108–109
legitimizing current regime, 80
Putin's view of, 12, 21
parliamentary politics in, 54–55
rehabilitation of, 68, 72
social policy in, 151
soviets (councils), 2
Soyuz Pravykh Sil (SPS). *See* Union of Right Forces
Sputnik, 102
Sretensky Monastery, 76
St Petersburg, 77
as federal entity, 120
lawyers and economists, 32–33
political-business elements, 33
political machine in, 209
stability
vs. democracy, 13
importance to public, 116, 211
military reform for, 181
vs. order, 14
under Putin, 11, 12, 20, 186
separatism challenging, 183
West as threat to, 186
stagnation *(zastoi),* 4, 139–141
Stalin, Joseph Vissarionovich, 3, 72
Stalinism, 6
START II (Strategic Arms Reduction Treaty), 166
State Council *(Gossovet),* 30, 128, 131–132
State Duma, 56–59, 215. *See also* Constitution; elections; Federal Assembly; Federation Council; parliament; political parties
approving prime ministers, 30
blocking foreign policy, 166
chairs of, 57

State Duma (*cont.*)
  commissions in, 57
  committees in, 57, 60
  decline of debate, 62–63
  election protests, 88–89
  ideology shaping, 58–59
  leadership hierarchy, 57
  limiting presidential power, 11
  partisan composition, 57–58
  recent developments, 64–65
  role in law-making, 60–61
  political parties in, 39, 48–51
  United Russia majority in, 42–43
Stavropol, 77
Stolypin Club, 147
'Strategic Course of the Russian Federation
    with Respect to the Member States of
    the Commonwealth of Independent
    States,' 193
Strategy of the Economic Security of the
    Russian Federation, 142
'Strategy 31,' 86–87
'Strategy-2020,' 150, 161, 162
strikes, 83, 87, 92–93, 98
Supreme Court, 111
Supreme Soviet, 7, 54
Surkov, Vladislav, 13–14, 42, 146
symbols, national, 71–74
Syria, 170, 176, 177, 180, 188, 190
systemic opposition, 48

T
Tajikistan, 195
tandem rule, 14–15
Tashkent Treaty, 195
Tatarstan, 83, 121, 122, 207
  Islam in, 69
  political machine in, 209
  special provisions for, 120, 122, 123
taxes and taxation, 119, 159–160
technocracy, 12, 14
technology, 4, 141, 190
teleological approach, 16
'telephone law,' 114, 118
television, 94–98. *See also* audiences;
    media
  audience size, 94
  coverage of opposition, 95–98
  hypodermic needle model, 94
  Kremlin controlling, 94
  national channels, 94, 95

range of programming, 95–98
  Russia Today (RT), 102–104
  supporting regime, 97, 213
term limits, 27–28
terrorism, in Chechen war, 84
Tikhon (Bishop Shevkunov), 76
Time of Troubles, 81
Titov, Boris, 147
Tkachenko, Natalia, 61, 63, 64
Tomsk-2, 96
trade. *See also* economic policies; economy
  Association Agreements, 197–198
  with China, 203–204
  in Eurasian region, 195, 197–203
Transnistria, 194
Trenin, Dmitry, 175
truckers, protesting, 92–93, 98
Trutnev, Yuri, 121
'tsar-father,' Putin as, 21
Tskhinvali, 196
Tulip Revolution, 173–174
Turchak, Andrei, 45
Turkey, 213
Turkmenistan, 194
TV Rain (*Dozhd*), 97, 99, 100
Twitter, 52, 100, 105
2007 Munich Security Conference, 174

U
Udaltsov, Sergei, 91, 100
Ukraine. *See also* Crimea; foreign policy;
    sanctions
  annexation of Crimean Peninsula,
    91–92, 150, 170, 175
  Association Agreement for, 175
  crisis in, 36, 91–92, 133, 150,
    198–202
  ending USSR, 8
  in Eastern Partnership, 197
  and economic sovereignty, 133
  in Eurasian economic strategies,
    177–178, 195
  frozen conflict in, 202
  Holodomor, 3
  Maidan Revolution, 199
  media coverage of, 92, 97, 100
  migrants leaving, 70
  Minsk II reshaping, 201–202
  nationalism in, 76, 77
  NATO membership, 176, 196, 199
  Novorossiya, 76, 77

Orange Revolution, 14, 168, 173–174, 175, 186
protests in, 91, 175, 199
and Putin's popularity, 91–92, 178
Russian objectives in, 170, 175, 179, 193, 195, 200–202
separatists in, 170, 175, 177–178, 201
trade sanctions, 198–199
and Western sanctions, 36, 96, 150, 210
Ulyukaev, Aleksei, 145
unconventional politics, 80–81
unemployment, 137, 152
Union of Right Forces (SPS), 46, 51, 86, 126
Union of Soviet Socialist Republics (USSR), 4, 5, 8, 12. See also post-communism; Soviet system
Union Treaty, 7
United Nations Security Council (UNSC), 9, 167, 177
United Russia, 41, 42, 215. See also party system; political parties
dominating party system, 47
and elections, 38, 42–47, 122
elements of popularity, 45–46
elites in, 210
FAR and Unity merging, 42
ideologies, 46–47
influencing government, 19, 38, 62, 123
and Kremlin, 42–43, 44, 215
limitations on, 44
media supporting, 45
and opposition parties, 47–52
relationship with Putin, 44, 207, 210
role in political system, 13, 26, 43–45, 57
Young Guard, 45
Unity, 42
United States (US). See also European Union; West
challenging relations with, 167–168
election interference, 102–103, 107, 177
military strength of, 189
negotiating terms in Ukraine, 200
orchestrating revolutions, 174
inequality in, 153–157, 160, 161–162
security concerns, 176–177, 180
uskorenie (acceleration), 5
Uzbekistan, 194, 195

V

Vaino, Anton, 29, 32
Valdai Discussion Club, 25

Vedomosti, 99, 100
Venediktov, Alexei, 98
vertical power, 31, 75, 120–126. See also political system
vertikal vlasti, 120–126
vetoes, 61, 62
VKontakte, 52, 100
Volodin, Vyacheslav Viktorovich, 57, 64, 65–66
'Vremya,' 95

W

wages, 21, 24, 36, 160. See also employment; pensions; social policy; workers
affected by floating rouble, 135–137
benefits of rising, 155
effect on regional budgets, 124
over time, 136
and Soviet pension model, 158
'war on terror,' 168, 173
wealth concentration, 156–157. See also inequality
'weaponized' information, 102–103
West, 171–176. See also European Union; sanctions; United States
challenging, as policy, 174–176
competition with, 173–174
counter-sanctions against, 146, 203
countering revisionism of, 179
criticisms of, 168–169
and economic reform, 172
imposing sanctions, 138–139, 150, 175, 203, 210
influencing Eurasian region, 193, 199–200
negotiating terms in Ukraine, 200, 201–202
Russia balancing, 172–173
security concerns, 180–181, 184, 188–189
supporting Russian peacekeeping, 194
as threat to stability, 186
WhatsApp, 100
White House, shelling of, 54
WikiLeaks, 102
Willerton, John, 18–37
workers. See also employment; pensions; wages
enhancing to increase growth, 140–141
protests by, 87
Putin's popularity with, 21
in Yeltsin era, 83

World Trade Organization (WTO), 197
World War I, 2
World War II, 3, 71, 78, 80
World Wealth and Income Database
    (WID.world), 153

X
xenophobia, 70, 76, 79

Y
Yabloko, 41, 46, 51
Yakovlev, Alexander, 5
Yakunin, Vladimir, 78
Yamalo-Nenets, 126
Yanukovych, Viktor, 14, 91, 175
Yaroslavl, 126
Yavlinsky, Grigory, 41, 51
Yeltsin, Boris Nikolaevich, 1, 3, 8–11, 40,
    166, 212
    'divide-and-rule' strategy, 182–183
    ethnic and regional conflicts under,
        83–84, 193
    and media, 10, 95
    1993 constitutional crisis, 55–56, 95

and oligarchs, 207
presidential powers, 7–8, 26–27, 82–83
and Rossian identity, 68
vs. Ruslan Khasbulatov, 54
security policy, 180, 181–184
seeking Western integration, 171–172
shaping parliamentary power, 7, 9,
    55–56
shaping political system, 9, 11, 82,
    119–120, 207–208
Yerevan, 194
Young Guard, 45
youth and young adults, 18, 79, 100
YouTube, 52, 104
Yugoslavia, 167, 173, 183
Yukos, 108, 186, 210
Yushchenko, Viktor, 14
Yves Rocher, 91

Z
zastoi (stagnation), 4
Zhirinovsky, Vladimir, 41, 48–49, 74
Zucman, Gabriel, 155
Zyuganov, Gennady, 10, 41, 49, 74, 88, 208